THE LIBRARY OF WORLD AFFAIRS

Editors

GEORGE W. KEETON

AND

GEORG SCHWARZENBERGER

D0264346

Number 60

The Law of
INTERNATIONAL INSTITUTIONS

AUSTRALIA
The Law Book Company Ltd.
Sydney : Melbourne : Brisbane

CANADA AND U.S.A.
The Carswell Company Ltd.
Agincourt, Ontario

INDIA
N.M. Tripathi Private Ltd.
Bombay
and
Eastern Law House Private Ltd.
Calcutta *and* Delhi
M.P.P. House
Bangalore

ISRAEL
Steimatzky's Agency Ltd.
Jerusalem : Tel Aviv : Haifa

MALAYSIA : SINGAPORE : BRUNEI
Malayan Law Journal (Pte.) Ltd.
Singapore

NEW ZEALAND
Sweet and Maxwell (N.Z.) Ltd.
Auckland

PAKISTAN
Pakistan Law House
Karachi

The Law of

INTERNATIONAL

INSTITUTIONS

D. W. BOWETT, Q.C., LL.D.
*Whewell Professor of International
Law in the University of Cambridge*

FOURTH EDITION

Published under the auspices of
THE LONDON INSTITUTE OF WORLD AFFAIRS

LONDON
STEVENS & SONS
1982

First Edition 1964
Second Edition . . . 1970
Third Edition 1975
Fourth Edition 1982
Reprinted 1986

Published in 1982 by
Stevens and Sons Limited of
11 New Fetter Lane, London
and printed in Scotland.

British Library Cataloguing in Publication Data

Bowett, D.W.
    The law of international institutions.—4th ed.
    1. International agencies   2. International law
    I. Title
    341.2   JK4001

    ISBN 0–420–46010–1
    ISBN 0–420–46020–9 Pbk

©
Stevens and Sons Limited
1982

Contents

PART ONE

GLOBAL INSTITUTIONS

A. *Organisations of general competence*

v

B. *Organisations of limited competence*

PART TWO

REGIONAL INSTITUTIONS

PART THREE

JUDICIAL INSTITUTIONS

PART FOUR

COMMON INSTITUTIONAL PROBLEMS

ABBREVIATIONS

Abbreviations of titles of institutions and organs

A.C.C.	Administrative Committee on Co-ordination
ALADI	Latin-American Integration Association
ANZUS	Australia, New Zealand and United States Security Pact
ASEAN	Association of S.E. Asian Nations
ASPAC	Asian and Pacific Council
CACM	Central American Common Market
CARIFTA	Caribbean Free Trade Area
CENTO	Central Treaty Organisation
CERN	European Organisation for Nuclear Research
COMECON	Council for Mutual Economic Aid (CMEA)
COMINFORM	Communist Information Bureau
ECA	Economic Commission for Africa
ECAFE	Economic Commission for Asia and the Far East
ECE	Economic Commission for Europe
ECLA	Economic Commission for Latin America
ECOSOC	United Nations Economic and Social Council
ECSC	European Coal and Steel Community
EFTA	European Free Trade Area

EDC	European Defence Community
EEC	European Economic Community
EFTA	European Free Trade Association
ENEA	European Nuclear Energy Agency
EPU	European Payments Union
Euratom	European Atomic Energy Community
FAO	Food and Agriculture Organisation
G.A.	General Assembly of the United Nations
GATT	General Agreement on Tariffs and Trade
IAEA	International Atomic Energy Agency
IA-ECOSOC	Inter-American Economic and Social Council
IBRD	International Bank for Reconstruction and Development
ICAO	International Civil Aviation Organisation
I.C.J.	International Court of Justice
ICSID	International Centre for Settlement of Investment Disputes
IDA	International Development Association
IDB	Inter-American Development Bank
IFC	International Finance Corporation
I.L.C.	International Law Commission
ILO	International Labour Organisation
IMCO	Intergovernmental Maritime Consultative Organisation
IMF	International Monetary Fund
IRO	International Refugee Organisation
ITO	International Trade Organisation
ITU	International Telecommunications Union
LAFTA	Latin-American Free Trade Area
NATO	North Atlantic Treaty Organisation

OAMCE	Organisation Africaine et Malagache de Co-operation Economique
OAS	Organisation of American States
OAU	Organisation for African Unity
OCAM	Organisation Commune Africaine et Malagache
ODECA	Organisation of Central American States
OECD	Organisation for Economic Co-operation and Development
OEEC	Organisation for European Economic Co-operation
ONUC	United Nations Operations in the Congo
OPEC	Organisation of the Petroleum Exporting Countries
P.C.A.	Permanent Court of Arbitration
P.C.I.J.	Permanent Court of International Justice
P.C.O.B.	Permanent Central Opium Board
SACEUR	Supreme Allied Commander in Europe
S.C.	Security Council
SEATO	South-East Asia Treaty Organisation
Sec.-Gen.	Secretary-General of the United Nations
T.A.A.	Technical Assistance Administration
T.A.B.	Technical Assistance Board
T.A.C.	Technical Assistance Committee
UCAS	Central African Union
UDEAC	Central African Economic and Customs Union
UN	United Nations
UNCIO	United Nations Conference on International Organisation, Documents, 15 vols. (1945)
UNCITRAL	United Nations Commission on International Trade Law
UNCOK	United Nations Commission on Korea

UNCTAD	United Nations Conference on Trade and Development
UNEF	United Nations Emergency Force
UNDP	United Nations Development Programme
UNESCO	United Nations Educational, Scientific and Cultural Organisation
U.N.J.Y.	United Nations Juridical Yearbook
U.N.T.S.	United Nations Treaty Series
W.E.U.	Western European Union
Yale L.J.	Yale Law Journal
Y.B.W.A.	Year Book of World Affairs
Z.f.a.ö.r.u.V.	Zeitschrift für ausländisches öffentliches Recht und Völkerrecht

LIST OF CHARTS

Chapter i

HISTORICAL INTRODUCTION

THE development of international organisation has been, in the main, a response to the evident need arising from international intercourse rather than to the philosophical or ideological appeal of the notion of world government. The growth of international intercourse, in the sense of the development of relations between different peoples, was a constant feature of maturing civilisations; advances in the mechanics of communications combined with the desire for trade to produce a degree of intercourse which ultimately called for regulation by institutional means.

The institution of the consul, an official of the State whose essential task was to watch over the interests of the citizens of his State engaged in commerce in a foreign port, was known to the Greeks and the Romans. It survives to this day as one of the less spectacular, but important, institutions of international law. The consul was not, however, concerned with representing his State as such, and for this purpose ambassadors were used, being despatched for the purpose of a specific negotiation. By the fifteenth century this intermittent diplomacy had been replaced in the relations of certain of the Italian States by the institution of a permanent diplomatic ambassador in the capital of the receiving State, and the practice of exchanging ambassadors, complete with staff and embassy premises, is now a normal (albeit not compulsory) feature of relations between States. It is not the purpose of this book to survey the development of consular and diplomatic relations; suffice it to say that in these two institutions can be found the origins of the subsequent and more complex institutions.

Situations soon arose in which the essentially bilateral relationships established by diplomatic embassies or missions were inadequate. For example, a problem would arise which concerned not two but many States, and whether what was proposed was a series of negotiations or even a formal treaty, there had to be found a means for representing the interests of all the States concerned.

The means was the international conference, a gathering of representatives from several States; simply diplomacy writ large.

1

The Peace of Westphalia in 1648 emanated from such a conference, as did the settlement after the Napoleonic Wars in 1815 through the Congress of Vienna and, even later, the post–1918 settlement negotiated at the Paris Conference of 1919 and embodied in the Treaty of Versailles. Clearly, any general post-war settlement demanded a more general participation in the negotiations than could easily be achieved via the traditional methods of diplomatic intercourse. Bilateral negotiation also proved inadequate for other problems of a general nature. The Congress of Berlin of 1871 was convened to consider the Russian repudiation of the régime for the Black Sea which had earlier been established at the Paris Conference of 1856; conferences met in Berlin in 1884 and 1885 to attempt to regulate the "scramble for Africa" which was leading to commercial rivalry and political antagonism between the European Powers. The Hague Conferences of 1899 and 1907 were an effort to secure, on a multilateral basis, agreement on different aspects of the law relating to the conduct of warfare on land and on the sea, and on the duties of neutral States. These are but a few examples of the many conferences which were called to solve problems on a multilateral basis.

The Congress of Vienna of 1815 had seen the initiation of the "concert system" which, for the purposes of any study of international organisation, constituted a significant development. As sponsored by the Czar Alexander I, what was envisaged was an alliance of the victorious powers pledged to conduct diplomacy according to ethical standards, which would convene at congresses held at regular intervals.[1] In fact four congresses were held between 1818 and 1822—at Aix-la-Chappelle (1818), at Troppau and Laibach (1820,1821), and at Verona (1822)—but the idea of regular congresses was thereafter abandoned and meetings took place as occasion required. The attempt to secure regular meetings was, however, a significant recognition that the "pace" of international relations demanded some institution for regular multilateral negotiations. The "Concert of Europe" remained a quasi-institutionalised system even after the Holy Alliance had broken up, until the First World War destroyed the balance of

---

[1] It gave to each of the members of the Holy Alliance a right to consultation and a right to propose a conference.

power on which it rested (or rather confirmed its demise); the London Conferences of 1912–13, at the end of the Balkan Wars, were the last conferences or congresses convened within the framework of the "concert system." The conclusion of a conference would normally be accompanied by a formal treaty or convention, or, where no such binding agreement was desired or obtainable, by a memorandum or minutes of the conference.

The disadvantages of this system of ad hoc conferences were, first, that for each new problem which arose a new conference had to be convened, generally upon the initiative of one of the States concerned. The necessity of convening each conference anew complicated and delayed international co-operation in dealing with the problem. Second, the conferences were not debating forums in the same way as the later assemblies of the League and the United Nations; delegations attended very much for the purposes of delivering statements of State policy and, though concessions were often made, the conferences had a rigidity which disappeared in the later "permanent" assemblies of the League and the United Nations. Third, the conferences were held by invitation of the sponsoring or host State; there was no principle of membership which conferred an automatic right to representation. Fourth, the conferences adhered to the strict rule of State equality, with the consequence that all States had an equal vote and all decisions required unanimity. As will presently be shown, there are matters in which it is necessary to subjugate the will of the minority to that of the majority if progress is to be made, and the unaminity rule represented a serious restriction on the powers of the ad hoc conference.

It might also be said to be a disadvantage of the conference system that, as a political body, the conference was not ideally suited to the determination of legal questions. There were many cases in which the issues before a conference, although of a primarily political character, involved questions of law, of the rights or duties of the States under international law. The Paris Conference of 1856 and the Berlin Conference of 1871, in dealing with the régime in the Black Sea, dealt very largely with legal issues. However, it must be remembered that there existed side by side with the conference system the traditional means of solving legal disputes, by mediation, conciliation or arbitration, although there was in this field, as in the field of political settlement, an

3

equal need for the creation of some permanent machinery.[2] It is also unlikely that a rigid separation between "political" and "legal" questions can ever be achieved so as to allocate the latter exclusively to judicial tribunals; politics are rarely "pure" and political matters do not cease to be such because they involve legal rights.

However inadequate the system of ad hoc conferences was for the solution of the political problems arising from international intercourse, it was even more inadequate for the regulation of the relations between groups of people in different countries arising from their common interests. The nineteenth century saw, therefore, an impressive development of associations or unions, international in character, between groups other than governments. This was followed by similar developments between governments themselves in the administrative rather than the political field. These developments, of the private international unions and of the public international unions (the former non-governmental, the latter governmental) must now be briefly summarised, for they foreshadowed the trend of development of international organisations generally.

I. THE PRIVATE INTERNATIONAL UNIONS

These unions or associations sprang from the realisation by non-governmental bodies, whether private individuals or corporate associations, that their interests had an international character which demanded the furtherance of those interests via a permanent international association with like bodies in other countries. The World Anti-Slavery Convention of 1840 was perhaps the first of these "private" conferences, many of which led to the establishment of some permanent machinery of association. Between 1840 and the beginning of the First World War something like 400 permanent associations or unions came into existence. The variety of interests thus organised can be seen from the following examples of unions of this kind: the International Committee of the Red Cross (1863), the Inter-Parliamentary Union (1889), the International Law Association (1873), the International Dental Federation (1900), the International Literary and Artistic Association (1878), the International Chamber of

[2] *Post*, pp. 255–257.

4

Commerce (1919). So great was the growth of these private unions that in 1910 an association, the Union of International Associations, was formed to co-ordinate their activities and to lay down the conditions of membership. These conditions are not without interest; they were (1) the possession of a permanent organ, (2) that the object must be of interest to all or some nations and not one of profit, and (3) that membership should be open to individuals or groups from different countries. A glance at the current *Yearbook of International Organisations* will give some indication of the proliferation of these private unions at the present day.

From the constitutional standpoint these private unions had a number of interesting features. They emphasised the need for permanent, as opposed to ad hoc, association and for periodic, regular meetings. Many set up a small, permanent secretariat. Many demonstrated by their membership the artificiality of a rigid distinction between "public" and "private" unions based upon function; membership sometimes comprised States, municipal authorities, national groups and societies and private individuals. Today, bodies like the International Council of Scientific Unions, the International Commission for the Scientific Exploration of the Mediterranean Sea, the International Statistical Institute, and the International Hospital Federation demonstrate the co-operation of States and individuals within the same association.

The activities of these private unions underlined, in many cases, the need for State action. In some cases this was brought about by treaty, and the work of the International Committee of the Red Cross in promoting the Geneva Conventions of 1864, 1906, 1929 and 1949, or that of the International Maritime Committee in promoting the Conventions on the Safety of Life at Sea of 1914 and 1929 are good illustrations of this. In other cases the success of the private unions led directly to the establishment of a public union in the same field; private activity led and State activity followed. In this sense the International Congress of Weights, Measures and Moneys in 1867 was the forerunner of the Metric Union, the International Association of the Legal Protection of Labour that of the ILO, and the International Literary and Artistic Association that of the International Bureau of Literary and Artistic Property.

It is not the purpose of this book, with its emphasis on the

5

organisations of the present day, to deal in detail with the history of the development of the private unions. Mention will be made, at a later stage, of their relationship (as non-governmental organisations) with the Economic and Social Council of the UN. This brief treatment is intended solely to demonstrate the manner in which the private unions anticipated the development of the public unions and to stress that the growth of international organisation came as a response to a demonstrated human need.

II. THE PUBLIC INTERNATIONAL UNIONS

In those fields where co-operation between governments became imperative, there developed the public international unions; these were, in fact, an essay into international organisation in the administrative sphere. The transition from private to public organisations was gradual, and no generally accepted definition of the public international union has ever been reached.[3] In general, however, they were permanent associations of governments or administrations, (*i.e.* postal or railway administrations), based upon a treaty of a multilateral rather than a bilateral type and with some definite criterion of purpose.

In the field of communications, the Congress of Vienna of 1815 established the Rhine Commission, invested with considerable powers. The Commission had power to amend the Règlement (though not the Convention) and had, in addition to this legislative power, a judicial power in its capacity as a court of appeal from the local courts in each littoral State established for the purpose of implementing the Convention and the Règlement. Each littoral State had one vote within the Commission, and whilst equality and unanimity were the normal rule, in certain administrative matters voting power varied with the length of the river bank of the member State. The European Commission for the Danube, established in 1856, similarly had administrative and legislative functions. Its budget came from tolls levied on river traffic, it frequently resorted to a majority vote, and the members of the Commission enjoyed diplomatic immunities. An "International Commission" for the Danube, with competence over the Upper Danube was established after 1919. Other international commis-

---

[3] See Eagleton, *International Government* (1948), pp. 177–179, and the literature there cited.

6

sions existed for the Elbe (1821), the Douro (1835),the Po (1849) and the Pruth (1866), though none of these compared in importance and power with the Rhine and the Danube. Railways, another means of transport susceptible to international administration, gave rise to many international conferences, and the International Union of Railway Freight Transportation, set up in 1890, in effect abolished the complete independence of the national administrations. Whilst it possessed an Administrative Bureau it had no legislative power other than via the conference of member States meeting at a regular intervals. Worthy of note is the fact that the Bureau had power to arbitrate over disputes. Other unions, dealing with various aspects of rail communications, have been established and, in the European Conference on Time Tables (1923), there assembled delegates of States, of railway and steamship administrations, and of Pullman and air companies.

The advent of wireless telegraphy similarly brought forth problems which called for international control, and in 1865 the International Telegraphic Union was established with a permanent bureau. The Conference of the Union had power to alter the Règlement (though not the Convention), and admitted representatives of private telegraph companies but without the right to vote. In 1906 the Radiotelegraphic Union was established, modelled on the Telegraphic Union and using the same permanent bureau.

The Universal Postal Union, established in 1874, provided for a five-yearly congress of plenipotentiaries, a conference of delegates of administrations, and a permanent international bureau. This combination of a diplomatic conference with a conference of postal administrations was not successful, and the latter ceased to meet. The conference had power to amend either Convention or Règlement and frequently used the majority vote. Moreover, in order to eliminate the need for a formal conference for any and every amendment, the practice developed whereby the Bureau would circulate proposals for amendment by post and, depending on the amendment, a notification of acceptance by either two-thirds or a simple majority would make the amendment binding on all members; this was a marked departure from the requirement of specific consent in the traditional "political" conference of States. The postal administrations of colonies and dependencies acquired separate representation and, in the case of the British Empire, did not always vote with the Mother Country. The financing of the permanent bureau was by a technique, now common, of dividing members into seven classes and varying the contribution according to the class.

In the field of health, since disease was no respecter of the national boundaries, much could be accomplished by international co-operation. After a number of conferences, sanitary councils on which several States were represented were set up at Constantinople, Tangiers, Teheran and Alexandria. The first was unsuccessful, being frustrated by Great Power rivalry. The last affords an example of moderate success, for with a staff of eighty-seven international health officers it regulated shipping and enforced quarantine regulations, having power to fine for the breach of those regulations. In 1903 the International Office of Public Health was established in Paris, with a much wider competence, and can be regarded as the predecessor of the World Health Organisation.

In the economic field the Metric Union (1875), the International Copyright Union (1886), the International Sugar Union (1902), and the International Institute of Agriculture (1905) serve to illustrate the breadth and kind of activity undertaken. The Sugar Union had a permanent commission which, by majority vote, could order a change in municipal legislation which, for example, granted unfair bounties or imposed unfair tariffs—a remarkable abandonment of sovereignty. The Institute of Agriculture provided for a quorum of two-thirds for voting purposes and for the balancing of votes according to the size of the budgetary contributions.

This survey of some of the earlier public unions does not purport to be exhaustive, but simply illustrative of their kind and variety. There is no agreement on their classification[4] and one need not be attempted here. Of more immediate interest are the constitutional developments and innovations made by the public unions, for they anticipated those made by present-day inter-governmental organisations.

In the first case, the trend towards permanence of association is very marked, whether in the form of permanent deliberative or legislative organs working with administrative organs (as in the

---

[4] See the classification of Woolf, *International Government*, p. 102, or of Eagleton, *International Government*, p. 177.

Telegraphic Union, Metric Union, UPU, etc.) or of periodic conferences working in conjunction with a permanent bureau (Industrial Property, Railway Freight Transportation). The departures from the unanimity rule are equally striking, particularly when coupled with the grant of legislative powers in the Rhine Commission. Useful, also, was the tendency to distinguish the Convention, embodying general rules, from the Règlement, which contained the detailed implementation of those rules and permitted amendment by a much simpler process. The representation of interests other than those of States, whether they be dependent territories, private companies or associations, and with or without the right to vote, injected a realism and degree of practicality which was of the utmost significance for future development. The techniques of weighted voting and of proportionate budgetary contributions pointed the way to the solution of extremely difficult problems to which the principle of the equality of States provided no effective answer. The outstanding problem was one of co-ordination of the activities of the many unions, and at this juncture one may profitably pass to the attempt by the League of Nations to secure some form of overall direction and co-ordinating authority.

III. THE UNIONS AND THE LEAGUE OF NATIONS

Article 24 of the Covenant of the League offered a means of co-ordination through the direction of the League. It provided that "there shall be placed under the direction of the League all international bureaux already established by general treaties if the parties to such treaties consent. All such international bureaux and all commissions for the regulation of matters of international interest hereafter instituted shall be placed under the direction of the League." The "direction of the League" was conceived, not as absorption of the bureaux or unions, but as the giving of support and the prevention of overlapping or duplication of activities, or of an unreasonable refusal to co-operate with other unions or the League itself. Few of the older unions consented to this direction, partly due to their desire for independence and partly due to the fact that often their members were not all members of the League, and those that were not were reluctant to accept the League's direction. Of the newly created unions, only five were admitted.

Those refused admission were generally not strictly "intergovernmental" and, therefore, not "established by general treaties" as the article demanded; the application of the International Agricultural Committee in 1923 was rejected on this ground, although where, as in the case of the International Relief Union, membership was largely confined to States, admission was granted as an exceptional case.

In the event, therefore, the League never became the effective co-ordinator of the activities of these many administrative unions. The greater success of the United Nations in its relationship with the "specialised agencies" will be dealt with at a later stage. One may, even here, however, raise the question of the desirability of associating these administrative unions too closely with the world political organisation. The fear is that, should the political organisation fail, the failure might extend to everything associated with it.

IV. CLASSIFICATION OF ORGANISATIONS

In concluding this introductory chapter, a word must be said of the classification of international organisations.[5] Quite apart from the intrinsic interest of the problem of classification, the reader is entitled to know the reason for the adoption of a particular scheme of presentation of these organisations in the present book.

From the descriptions of many of the public international unions in this chapter it will be readily apparent that organisations of an administrative character preceded those of a predominantly political character, like the League or the UN. A distinction based on function automatically suggests itself, and it is broadly possible to distinguish between the "political" organisations, concerned primarily with the preservation of international peace and security, and the administrative organisations of more limited aims. The distinction is perhaps more accurately stated as one between organisations of comprehensive competence and organisations of limited competence. Prima facie, one should also distinguish the institutions for the judicial settlement of disputes, such as the Permanent Court of International Justice. In fact this broad classification into political, administrative and judicial organisa-

---

[5] For detailed treatment of classification see Schermers, *International Institutional Law* (1980), Ch. 3.

tions is the one adopted in this book, in so far as the United Nations, the specialised agencies and judicial institutions are each given their respective sections. Its justification is not, however, its scientific accuracy, but simply its convenience for purposes of presentation and description. As we shall see, no rigid distinction in function is made in practice. The "political" organisation, the United Nations, has amongst its organs the Trusteeship Council, with primarily administrative functions, and the I.C.J., a purely judicial body. The co-ordination achieved by bringing the specialised agencies into relationship with the UN also makes any clear classification by function difficult.

Another possible basis of classification is the fact that some organisations are "global" whereas others are "regional." Therefore, in this book a separate section is devoted to regional organisations and, within Europe at least (because of the diversity of the organisations involved), it has been possible to make the same broad division between organisations of general competence and those of limited competence. Even the notion of a"regional" organisation is convenient rather than accurate, for in some organisations the "region" is based upon a political rather than a geographical test (*i.e.* NATO, the Warsaw Treaty Organisation). Moreover, a "global" organisation like the UN has within it many "regional" bodies such as the regional commissions of Ecosoc (the Economic Commissions for Asia, the Far East, Europe, Latin-America, Africa).

It has also been suggested that there is a fundamental distinction, and therefore a basis for classification, between organisations founded on a treaty between States and a treaty between governments. Jenks has described this distinction as having an importance comparable to that of the classical distinction between a confederation and a federation in the evolution of the public law of the principal federal states.[6] The idea is, essentially, that the inter-state treaty-form embraces the totality of the State's institutions, its legislative and judicial machinery as well as the administrative, whereas the inter-governmental treaty form embraces only the administrative. It would seem, however,

---

[6] "Some constitutional problems of international organisations" (1945) 22 B.Y.B.I.L. 18–20; see also Parry,(1946) 23 B.Y.B.I.L. 397, and, more in line with the present author's views, Starke, *Introduction to International Law*, 4th ed., p. 416.

that in practice the distinction is not regarded as having this significant difference in effect. The UN Charter itself refers indiscriminately to "peoples," "governments" and "States," so that it is difficult to see who the parties really are. Organisations like the IMF or the newer IMCO are based on inter-governmental treaties, whereas the FAO or WHO are inter-State; yet there is no observable difference in the view that States take as to their commitments according to the form used. The most that might be said is that, from the point of view of drafting technique, these variations leave much to be desired. The only possible justifications for the difference are first that the inter-governmental form would be satisfactory for a non-permanent organisation, like UNRRA, and second that some States might find it easier, from their constitutional position, to accept the inter-governmental form. The distinction between inter-governmental and non-governmental organisations is, of course, a quite different matter. The importance of this distinction will be brought out in discussing the relationships between the UN and the specialised agencies (inter-governmental) on the one hand and the NGO's on the other.[7]

It is also possible to distinguish organisations with "supra-national" powers, *i.e.* power to bind member States by their decisions, from those without such powers. But this is often the characteristic of a particular organ, rather than the organisation as a whole, and whilst the possession of such powers will be pointed out where they exist, it is not intended to classify in this book on the basis of a distinction between powers.

The adequacy of the system of classification adopted in this book will be for the reader to judge; its purpose is to simplify presentation, and, in the absence of an agreed, scientific classification, this purpose seems a satisfactory guide.

[7] See *post*, p. 69.

Bibliography

CHAUMONT: Les organisations internationles (1963).
COLLIARD: Institutions internationales (1966).
EAGLETON: International Government (1956), Chap. 7.

12

HILL: The Public International Conference (1929).
HILL: International Administration (1931).
KIRGIS: International Organisations in their legal setting (1977).
LEONARD: International Organisation (1951), Chap. 2.
MANGONE: A short history of International Organisation (1954), Chap. 3.
MONACO: Lezioni di Organnizzazione Internazionale (1965), Chap.1.
POTTER: Introduction to the Study of International Organsiation (1948).
REINSCH: Public International Unions (1911).
REUTER: International Institutions (1958), Part III, ss. 1–3.
SAYRE: Experiments in International Administration (1919).
SCHERMERS: International Institutional Law (1980).
SERENI: Le Organizzazioni Internazionali (1959).
WOOLF: International Government (1916).

PART ONE

Global Institutions

A. ORGANISATIONS OF GENERAL COMPETENCE

CHAPTER 2

THE LEAGUE OF NATIONS

THE creation of a league of States, dedicated to the maintenance of peace, had long been advocated in philosophical and juristic writings[1] and in the aims of private organisations. The immediate source of the League of Nations was, however, a proposal introduced at the Peace Conference of Paris in 1919. In the drafting of the Covenant of the League the major powers played the decisive role; it emerged as a fusion of President Wilson's third draft and the British proposals emanating from the Phillimore Committee.

The League's objective was "to promote international co-operation and to achieve international peace and security." The system of collective security envisaged in the Covenant rested, essentially, on the notions of disarmament (Art. 8), pacific settlement of disputes and the outlawry of war (Arts. 11–15), a collective guarantee of the independence of each member (Art. 10), and sanctions (Arts. 16 and 17). The League's disarmament programme failed dismally. As envisaged in the Covenant, the pacific settlement of disputes likely to lead to a rupture of the peace was obligatory; parties to the dispute could choose to go to arbitration, judicial settlement or to the Council of the League. It was obligatory to accept the award or a unanimous report of the Council and there was an obligation on all members not to go to war with any State so accepting as well as a "moratorium" forbidding recourse to war within three months of the award or the Council's decision. The members agreed to respect and preserve the "territorial integrity and existing political independence" of all members against external aggression. War, as such, was not made illegal but only where begun without complying with the requirement of the Covenant with regard to prior resort to pacific settlement of the dispute. A State resorting to war in violation of its undertaking with regard to pacific settlement was deemed to

---

[1] For a brief review of the growth of the idea, see Leonard, *International Organisation*, (1951), Chap. 2; or Eagleton, *International Government*, (1948), p. 247.

have committed an act of war against all other members. Yet it was left to each member to decide whether a breach had occurred or an act of war had been committed, so that even the obligation to apply economic sanctions under Article 16 (1) was dependent on the member's own view of the situation. Military sanctions could be recommended by the Council, but the decision on whether to apply them rested with each member.

Such was the system; in itself a not unworkable one. After an initial success in dealing with the Graeco-Bulgarian crisis of 1925, and a less spectacular achievement in the Chaco dispute of 1928, the League witnessed the invasion of Manchuria in 1931, the Italo-Abyssinian War of 1934–5, the German march into the Rhineland in 1936, into Austria in 1938, into Czechoslovakia in 1939, the Soviet Union's invasion of Finland in 1939 and, finally, the German invasion of Poland in 1939. Apart from half-hearted economic sanctions against Italy in 1935, no sanctions were ever really applied by the League. To this extent the failure of the League was due, not to the inadequacies of the Covenant, but to the apathy and reluctance of the member States to discharge their obligations. This being said, it is still worthwhile to examine briefly the structure of the League to see how far it represented an adequate machinery for the achievement of its purposes.

The League had but three principal organs: the Council, the Assembly and the Secretariat.[2]

The Council was designed as the organ of limited membership, comprising originally "representatives of the Principal Allied and Associated Powers together with representatives of four other Members . . . selected by the Assembly from time to time . . . " (Art. 4 (1)). It was enlarged by stages. Germany became a permanent member and the non-permanent membership was

---

[2] Auxiliary organs consisted of the technical organisations (economic and financial organisation, organisation of communications and transit, health organisation), the permanent advisory commissions (mandates commission, opium commission, advisory committee of experts for slavery, intellectual co-operation commission, etc.), the temporary advisory commissions (study of European union, special committee on contributions in arrears), and the administrative or executive organisations (advisory commission for refugees, commissioner for Bulgarian refugees). There were also the autonomous organisations like the ILO and the P.C.I.J., and the special organisations brought into relationship under Art. 22, such as the International Institute of Intellectual Co-operation (Paris) and the Nansen Office for Refugees.

increased to six in 1922, then to nine in 1926 and finally to eleven in 1936 but at no time had a majority of major powers. In practice the Council met four times a year and could be specially convened in an emergency. Its decisions were to be reached by unanimous vote, subject to the exclusion of the vote of a party to a dispute (Art. 15), but were not, as such, binding on member States; the rule of unanimity naturally made a recommendaion for sanctions difficult to achieve in a Council plagued by great-power rivalry and, even where this could be achieved (as in the cases of the Italo-Abyssinian war or the invasion of Finland), no member was bound to. apply military sanctions. These are the defects inherent in any "de-centralised" system of sanctions, that is to say, a system in which the executive organ does not take decisions on behalf of all the members and binding upon those members. The Council combined with its political role the task of supervising the Mandates system and various other economic and administrative activities.

The Assembly was the plenary organ, meeting annually and including States signatories of the Versailles Treaty, "neutral" States named in the annex to the Covenant as States invited to accede, and "any fully self-governing State, Dominion or Colony" admitted to membership by a two-thirds vote of the Assembly. Its terms of reference were wide: "any matter within the sphere of action of the League or affecting the peace of the world" (Art. 3 (3)). The Assembly in practice met annually, working through six main committees, and acted as a deliberative organ; it had only power to make "resolutions" or "recommendations" and could bind no member State. Each State had one vote and its voting procedure required unanimity, except for matters of procedure or for the appointment of committees to investigate particular matters which required a simple majority of members present. However, the main committees made recommendations to the plenary by simple majority vote and the Assembly itself adopted the practice of making a recommendation or "voeu" by simple majority,[3] thus minimising to some extent the difficulties of securing complete unanimity.

The third organ, the Secretariat, was by far the most ambitious international civil service, or "bureau," ever established in

---

[3] Williams, "The League of Nations and Unanimity" (1925) 29 A.J.I.L. 475–488.

international organisation. Reference to the Secretariat will be made in a later chapter.[4]

It will be noted that, although the establishment of the Permanent Court of International Justice was anticipated in the Covenant (Art. 14), the Court was a separate body and not, as in the UN, an organ of the League itself.

The League experienced considerable constitutional development. Reference has already been made to the enlargement of the Council and to the inroads made into the unanimity rule by the Assembly. More significant, perhaps, was the gradual extension of the Assembly's role at the expense of the Council, an extension which came with the gradual disillusionment in the effectiveness of the Council and parallels the shift of power later experienced in the UN for the same reason. The Assembly's technique of securing agreement via inquiry and general debate proved more effective than the narrower diplomatic negotiation favoured within the Council. It is noteworthy, also, that the Assembly gradually took over control of the budget from the Council, and control of the purse-strings carries considerable weight.

From the constitutional standpoint the League had several defects. The inclusion of the Covenant within the four Peace Treaties led to certain legal difficulties and to a partial identification of the League with the victor States, even though later it came to be recognised as a treaty independent of the Peace Treaties and the League admitted to membership former enemy States. The unanimity rule, inherited from the traditional diplomatic conference, proved a severe hindrance and the Assembly's move towards simple majority was a clear recognition of this. Certain matters were within the exclusive jurisdiction of the Council (expulsion of members, for example,) others were within the exclusive jurisdiction of the Assembly (admission of new members, revision of treaties); there was, however, concurrent jurisdiction in the most important matter of maintaining peace and the lack of any clear separation of powers in this matter (or of any priority in the right to deal with them) might give rise to difficulty where the Council and the Assembly differed in their approaches to the solution of a given problem affecting international peace. The Council's functions were too wide, for they included not merely its "political"

[4] *Post*, Chap.3, s.V.

functions but also certain administrative functions such as supervision over the Mandates system and the economic and social activities of the League.[5] It was realised, too late, that the political impasse within the Council too easily spread to these other activities and it is significant that in the UN they are handled by separate organs. Amendment of the Covenant was by a process both vague[6] and difficult, requiring ratification by a majority of the Assembly and *all* members of the Council (Art. 26); the process over-estimated the adequacy of the initial drafting and under-estimated the rate at which development must take place, and thus introduced a static element into an inherently dynamic organisation. The wisdom of allowing for withdrawal from membership (Arts. I, 26 (2), 16 (4)) can be questioned in an organisation aiming at universality and perpetuity. Finally, as history proved, a "decentralised" system of sanctions was ineffective; there had to be some delegation of authority to an executive organ and an acceptance of the principle that its decisions would bind all members.

No lengthy appraisal of the League is required here. It never acquired a universal character; handicapped from the outset by the non-participation of the U.S.A., it remained predominantly a European organisation with at one time a maximum membership of fifty-nine. The "delinquent" States, such as Japan, Germany and Italy, simply withdrew to pursue their aggression unembarrassed by membership. The success of the League in the field of economics, finance, public health, mandates, transport and communications, social and labour problems, was overshadowed by its failure to prevent the Second World War. Potter has said of the League that it "made a far greater contribution to the progress of international organisation than any other institution in history . . . ."[7] It did, however, fail to fulfil the hopes which it engendered by its formation. But, at the expense of repetition, it is worthwhile repeating that its failure was not due to its constitutional defects; it failed because members were not prepared to fulfil their obligations and thus ensure its success. That, in conception, it showed the right approach to the problem of

[5] See *post*, p. 59.
[6] *i.e.* was it for the Assembly and Council to act as such, or in joint session, and by the normal unanimity rule under Art. 26?
[7] *Introduction to the Study of International Organisation* (1948), p. 257.

maintaining peace cannot be doubted. The determination to establish the UN as its successor proved that only by such or similar measures was mankind to be protected from the catastrophe of world conflict.

The formal demise of the League came on April 18, 1946. Its legal personality had been recognised as distinct from that of the member States, not, admittedly, in the Covenant expressly, but by necessary implication from the various rights and duties assigned to it. No other construction could be placed on the grant to the League by the Swiss Government of juridical capacity, protection and immunity for its property and immunities and privileges for its personnel.[8] Yet, since the creation of this separate personality had been by the will of the member States, expressed in treaty form, it was obvious that those States could bring an end to the personality by a similar method. However, since that method would involve all the delay of drafting a text, signing and ratifying the treaty,the Assembly of the League chose to dissolve the League by simple resolution (so also with the Permanent Court of International Justice). The actual liquidation was handed over to a Board of Liquidation and is described in greater detail in the latter part of this book, in the section dealing with dissolution of international organsiations.[9]

[8] *Post*, p. 335.
[9] *Post*, p. 377.

Bibliography

AUFRICHT: Documentary Guide to the League of Nations, 1920–1946 (1947).

EAGLETON: International Government (1948), revised ed., Chaps. 10 and 11.

FISCHER WILLIAMS: Some Aspects of the Covenant of the League of Nations (1934).

MANGONE: A short history of International Organisation (1954), Chap. 5.

MILLER: The Drafting of the Covenant (1928), 2 vols.

MUNCH: Les Origines et l'oevre de la S.D.N. (1923–24), 2 vols.

OPPENHEIM: International Law, 8th ed., Vol. II, pp. 380–400.

REDSLOB: Théorie de la S.D.N. (1927).

STONE: Legal Controls of International Conflict (1959), Chap. VI.

WALTERS: A History of the League of Nations (1952), 2 vols.

CHAPTER 3

THE UNITED NATIONS

THE failure of the League of Nations to avert a second world war did not destroy the conviction, shared by many, that only by some form of general organisation of States could a system of collective security be achieved which would protect the international community from the scourge of war. The Allies were, even in 1941, calling themselves "The United Nations" and by 1943 the Moscow declaration had recognised "the necessity of establishing at the earliest practicable date a general international organisation, based upon the principle of sovereign equality of all peace-loving States, large and small, for the maintenance of international peace and security." The formulation of definite plans for such an organisation took shape in stages, at Teheran in 1943, at Dumbarton Oaks in 1944, at Yalta in 1945 and, finally, at the San Francisco Conference in 1945 where fifty governments, upon the basis of the Dumbarton Oaks proposals prepared by the four sponsoring States, together drafted the United Nations Charter.

The Charter is, of course, a multilateral treaty establishing or restating the rights and duties of the signatory States; it is not, however, subject to reservation or denunciation, although, despite the absence of a "withdrawal" clause, it may be assumed that legally a State can withdraw subject to its fulfilment of any outstanding obligations, such as its budgetary commitments.[1] A withdrawal could, however, be politically more difficult than in the case of the League and it is probably true that exclusion from the United Nations is politically disadvantageous; this is symptomatic of the relatively more important role which the UN plays in international relations than did the League. If this be true, then the suspension of the rights and privileges of a State against which the Security Council takes preventive or enforcement action (Art. 5), or expulsion for persistent violation of the Charter principles (Art. 6), can be very real sanctions.

The Charter is also the basic constitutional document of the

[1] See *post*, p. 390.

23

Organisation and, as such, it has an inherently dynamic character (which can be seen in the various constitutional developments since 1945) quite unlike the normal multilateral treaty.

The Organisation created by the Charter is not a "super-State" or anything resembling a world government. As we shall see, it is first and foremost a collective security system far more centralised than the League. The Security Council can take decisions binding on the members, but, in the main, the Charter provides special forms of co-operation between sovereign States, supplementing the traditional methods of inter-State intercourse, and extending into fields of social and economic affairs which lie outside a system of collective security *simpliciter*. It proceeds essentially on the basis of voluntary co-operation by the members and "commands" only in the limited field of enforcement action via the Security Council. This reliance on co-operation can be regarded as a limitation on the powers of the Organisation but it is perhaps preferable to regard it as a characteristic of any organisation to which sovereign powers are not delegated by the members.

It follows, therefore, that, since each member remains sovereign, the Organisation as such has no competence in matters within the domestic jurisdiction of a State.[2] Thus Article 2 (7) provides:

> "Nothing contained in the present Charter shall authorize the United Nations to intervene in matters which are essentially within the domestic jurisdiction of any state or shall require the Members to submit such matters to settlement under the present Charter; but this principle shall not prejudice the application of enforcement measures under Chapter VII."

A review of the practice under this article gives some indication of the bitter controversies which have arisen over this question of competence.[3] The Assembly's recommendation in December 1946 that Spain be debarred from membership of any international organisation or conference connected with the United Nations, the discussions on the treatment of Indians within the Union of South

---

[2] See Rajan, *The United Nations and Domestic Jurisdiction* (1958): also Higgins, *The Development of International Law through the Political Organs of the United Nations*, (1963), Part II.

[3] *Repertory*, Vol. 1, pp. 27 *et seq*.

Africa, or on the policy of apartheid pursued by the government of the Union, the discussion of the Tunisian, Moroccan and Algerian questions, and eventually of the Cyprus question, have brought forward strong protests from the governments concerned. Indeed, on some occasions the delegates of South Africa and France withdrew in protest, and, in 1962, the British delegate withdrew when the Assembly called for a more liberal constitution for Southern Rhodesia. During the decade of the '60s it became clear that the Assembly would refuse to regard any colonial situation as a matter of domestic jurisdiction. It may, of course, be argued that discussion as such can never constitute "intervention" and is therefore not prohibited by the article.[4] Certainly a matter which becomes serious enough to threaten international peace and security would, *ipso facto*, cease to be essentially "domestic"; that is sufficiently recognised by the proviso to Article 2 (7) regarding enforcement measures.[5] Equally certainly where a State has assumed treaty obligations with respect to a certain matter it can no longer maintain that the matter is exclusively within the domestic jurisdiction. But beyond this the application of the article is more a matter for political judgment than legal interpretation. Action by the Assembly which might drive members out of the Organisation is of questionable value although, it must be stated frankly, the Assembly should never decline to fulfil its responsibility in taking up a matter simply because to do so would incur the displeasure of a particular State. What is required is a proper balance between fulfilling the duties of the Assembly and, on the other hand, allowing the Assembly to become a forum in which one State may seek to embarrass another with which it has political differences.

A second general limitation on the powers of the Organisation springs from the normal principle of the law of treaties, *pacta tertiis nec nocent nec prosunt*; the Charter, as a treaty, cannot bind non-members. In general, therefore, the Organisation must proceed on the basis that the Charter obligations, where these go

---

[4] Lauterpacht, *International Law and Human Rights*, (1950), pp. 166 *et seq.*
[5] But note that where, as in the Congo, the Security Council orders "provisional measures" under Art. 40, since these do not have the character of "enforcement action" the proviso to Art. 2 (7) does not apply and the principle of non-intervention constitutes a limit upon the powers of the Organisation (see *post*, p. 86).

beyond the obligations of general international law, do not bind non-members. However, in Article 2 (6) it is provided that:

> "The Organisation shall ensure that states which are not Members of the United Nations act in accordance with these Principles so far as may be necessary for the maintenance of international peace and security."

Although this does represent a technical variation from the maxim stated above the political justification for asserting the primacy of the Organisation's interest in maintaining international peace and security is undeniable. Resolution 232 (1966) of the Security Council, which decided upon economic sanctions against Rhodesia, specifically invoked Article 2 (6) in addressing itself to non-members and urging them to act in accordance with it.[6]

I. THE SECURITY COUNCIL

The Dumbarton Oaks proposals had envisaged the need for an executive organ of limited membership which would be entrusted with "primary responsibility for the maintenance of international peace and security." Indeed, the increased degree of centralisation of the procedures for maintaining international peace and security, as contrasted with the League, made the Security Council even more essential than the Council of the League. What was needed was a small, executive organ, functioning continually and able to take decisions quickly and effectively so as to bring into operation the enforcement machinery of Chapter VII of the Charter whenever international peace and security was threatened. Whilst it may be true that the Security Council is not, in practice, such an organ, the present chapter should show that any failure is due more to the attitude of its members than to any constitutional defects in the Charter provisions.

---

[6] For the somewhat equivocal responses of Austria (a member) and Switzerland (a non-member), based upon their special position as "neutralised" States, see S/7795 and S/7781, p. 58. See generally Falk, "The authority of the U.N. to control non-members" (1965) *Rutgers L.R.* 591. And see Gold, "The Fund and Non-Member States" *IMF Pamphlet Series* No. 7 (1966).

STRUCTURE OF THE SECURITY COUNCIL

GENERAL ASSEMBLY

COLLECTIVE MEASURES COMMITTEE

INTERNATIONAL ATOMIC ENERGY AGENCY*

SECURITY COUNCIL

CHIEFS OF STAFF OF THE PERMANENT MEMBERS OF THE SECURITY COUNCIL

MILITARY STAFF COMMITTEE

COMMITTEE ON THE ADMISSION OF NEW MEMBERS

COMMITTEE OF EXPERTS

DISARMAMENT COMMISSION

AD HOC BODIES

Namibia
Rights of Palestinian People
concerning Resol. 421 (1977)
South Africa
Benin
Apartheid
UNTSO
UNDOF
UNFICYP
UNMOGIP

* The International Atomic Energy Agency, an autonomous inter-governmental body under the aegis of the United Nations, reports annually on its activities to the General Assembly, and, as appropriate, to the Security Council and to the Economic and Social Council.

1. Composition

Article 23, as amended,[7] provides that the Security Council shall consist of 15 members of which five are "permanent members," namely China, France, U.S.S.R., United Kingdom and United States. These five permanent members enjoy an exceptional status not only by virtue of their permanency but also by reason of special voting rights amongst which, as we shall presently see, the most important is the power of "veto." The justification for granting this exceptional status to five members lies in the "inescapable fact of power differentials," to use Jessup's phrase. In other words, the basic premise was that upon these members would fall the brunt of the responsibility for maintaining international peace and security and, therefore, to them must be given the final or decisive vote in determining how that responsibility should be exercised. To this end, all the signatories of the Charter agreed to a system which might otherwise (*i.e.* without such agreement) have been contrary to "the principle of the sovereign equality of all its Members" upon which the Organisation is based (Art. 2 (1)).

The assumption made in 1945 that these five named States were the "great Powers" was, of course, a political judgment. The actual naming of them in the Charter introduces a static element into the Charter, for it cannot be assumed that these identical five will necessarily remain the five "great Powers," and in an organisation intended to endure problems may well arise when any marked shift of power does occur. Those problems will be rendered more acute by the procedure for amendment of the Charter which, under Articles 107 and 108, requires the consent of the named five members to any amendment; it is difficult to imagine a permanent member voting itself out of that status.

The 10 other members of the Security Council, the non-permanent members, are elected for two years by the General Assembly, and are not immediately eligible for re-election. In order to ensure a certain continuity, the elections are staggered, five States being elected each year, and by a two-thirds majority vote. Article 23 itself indicates certain criteria to be applied in these elections, namely, contribution to "the maintenance of

---

[7] See Amendments to Arts. 23, 27 and 61 which entered into force on August 31, 1965: UNJY (1965), 159.

international peace and security and to the other purposes of the organisation," and "equitable geographical distribution." The ten seats are now allocated according to the following formula: Afro-Asia (5), Eastern Europe (1), Latin-America (2), Western Europe and others (2). This allocation is based upon General Assembly resolution 1991 (XVIII)A and not upon the amending Protocol. However, it is clear that this formula now replaces the earlier "gentleman's agreement" of 1946.[8]

Apart from the question of which States shall be seated on the Council, there is a further question of whether a given government is to be recognised as entitled to represent a particular State. This question arises when two rival governments exist, both claiming to represent the State concerned, or when objection is taken to the circumstances in which a government achieved power. The examples of these two cases are, of course, China and Hungary; the manner in which the question has been dealt with in practice is discussed later.[9]

2. Voting Procedure

The voting procedure is stated in Article 27:

"1. Each member of the Security Council shall have one vote.

2. Decisions of the Security Council on procedural matters shall be made by an affirmative vote of nine members.

3. Decisions of the Security Council on all other matters shall be made by an affirmative vote of nine members including the concurring votes of the permanent members; provided that, in decisions under Chapter VI, and under paragraph 3 of Article 52, a party to a dispute shall abstain from voting."

The distinction between the procedures envisaged under paragraphs 2 and 3 rests on a distinction between "procedural matters" and "all other matters." There is, however, no enumeration of what matters fall into these two categories comparable to the enumeration of "important questions" in Article 18, which covers voting in the General Assembly. The Security Council is thus

[8] For the practice under this earlier agreement see *Repertory*, Vol. II, paras. 14 *et seq.*
[9] *Post*, p. 395,

faced with the problem of determining into which category any particular decision falls, a problem often referred to as the "preliminary question." In practice certain matters have been well-established as procedural,[10] but, when a dispute arises, the permanent members have relied upon the statement of the Four Sponsoring Powers at San Francisco,[11] which stated:

> "1. In the opinion of the Delegations of the Sponsoring Governments, the Draft Charter itself contains an indication of the application of the voting procedures to the various functions of the Council.
>
> 2. In this case, it will be unlikely that there will arise in the future any matters of great importance on which a decision will have to be made as to whether a procedural vote would apply. Should, however, such a matter arise, the decision regarding the preliminary question as to whether or not such a matter is procedural, must be taken by a vote of seven members of the Security Council, including the concurring votes of the permanent members."

The U.S.S.R. has relied upon this second paragraph and insisted upon deciding the preliminary question by a non-procedural vote, using its veto to determine that the main issue was non-procedural. Then, in the subsequent vote on the main issue, the U.S.S.R. would cast a second veto, exercising a "double-veto." This practice, if carried to its absurd conclusion, could mean that no matter could be considered as procedural against the wishes of a permanent member. Thus used, it would be contrary to the first paragraph of the statement quoted above which indicates that resort to a vote on the preliminary question should only be had when the Charter does not itself contain an indication of the nature of a given question. In fact the Charter does, in Chapters IV, V, X and XI, employ the heading "Procedure"to various articles and this, together with the application of accepted canons

---

[10] For example, decisions relating to the agenda, adjournment of meetings, conduct of business, invitation to States to participate in the meetings, postponement of consideration of a question: see generally *Repertoire of the Practice of the S.C.,* 1952–55 (ST/PSCA/1/Add. 1), pp. 63 *et seq.*

[11] *Repertory,* Vol. 11, p. 104. This statement, to which France later adhered, was prepared in answer to a lengthy questionnaire submitted to the Sponsoring Powers by the lesser Powers and concerning the operation of the voting procedure.

of treaty interpretation and including the use of analogy, should often provide an answer without resorting to a vote on the preliminary question. One means of avoiding a double-veto is for the President to rule that the matter is procedural; under rule 30 of the Rules of Procedure this ruling stands if nine members support it, and thus there is no place for a veto. The practice depends for its efficacy on the astuteness and fairness of the delegate in the Presidential Chair.

In Article 27 (3) the requirement of an affirmative vote of nine members "including the concurring votes of the permanent members" results in the power of any permanent member to prevent *by its sole vote* the taking of a decision which has the support of a majority of the Council, *i.e.* of nine members. This power, the power of veto, has been the instrument whereby much of the efficacy of the Council has been destroyed and the permanent members have not hesitated to use the veto when they felt their vital interests were at stake.

In many cases permanent members have chosen to abstain from voting rather than cast a negative vote which would prevent the Council from taking a decision. This practice of abstention,[12] though not envisaged in Article 27 (which might easily have added the proviso "present and voting,") has been generally accepted and must now be deemed to be a constitutionally valid interpretation of the notion of "concurrence." It has even been argued that not only is this practice of abstention unaffected by the Charter amendments to Article 27, but that a non-procedural vote might be taken with all permanent members abstaining.[13] In fact Portugal raised this very question with the Secretary-General apropos of the Council's resolution 221 (1966) on Rhodesia (on which two permanent members abstained) although the Secretary-General declined to give a legal opinion, maintaining that it was for the Council to interpret its own resolutions over procedures.[14] The crucial question, of course, is whether a resolution adopted with all the permanent members (or even some of them) abstaining would be not only constitutionally valid but also *binding*

---

[12] For the precedents, see *Repertory*, Vol. II, p. 81.

[13] Stavropoulos, "The Practice of Voluntary Abstentions by permanent members of the Security Council under Article 27 (3) of the Charter" (1967) 61 A.J.I.L. 737.

[14] S/7271 and S/7735/Rev.I.

to the extent that it embodies a decision which purports to be mandatory under Chapter VII: this question has yet to be settled in practice.[15] Although the I.C.J. did not specifically deal with this question, in its advisory opinion in 1971 on Legal Consequences for States of the continued presence of South Africa in Namibia, it upheld the practice of abstention by a permanent member as "not constituting a bar to the adoption of resolutions."[16]

A more difficult question arises where a decision is taken in the absence of a permanent member. Cases had occurred where the Council took a decision on a procedural matter in the absence of a permanent member without objection[17]; it is only in non-procedural decisions, where "concurrence" is required, that the real difficulty arises. In fact the decisions of June 25 and 27, 1950, determining a breach of the peace in Korea and recommending member States to take up arms to assist South Korea, were taken in the absence of the U.S.S.R., which thereafter denied their legality. Although, it must be added, the U.S.S.R. was in breach of Article 28 requiring her "to be represented at all times at the seat of the Organisation," there is some difficulty in arguing that this breach, or the precedents for abstention and for absence on a procedural vote, justify the decisions taken; when the permanent member abstains from using a veto there may be said to be an implied "concurrence" in the majority will, but this cannot be said when the member is not present at all. The political justification for those decisions is a separate question from that of their constitutional validity.[18]

Article 27 (3) does contain a proviso under which abstention is compulsory, *i.e.* "in decisions under Ch. VI, and under paragraph 3 of Article 52, a party to a dispute shall abstain from voting." This is a re-statement of the general principle of law, *nemo judex in sua causa*, albeit confined to "disputes"[19] dealt with under the specified provisions. It would not extend to the question of

---

[15] See Gross, (1968) 62 A.J.I.L. 315 who argues that such resolutions may be merely permissive and not binding on the entire membership.

[16] (1971) I.C.J. Reports, para. 22.

[17] See Stone, *Legal Controls of International Conflict* (1959), pp. 204–210, for a review of these cases.

[18] See, on the constitutional issues, Stone, *op. cit.,* pp. 210–212; Kelsen, *Recent Trends in the Law of the UN,* (1951), pp. 927–936.

[19] The Council's practice in defining a dispute is confused: see the debate in 1976 on the complaint by the Comoros against France.

determining the existence of a "threat to the peace, breach of the peace or act of aggression" under Article 39 of Chapter VII, even though there may be a complete "dispute" about this question. Hence, in this most vital question, there is no obligation to abstain, and a permanent member can use the veto to prevent a finding that it has itself (or any other State favoured by its support has) been guilty of aggression.

The early practice of the Council revealed a tendency to discuss whether what was involved was a "dispute" (as opposed to a "situation,"), whether the decision to be taken came under Chapter VI, and whether a particular State was a "party." Since 1947 this legalistic analysis has lost its appeal and members of the Council have abstained without forcing the Council to determine whether a legal obligation to do so exists.

3. Functions and Powers

These are stated in Articles 24–26 of the Charter. In conferring on the Council "primary responsibility for the maintenance of international peace and security," the members of the Organisation agree that it "acts on their behalf." The Council thus acts as the agent of all the members and not independently of their wishes; it is, moreover, bound by the Purposes and Principles of the Organisation, so that it cannot, in principle, act arbitrarily and unfettered by any restraints. At the same time, when it does act *intra vires*, the members of the Organisations are bound by its actions and, under Article 25, they "agree to accept and carry out the decisions of the Security Council in accordance with the present Charter." This agreement would not extend to a mere "recommendation" as opposed to a "decision."[20]

Although Article 24 (2) refers to "the specific powers granted . . . in Chapters VI, VII, VIII and XII," practice has now confirmed the view that this enumeration is not exhaustive. There exist such other "implied" powers as may be required in the execution of its overall responsibility.[21]

The Council's primary function, the maintenance of inter-

---

[20] But "decisions" are not confined to decisions under Chapter VII of the Charter: see the *Namibia* case, (1971) I.C.J. Reports, para. 113.

[21] See *Repertory*, Vol. II, pp. 19–25: a good example is the responsibility the Security Council was to assume under the Statute of the Free Territory of Trieste, including a power to appoint a Governor.

national peace and security, is to be exercised by two means; the first is the pacific settlement of such international disputes as are likely to endanger international peace and security, and the second (which presupposes the failure or inapplicability of the first) is the taking of enforcement action.

(a) *Pacific settlement of disputes*

Chapter VI sets out the various means by which the Council may assist in the settlement of disputes and, as Article 33 makes clear, the methods of Chapter VI are supplementary to those methods traditionallly established in international law and which the parties must "first of all" utilise, as appropriate. Moreover, it is with disputes "likely to endanger international peace and security" that the Council is concerned, and not with all disputes.

The following have a *right* to submit disputes to the Council: the Assembly (Arts. 11 and 12), the Secretary-General (Art. 99), member States (Art. 35 (1)), and non-member States (Art. 35 (2)). It will be noted that the non-member States are bound, in so doing, to accept in advance and for the purposes of the dispute "the obligations of pacific settlement provided in the present Charter." There is also a *duty* imposed on parties to a dispute likely to endanger international peace and security to submit the dispute to the Council if they cannot settle it by the traditional means enumerated in Article 33; this is provided for in Article 37, but would, presumably, only apply to member States and not non-members.

The dispute, once submitted, is not automatically incorporated on the Council's agenda. The Council itself decides, by a majority of nine (*i.e.* a procedural decision), whether or not to place the matter on the agenda and even this decision is without prejudice to the question of competence. It may well be that the Council, after considering the matter, decides that the dispute is not an "international" one—in other words it is precluded from exercising any jurisdiction by virtue of the domestic jurisdiction clause of Article 2 (7). Similarly, it is for the Council itself to decide whether and when a dispute shall be removed from its agenda, and again by a procedural vote.[22]

---

[22] For details of the controversy which arose over this question in the Iranian dispute of 1946, see *Repertoire*, 1946–51, pp. 92–93.

Once seised of a "dispute" the Council is *bound* under Article 32 to invite the parties to participate in the discussion (but without the right to vote); the Council *may* invite member States under Article 31 'to participate in the discussion of "any question," whether or not a "dispute," when the Council considers the interests of that State are specially affected. Naturally the Council is not limited by the statements of the parties. It may undertake its own investigations[23] of the matter by setting up an investigation under Article 34, using a subsidiary organ for that purpose. If the purpose of the investigation is as defined in that Article, it is not permissible for the Council to utilise its general power under Article 29 to establish subsidiary organs. Under Article 29 the vote is procedural; under Article 34 it is non-procedural and the Council's decision to investigate a dispute should, as agreed at San Francisco, be made only with the concurrence of the five permanent members.[24] There is no legal obligation spelt out in the Charter to the effect that a State must comply with the decision of the Council in the sense of permitting a commission of investigation to have access to its territory. Yet, without such access, the value of a commission is much decreased and it can be, and has been, argued that such an obligation exists by virtue of the general terms of Article 25.

In dealing with a dispute the Council has a number of alternative ways of proceeding open to it. It may, under Article 33 (2), simply call upon the parties to utilise the traditional means of settlement, leaving the choice of any particular means to the parties. Or it may, under Article 36 (1), recommend a particular means of settlement, but taking into consideration that "legal disputes should as a general rule be referred by the parties to the International Court of Justice . . . " (Art. 36 (3)).[25] The Council may even go further and, under Article 37 (2), recommend the actual terms of a settlement in addition to the means or procedures for settlement; this is tantamount to assuming a quasi-judicial function where the dispute affects the legal rights of the parties.

[23] See Kerley, "The powers of investigation of the UN Security Council" (1961) 55 A.J.I.L. 892.

[24] See, as an example of controversy on this point, the discussion in the Czechoslovakian question in 1948: *Repertory*, Vol. II, pp. 231–233.

[25] Only in the *Corfu Channel* case did the Council ever so recommend, although it recommended arbitration in the *Suez Canal Company* case, the India/Pakistan dispute in 1951 and the Indonesian dispute in 1947.

This way of proceeding is available only where the dispute is considered by the Council to endanger international peace and security; otherwise the Council could only so act, under Article 38, with the consent of all the parties. A final alternative is for the Council to set up a machinery for settlement within the United Nations—such as the Committee of Good Offices in Indonesia in 1947 or the Mediator between India and Pakistan over Kashmir—or to refer the dispute to an existing organ, as was done by the Council in referring the Palestine question to the General Assembly.

Whatever the course adopted under Chapter VI, it must be adopted by a non-procedural decision. The justification for this lay in the so-called "chain of events" theory. This was that, it being granted that any permanent member could veto enforcement action, it was necessary to grant the same veto in matters of pacific settlement lest the permanent member should otherwise become committed to a course of action against its wishes which might ultimately lead to taking enforcement action. This reasoning does not really bear close examination. As we shall see, any permanent member can, whatever course has been adopted under Chapter VI, cast its veto to prevent the determination of a "threat to the peace, breach of the peace or act of aggression" under Article 39 without which none of the enforcement measures under Chapter VII can be applied.

One final point must be noted in connection with Chapter VI, and that is that the powers of the Security Council are to make "recommendations." These are not binding on the States to whom they are addressed, for Article 25 relates only to "decisions." Hence the recommendation by the Council to the parties in the Corfu Channel dispute, that they submit their dispute to the International Court of Justice, was not regarded by the majority of the Court as creating a legal obligation to submit to the Court's jurisdiction.

(b) *Enforcement action*

The striking difference between the Covenant of the League of Nations and the Charter of the United Nations lies in the degree of centralisation accorded to the Council—the executive organ of limited membership. Under the League each member State reserved the right to determine for itself whether a particular State had resorted to war in breach of the Covenant, and also whether or not to comply with the recommendation of the Council with regard to the "sanctions" to be taken. In the United Nations the Security Council has the power, under Article 39, to determine, on behalf of the Organisation as a whole, whether or not there has been a "threat to the peace, breach of the peace or act of aggression," and its decisions with regard to any enforcement action to be taken are, theoretically at least, binding on the member States by virtue of Article 25.

The Security Council has two forms of enforcement action available to it; those described in Article 41, *i.e.* not involving the use of armed force, and those described in Article 42, *i.e.* involving action by air, sea or land forces. Before deciding upon either it is necessary for the Council to "determine the existence of any threat to the peace, breach of the peace, or act of aggression" under Article 39. This determination, as with all other decisions under Chapter VII, can only be made by a non-procedural vote. The unanimity (or abstention) of the permanent members is, therefore, essential and it is unlikely that any enforcement action can be taken under Chapter VII against any of the permanent members or any other State securing their support; the veto ensures that result. It is for this reason, above all others, that the measures envisaged in Chapter VII are virtually useless in an age in which the threats to the peace, breaches of the peace or acts of aggression occur in situations in which there is a conflict of interests between, notably, the U.S.A. and the U.S.S.R. and, consequently, no unanimity amongst the permanent members. Hence, after the Indonesian affair in 1947 (in which there was unanimity) and until the Congo crisis of July 1960, there had been no occasion on which the Security Council effectively used its powers under Chapter VII, except that of Korea in 1950, and this only due to the fortuitous absence of the U.S.S.R.[26] The successive crisis of Berlin, Palestine, Indo-China, Hungary and Suez, to pick random samples, have all involved the East-West conflict of interests and, therefore, the Council has never used its enforcement powers. The East-West conflict destroyed the principle of unanimity upon which the whole structure of Chapter VII (and indeed UNO itself) depends for its ability to work as intended

[26] See *ante*, p. 32.

under the Charter. The Congo crisis of 1960 appeared, at the outset, to be a unique example of a situation which called for UN action but which did not involve the East-West conflict. Hence the three major resolutions of July 14, 22 and August 9 came from the Security Council, enabling the Secretary-General to provide military assistance to the government of the Congo. Admittedly the action taken was not "enforcement action" under Articles 41 or 42, but rather the "provisional measures" envisaged in Article 40,[27] but it nevertheless marked an unprecedented and initially successful use by the Security Council of its powers under Chapter VII. However, in due course the conflict between East and West re-emerged even here, and with the loss of unanimity effective control passed to the Assembly, convened in emergency session under the Resolution on Uniting for Peace procedure by the Security Council on September 17, 1960, against the votes of the U.S.S.R. and Poland. Some semblance of unanimity—or at least the absence of a veto—returned during the Council's handling of the Rhodesian affair: the resolutions of April 9, 1966 (221 (1966)), December 16 1966 (232 (1966)) and May 29 1968 (253 (1968)) envisaged sanctions under Chapter VII, the later two resolutions in fact specifically invoking Articles 39 and 41. On November 7, 1977 the Council also unanimously imposed an arms embargo against South Africa under Chapter VII. However, as a general rule it is certainly true that the veto has invariably frustrated the Council's enforcement powers, so that the following discussion of Chapter VII is necessarily of a somewhat cursory character. It must be emphasised that by the end of 1980 the only true "sanctions" ordered by the Council, and made mandatory for all members, have been the economic sanctions against Rhodesia and South Africa.[28]

The determination of a "threat to the peace, breach of the peace

---

[27] See Schachter, "Legal Aspects of the UN Action in the Congo" (1961) 55 A.J.I.L. I. The I.C.J., in its advisory opinion of July 20, 1962, on *Certain Expenses of the UN*, took the view that ONUC was not "enforcement action" against any State, and that the S.C. could "police a situation" (p.167) without agreements existing under Art. 43, and without characterising its actions as "enforcement action."

[28] The U.S.A. imported chrome-ore from Rhodesia under Act of Congress (the Byrd amendment) despite the mandatory sanctions. In *Diggs* v. *Shultz* U.S. Court of Appeals, D.C. Circuit, 1972 the Court accepted that this was a "blatant disregard of our treaty undertakings."

or act of aggression" under Article 39 must precede the use of the Council's powers under Articles 41 and 42, whether or not that Article is specifically invoked or cited. With the exception of the resolutions 232 (1966) and 253 (1968) on Rhodesia, the practice of the Council has been to avoid specific reference to that Article[29] (a practice, incidentally, not limited to Article 39); even in determining that the armed attack upon the Republic of Korea constituted a "breach of the peace," no specific reference to Article 39 was made by the Council in its resolution of June 25, 1950.[30] Two difficulties in the making of this determination call for comment. The first is that the "peace" referred to must mean "international" peace. It would be contrary to the intention of the Charter to assume that the Council could forcibly intervene in any civil strife which did not threaten international peace, and both in the Korean question and in the earlier Indonesian question the argument was advanced that action by the Council was barred on the ground that it intervened in the purely domestic jurisdiction of the State concerned. However, that argument was in both cases implicitly rejected. In the Congo affair, although the Council probably acted under Article 40, and although there was there a specific request from the government for UN intervention, it may also be recalled that the principle of non-intervention guided the Secretary-General in instructing the UN Force not to intervene in the internal struggle for political power but to confine its activities to the maintenance of law and order, the protection of human life and the elimination of the foreign elements (originally Belgian troops and later mercenaries) which tended to create a threat to *international* peace.[31] The second difficulty arose from the lack of any definition in the Charter of the terms used, *i.e.* "threat to the peace, breach of the peace or act of aggression." This lack was intentional. At San Francisco an area of discretion was intentionally left to the Council and although, in Res. 3314 (XXIX) in 1974 the General Assembly succeeded in adopting a definition of

---

[29] See *Repertory*, Vol. II, pp. 334 *et seq.*

[30] S/1501; similarly in the resolution of June 27, 1950 (S/1511). It may be noted that neither resolution, the latter of which recommended Members to furnish assistance to the Republic of Korea, cited Articles 41 or 42. One construction of these resolutions is that they were in exercise of the power of "recommendation" under Art.39.

[31] Schachter, *Loc. cit.,* pp.15–20, and see especially the S.G.'s statement to the Security Council (UN Doc. S/P.V 887).

aggression, this is only for the "guidance" of the Council and the list of aggressive acts is not exhaustive. In practice the problem may be one of acquiring accurate factual knowledge of events, rather than one of legal definition, and in Korea the Council relied heavily on the report of UNCOK (UN Commission on Korea) then in Korea, just as in considering the situation in Lebanon in 1958 it relied on the reports from UNOGIL (UN Observer Group in Lebanon). The presence of such groups "on the spot" is a tremendous advantage and, as has already been suggested, the Council has the power under Article 34 to send a committee or group where none already exists.

The practice of the Council rather suggests that the power under Article 40 to call upon the parties to comply with "provisional measures" does not depend upon a prior determination under Article 39. In the Palestine question Article 40 was specifically invoked, in ordering a cease-fire and calling for a withdrawal behind provisional truce-lines; similar measures were ordered by the Council in Kashmir. In the Congo, whilst there was abundant evidence, both in the terms of the request for assistance by the government of the Congo and in statements by representatives in the Security Council, that a "threat to international peace" existed, no specific determination under Article 39 was made. The resolutions of the Council were, however, probably based upon Article 40. The question whether a resolution "calling upon" States or other bodies to comply with the provisional measures is mandatory cannot be answered in the abstract. It was, however, clear that the three resolutions of July 14, 22 and August 9 were considered as mandatory, for the Secretary-General's conclusion[32] that Articles 25 and 49 applied was confirmed by the Security Council in the resolution of August 9. Both those articles refer to the *decisions* of the Security Council which are, of course, binding on all members.[33] The "provisional measures" ordered under Article 40 do not prejudice the rights of the parties; they are simply a means of preventing an aggravation of the situation and

[32] Statement to the S.C. on August 8; Doc. S/P.V 884, pp. 9–10.
[33] Note that the U.K. (Letter of December 12, 1979, S/13688) took it upon itself to decide that the obligations under Article 25 in relation to sanctions against Rhodesia were at an end. The Council, in its resolution of December 21, 1979 and the Assembly in Resol. 34/192 of December 18, took the view that this was for the Council to decide.

the Council may take account of a failure to comply with such provisional measures.

The crux of the scheme envisaged in Chapter VII lay in the provision to the Security Council of the armed forces necessary to enforce its decisions against recalcitrant States, and this was to be effected by agreements between the member States and the Council, for which provision is made in Article 43. No such agreements have ever been concluded, so that the Council lacks the "teeth" with which to bite, and the Military Staff Committee for which provision is made in Articles 46 and 47 (although established since 1946) has no real function since its purpose was to make plans for the application of armed force and to advise and assist the Council in the use of forces placed at its disposal. The absence of agreements under Article 43 would not, however, prevent member States from agreeing ad hoc, and in relation to a particular situation, to place forces at the disposal of the Council; in fact this is precisely how the United Nations Command was composed in Korea in 1950 and how the UN Force in the Congo was subsequently constituted. However, dependence on "voluntary contributions" cannot be said to be the surest guarantee of effectiveness.

The failure of the Security Council to fulfil its primary purpose of maintaining international peace and security has led to three major developments which will be considered later. The first is the assumption by the General Assembly of a role which was certainly never intended for it, namely that of determining a breach of the peace or an act of aggression and recommending action by members, including the use of armed forces.[34] The second is the development of powerful regional security systems or alliances outside the UN, such as NATO or the Warsaw Treaty Organisation, a development symptomatic of the breach of unity between the permanent members and the lack of confidence in the efficacy of the general collective security system based on the Security Council.[35] The third is the development of "peacekeeping" operations under either Chapter VI or Chapter VII of the Charter, using limited military forces, voluntarily contributed by Member States, for observation and fact-finding (*e.g.* UNTSO, UNMOGIP

---

[34] See *post*, p. 49.
[35] See *post*, p. 180.

(Kashmir), UNYOM (Yemen), UNIFIL (Lebanon), UNDOF (Golan Heights)) or maintaining law and order in a situation involving an actual or incipient threat to peace (*e.g.* ONUC (Congo), UNFICYP (Cyprus)). This role falls between Chapters VI and VII—some have advocated a new Chapter VIA—and, since it is one shared by the Assembly, will require further discussion at a later stage.

II. THE GENERAL ASSEMBLY

1. Composition

The General Assembly is the plenary organ of the United Nations, consisting of all the member States, each with one vote but entitled to five representatives. It would be this organ, therefore, which would reflect the extent to which the Organisation had become truly universal and thus a "world forum," an effective sounding-board for world opinion. For many years the Organisation fell far short of universality, for admission to membership was dependant on the fulfilment of certain conditions, and was to be achieved via a certain process, as Article 4 makes clear:

"1. Membership in the United Nations is open to all other peace-loving states which accept the obligations contained in the present Charter and, in the judgment of the Organisation, are able and willing to carry out these obligations.

2. The admission of any such state to membership in the United Nations will be effected by a decision of the General Assembly upon the recommendation of the Security Council."

Thus Statehood is not alone sufficient; the applicant for membership has to satisfy the Organisation that it is "peace-loving," that it "accepts" the Charter obligations and, moreover, is "able and willing" to carry them out. The criteria are all capable of subjective appreciation by the existing member States in voting on an application for admission. However, the repeated failure of the Security Council in the first ten years of the Organisation's history to admit many States was due more to the East-West conflict, in which each side sought to keep out States politically sympathetic to the other. The General Assembly frequently expressed its concern over the Security Council's failure to make favourable recommendations on admission and eventually requested an Advisory Opinion from the International Court of Justice on whether a State, in voting upon an application for admission to membership, was legally entitled to make its vote dependent on conditions other than those enumerated in Article 4 (1); the Court advised that it was not and, in particular, was not entitled to make its affirmative vote subject to the condition that other States be admitted together with a particular State or States.[36] The practice of the Security Council showed no significant change, and there was some indication of a will in the Assembly to "by-pass" the Council and proceed unilaterally to admit to membership. However, the Assembly requested a second Advisory Opinion on the legality of such a course, and the Court advised that the Assembly had no power to admit an applicant in the absence of a favourable recommendation from the Council.[37] It is a sad commentary on the respect shown by some member States for the Court's opinions that it was not until 1955 that the impasse was broken and, as a result of a political compromise, 16 new members were admitted out of a proposed bloc of 18. By the end of 1980 the membership stood at over 150, a figure which offers a favourable comparison with the League so far as universality is concerned.

It would be unwise to assume universality, or rather the lack of it, was the only problem on membership. Changes in the character of members, for example those arising from secession or from union, can and do occur. In the case of the division of India (an existing member) into the two States of India and Pakistan in 1947, the course taken was to regard the new "India" as a continuation of the old for the purpose of membership and to admit Pakistan as a new member. When the union between Egypt and Syria occurred in 1958 the U.A.R. was not admitted to membership as a new State; the Secretary-General simply informed all members of

---

[36] (1948) *I.C.J. Reports,* 65 (Advisory Opinion of May 28, 1948). As late as 1975, however, the U.S.A. was adamant in making its vote in the Security Council to admit the two Vietnams to membership dependent on the Council's willingness to admit South Korea.

[37] *Ibid.* (1950) 10 (Advisory Opinion of March 30, 1950).

the change and the U.A.R. henceforth sat in place of the two States with, of course, only one vote instead of two. The reverse process was applied when the union was subsequently dissolved.

2. Voting procedure

The voting procedure of the Assembly is provided for in Article 18; it consists essentially in one vote for each member, with decisions on "important questions" being taken by a two-thirds majority of the members present and voting, and decisions on other questions by a simple majority of members present and voting.

The equality of voting power of all members, irrespective of size, power or population, is at present the only acceptable solution in a political organisation based on the principle of sovereign equality. It may be somewhat unreal to equate, for voting purposes, Yemen and the U.S.A., but no other acceptable formula has yet been found.[38] The unreality of the system is most marked when, on given issues, States group into "blocs,"[39] for example the Latin-American "bloc," or the Afro-Asian "bloc,"for in the bloc a number of States may, by their voting power, acquire a degree of political influence within the Assembly which is disproportionate to their real political influence in the world at large. There is also increasing concern over the unreality of some of the resolutions passed: a resolution passed in the teeth of opposition by States which alone have power to implement the resolution, and which therefore stands little chance of implementation, adds little to the prestige of the Assembly.

Decisions of the Assembly cover all types of action taken by vote, whether framed as "recommendations," "resolutions" or the like. The vote can be by "acclamation" (in effect an expression of unanimity without resort to vote), or by show of hands or, if demanded, by roll-call; secret ballots are also used in certain cases, notably for elections. The nineteenth session of the Assembly

---

[38] For one interesting suggestion see Clark and Sohn, *World Peace through World Law*, (1958), pp. 19–30; representation is based on population in the revised Charter suggested by the authors.

[39] See Lijphart, "The analysis of bloc voting in the General Assembly" (1963) 57 *A. Pol. Sci. Review* 902.

witnessed the extraordinary practice of taking all motions and resolutions by "consensus" so as to avoid a confrontation over the question whether Article 19 should be applied so as to deprive of a vote those Members in arrears with their contributions to an amount exceeding two years' contributions.

In the main the distinction between "important questions"and "other questions," although vague, has not led to undue difficulty. The fact that there is a non-exhaustive list of important questions does, of course, help in making the distinction, just as the phrase "present and voting" helps to avoid the problems of abstention and absence which plague the Security Council.[40] Although new categories of important questions can be created by a simple majority, the Assembly has tended not to create categories but to decide specific cases on an ad hoc basis[41]; thus the request for an Advisory Opinion on S.W. Africa in 1950 was ruled procedural (or rather not "important") without creating a general rule for all requests for Advisory Opinions. A "question" is treated as being the individual resolution and not the problem which the resolution concerns.

3. Functions and powers

The Assembly is a deliberative organ which proceeds via recommendation rather than binding decision; any attempt to draw analogies with a national assembly, parliament or legislature, is apt to be dangerous unless this fundamental difference in powers is grasped—the Assembly cannot directly legislate for the member States. Although as a general rule it can have no legally binding effect on the members, there are some circumstances in which a recommendation may create direct legal obligations for members, for example by the Assembly's approval of the budget which creates an obligation on a State to pay its contribution or by decisions on elections to various organs or admission to membership; such matters normally relate to the internal working of

---

[40] *Ante*, p. 31.

[41] Kerley, "Voting on Important questions in the UN General Assembly" (1959) 53 A.J.I.L. 324. Note that the General Assembly, at its sixteenth session and again at its twentieth session, voted that any proposal to change the representation of China was an "important question."

the Organisation as distinct from a recommendation addressed to a member.[42]

What is of great, contemporary interest is the way in which certain resolutions of the Assembly assume a "quasi-legislative" role. While they cannot create direct legal obligations for member States they can embody a consensus of opinion about what the law is so that, indirectly, they become evidence of international law. The repeated affirmations of the right of self-determination have probably given normative status to what was originally regarded as a political doctrine. The celebrated resolution 1803 (XVII) on permanent sovereignty over natural resources, or resolution 2131 (XX) on non-intervention, or resolution 2312 (XXII) embodying a declaration on territorial asylum, or resolution 3281 (XXIX) on the Economic Rights and Duties of States, are examples of resolutions which cannot be ignored in any contemporary evaluation of what is the relevant rule of law. Of course, where the resolution has not gained the support of many of the States principally concerned—as is the case with resolution 1653 (XVI) on the illegality of nuclear weapons—its evidential quality is correspondingly weakened.[43] A quite distinct legislative role is played by the Assembly in formulating treaties open for accession by members, such as the Treaty on Principles governing the exploration and use of Outer Space (annexed to resol. 2222 (XXI) or the Covenants on Economic Social and Cultural Rights and on Civil and Political Rights (annexed to resol. 2200A (XXI). Here, of course, the normative character will arise not so much from this resolution but more from the accessions of member States. However, important though these "quasi-legislative" functions

---

[42] See D. H. N. Johnson, "The Effect of resolutions of the General Assembly of the UN," *ibid.* 32 (1955–56), 97; Falk, "On the quasi-legislative competence of the General Assembly" (1966) 60 A.J.I.L. 782; Arangio-Ruiz, "The normative role of the General Assembly" (1972) 137 R.C., 431; Higgins, *op. cit.,* pp. 1–10; Schermers, *op. cit.,* (1980), 598–619; Schreuer, "Recommendations and the traditional sources of international law" (1977) 20 German Y.I.L., 103–118; the views of Judge Lauterpacht in the *A.O. on S.W. Africa—Voting Procedure,* (1955) *I.C.J. Reports,* 118–119, and, more recently, in the A.O. of July 20, 1962, on *Certain Expenses of the UN,* the separate opinion of Fitzmaurice (pp. 208–211) and of the majority (p. 164).

[43] See the Award of Dupuy, making this point in relation to the 1974 Charter on Economic Rights and Duties of States in *Texaco* v. *Libya* (1977) 53 *I.L.R.* at 485.

may be, the Assembly remains primarily a deliberative ⟨
not a legislative organ. The objection to conferring on re
of the Assembly a direct, legislative effect so as to bind l
stems from two separate considerations. First, there   ᴜᴇ
objection to a two-thirds majority binding the minority. Second,
there is the objection that this circumvents the traditional
treaty-making process, avoiding the need for ratification which,
under the constitutions of some States, is regarded as essential if
new obligations are to be assumed.

The deliberative character of the plenary organ is reflected in
Article 20 which provides for "regular annual sessions" and for
special sessions to be convened by the Secretary-General at the
request of the Security Council or of a majority of the members of
the UN. This is to be contrasted with the capacity for continous
functioning of the Security Council, the executive organ.

The powers of the Assembly are broadly stated in Chapter IV
and include power "to discuss any questions or any matter within
the scope of the present Charter or relating to the powers and
functions of any organs provided in the present Charter" (Art.
10). This provides the basis for the overall authority of the
Assembly over the various organs of the UN although, clearly, in
relation to the Security Council and the Court, this authority is
limited. This "supervisory" role in relation to other organs is
further specified in Chapters IX, X and XII which give the
Assembly a general power of supervision over the arrangements
made by the Economic and Social Council (ECOSOC) with the
specialised agencies, and an overall control over ECOSOC
generally and also the Trusteeship Council. Further elements in
this control are the Assembly's power to approve the budget (Art.
17), which necessarily affects the scope of the activities of other
organs, and the right to receive reports from these organs (Art.
15). In practice detailed examination and discussion does not take
place on reports from the Security Council, but it does on reports
from ECOSOC and the Trusteeship Council; this emphasises what
was said above, namely, that control over the Security Council is
not of the same order as that exercised over other organs.

A further power is "to consider the general principles of
co-operation in the maintenance of international peace and
security" (Art. 11 (1)) and "to discuss any questions relating to the
maintenance of international peace and security" (Art. 11 (2)). In

47

this lies the basis of the Assembly's political power, albeit power in a deliberative sense, and this power overlaps considerably with that of the Security Council. So also does the power to make recommendations with regard to "the peaceful adjustment of any situation regardless of origin, which it deems likely to impair the general welfare . . . " (Art. 14); a glance at the Security Council's own powers in relation to pacific settlement under Chapter VI will demonstrate this. However, whilst a concurrent jurisdiction may exist in these spheres, a conflict is sought to be avoided by Article 11 (2) which, in the last sentence, provides that: "Any such question on which action is necessary shall be referred to the Security Council by the General Assembly either before or after discussion." This stresses the fact that, so far as "action" may be required, it is the Council and not the Assembly which is competent; in other words it underlines the distinction between the executive and the deliberative organ. Further, under Article 12 (1) (to which Articles 10 and 11 (2) are subject) the Assembly may not make recommendations with regard to a dispute of situation in respect of which "the Security Council is exercising . . . the functions assigned to it . . . " Thus the priority of the Council in such matters is maintained, and the Assembly is kept notified by the Secretary-General of the matters with which the Security Council is seised (Art. 12 (2)). Normally, when the Council wishes the Assembly to deal with a matter, it removes the item from its own agenda; this procedure was followed on the Spanish question on November 4, 1946, on the Greek question on September 15, 1947, and on the complaint of Chinese aggression against South Korea on January 31, 1951. The difficult problem arises where this procedure is not followed and the Assembly places a matter on its agenda whilst it still remains on the agenda of the Council[44]; this occurred, for example, when the Assembly proceeded to discuss the Soviet Union's complaint that the U.S.A. had committed aggression against China by invading Formosa, despite the fact that the Council had decided "to defer consideration" of this same question on September 29, 1950. The justification for such action by the Assembly can be sought in part in the argument that the Council had ceased to, or was unable to, exercise the function

---

[44] See Memorandum on the Practice of the UN as regards the consideration of the same questions by the SC and the GA, (1964) *U.N.J.Y.*, 228.

assigned to it in this matter, or that discussion in the Assembly could not constitute "action"; the larger part of the justification is not, however, one of legal interpretation but of the necessity for the Assembly to promote the aims of the Charter when the Security Council cannot or will not do so.

The possibilities of a clash in competence between the Assembly and the Council have been increased by the tendency of the Assembly to assume a larger role than that which the Charter would at first sight suggest. This larger role has sprung from the reaction of member States to the frustration of the Council consequent upon the East-West rivalry; there is a clearly apparent resolve to use the Assembly to achieve the aims of the Charter when the Council cannot do so. This may be illustrated by two important and controversial developments.

Added political responsibility was difficult for the Assembly to assume when it met in short annual sessions. In 1947, therefore, the Assembly established, as a subsidiary organ under Article 22, the Interim Committee to function inbetween the sessions of the main Assembly; its purpose was to ensure continuity in the control the Assembly could exercise over major political problems. The Interim Committee was to have represented on it all the member States (though with only one delegate instead of five) and its competence was more restricted than that of the Assembly itself. It did, however, have power to discuss important disputes or situations submitted to the Assembly, to conduct investigations and to advise the summoning of a special session of the Assembly. This Committee was boycotted by the U.S.S.R. on the ground that it was a perpetuation of the Assembly, contrary to Article 20, which provided for annual sessions, and a usurpation of the Council's role. The Committee was re-established in 1948 and 1949 but, since that time, the Assembly has been able to exercise sufficient control by either convening a special session or else adjourning its regular session in December and continuing in the New Year.

The second development came after a United Nations force had been established in Korea by the resolutions of the Council of June 25 and 27, 1950. These, it will be recalled, were passed only due to the fortuitous circumstance of the absence of the U.S.S.R. from the Council. The unlikelihood of a repetition of that circumstance led the Assembly, on November 3, 1950, to pass the Resolution on

49

Uniting for Peace[45]; this was done in the face of the strongest opposition by the Soviet Union. The Assembly thereby assumes the power to determine a threat to the peace, breach of the peace or act of aggression and to recommend action by members including the use of armed force. This power is to be exercised only "if the Security Council, because of lack of unanimity, fails to exercise its primary responsibility for the maintenance of international peace and security"; it is virtually an assertion of a secondary responsibility. A Peace Observation Commission of fourteen members is established which can be despatched to any "trouble-area" so as to advise the Assembly of any necessary action, and a Collective Measures Committee of 14 members is established to co-ordinate the action taken by members on the Assembly's recommendation. In the event of a breach of the peace or act of aggression the Assembly will, if not in session, meet within 24 hours of a request being made by nine members of the Security Council or a majority of the members of the Assembly. This procedure has in fact been used on October 31, 1956, when, after the United Kingdom and France had voted against the U.S. resolution in the Security Council proposing measures for the cessation of the military action against Egypt, the Suez question was transferred to the Assembly. Four days later, on November 4, following a Soviet veto, the Hungarian question was similarly referred to the Assembly. More recently, on September 17, 1960, and again following a Soviet veto, the Congo question was referred by the Council to the Assembly.[46] The extent to which practice has so far demonstrated an acceptance within the Security Council of the Resolution on Uniting for Peace is not entirely clear. Two issues must be separated. The first is that of the appropriate procedure for convening an emergency session of the Assembly, for, whereas the resolution, as amended, provides for this by a vote of "any nine members of the Security Council" the Soviet Union contested the legality of this at the time of the adoption of the resolution on the ground that Article 20 governs the convening of emergency sessions and the vote of the Security Council is a non-procedural one to which, therefore, the veto applies. However, the resolutions of the Council of October 31 and November 4, 1956, which both referred specifically to the Resolution on Uniting for Peace, were adopted against the votes

[45] Resol. 377 (V).   [46] UN Doc. S/P.V. 906, p. 116.

of Britain and France in the first case and of the U.S.S.R. in the second case. On neither occasion did the U.S.S.R. raise the Article 20 argument and, indeed, it voted for the resolution of October 31. However, somewhat inconsistently, the U.S.S.R. again raised this particular argument when on September 17, 1960, it opposed the convening of the emergency session of the Assembly to deal with the Congo. In 1971 the U.S.S.R. abstained in the vote of the Council referring the Bangladesh issue to the Assembly under Uniting for Peace.[47] Again, in January 1980 the U.S.S.R.'s negative vote failed to stop the Assembly convening to discuss the Soviet invasion of Afghanistan, and calling for the withdrawal of all foreign troops.

The second issue is the more substantive one of the capacity of the Assembly to establish, even by recommendation, a UN Force. The U.S.S.R. has constantly opposed this as being in breach of Articles 11 (2) and 12 and the force monopoly of the Security Council envisaged under Chapter VII, and this became one of the principal Soviet contentions before the Court in the proceedings on the request for an advisory opinion on *Certain Expenses of the United Nations.*[48] The U.S.S.R. took the view that it was under no obligation to contribute towards the maintenance of UNEF since the force was illegal under the Charter. Although a number of States suggested to the Court that it was not necessary, in order to answer the actual question put to the Court,[49] that the Court should consider the validity of the powers assumed by the General Assembly under the Resolution on Uniting for Peace, the Court did in fact examine the respective functions of the Assembly and the Securiy Council with respect to the maintenance of international peace and security.[50] Briefly summarised, the Court, in the majority opinion (9 votes to 5), advised that the Security Council had "primary" and not exclusive authority, and that whilst the

[47] Resol. 303 (1971), December 6, 1971.
[48] Advisory Opinion of July 20, 1962; for the oral statement of Profesor Tunkin of the U.S.S.R., see C.R. 62/32. He met the argument that, by voting for the resolution of October 31, 1956, the U.S.S.R. had already accepted the legality of the resolution on Uniting for Peace by saying "but the S.C. did not ask the G.A. to take action for maintaining peace and security, which under the Charter the S.C. alone is competent to take" (*ibid.* p. 8). This is scarcely adequate, for the Resolution for Uniting on Peace clearly gives the Assembly such power, and the Resolution was specifically referred to in the resolution of October 31, 1956.
[49] See *post*, p. 418.
[50] (1962) *I.C.J. Reports*, 163 *et seq.*

51

taking of enforcement action was the exclusive prerogative of the Council under Chapter VII, this did not prevent the Assembly from making recommendations under Articles 10 and 14; the limitation of Article 11 (2) does not apply in such cases, since the "action" there referred to means only "enforcement action" which is in the nature of coercive action directed *against* a State. The UNEF "action" was not, in the Court's view, enforcement action, but rather "measures" recommended under Article 14.[51] It would therefore seem that, whilst the Court did not explicitly hold that the Resolution on Uniting for Peace was a lawful assumption of power by the Assembly, it implicitly did so, to the extent that the General Assembly may make recommendations which do not envisage "enforcement action" against States.

Hence, whatever be the arguments based on Articles 11 (2) and 12 of the Charter and the absence of any specific power to determine a threat to the peace, breach of the peace or act of aggression,[52] the resolution may now be treated as justifiable, at least to the extent that it envisages a "peace-keeping" operation as opposed to "enforcement action," on the basis of the purposes and principles of the organisation. Naturally, the co-operation of members is entirely voluntary, for the Assembly has only the power to "recommend." The Assembly has used its powers under this resolution to condemn the Chinese intervention in Korea as aggression,[53] to recommend economic sanctions against China[54] and to bring about the withdrawal of British and French forces from Egypt in 1956.[55] It must be added that the future of the Assembly's peace keeping powers insofar as these involve the use of military forces is in doubt. Part of the problem is budgetary, or financial,[56] but the larger part is the refusal of the Soviet bloc to concede such powers to the Assembly. So far, after several years

---

[51] *Ibid.* 172. Note that the validity of the Congo operations was not contested on the same grounds, because it was the S.C., not the G.A., which initiated them, hence the Resolution on Uniting for Peace was not in question. The principal argument relating to the Congo was that the Secretary-General had exceeded and abused the powers conferred on him: this, too, was rejected by the Court.

[52] For a summary of the original arguments in 1950 on the legality of the resolution, see *Repertory,* Vol. I, summary of practice under Art.11, paras. 53–167.

[53] Resol. 498 (V) of December 14, 1950.

[54] Resol. 500 (V) of May 18, 1951.

[55] Resolutions 997 (ES–I), 1002 (ES–I) and 1120 (XI) of November 2, 7 and 24, 1956.

[56] See *post,* p. 418.

of search for a compromise, the Special Committee on Peace Keeping Operations (Committee of 33) has failed to reach agreement on this central issue. Significantly, when UNEF was re-instated in the Middle East in 1973, it was done by resolution of the Security Council and not the Assembly.[57] So, too, UNDOF and UNIFIL were established in 1974 and 1978 (in the Golan Heights and the Lebanon) by the Council, not the Assembly.

The additional and specific powers given to the Assembly under Chapter IV do not raise so acutely the problem of a conflict of jurisdiction with the Council. Article 13 lists a number of purposes for which the Assembly may make recommendations. Article 14 gives power of recommendation of measures for the peaceful adjustment of situations likely to impair the general welfare; under this article it put forward the famous and abortive Plan of Partition with Economic Union for Palestine in 1947, and UNEF must be regarded as established within this article. It has not so far become clear whether it gives the Assembly power to recommend treaty revision as an instrument of peaceful change. Article 15, as has been previously mentioned, gives power to receive reports from other organs, and Article 16 refers to its functions relating to the Trusteeship system.[58] Article 17 confers on the Assembly the power to consider and approve the budget of the Organisation. This is initially prepared by the Secretary-General and goes through the Advisory Committee on Administrative and Budgetary Questions, then the 5th Committee, and then before the Assembly itself. The actual contributions of the members are on a scale fixed by the Committee on Contributions, broadly according to capacity to pay (ascertained from national income, *per capita* income) and are subject to annual review. The Secretary-General has at his disposal for unforeseen expenses a Working Capital Fund and can submit supplementary budget estimates. A major budgetary problem for some years was the upkeep of UNEF and the UN Force in the Congo (ONUC) since some States which contested the legality of the setting up of UNEF or the uses made of the UN Force in the Congo had repeatedly refused to pay their contributions; other States had failed without even this pretext. The Court's opinion, to the effect that the expenses of UNEF and

---

[57] UNEF was disbanded and its functions assumed by UNTSO on July 24, 1979, by decision of the Council.

[58] See *post*, p. 79.

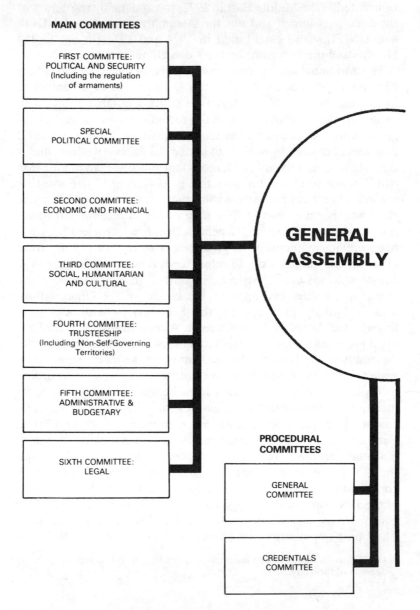

MAIN COMMITTEES

FIRST COMMITTEE:
POLITICAL AND SECURITY
(Including the regulation
of armaments)

SPECIAL
POLITICAL COMMITTEE

SECOND COMMITTEE:
ECONOMIC AND FINANCIAL

THIRD COMMITTEE:
SOCIAL, HUMANITARIAN
AND CULTURAL

FOURTH COMMITTEE:
TRUSTEESHIP
(Including Non-Self-Governing
Territories)

FIFTH COMMITTEE:
ADMINISTRATIVE &
BUDGETARY

SIXTH COMMITTEE:
LEGAL

**GENERAL
ASSEMBLY**

**PROCEDURAL
COMMITTEES**

GENERAL
COMMITTEE

CREDENTIALS
COMMITTEE

Other Existing Bodies Set Up
by General Assembly

Interim Committee of the General Assembly
Disarmament Commission
Commission of Conciliation for the Congo
Sub-Committee on the Situation in Angola
United Nations Conciliation Commission for Palestine
United Nations Relief and Works Agency for Palestine
    Refugees in the Near East (UNRWA)
Panel for Inquiry and Conciliation
United Nations Scientific Advisory Committee
United Nations Scientific Committee on the Effects of
    Atomic Radiation
Committee on the Peaceful Uses of Outer Space
United Nations Representative on Hungary
Peace Observation Commission
Collective Measures Committee
United Nations Commission for the Unification and
    Rehabilitation of Korea (UNCURK)
United Nations Children's Fund (UNICEF)
Office of the United Nations High Commissioner for
    Refugees
Committee on Establishment of United Nations Capital
    Development Fund
Committee on Information from Non-Self-Governing
    Territories
Special Committee of Twenty-four
Negotiating Committee for Extra-Budgetary Funds
United Nations Staff Pension Committee
Investments Committee
Board of Auditors
Panel of External Auditors
Consultative Panel on United Nations Information Policies
    and Programmes
Committee of Experts on the Review of the Activities and
    Organization of the Secretariat
Working Group to Examine Administrative and Budgetary
    Procedures of United Nations
United Nations Administrative Tribunal
Committee on Applications for Review of Administrative
    Tribunal Judgments
International Law Commission
Committee on Arrangements for a Conference for the
    Purpose of Reviewing the Charter
Committee on Government-Replies on the Question of
    Defining Aggression.
United Nations Commission on Permanent Sovereignty
    over Natural Resources
United Nations Commission on International Trade Law
    (UNCITRAL)
United Nations Development Programme (UNDP)
United Nations Institute for Training and Research
    (UNITAR)
United Nations Environment Program (UNEP)
United Nations Council for S. W. Africa
United Nations Special Fund (UNSF)
World Food Council (WFC)

**STANDING
COMMITTEES**

ADVISORY COMMITTEE
ON ADMINISTRATIVE
AND BUDGETARY
QUESTIONS

COMMITTEE ON
CONTRIBUTIONS

ONUC were "expenses of the Organisation" within the meaning of Article 17 (2) of the Charter will be discussed in detail later.[59]

This brief review of the functions and powers of the Assembly will demonstrate both their complexity and variety. Accordingly, a complicated structure of committees and subsidiary organs is required to enable the Assembly to discharge them.

The Assembly has seven Main Committees: First Committee, Political and Security; Special Political Committee; Second Committee, Economic and Financial; Third Committee, Social, Humanitarian and Cultural; Fourth Committee, Trusteeship (including non-self-governing territories); Fifth Committee, Administrative and Budgetary; Sixth Committee, Legal. There are two "procedural" committees, the General Committee and the Credentials Committee, and there are two Standing Committees, the Advisory Committee on Administrative and Budgetary Questions, and the Committee on Contributions.

At the beginning of each Assembly the General Committee, a kind of steering committee, allocates to each Main Committee those agenda items which, by reason of the subject-matter, fall within its competence. All Main Committees are plenary in composition and the bulk of the discussion takes place in the committees, the Assembly being called to meet towards the end of the session to vote on the reports from the various Main Committees; discussion of the substance of an issue is rarely renewed in the Assembly.

In addition to these, the Assembly has power under Article 22 to establish "such subsidiary organs as it deems necessary for the performance of its functions."[60] It has, therefore, established a great variety of subsidiary organs (including UNEF), differing in function, membership, duration and other respects. Most are established by a resolution of the Assembly itself, although in

[59] *Post*, p. 418.
[60] "Subsidiary organs" is a phrase apt to include any organ established by or under the authority of a principal organ of the UN in accordance with Art. 7 (2); such organs are an integral part of the Organisation. They must be distinguished from, on the one hand, the "specialised agencies" (as to which see *post*, Chap. 4), and on the other the "special bodies" such as the Permanent Central Opium Board (P.C.O.B.) or the Narcotic Drugs Supervisory Body, both of which were established by multilateral treaty prior to the establishment of the UN and have been given a special status within the UN. See generally the "Summary of internal Secretariat Studies of constitutional questions relating to agencies within the framework of the UN," Doc. A/C.1/758 (1954).

certain cases the Secretary-General has been requestd to establish the organ. Membership is sometimes dealt with in the resolution, sometimes separately by the Assembly or by the Assembly upon the recommendation of the President of the Assembly or of a Main Committee, and sometimes by election where the members of the committee or organ are individuals and not States. This is true of organs like the UN Administrative Tribunal or the International Law Commission (I.L.C.), although in the case of the Special Committee on the representation of China or the 29 member UN Commission on International Trade Law (UNCITRAL), the elective process was also applied to an organ composed of States.

In function these subsidiary organs include "study" committees, such as the Committee on International Criminal Jurisdiction, or the UN Institute for Training and Research (UNITAR) which is an autonomous institution, which study a matter and report back to the Assembly, to the Secretary-General, to one of the other principal organs of the UN or even, as in the case of the Disarmament Commission, to a conference of States. They include organs with political responsibilities, such as the UN Special Committee on Palestine or the UN Council for S.W. Africa; some even have power of independent decision, such as the Conciliation Commission for Palestine, and some have power to negotiate directly with governments, for example UNRWA and the Office of the High Commissioner for Refugees. There are also "administrative" committees, of which the two standing committees referred to above, the Committee on Contributions and the Advisory Committee on Administrative and Budgetary Questions, are examples. There are "operational agencies," such as UNICEF or UNRWA, which have a distinctive secretariat, budget, and governmental committee or board to give policy directives. There are also "judicial" organs, such as the Administrative Tribunal, and organs *sui generis*, such as the I.L.C., this last being established specifically for the furtherance of the Assembly's duties under Article 13 (i) (a) of the Charter. A fairly recent tendency is to establish subsidiary organs with an "autonomous" status, such as UNITAR, UNCTAD,[61] UNIDO,[62] UNEP or the

---

[61] See Gardner, "UNCTAD" in (1968) 22 *Int. Org.*, 99 for an excellent summary of this organ.
[62] Established by resol. 2152 (XXI), this "autonomous organisation within the U.N." became a specialised agency in 1979.

World Food Council. The latter two, in particular, fall between the normal categories of subsidiary organs and specialised agencies. Equipped with separate budgets, secretariats and organs they do raise difficult problems of relationship to the parent organ, the Assembly. They also raise specific problems of co-ordination with both ECOSOC and the specialised agencies about which more must be said later.[63]

The question of the competence of the Assembly to establish a particular organ has been raised on a number of occasions, and reference has already been made to the opposition to the establishment of the Interim Committee in 1947. In general the Assembly can only establish organs with powers which fall within the scope of the Assembly's own powers; however, these must be ascertained not simply by reference to specific provisions of the Charter but by necesssary implication from the powers and duties of the Assembly in general. Hence the I.C.J. did not doubt that the Assembly could establish the Administrative Tribunal with power to render judgments binding on the UN, even though no *specific* power to that effect was given in the Charter.[64] Moreover, in the same opinion, the Court expressed the view that the Assembly could establish a judicial organ with power to take decisions binding on the Assembly itself.[65]

In concluding, therefore, the overall picture which the Assembly gives is of an organ which has assumed more and more political power as the Security Council has shown its inability to act so as to achieve the purposes and principles of the Charter. This *de facto* amendment of the Charter has posed questions of the constitutional validity of the various steps in this development, but, by and large, the Assembly has sought to regulate its actions by reference to those purposes and principles and has been undeterred by the narrower questions of the legal interpretation of specific articles of the Charter.

III. THE ECONOMIC AND SOCIAL COUNCIL (ECOSOC)

Before dealing in any detail with the structure and functions of ECOSOC it is as well to review, historically, the trend of

---

[63] *Post*, p. 65.
[64] (1954) *I.C.J. Reports*, 47.
[65] See *post*, p. 324.

governmental co-operation in the economic and social fields; only in this way can the present importance of ECOSOC be really appreciated.

In the first chapter mention was made of the prolific growth of international public unions in these fields; the various river commissions, the U.P.U., the I.T.U., the Metric Union and the Sugar Union are but a few of the many instances of governmental co-operation which preceded the League. During the First World War co-operation between the Allies reached an impressive stage through various bodies such as the Wheat Executive (1916) and Allied Maritime Transport Council (1917), although, be it added, this was based on the personal integration of the national administrations rather than on any formal delegation of executive power. The League, however, failed to make full use of this background of co-operation. Not only, as has been pointed out, was the League's co-ordination of the work of the public unions superficial, but the Covenant did not reflect any real appreciation of the relationship of international economic and social stability to world peace[66]; these matters received the briefest of mention in the Preamble and Article 23 (e). No special responsibilities were assigned to the Assembly or the Council and no special organ was created to undertake such responsibilities. There developed, instead, an elaborate structure of advisory committees, working under the Council, which together constituted the Economic and Financial Organisation of the League.[67]

Of these the two principal committees were the Economic Committee and the Financial Committee, composed of technical experts serving in their personal capacity rather than as governmental representatives; their work was purely advisory. There were, in addition, various subsidiary committees, also advisory, such as the Fiscal Committee, the Committee of Statistical

---

[66] Part XIII of the Versailles Treaty, the Constitution of the ILO, contained fuller recognition of this relationship.

[67] See generally Martin Hill, *The Economic and Financial Organization of the League of Nations* (1946). There was also the Organisation of Communications and Transit, which originated in Part XII of the Treaty of Versailles and was founded on a Statute provided by the Barcelona Conference of 1926; this had a general conference (four yearly) which drafted treaties, an Advisory and Technical Committee (twice yearly) and six permanent committees. Then there was the Health Organisation, which drafted treaties and provided assistance to States.

Experts, the Co-ordination Committee and the International Loan Contracts Committee.

As the years progressed the League was, almost against its own inclination, forced into more and more economic and social activity. Indeed, the trend of events, of which the general depression of 1928–31 is a singular example, made this inevitable. The League convened various conferences, such as the Monetary Conference of 1933 and the World Economic Conference of 1927, it made reconstruction loans to countries like Austria and Bulgaria, it established the International Relief Union, the Communications and Transit Organisation, the Bank for International Settlements, and so on. By a curious irony of events, the League's economic and social activities, on which so little emphasis had originally been placed, became far more impressive than its political activities. By 1939 the Bruce Committee, set up by the League to review these activities, recommended that the Council be relieved of them, or rather of responsibility for them, and that a separate Central Committee of 24 governmental representatives and eight experts should assume direct responsibility.

The Second World War, repeating the experience of the First World War, produced an impressive record of inter-allied co-operation in the economic field. Combined boards were set up, allocating essential supplies and materials, pooling resources and sublimating national interests in the common aim of victory.[68]

During the War, on a larger basis of participation, a United Nations Conference on Food and Agriculture in May 1943 laid the foundations for FAO[69] and in November 1943, 44 governments established the United Nations Relief and Rehabilitation Administration (UNRRA). In July 1944 the Bretton Woods Conference established the International Monetary Fund (IMF) and the International Bank for Reconstruction and Development. In December 1944 at Chicago the Convention on Civil Aviation was signed, which provided for the new organisation ICAO.

When, therefore, the San Francisco Conference met to sign the UN Charter there existed an impressive history of co-operation in the economic and social fields. The League's history suggested a

[68] See Schwarzenberger, *Power Politics*, (1951), Chap. 21.
[69] See *post*, p. 112.

need for greater emphasis on these fields and a separate organ to deal with responsibility for them. The existence of the older specialised organisations (unions), coupled with the creation of the new ones referred to in the previous paragraph, pointed to the necessity for co-ordination within the framework of the new, general organisation.

1. Composition

As a principal organ of the UN, the Economic and Social Council now has 54 members, elected by the General Assembly by "staggered" elections so as to ensure some continuity. There is no permanent membership as of right, as in the Security Council (though in practice the "big five" are always elected), and, as we shall see, the principle of equality is also applied to voting power. In the elections an attempt is always made to represent a variety of social, economic, cultural and geographical interests. The amendment of Article 61 of the Charter, decided upon in Resolution 2847 (XXVI), establishes five categories of members corresponding to the following groups: African, Asian, Latin-American, W. European and others, E. European. Article 69 gives a right of participation to any member of the UN "on a matter of particular concern to that Member," but without a right to vote.

2. Voting procedure

This is on the basis of one vote for each member, with decisions (albeit of a non-obligatory character) being made by a simple majority of the members present and voting. The Council normally meets twice a year for about a month at a time (although it does have certain permanent commission).

3. Functions and powers

The Secretary-General has described the Council as "the pivot of the economic and social organisation under the auspices of the UN". It operates "under the authority of the General Asembly" (Art. 60) in assuming responsibility for the discharge of the functions of the Organisation set out in Chapter IX, *i.e.* in Articles 55–60. These call for some comment. Article 55 sets out three heads of "aims" which the UN shall promote and, from a reading of that article, it becomes apparent that these could touch upon matters which are normally essentially within the domestic jurisdiction of States. At San Francisco Committee II/3, dealing with the articles on economic and social co-operation, took note of the general application of Article 2 (7) and recognised that nothing in the new Chapters IX and X warranted intervention by the UN in a State's domestic jurisdiction. The impact of these aims should not, therefore, be exaggerated and it will be noted that Article 56 contains a mere pledge to co-operate on the part of members in the promotion of those aims. Moreover, the Council has only power to "recommend" to States, to the Assembly and to the specialised agencies (Arts. 58, 62); it has no sort of "executive" power.

The Council is, therefore, an organ of very wide terms of reference but of limited powers. Since much of the economic and social field falls directly within the competence of the specialised agencies, the Council is to a large extent a "residuary legatee" and, in order to avoid duplication, operates in those areas for which no agency exists. As outlined in Article 62, it may operate in various ways.

(a) *Functions and powers under Article 62*

(i) *Studies.* The Council may make or initiate studies which, in practice, range from those of a very general character, such as the study requested of the Secretary-General on the economic development of under-developed countries,[70] to those which are quite specific and restricted, such as the study of the effects of chewing coca leaf undertaken by a commission of inquiry despatched to Peru.[71] The requests for studies are addressed to the Secretary-General, to the regional economic commissions, to ad hoc committees, bodies of experts or the specialised agencies. In most cases the recommendations of the Council are directly based upon such studies.

(ii) *Recommendations.* The Council may make recommendations, either under Article 62 (1) or, without being related to any particular study, under Article 62 (2). The word "recommendation" signifies the non-obligatory character of the resolution, for in practice many different terminologies are used such as "com-

[70] Resol. 416F (XIV).
[71] Resol. 159, IV (VII).

mends," "refers," "calls upon," etc. The recommendations are addressed to States, sometimes calling for specific legislative action by them as in resolution 368 (XIII) dealing with methods of financing development in under-developed countries; to the Assembly, especially where, as in budgetary matters, action is required by the Assembly pursuant to the Charter; or to the specialised agencies: Article 62 (2) in fact places no limit on the possible addressees.

(iii) *Draft conventions.* These may be prepared for submission to the Assembly, which adopts them and opens them for signature; the Convention on the Prevention and Punishment of the Crime of Genocide was dealt with in this way. Or, where a draft calls for detailed discussion, it may be referred to a special international conference of States convened for that purpose; the Draft Protocol relating to the Status of Stateless Persons was thus referred to a special UN Conference in 1954.

(iv) *Calling of conferences.* These may be called under Article 62 (4), quite apart from their function in relation to a draft convention prepared by the Council, where the work cannot be done by an organ of the UN. They may be of an international or a regional character and, in fact, have already been called into being on matters such as health, trade and employment, transport, refugees and stateless persons. The conferences can also be non-governmental in character, such as the World Population Conference of 1954, or even conferences of experts, such as the UN Scientific Conference on the Conservation and Utilisation of Resources, 1949; there is no basis for construing "international" conferences as meaning solely conferences of States.

(b) *Assistance to other organs, States and specialised agencies*

The Council also acts as an organ of assistance to two other main organs; to the Security Council under Article 65, and to the Assembly under Article 66 (1) and (3). It may, also, with the approval of the Assembly, assist member States and specialised agencies.

The most striking example of assistance to States lay in the field of technical assistance which, until the end of 1965, flowed through three main channels. First, there was the "regular" programme carried on by ECOSOC independently of the specialised agencies.

Second, there was the Expanded Programme of Technical Assistance (EPTA) carried out by ECOSOC together with 10 participating specialised agencies with a Technical Assistance Committee (TAC) of the Council determining basic policy questions and the execution of the policy being entrusted to the Technical Assistance Board (TAB) in which the specialised agencies participated. Third, there was the Special Fund, first established in 1958 and based entirely on voluntary contributions from member States and controlled by its own Governing Council and Consultative Board. However, in 1965 by resolution 2029 (XX) the General Assembly fused the EPTA and the Special Fund into one programme, the UN Development Programme (UNDP).

UNDP will maintain the special characteristics of the two earlier programmes, and contributions may be pledged separately, but there is a unified 48 Nation Governing Council[72] (replacing the Governing Council of UNDP and the TAC) and a new Inter-Agency Consultative Board (replacing the Consultative Board of the Fund and the TAB). The fusion is likely to increase efficiency in the use of resources but the real handicap remains the lack of sufficient financial support. Although the level of projects is impressive,[73] the fact remains that the first UN Development Decade was something of a failure because of lack of funds and the ominous "North-South Gap" (the Developed and the Developing Countries) is increasing rather than decreasing.[74]

In an attempt to meet this need, General Assembly resol. 2186 (XXI) established a new Capital Development Fund, equipped with its own Executive Board of 24 States elected by the Assembly, a Managing Director and staff. Moreover, a second Development Decade was begun in 1971.[75] In May 1974 the UN Special Fund was established to provide emergency economic relief.

---

[72] See resol. 2813 (XXVI) for the detailed distribution of the 48 seats. See the proposal of the Group of Experts to bring all funds into a new U.N. Development Authority (E/AC.62/9).

[73] The 1959–69 decade saw the provision by UNDP of $1,200 million in aid: direct investment follow-up exceeded $2,000 million.

[74] In 1980 UNDP approved projects totalling $144 million.

[75] G.A. Resol. 2626 (XXV). This aims at a 6% annual growth rate, with the economically advanced countries giving 1% of their G.N.P. By 1980 its resources had reached $121.5 million. The 1979 Program of Action visualised a 14% growth rate annually, regarded sceptically by Western Powers.

(c) *Co-ordination of work with and between the specialised agencies*[76]

As has been stressed previously, one of the main tasks envisaged for the Council was the co-ordination of the work of the various specialised agencies which, to that end, were to be brought into relationship with the UN. That relationship was to be established by agreements, concluded under Articles 57 and 63, with organisations fulfilling the criteria of Article 57 (1), namely, establishment by inter-governmental agreement (thus excluding NGO's), having "wide international responsibilities," and in "economic, social, cultural, educational, health and related fields." The second criterion has been interpreted in both a geographical and a functional sense, thus excluding regional organisations and those with a limited responsibility. The Preparatory Commission at San Francisco had not excluded the bringing into relationship of other inter-governmental agencies, but these were not to be termed "specialised agencies."[77]

The agreements contemplated were negotiated at the initiative of the Council (since Article 57 is mandatory) and through a Negotiating Committee which negotiated directly with the organisation concerned; they were then submitted to the Council and, finally, for approval by the Assembly. At present there are agreements with 12 "specialised agencies,"[78] the International Telecommunications Union (ITU), the Universal Postal Union (UPU), the International Labour Organisation (ILO), the Food

---

[76] See generally Hill, *The United Nations System* (1978); also Jenks, "Co-ordination in International Organisation" (1951) 28 B.Y.B.I.L. 78 *et. seq.*, and (same author) "Co-ordination: a new problem of international organisation" R.C. 1950 (11), p. 156, espec. Chap. III; Dupuy, "Le droit des relations entre les organisations internationales" R.C. Vol. 100 (1960), p. 461.

[77] UNCIO, Docs. Vol. 10, p. 269.

[78] The International Atomic Energy Agency (IAEA) is not a specialised agency; the Agreement with the UN, approved by the G.A. on November 14, 1957, is modelled on the agency agreements except that the IAEA is more autonomous and, because of the implications for peace and security of the development of nuclear energy, the G.A. and S.C. are the organs with which the main relationship exists, and not ECOSOC: U.N.T.S., Vol. 281, p. 369. See Bechhofer, "Negotiating the Statute of the IAEA" (1959) 13 *International Organisation*, 38. Of the other agencies, the International Refugee Organisation (IRO) has been discontinued and the Charter of the International Trade Organisation (ITO) has never been ratified. The International Development Association is an affiliate of the Bank and is not, technically, a separate specialised agency.

and Agriculture Organisation (FAO), the International Monetary Fund (IMF), the International Bank for Reconstruction and Development (IBRD), the International Finance Corporation (IFC),[79] the United Nations Educational, Scientific and Cultural Organisation (UNESCO), the International Civil Aviation Organisation (ICAO), the World Health Organisation (WHO), the World Meteorological Organisation (WMO), and the Inter-Governmental Maritime Consultative Organisation (IMCO).

Whilst the agreements all follow a general pattern,[80] with a number of common features, certain differences do occur, notably in the greater degree of autonomy possessed by the Fund, the Bank and the Finance Corporation. The common features are the following. A recognition of the status of the organisation as a "specialised agency," but with the Fund, Bank and Finance Corporation agreements stressing their independent character. A clause linking membership to some degree[81]; hence UNESCO gives ECOSOC a right to recommend the rejection of applications and ties loss of membership to suspension or expulsion from the UN. A clause for reciprocal representation (but without right of vote) at each other's meetings, but with a good deal of variation in the bodies to which this applies. A clause giving reciprocal rights to propose agenda items, after any necessary consultation, to the appropriate organ; this is not always in the UN, the General Assembly, and IMCO, for example, has this right *vis-à-vis* ECOSOC and the Trusteeship Council. The Bank, Fund and Finance Corporation undertake only to give "due consideration" to the inclusion of any item proposed by the UN. Another common clause allows the General Assembly or the Council to make recommendations to the agency, which is then obliged to submit them to the appropriate organ; again, in the case of the Fund, Bank and Finance Corporation, the obligation is weaker, for the Assembly can only make recommendations after prior consultation with the agency and there is also a "hands-off" clause whereby the UN undertakes to respect the autonomy of the

---

[79] The UN-IFC Agreement was concluded by the Bank on behalf of the IFC and simply adopts the UN-Bank Agreement with a few amendments: 265 U.N.T.S. 314.

[80] For details see Jenks, (1951) 28 B.Y.B.I.L. 67; Parry, *ibid.*, 26 (1949) 138–139; Weissberg, *International Status of the UN* (1961), pp. 41–50.

[81] See *post*, p. 384.

agencies in matters affecting their loan and financing policy. The Bank has accordingly taken the view that it is under no obligation to comply with the General Assembly resolutions requesting the specialised agencies to refrain from giving aid to Portugal (because of the latter's non-implementation of resolution 1514 (XV) on the Granting of Independence) and is by its own constitution precluded from adopting a policy based on other than economic considerations.[82] Other clauses relate to the exchange of information and documents and the transmission of regular (or annual) reports by the agency; to assistance to be rendered by the agency to the Security Council and, in some cases, other principal[83] and even subsidiary organs; to furnishing information to the I.C.J. and to the right of the agency (other than the UPU) to request an advisory opinion from the Court on questions falling within its competence. Some agreements contain undertakings by the agency to associate regional offices with those of the UN; there is, be it noted, no evidence of any wish to combine the headquarters of all the agencies and the UN in one central location.

One standard clause (except for the UPU, ITU, Fund, Bank and Finance Corporation) recognises the desirability of a "single unified international civil service" and the agencies agree to develop "common personnel standards" and to consult regarding the establishment of an International Civil Service Commission. There is, in practice, no real unification of Secretariats and the wisdom of this, in the immediate future, is highly doubtful. There have been, however, frequent consultations and liaison on a number of matters such as salaries and allowance scales and recruitment policies; and several agencies participate in the UN Joint Staff Pension Fund. There is also an International Civil Service Advisory Board, a body of experts, which advises the Administrative Committee on Co-ordination (ACC) which is itself a main channel of consultation and co-ordination (and this will be mentioned shortly). The Staff Rules and Regulations of the various Secretariats follow a similar pattern and the agencies

---

[82] A/C.4/SR. 1645, 11–15, 23, 27: and for the UN Legal Counsel's view that both the UN and the Bank were in breach of the 1947 relationship agreement in failing to consult see A/C.4/SR. 1653.

[83] In 1951, at the request of ECOSOC, the ILO, UNESCO, FAO, WHO and ICAO undertook to give assistance to the General Assembly, on request, in action taken by it under the Resolution on Uniting for Peace (Resol. 377 (V)).

subscribe either to the UN Administrative Tribunal or to the ILO Administrative Tribunal, except for the Bank.[84]

Other clauses deal with the desirability of co-operation in statistical compilations, in efficiently using administrative and technical services, with revision of the agreements, supplementary agreements to be concluded by the Secretary-General and his counterpart in the various agencies, and, for those agencies established after August 1947, the right to use the UN laissez-passer.

The clauses on budgeting and financial arrangements are complex and varied. Most agreements recognise the desirability of close relationship in these matters, but there is no common or over all budget; the autonomy of the Fund, Bank and Finance Corporation is particularly striking. The budgets of the agencies are, in practice, considered by the Assembly's Advisory Committee on Administrative and Budgetary Questions and the attention of the agencies is invited to comments made there and in the 5th Committee.

Clearly these agreements provide a useful basis for co-ordination. The submission of reports by the agencies, the examination of these reports by the Council and the power to make recommendations to the agencies are useful factors in securing co-ordination and avoiding duplication. There are, however, additional means of co-ordination. The first, already referred to, is the Administrative Committee on Co-ordination (ACC) which, comprising the Secretary-General and the administrative heads of the agencies,[85] directly and through its sub-committees, can review the whole field of operations of the various organisations in the light of the need for co-ordination, fixing priorities and enabling a concentration of efforts and resources. ECOSOC has itself established a Committee for Programme and Co-operation which holds joint meetings with the ACC. And, of course, on the technical assistance side, all the agencies are represented on the Inter-Agency Consultative Board of UNDP. The second is co-ordination at the national level. The membership of the UN and the specialised agencies is, whilst not identical,

---

[84] See *post*, p. 318.
[85] Under Art. XI of the Agreement with the IAEA, the Agency agrees to participate in the work of the ACC, even though the Agency is not a specialised agency.

sufficiently approximate to enable each individual member to ensure that its own efforts in each organisation are co-ordinated, and the General Assembly, in a resolution of November 20, 1947, has stressed the need for this co-ordination at the national level; an obvious but apparently necessary admonition!

(d) *Relations with other inter-governmental organisations and non-governmental organisations*

As has been previously mentioned, the Preparatory Commission did not exclude the possibility that the Council should effect a relationship with inter-governmental organisations other than the "specialised agencies." No formal relationships comparable to those with the specialised agencies have been established, but both the Council and the Assembly have on occasions invited observers from the League of Arab States and the Organisation of American States to attend their meetings. There are, moreover, informal arrangements for reciprocal representation, consultations, exchange of documents and information with various other organisations; the Council of Europe is one example.

Relations with non-governmental organisations (NGO's) are on a far more formalised plan. Article 71 specifically provides for "suitable arrangements" and in practice the Council has established three categories in which NGO's, on their application, may be placed. Category A includes organisations which have a basic interest in most of the activities of the Council; Category B those with a special competence in some of the aspects of the Council's work; and "The Register"—a third category—has on it those which, by means of ad hoc consultation, are able to make a significant contribution to the work of the Council. In no case does an NGO have rights comparable to States under Article 69, or specialised agencies under Article 70; the difference between "participation" and "consultation" is fundamental. However, all three categories may send[86] observers to public meetings of the Council and its commissions; organisations in categories A and B may submit written statements for circulation to the members of

---

[86] Representatives of NGO's enjoy no privileges and immunities, and whilst s. 11 of the Headquarters Agreement with the U.S. provides for freedom of access to the Headquarters District for representatives of NGO's recognised under Art. 71 of the Charter, the U.S. authorities have occasionally denied visas to particular persons. See Weissberg, *The International Status of the UN*, pp. 158–161.

the Council, and those in A may even present their views orally and propose agenda items. Organisations merely "on the Register" may be *invited* to submit written statements or, *at the request of a commission*, may be heard orally by the Council. The number and variety of NGO's is astonishing and nearly 400 enjoy consultative status in one or other category. The value of their contribution to the work of the Council is often regarded with scepticism, and the present record is not too impressive, but if the UN is to be regarded as an organisation representing "We, the peoples . . . ," as the Preamble states, then in principle the development of this consultative process is a worthy aim.

4. The committee structure of ECOSOC

The diversity of the work of the Council makes it essential that it should work through subsidiary bodies. There are three plenary "sessional" committees (economic, social, programme and co-operation) and, in addition, several "standing" committees. Article 68 gives specific power to set up commissions. These vary considerably in type, structure, functions and composition, but may be grouped into three classes.[87]

(a) *Functional commissions*

These are established and defined by subject-matter. They are six in number, with one sub-commission, and include bodies such as the Commission on Human Rights; the Commission for Social Development, The Population Commission, the Statistical Commission, the Commission on Narcotic Drugs, and the Commission on the Status of Women. Whilst varying in the number of States represented, these commissions are essentially composed of representatives of States, assisted by technical experts. The Council decided in 1946 against a proposal to have on these commissions independent experts who would consider these problems as experts and unfettered by governmental instructions.

(b) *Regional commissions*

These were unforeseen at San Francisco, but experience has shown that economic and social problems vary tremendously by

[87] The GA resol. 32/197 of January 9, 1978 accepted the recommendations of its ad hoc Committee on the Restructuring of the Economic and Social Sectors of the U.N. system and called for ECOSOC to take over the work of many of its subsidiary bodies.

region and can thus often be better considered at a regional level. There now exist five such commissions: The Economic Commission for Europe (ECE), the Economic and Social Commission for Asia and the Pacific (ESCAP), the Economic Commission for Latin-America (ECLA), the Economic Commission for Africa (ECA) and the Economic Commission for Western Asia (ECWA). They are primarily operational commissions, as distinct from the functional commissions, and can deal directly with governments as well as reporting back to the Council. Even non-UN members are associated with their work; ESCAP and ECLA provide for associate membership and ECE for consultative status. The General Assembly has insisted upon decentralisation of the economic and socal activities of the UN so that the regional commissions have assumed increasing importance over recent years.

(c) *Other bodies*

Certain other bodies have been established to respond to a special need which falls into neither of the above two categories. The UNDP works in close relationship with the Council, reporting to it annually. The office of the UN High Commissioner for Refugees, the Permanent Central Narcotics Board, the Drug Supervisory Body, UNITAR, the Interim Co-ordinating Committee for International Commodity Arrangements, UNICEF, UNEP, UNCTAD and the UN Capital Development Fund are other bodies falling within this residuary category.

In conclusion, although what has been said above is largely of a descriptive or analytical character, a word of evaluation on the work of the Council might be ventured. Given the absence of any power to legislate on economic and social matters, the Council is bound to be a forum of discussion, from which, admittedly, recommendations ensue. A general criticism has been that the Council attempted too much, and diversified its activities too greatly. Yet it has substantial achievements to its credit. The statistical and economic reporting is indispensable, and the initiative in inaugurating conference work considerable. It is, however, true that dissatisfaction with ECOSOC on the part of the developing countries has led to the creation of both UNCTAD and UNIDO, as autonomous bodies responsible to the Assembly. The terms of reference of the former include the duty "to review and facilitate co-ordination of activities of other institutions within the UN system in the field of international trade and related problems of economic development . . . ."[88] Even with UNIDO the overlap of functions with ECOSOC and the specialised agencies is clear. Admittedly, both are enjoined to respect the co-ordination responsibilities of ECOSOC and the relationship agreements, but there is evidence of rivalry and very serious problems of co-ordination. The situation has not yet acquired major proportions, due so far as UNCTAD is concerned to its relative failure to move beyond the stage of enunciating general principles.[89] So far as UNIDO is concerned, it became operational and in April 1979 was upgraded to a specialised agency. The problem of duplication and co-ordination is however inherent in the technique of establishing autonomous bodies with functions cutting across those assigned to ECOSOC and the specialised agencies. If this problem, together with that of the paucity of resources for development, can be overcome it may well be that ECOSOC will come to the fore as a most active and useful organ of the UN.[90]

IV. THE TRUSTEESHIP COUNCIL

1. The Trusteeship system
Before dealing with the Council and the machinery of supervision, something must be said of the system under supervision. The trusteeship system has been of considerable historical interest, and it remains open for further use in the future, so that a description of the system continues to be justified. The Trusteeship system is the obvious successor to the Mandates system under the League; both rest, essentially, on the idea of an administering authority, normally a State, assuming responsibility for the government of a territory whose peoples have not developed to the stage necessary for independence or self-government, and being in some measure accountable internationally for the administration of the territory.
Under the League the territories placed under the Mandate system were those detached from Turkey and Germany at the

[88] G.A. resol. 1995 (XIX).
[89] Although its 1980 budget is $50 million.
[90] For a fuller evaluation see "The Global Partnership: international agencies and economic development" (1968) 22 *Int. Org.* No. 1; Mangone, *UN Administration of economic and social programs* (1966).

conclusion of the First World War. They were placed in three categories, A, B, and C according to the stage of development reached. No express provision for termination of the system was to be found in the Covenant, but for those in category A it was clearly implied that independence would eventually be granted, for those in category B the implication was less clear, and for those in category C the contrary implication arose by reason of the fact that such territories were to be administered as an "integral part" of the territory of the administering State.

The Trusteeship system is potentially wider in scope, for Article 77 contemplates three categories to which it might apply:

(a) territories now held under mandate;
(b) territories which may be detached from States as a result of the Second World War;
(c) territories voluntarily placed under the system by States responsible for their administration.

Only territories within the first two categories have so far been placed under trusteeship, and of the second category there was but one example, Somaliland, a territory which has now achieved independence. Thus, in practice, the scope of the system is narrower than that of the League. The third category, the real "innovation" of the Charter, has never been used, although trusteeship has often been suggested for "problem areas" such as Jerusalem, Trieste, Berlin, and even the Congo (always, however, with the UN as the possible administering authority). The Trusteeship system therefore applied in practice to territories formerly under mandate, and all such territories, with one exception, were voluntarily placed under the system. The exception was the territory of S.W. Africa which the mandatory power, South Africa, refused to place under trusteeship and, instead, proposed to incorporate into its own territory. The controversy which this proposal unleashed still continues, and certain aspects of it have led to four advisory opinions and one judgment of the I.C.J., which must now be considered. In 1950 the Court, at the request of the General Assembly, gave an opinion[91] which made three points. First, that South Africa's rights over the territory, and the present status of the territory, arose from Article 22 of the

---

[91] A.O. on *International Status of S.W. Africa*, (1950) *I.C.J. Reports*, 128.

Covenant and the Mandate itself; South Africa had therefore no power to modify the international status unilaterally, and such competence lay only with the Union of South Africa acting with the consent of the UN. Second, that the placing of mandated territory under trusteeship was not compulsory, since the language used is permissive in its phrasing and clearly envisages this step to be by way of an agreement. Third, that in the case of a territory remaining under mandate, the supervisory functions previously exercised by the League now rest in the General Assembly of the UN, provided that the degree of supervision exercised should not exceed that which applied in the Mandates system and should conform, as far as possible, to the procedure followed by the Council of the League. This qualification, that the degree of supervision should not exceed that under Mandate and the procedure should be similar, led to two further opinions. Under Rule F of its rules of procedure the Assembly's decisions on reports and petitions on S.W. Africa require a two-thirds majority vote, whereas under the Mandates system the League Council had required unanimity. The Court, by an advisory opinion of June 7, 1955,[92] took the view that the Assembly's rule was permissible, for the "degree of supervision," as used in the Court's earlier judgment, referred to the "extent of the substantive supervision thus exercised, and not to the manner in which the collective will of the General Assembly is expressed." In 1956 the Court gave an opinion[93] on yet another question, namely, whether the Assembly's Committee on S.W. Africa[94] could grant oral hearings to petitioners (a practice never followed by the League). It held that it could, since the League Council had always had the *right* to grant oral hearings, even though not exercised, and, moreover, the practice did not increase the obligations placed upon the Mandatory Power. Liberia and Ethiopia brought a complaint against S. Africa, alleging that by the practice of *apartheid* and by its general economic, political and social policies in the Territory, S. Africa was in breach of Articles 2 and 22 of the Mandate. Initially, S. Africa contested the jurisdiction of the I.C.J., claiming that under the jurisdictional clause of the Mandate (Article 7), the

[92] A.O. on *S.W. Africa—Voting Procedure,* (1955) *I.C.J. Reports,* 67.
[93] A.O. on *Admissibility of Hearings of Petitioners by the Committee on S.W. Africa,* (1956) *I.C.J. Reports,* 23.
[94] This is now dissolved.

claimant States had no *locus standi*: this was rejected by the Court in a judgment of December 21, 1962.[95] On July 18, 1966 the Court gave its main judgment[96] which to the surprise of many, instead of dealing with the merits of the complaint, returned to the jurisdictional issue and found, contrary to its earlier judgment, that it had no jurisdiction. Limitations of space do not permit full discussion of the reasoning by which the Court distinguished its two judgments. The author would, however, wish to record his own disagreement with that reasoning.[97]

The dissatisfaction with this judgment within the General Assembly was so great that by resol. 2145 (XXI) of October 27, 1966, the Assembly recorded its own conviction that there had been a breach of the mandate, of the UN Charter and of the declaration on Human Rights and terminated the mandate. It also established an ad hoc Committee to consider means whereby the Territory might be administered and by resol. 2248 (S–V) of May 19, 1967 established an 11-Member UN Council for S.W. Africa and a UN Commissioner to administer the territory, which, by resol. 2372 (XXII), is henceforth to be called Namibia. By the end of 1968 the UN Council for Namibia had failed to secure admission to the Territory. The Territory is now considered by the Assembly to be no longer under mandate but held, illegally, by S. Africa: legally, "sovereignty" must be regarded as in suspense but the right of administration is vested directly in the UN.

In 1970, by resolution 284 (1970), the Security Council requested an advisory opinion from the Court, posing the question "What are the legal consequencese for States of the continued presence of South Africa, notwithstanding Security Council resolution 276 (1970)?"[98] The Court advised[99] that all member States were bound to recognise the illegality of the South African presence and to refrain from any acts or dealings which might imply the legality of that presence.

---

[95] (1962) *I.C.J. Reports*, 319: by a majority of 8 to 7.

[96] (1966) *I.C.J. Reports*, 6.

[97] The author shares the views expressed in his Dissenting Judgment by Judge Jessup.

[98] This resolution re-affirmed the General Assembly's termination of the mandate and declared the continued presence of South Africa in Namibia to be illegal.

[99] *Namibia* case, (1971) *I.C.J. Reports*, 16. See generally Dugard, *S.W. Africa Namibia Dispute* (1973).

2. The Trusteeship Agreements

From what has been said above it will be clear that no territory can come under trusteeship except when an agreement to that effect is concluded. An initial question, therefore, is at whose initiative is this agreement reached, and who are the parties to it? In practice the initiative (in the sense of proposing a draft agreement) has come from the State administering the territory, the former mandatory Power[1]; the "agreement" is contemplated by Article 79 as being between "the States directly concerned." Yet no criteria are stipulated for determining which these States are, and in practice the various administering authorities reached their own decisions on this, submitting the draft agreement to certain States and to others "for information purposes only." The role of the Assembly, or the Security Council in the case of "strategic areas," is limited to the mere "approval" of the agreement reached; it may well be that the UN is not a "party."[2] However, under Article 81 the administering authority may be "one or more States or the Organisation itself," so that if the UN ever did assume the administration of a territory it would be in the curious situation of having to give its "approval," via the Assembly or Security Council, to an agreement already reached between itself and any "States directly concerned."

The Agreements form the legal basis for the supervision by the UN and the administration by the administering authority and, in the main, repeat and supplement the relative Charter provisions to which, by Article 103, they must be subject. Some provisions in the Agreements go beyond the Charter provisions, either by according additional rights or obligations to the administering authority or by giving additional guarantees to the inhabitants of the territory. In the former category are provisions allowing the authority to exercise a discretion in extending to the territory the application of international conventions to which the authority is a

---

[1] Except in the case of Somaliland when the agreement was drafted by the Trusteeship Council, and Italy, the chosen administering authority, had no vote in the drafting committee: the case was exceptional because Italy was not at that time a UN Member.

[2] Kelsen, *Law of the UN*, pp. 586, 608–609, and Toussaint, *The Trusteeship System of the UN*, p. 78, regard the agreements as embodying in reality two agreements, the first between States directly concerned and the second between the administering authority and the UN. Parry, "The Legal Nature of the Trusteeship Agreements" (1950) 27 B.Y.B.I.L. 166, and Schachter, *ibid.* 25 (1948) 130–131 deny that the UN is a party.

party; or provisions allowing for reference of disputes between the authority and other UN member States to the I.C.J.; or provisions allowing for the creation of administrative unions; or (as in the case of New Guinea) provisions allowing the authority to administer as an integral part of its own territory. In the latter category fall provisions forbidding the alienation of rights over native land and resources to non-natives; or amplifying the human rights provisions.

The Agreements may be altered or amended, under Article 79, by agreement between the "States directly concerned," subject to the approval of the Assembly or Security Council. Termination is, however, another matter, for the Charter says nothing of this and only the Agreement for Somaliland included a termination date (ten years from the signing of the Agreement). The administering authorities have strongly resisted being tied down to a specific time within which "independence or self-government" will be achieved and, therefore, the trusteeship terminated. Of course, the achievement of independence or self-government is not the only possible cause for termination, and at San Francisco there was some speculation over the effect of the administering authority ceasing to be a member of the UN. A statement made by the U.S.A. and United Kingdom at that time put the view that loss of membership would not automatically lead to termination and the circumstances of each case would have to be examined. No doubt much would turn on the reason why membership had been lost.

3. Objectives of the system

These are set out principally in Article 76, although supplemented by Articles 73[3] and 84. What stands out, as compared to the Mandates system, is the emphasis on the contribution of the Trusteeship system to international peace and security; this objective is, significantly, the first of the four enumerated in Article 76. The whole of Article 84 is to the same effect. Moreover, there is the quite novel distinction between territories or parts of territories which are "strategic areas" and those which are not (Art. 82), and in the case of the former it is the Security Council rather than the General Assembly which approves the trusteeship agreement and exercises the supervisory functions of

---

[3] See *post*, p. 84.

the UN. Clearly, therefore, the trusteeship system aims not simply at removing these territories from possible competition by States for their possession, but also of ensuring that they play a part in the collective security system envisaged by the Charter. Hence Article 84 permits the use of *volunteer* forces, facilities and assistance from the territory either in carrying out obligations towards the Security Council assumed by the administering authority (either under Article 43 or ad hoc, presumably) or in defence of the territory: such use would not be justified in defence of the metropolitan territory.

Under Article 76 (b) is stated the goal of "self-government or independence," as may be appropriate in the circumstances and according to the wishes of the peoples concerned. In fact no trust agreement has omitted "independence" as the goal although, with the exception of Somaliland, no time-limit was set for its achievement. Undoubtedly the political sentiment of the majority of the UN members is in favour of early independence, and the administering authorities are under a fairly constant pressure within the UN to bring this about. However, the assumption that independence is the proper goal for *all* trust territories is one which is difficult to justify on political and economic grounds. In relation to Nauru, with an indigenous population of 2,800 on an island of 5,263 acres, the independence achieved in January 1968 raised the crucial question of whether the inhabitants were to be re-settled or, as eventually decided, the land excavated for phosphates should be rehabilitated. Indeed, the Trusteeship Council appears to have set its face against any alternative to independence. The people of the trust territory of the Pacific Islands have expressed a desire for integration with the U.S.A., a wish simply "noted" by the Trusteeship Council; its fulfilment would be neither independence nor self-government. In fact, the U.S.A. has set 1981 as the date for termination of the trusteeship agreement and full self-government for "Micronesia."

One aspect of this political insistence on independence has been the criticism of administrative unions formed between a trust territory and adjacent non-self-governing territories. In 1948 the Assembly endorsed the view that such unions must remain strictly administrative in nature and not impede separate development of the territory, and there now exists a Standing Committee on Administrative Unions to watch over this development.

Article 76 (c) is really inserted for purposes of emphasis, for almost identical provisions appear in the Preamble and, moreover, Article 2 of the Universal Declaration of Human Rights states the applicability of that declaration to trust territories. Article 76 (d) is of interest in that it applies the "open-door" policy to all trust territories whereas, under the Mandates system, it applied only to B Mandates. This is qualified in that the objectives of the trusteeship system and the guarantee of existing rights under Article 80 take precedence over this policy. By a curious paradox (for the U.S.A. was the staunchest advocate of this policy) the U.S. Agreement relating to the Pacific Islands alone of the trusteeship agreements does not provide for this but substitutes most favoured nation treatment amongst all UN members *other than* the administering authority; the U.S.A. can, therefore, arrogate to itself a preferential treatment by a provision of doubtful legality.

4. The machinery of supervision

The supervisory powers of the United Nations are based on the Charter and on the trusteeship agreements and, in the event of any conflict between the provisions of the two, the Charter prevails (Art. 103). In fact four organs participate, to a greater or lesser extent, in the supervision.

(a) *The General Assembly*

It is this organ which, under Article 85, exercises the functions of the UN with regard to all areas not designated as "strategic," although, as we shall see, much of the actual supervisory function is delegated to the Trusteeship Council which, under Article 85 (2) "shall assist" the General Assembly. As has already been mentioned, it is the Assembly which approves the terms of the trusteeship agreements and any alteration or amendment of those terms. The means of supervision set out in Article 87, namely, consideration of reports, acceptance of petitions, periodic visits and other actions are all available to the Assembly. In practice, however, the Assembly (acting through its 4th Committee (Trusteeship)) does not generally examine reports from the administering authorities; this is left to the Trusteeship Council and it is the reports of that Council which form the basis of the 4th Committee's work. The 4th Committee has occasionally granted requests for oral hearings to individuals and organisations, although the normal examination of written petitions is left to the Council. The 4th Committee has also established a Sub-Committee on the Questionnaire, reporting to the Trusteeship Council and suggesting certain modifications in the Questionnaire.[4]

(b) *The Security Council*

This organ exercises the functions of the UN with regard to "strategic" areas. Presumably, though this not clearly stated, it too could use the means of supervision set out in Article 87 and, indeed, the agreement on the Pacific Islands specifically provides that the provisions of Article 87 are applicable to that territory. In practice the Security Council does not itself undertake detailed supervision and uses the power given under Article 83 (2) to "avail itself of the assistance of the Trusteeship Council . . . ."

(c) *The Economic and Social Council*

This organ is only involved in a subsidiary sense, for Article 91 provides that the Trusteeship Council "shall, when appropriate, avail itself of the assistance of the Economic and Social Council and of the specialised agencies . . . ." The Rules of Procedure of the Economic and Social Council and the agreements with the specialised agencies provide for the giving of this assistance.

(d) *The Trusteeship Council*

Whereas, under the League, the supervision of the Mandates system lay with the Council, assisted by the Permanent Mandates Commission, the deliberate decision was taken at San Francisco to set up a special organ to deal with Trusteeship and, moreover, an organ answerable to the Assembly rather than to the Security Council. The Trusteeship Council is answerable to the Security Council only to the extent that it assists the Security Council with functions relating to "strategic areas."

(i) *Composition and voting.* The composition of the Council is based upon the principle that administering and non-administering member States shall be equally represented; the application of that principle is set out in Article 86 and is slightly complicated by

[4] As to this see *post*, p. 82.

Article 86 (1) (b), which gives to the "Big Five," the permanent members of the Security Council, a right to membership of the Trusteeship Council. Equal representation is ensured via the election of other non-administering States, for three-year terms, by the Assembly. There are certain hidden defects in the system of membership. For example, whilst it is clear that an administering authority can be a non-member State, the membership of the Council is open to UN member States; hence, Italy, as the administering authority for Somaliland, was denied membership until her admission to the UN. During that period Italy's rights of participation, whenever matters affecting Somaliland were under discussion, was secured by the Rules of Procedure of the Council but no voting rights could be conceded to Italy. This contrasts strangely with the practice of the League Council, which was to accord a right to vote in such cases. A further defect of the system was that it assumed a continuing balance in the membership between administering and non-administering States yet gave permanent membership to the Big Five. By 1976, only the U.S.A. remained as an administering State and this formula became strictly unworkable. The Assembly, however, accepted the Secretary-General's suggestion that the purpose of the formula was to ensure outside supervision of the administering States, so that the essential aim of the Charter would continue to be achieved if the Council comprised only administering States and the Big Five.[5] The Rules of Procedure also allow for the representation, without vote, of any UN member or specialised agency proposing an item on the agenda of the Council.

Members of the Council are represented by governmental representatives who are "specially qualified"; they are not independent experts as was the case in the Mandate Commission.

The voting procedure is simple; each member has one vote and decisions are taken by a majority of the members present and voting; there are thus no problems of a "veto," of "abstention," or "absence."

(ii) *Functions and powers.* The only function exclusively assigned to the Council by the Charter is the formulation of the Questionnaire (Art. 88). This apart, the Council functions under the authority of the General Assembly and "assists" the Security

[5] Annual Report of the S.G. 1967–68 (A/6201), p. 95.

Council. In practice the Council's relationship to these two organs is not substantially different, in the sense that its functions with regard to "strategic" and "non-strategic" areas are regarded as identical. The Council considers the reports submitted by the administering authorities, on the basis of the Council's Questionnaire, and then reports to the Assembly or the Security Council, as appropriate. The Council may also make recommendations to either of these two organs, or to member States; these, despite the use of the word "decisions" in Article 89, are entirely non-binding. The same is, of course, true with regard to any recommendations to members which the Assembly itself might make on trusteeship matters, although the Security Council could take a binding decision with regard to a strategic area.

The Council has established both ad hoc and standing committees. There are two of the latter, the Standing Committee on Administrative Unions and the Standing Committee on Petitions. In the past, the committees of the Council have reflected the same equality of representation between administering and non-administering States.

5. The forms of supervision

Article 87 sets out the various means or forms of supervision and the general reference to "these and other action" in (d) is a clear indication that heads (a), (b) and (c)—reports, petitions and visits—are not exhaustive. There has been a marked tendency in the Council to regard its function as one of making to the administering authorities positive, constructive proposals as opposed to a simple review and criticism of accomplished acts.

The reports referred to under (a) are, by virtue of Article 88, to be submitted annually[6] by the administering authority. The reports are to be based upon the questionnaire formulated by the Trusteeship Council consisting of some 190 questions and dealing with a whole range of topics from political, economic and social advancement down to the educational advancement of the people of the territory and the action taken on previous resolutions and recommendations of the Assembly and the Trusteeship Council. The reports are transmitted by the Secretary-General to all

---

[6] This is not so clearly an obligation in the case of strategic areas, for Art. 88 speaks only of an annual report to the Assembly, whereas the report on strategic areas is due to the Security Council.

members of the Council and, when examined by the Council, the administering authority is entitled to have a special representative present who will normally make a statement prior to discussion and give both written and oral answers to any questions put by members of the Council. It is on the basis of these reports that the Council will make its own report to the Assembly or Security Council on each of the trust territories and this report will also contain any recommendations to the Assembly or Security Council. These organs will then, when necessary, make recommendations to the administering authority.

The petitions referred to under head (b) are a device, previously used by the League, for the hearing of grievances; in contrast to the League, they are no longer accepted only through the mandatory power or administering authority. They may now be accepted directly by the Assembly or the Council (or even visiting missions) and, in that event, are sent to the administering authority for comment. The Charter does not specify the "source" of such petitions, so that the fact that they are anonymous or stem from outside the territory in question is not a ground of inadmissibility. Admissibility is a question for the Council and the Standing Committee on Petitions screens such petitions in a preliminary investigation. Petitions are quite often rejected and Rule 81 of the Council's rules of procedure regards as normally inadmissible petitions directed against the judgments of courts within the territory or dealing with a justiciable dispute—a kind of "exhaustion of local remedies" rule. This is not, however, the *sole* ground of inadmissibility. Petitions may be written or oral, although the latter kind was never in practice received by the League's Mandates Commission. The Council may refer to such petitions in its report, or pass a resolution based on the petition, or even despatch a visiting mission to make further enquiries.

The power to despatch missions, or make "periodic visits," is found under head (c); it is quite new, for it was rejected under the Mandates system as likely to undermine the authority of the administering authority.[7] Each mission is given its own terms of reference and a territory is visited at least once every three years;

---

[7] The League did, however, despatch missions when a specific dispute arose over a territory, but not as a regular thing. In May 1962, after protracted negotiations, the Chairman and Vice-Chairman of the UN Special Committee on S.W. Africa were allowed to visit S.W. Africa.

the mission reports back to the Council. In composition the mission will normally reflect the same balance of administering and non-administering States, and the members of the mission are States, not individuals, although the persons they nominate to represent them are subject to the approval of the Council itself. This power is exercisable "at times agreed upon with the administering authority"; there is no right to spring a surprise visit. For an administering authority to consistently refuse to agree upon a time would, of course, be contrary to its obligation under Article 2 (5) to "give the United Nations every assistance in any action it takes in accordance with the present Charter . . . ."

6. Non-self-governing territories

The relation between Chapter XI of the Charter, containing the Declaration regarding Non-Self-Governing Territories, and the trusteeship provisions we have just considered, often causes difficulties to the student. The apparent similarity in subject-matter justifies treatment of Chapter XI at this juncture. However, it is essential to grasp the fact that "supervision" envisaged in Chapter XI is not within the scope of the functions of the Trusteeship Council, but of the General Assembly by virtue of Article 10.

The Declaration covers all dependent territories, whether these are within or without the Trusteeship system; in the case of territories under trusteeship the obligations of the administering State or authority are additional to whatever obligations arise under the Declaration. How far this declaration imposes obligations in the legal sense is a matter of some dispute, for the extreme "colonialist" view has been that Chapter XI is a mere declaration of aims which imposes no legal obligations *stricto sensu*. In practice such an extreme view has scarcely been adhered to, and has been bitterly opposed by many States. Article 73 speaks of the acceptance of "the obligation" to promote the well-being of the inhabitants of "territories whose people have not yet attained a full measure of self-government" and lists five heads of means whereby this can be carried out.

A paramount difficulty has been the absence of any definition of what are "non-self-governing territories." Almost certainly indigenous minority groups within a metropolitan territory cannot be within the definition, for they have no "territory" capable of separate recognition in the international sphere; any other construction would bring about a conflict with Article 2 (7) of the Charter, the "domestic jurisdiction" clause. The disagreements which have arisen have resulted not so much from the failure of a State to include a particular territory within its reports but more on the discontinuance of such reports in respect of a territory which, because of some constitutional change, the State has henceforth regarded as self-governing. Thus, for example, the United Kingdom discontinued reports on Malta, the U.S.A. on Puerto Rico, and the Panama Canal Zone, and the Netherlands on Surinam. In 1953 the General Assembly adopted[8] a "list of factors" as a guide to determine whether a territory is or is not "self-governing"; these factors have never been accepted by the administering States as an exhaustive, binding definition. However, and despite the lack of an agreed definition, the Assembly has assumed competence to decide whether or not a territory is "self-governing"[9]; a decision of the Assembly on such an issue could not, however, bind the administering State.[10]

A further difficulty has been the absence of any organ, prescribed by the Charter, to "supervise" the implementation of the obligations under Chapter XI. After stormy opposition to the establishment of any such organ, and especially to the assignment of this role to the Trusteeship Council, the Assembly established the Committee on Information from Non-Self-Governing Territories composed of sixteen States drawn equally from administering and non-administering States. The former constantly but vainly opposed any move to give it permanence. With the adoption of the celebrated General Assembly resolution 1514 (XV) of December 14, 1960 on the Granting of Independence to

---

[8] Resol. 742 (VIII).

[9] See resols. 748 (VIII), 849 (IX), 1542 (XV) (Portuguese territories), 1747 (XVI) (S. Rhodesia).

[10] *Ante*, p. 45. On November 12, 1960, the Trusteeship Committee asked Portugal to submit information on ten territories which it controls, despite Portugal's contention that under the 1951 amendments to the Constitution those territories became overseas provinces of Metropolitan Portugal and, therefore, ceased to be non-self-governing territories. Similarly, the U.K. has discontinued reporting on Antigua, Dominica, Grenada, St. Kitts-Nevis-Anguilla and St. Lucia following their attainment in 1967 of a "full measure of self-government" as associated States within the Commonwealth. The Committee of 24 has refused to accept the view that these territories are no longer "non-self-governing." See Barbier, *Le Comité de décolonisation des Nations Unies* (1974).

Colonial Peoples and Territories a new committee, the "Committee of 24," came into being and in 1963 this took over the functions of the earlier committee.

The work of this Committee is based partly upon the reports submitted to the Secretary-General under Article 73 (c) and partly upon a method of work which, though endorsed by the Assembly, has no basis in any specific provision of the Charter. This method is closely analogous to the method of the Trusteeship Council: it includes the determination of which territories fall within the purview of the 1960 resolution; the examination of an information paper prepared by the Secretariat on each territory and of information submitted by the administering Power at the Committee's request or unilaterally; the hearing of petitioners (despite opposition from the United Kingdom, U.S.A. and Australia) and visits to territories (also against opposition by these three States). States like Portugal and S. Africa have virtually boycotted this Committee, whereas the United Kingdom has co-operated in some degree but protested over various steps taken. For example, in April 1967 the United Kingdom protested against the decision of the Sub-Committee on Petitions *not* to circulate communications on Aden because they embodied complaints against the U.A.R. and Saudi Arabia rather than the United Kingdom. The United Kingdom has also protested against the Committee's resolution and General Assembly resol. 2429 (XXIII) on Gibraltar which, contrary to the express wish of the inhabitants of the territory, has rejected the idea of a continued association with the United Kingdom. The Committee's discussions on the Falkland Isles have disclosed the same trend.

Whatever the disputes which earlier marked the attempts to transform the system of supervision under Chapter XI into something akin to the Trusteeship system, it is clear that, following the 1960 resolution, the activities of the Committee of 24 have given rise to increasing controversy. By 1970 the General Assembly had moved to the position of condemning colonial rule as a breach of international peace, a crime against humanity, and called on States to assist colonial peoples in their struggle for independence. By 1971 the U.S.A., United Kingdom and Australia withdrew from the Committee of 24, although Australia subsequently returned.

One very important offshoot of this development relates to the future status of the remaining, and generally rather small, territories.[11] If no alternative to independence is to be accepted, the "micro-State" presents not only considerable economic problems, but also problems of political Statehood and, in particular, whether this will carry the right to full membership of the United Nations. Proposals by a committee of experts of the Security Council for associate membership, or a form of membership which allowed a State to opt out of participation of certain U.N. organs were regarded as incompatible with the Charter and not proceeded with.[12]

V. THE SECRETARIAT

The Secretariat is described in Article 7 of the Charter as one of the "principal organs" of the Organisation, and Article 97 provides that the Secretariat "shall comprise a Secretary-General and such staff as the Organisation may require." For the purposes of presentation in this chapter the Secretary-General and his staff will be dealt with separately. However, it must always be borne in mind that no such rigid separation occurs in practice. In the exercise of his office the Secretary-General draws upon the advice and the resources of all branches of the Secretariat and assumes final responsibility for its conduct.

1. The Secretary-General

Prior to the establishment of the League, the idea of a "Chancellor," a world statesman playing an active and dominant role in world politics, was seriously entertained. In the outcome, however, the League Covenant provided for a "Secretary-General," and the history of this office under the League shows that the interpretation placed upon the powers accorded to the Secretary-General depends very largely upon the individual characters of the office-holder. The contrast between the office under its first holder, Sir Eric Drummond, an eminent British civil servant, and the second, M. Avenol, a French diplomat by

---

[11] There are 65 territories with populations of less than 30,000: three of them, Barbados, Iceland and the Maldive Islands are already UN members.
[12] S/9836. And see Schwebel, (1973) 67 A.J.I.L. 108; Rapaport, *Small States and Territories,* (1971), a UNITAR study.

training, is not a contrast between different functions (for these remained the same) but between the individuals to whom responsibility for carrying out those functions was given. The development of the office of Director-General of the ILO under the dynamic leadership of M. Albert Thomas, particularly in its policy-making powers, was due more to the character of M. Thomas than to any difference in the formal powers and functions given to his office. Similarly, in the United Nations, any differences in the interpretations placed upon the office of Secretary-General under Mr. Trygvie Lie and Mr. Dag Hammarskjold until his tragic death on September 17, 1961, are explained mainly by the difference in character and temperament.[13] Naturally, prevailing political conditions will also influence the scope of a Secretary-General's political powers, and the somewhat less dynamic character of the office under U Thant was probably attributable both to personal temperament and to changed political conditions. However, it is clear that the way in which the office develops depends as much upon the personality of the office-holder as upon the definition of the office in the treaty constituting the organisation.

Within the United Nations the Secretary-General is, at one and the same time, both chief administrator and chief executive. There was, prior to the San Francisco Conference, a plan to divide the functions between a Secretary-General, who would be the chief administrator, and a President, who would be the chief executive. However, in the Charter the office of Secretary-General combines both roles, as a survey of his functions will presently show.

(a) *Appointment of the Secretary-General.*

The interpretation given to Article 97 in practice has resulted in the following procedure. The Security Council discusses candidates in private meeting and, after a non-procedural vote, proffers but one candidate in its recommendation to the General Assembly. The justification for this practice lies in the need for the Secretary-General to be a person acceptable to all the permanent members, for experience has shown that the office-holder is most

---

[13] Hammarskjold's own conceptions of his office can be seen in his address to Oxford University on May 30, 1961, entitled "The International Civil Servant in Law and in Fact" (Clarendon Press).

effective when commanding the support of all the permanent members.[14]

Upon receiving the recommendation of the Security Council, the Assembly conducts its own discussions in private and then holds the actual vote by secret ballot but in public meeting; the decision is by a simple majority vote.

The term of office is nowhere specified in the Charter, but in 1946 the Assembly fixed a five-year term, which can be renewed or extended. The only real constitutional difficulty which has arisen over this procedure was when Mr. Lie's first term expired in 1950. The Security Council reported to the Assembly that it was unable to formulate any recommendation. The Assembly thereupon, and against the opposition of the U.S.S.R., placed the matter of the appointment of the Secretary-General on its own agenda and by resolution 492 (V) decided to continue Mr. Lie in office for a further period of three years.[15] Upon the death of Mr. Hammars-kjold his successor, U Thant of Burma, was elected acting Secretary-General for the unexpired portion of Mr. Hammars-kjold's term by the General Assembly on November 3, 1961, and upon the recommendation of the Security Council; he was later confirmed by both organs.

(b) *Functions and powers of the Secretary-General*

In addition to the specific functions contained in Articles 12 (2), 20, 73 (e), 101, 110, the Statute of the I.C.J., and many international treaties which nominate the Secretary-General as depositary of the treaty, the functions and powers of the Secretary-General are broadly stated in Articles 97, 98, 99, 100 and 101. These can be briefly outlined under two heads: the first, administrative, really includes a variety of functions and powers which are administrative, technical and financial; the second, executive, relates to those functions which are pre-eminently political in character.

---

[14] The administrative heads of the specialised agencies do not, in the procedures for their appointment, have to face a possible veto; they do not possess the political powers comparable to those of the S.G. under Art. 99 of the Charter.
[15] For a survey of the legal arguments for and against this action see *Repertory*, Vol. V, pp. 115–116.

(i) *Administrative.* The Secretary-General is, as Article 97 states, the "chief administrative officer" of the Organisation.[16] Amongst his primary duties is that of ensuring the efficient working of the meetings of the organs and committees, and also of such conferences as may be convened under UN auspices. In this connection he draws up provisional agenda, notifies invited States and other bodies of the convening of the sessions and meetings, provides staff and facilities, examines the credentials of representatives and reports thereon to the organ concerned. For special conferences he may submit proposals regarding their method of work and procedure, and provide draft agenda and rules of procedure. During the course of a meeting or conference he, through his staff, will undertake studies, advise on matters of procedure, and assist in the drafting of documents, resolutions, and reports, as well as giving legal and technical advice.

Another primary duty is to secure adequate co-ordination and integration of the work programmes of the various branches of the Secretariat and of the specialised agencies and other intergovernmental organisations. This need for co-ordination has been particularly evident in the economic and social fields. Generally, it covers problems such as the elimination of duplication of work, fixing responsibility for and priority of projects, preparation of budgets, allocation of staff, scheduling of meetings and conferences, and the dissemination of information. It is true that, in relation to the specialised agencies, the primary responsibility lies with the General Assembly and the Economic and Social Council. However, under the agreements with the specialised agencies, specific powers have been assigned to the Secretary-General and, in addition, as Chairman of the Advisory Committee on Co-ordination (ACC), he can consult with the heads of the specialised agencies in a practical way so as to co-ordinate policies and work programmes.

[16] As initially organised in 1946 there were eight Assistant Secretaries-General, forming a kind of advisory council and chosen on a political basis. In 1953 Hammarskjold fused this category and that of the "Principal Directors" into one category of Under-Secretaries, thus broadening the basis of consultation but, at the same time making the responsibility for decisions a more personal one. This structure was severely criticised by the U.S.S.R. during the Congo crisis, and U Thant attempted to meet this criticism (which involved a proposal to replace the S.G. by a commission of three—"troika,") by appointing eight Under-Secretaries as "principal advisers." In 1968 U Thant divided the level of Under-Secretary into two, with a higher level of 11 Under-Secretaries-General.

Many of the decisions of UN agencies and committees embody a request for the preparation of studies and reports. The Secretary-General assumes responsibility for this work, and such studies extend over all aspects of the Organisation's work. The work actually requested is, however, only a fraction of the informative work and study which the Secretariat undertakes as part of its normal work programme. This work supplies much of the essential data upon which the UN organs rely in reaching decisions; it is generally of a high standard although occasionally, in an understandable attempt to be impartial, it may lack positive opinions or proposals. The independent secretariat of UNCTAD, at least during the period of office of Prebisch as Secretary-General, has been somewhat exceptional in its advocacy of the policies and aims of the developing countries.[17]

In financial matters the Secretary-General assumes responsibility for the preparation of the annual budget of the Organisation, which then goes before the Advisory Committee on Budgetary Questions, then to the 5th Committee, and ultimately to the Assembly itself. He also assumes custody of all UN funds and responsibility for their expenditure. Even outside the specific budgetary appropriations, he retains a limited authority to enter into commitments not provided for in the budget, as, for example, where necessary in the interest of international peace and security or for urgent economic rehabilitation.

There are more than 60 multilateral treaties which entrust the Secretary-General with depositary and other functions, quite apart from those treaties which are registered with the Secretariat under Article 102 and require publication under that article. In respect of such multilateral treaties the Secretary-General may be required to undertake the notification of signatures, accessions, and reservations to the States concerned.

A final function of the Secretary-General is the submission of the annual report on the work of the Organisation, provided for in Article 98. This is a comprehensive summary of the work undertaken, and has great value as a source of information. However, it is also used as a means of exercising the Secretary-General's political powers, in so far as that report contains, as it frequently does, suggestions and proposals relating to political questions.

[17] Gardner, "The UNCTAD" (1968) 22 *Int. Org.* 106.

(ii) *Executive.* The power given to the Secretary-General under Article 99 was regarded by the Preparatory Commission at San Francisco as "a quite special right which goes beyond any power previously accorded to the head of an international organisation."[18] It has, however, been specifically invoked on rare occasions as when, on June 25, 1950, the Secretary-General brought to the attention of the Security Council the aggression upon the Republic of Korea and when, on July 13, 1960, the Secretary-General convened the Council to deal with the Congo crisis. The reason why the power has not been invoked more frequently is not that there is any lethargy in the Secretary-General, but rather that member States are usually quick to bring any threat to international peace and security to the attention of the Council themselves. And it may be noted that, in this respect, the Secretary-General's power under Article 99 is equivalent to that of a member State under Article 35, or to that of the General Assembly under Article 11 (3). Of course, in the discussion of any matter within the Council, the Secretary-General has no vote.

Although the power is, under this article, limited to the Security Council, the rules of procedure of the Assembly give the Secretary-General a general power to place matters on its provisional agenda and, not unnaturally, this has been interpreted in practice to include items of a political character. A good example of this was the Secretary-General's memorandum concerning a 20-year programme for achieving peace through the United Nations, placed on the agenda of the fifth session.

This power of the Secretary-General to bring matters to the attention of the UN organs carries with it the power to make such investigations and inquiries, on his own initiative, as may be necessary in order to fully inform the appropriate organ of the matter. Such implied power had been claimed by the Secretary-General as early as 1946 in connection with the Greek question,[19] and has never been disputed.

In addition to the specific power of Article 99, Article 98 provides that the Secretary-General shall act in the capacity of chief administrative officer of the principal organs (other than the Court), and the rules of procedure of these organs authorise the

---

[18] Preparatory Commission, Report, Doc. PC/20, p. 87.
[19] *Off. Rec. S.C.,* 70th Meeting, Doc. S/P.V./70, Sept. 20, 1946.

Secretary-General to place items on their provisional agenda, to make statements, to submit proposals or draft resolutions, and to submit amendments to other proposals. These further powers afford to the Secretary-General a sufficient basis upon which he can exercise considerable political influence in these organs. An example of the extent of these powers is to be found in the Secretary-General's statement before the third emergency session of the General Assembly on August 8, 1958. This statement outlined a comprehensive programme of far-reaching political importance for the solution of the Middle East crisis in which U.S. and British forces had landed in Lebanon and Jordan. A reading of the subsequent debate shows how greatly this influenced the views of many member States and the action taken.

Yet another means by which the Secretary-General can develop his initiative in the political field is his annual report on the work of the Organisation. This, as has already been mentioned, has tended to become in part a "review of the world situation," and, as such, contains constructive proposals by the Secretary-General.

The Secretary-General has also claimed, and exercised, a general power to act on his own initiative whenever such action seemed to him necessary in the interests of international peace and security. On accepting a further term of office on September 26, 1957, Hammarskjold stated that he would act "to help in filling any vacuum that may appear in the systems which the Charter and traditional diplomacy provide for the safeguarding of peace and security."[20] Many instances of this are to be found: his decision in July 1958 to enlarge UNOGIL (UN Observer Group in Lebanon), his role in Laos in 1959, or his discussions with the government of the Union of South Africa in 1960 on the segregation issue. This last is, moreover, an example of a situation in which the government concerned rejected the competence of the Security Council, but accepted that it was a matter upon which the Secretary-General had the initiative to act. U Thant's proposals on Vietnam, in 1966 and 1968, are another example.[21] So also is his decision in May 1967 to withdraw UNEF, without reference to the General Assembly (a decision which, on legal grounds, is extremely difficult to justify). Another example is his extending his

---

[20] A/P.V. 690.
[21] *UN Yearbook* 1966, 151; *UN Monthly Chronicle,* Feb. 1968, 47.

good offices in 1970 over the Bahrain dispute, although he exercised great care in emphasising that any findings would require endorsement by the Security Council.[22] In all such cases where the Secretary-General so acted he did so, not arbitrarily, but guided by the purposes and principles of the Charter which he regarded as setting the *legal* limits to his political discretion.[23]

There are other situations in which the Secretary-General carries out "such other functions as are entrusted to him" by the UN organs (Art. 98). For example, at its third emergency session on August 21, 1958, the Assembly, by resolution 1237 (ES-III), requested the Secretary-General to make "such practical arrangements as would adequately help in upholding the purposes and principles of the Charter in relation to Lebanon and Jordan in the present circumstances." The margin of discretion left to the Secretary-General under this general directive needs no emphasis. Yet, in this and every such case, where the Secretary-General acts under a specific resolution, it is his practice to regard this as a mandate with terms of reference binding upon him.[24] The Congo situation affords a remarkable illustration of an organ, the Security Council, authorising the Secretary-General, in the widest possible terms, to take action.[25] When, in due course, criticism developed of his adherence to a policy of non-intervention in the sense of refusing to allow UN troops to be used for the conquest of Katanga, he referred back to the Security Council for explicit guidance. Tragically, no such guidance was forthcoming in any formal resolution, for the lack of unanimity of the permanent members had again appeared; however, as he declared to the Council, "I have the right to expect guidance. But . . . if the Security Council says nothing I have no other choice than to follow my conviction."[26] His subsequent action was thus once more

---

[22] 9.I.L.M., 787–805.

[23] Schachter, "Dag Hammarskjold and the relation of Law to Politics" (1962) 56 A.J.I.L. I.

[24] See the Secretary-General's subsequent report on his activities under this resolution. Doc. A/3934, Sept. 29, 1958.

[25] The resolution of July 14, 1960, authorised the Secretary-General "to take the necessary steps, in consultation with the government of the Republic of the Congo, to provide the government with such military assistance, as may be necessary, until . . . the national security forces may be able, in the opinion of the government, to meet fully their tasks."

[26] August 21, 1960, 888th Session.

guided by the principles and purposes of the Charter as conceived by him. Thus the differences between his powers under Article 99, his residuary powers to act, and his powers under a mandate from an organ are real, but possibly deceptive: his discretionary powers obviously increase, even when acting under a mandate, in proportion to the generality of the terms of the mandate.

Another important political role of the Secretary-General is to act "as a mediator and as an informal adviser of many governments," to quote from the report of the Preparatory Commission. This role was a familiar one under the League and its usefulness is increasingly evident in the United Nations. In some cases, as in the question of the treatment of people of Indian origin in the Union of South Africa,[27] the Secretary-General may be specifically requested by the Assembly to undertake such a role. In others he may undertake this role on his own initiative, often with the minimum of publicity, and this was a technique much favoured by Mr. Hammarskjold in his "quiet diplomacy." He may do this personally or through a representative.[28] Governments tend to prove far more tractable in private discussion than in the full glare and publicity of an open debate in the Council or the Assembly.

The political role of the Secretary-General is, therefore, an essential part of the office as now constituted. The Soviet proposal for a "troika,"[29] in 1961 as a consequence of the Soviet Union's dissatisfaction with Hammarskjold's use of the role, would inevitably destroy that role and reduce the Secretary-General to an administrative head and little more. It found little support in the Assembly.

The Secretary-General also has a certain representational function whereby he acts as agent or representative of the United Nations. The function is apparent not only when he speaks publicly about the UN but, more important, when he undertakes agreements on behalf of the UN. These agreements may have to be negotiated and concluded with governments, as for example the

---

[27] G.A. resolution 511 (VI).

[28] See S.C. resol. 242 of November 22, 1967 on the Middle East crisis in which the Council asked the S.G. to appoint a Special Representative (Ambassador Jarring being subsequently appointed).

[29] *i.e.* a body of three: one Western nominee, one Socialist and one "neutral", in which there would be virtually a veto. See Bailey, "The Troika and the future of the UN" *Int. Conciliation* (1962), No. 538.

Headquarters Agreement with the U.S.A., or with other organisations; such is the case with the agreements between the UN and the specialised agencies which are concluded by the heads of the organisations. The Headquarters Agreement also provides for consultation and negotiation on several matters between the Secretary-General and the U.S. Government *after* the agreement has come into force.

As a general rule such agreements are concluded by him at the request of one of the UN organs, but in certain cases, notably in those which concern agreements on the privileges and immunities of the UN, the Secretary-General will act on his own initiative.

Apart from the negotiation and conclusion of treaties, there are many other agreements and contracts which the Secretary-General concludes under private law with private agencies for supplies and services and, of course, with individuals who become staff members.

These representational functions also extend to the conduct of court proceedings on behalf of the UN. The Secretary-General has, through his representatives, made statements in the interest of the Organisation before the I.C.J. on several occasions on which the issues raised affected the Organisation.[30] He also represents the Organisation before national tribunals in matters affecting the Organisation's property, or privileges and immunities, and before the Administrative Tribunal on staff matters. Many treaties to which the UN is a party provide for the arbitration of disputes, and in all such disputes it would be for the Secretary-General to represent the Organisation. There is, of course, no possibility under the statute of the I.C.J. of the UN appearing as a *party* in contentious proceedings as opposed to the advisory proceedings mentioned above, although the Reparations Case left no doubt as to the capacity of the Organisations to present claims for damage to its property or its agents before other tribunals, be they national or international. Where, in any judicial proceedings, the questions of immunity arises for a UN official, it is for the Secretary-General to decide whether to waive or maintain the immunity.

---

[30] For example, *Reparation for Injuries suffered in the service of the UN, I.C.J., Oral Statement,* pp. 3–4; *Reservations to the Convention on the Prevention and Punishment of the Crime of Genocide, I.C.J., Oral Statement* (Extract), p. 20.

2. The Secretariat

(a) *Its international character*

The most important single characteristic of an international civil service is its international character. This is safeguarded in the United Nations Charter by Article 100 which, in its first paragraph, enjoins the Secretary-General and his staff to, in effect, acknowledge their primary allegiance to the Organisation, and, in its second paragraph, states the corresponding obligation of all member States to respect this international character.[31] This article is supplemented by Regulations 1.1, 1.2, 1.3 and 1.4 of the Staff Regulations, and by the oath taken by staff members upon appointment.

The Staff Regulations, and the Staff Rules which supplement them, further protect this international character by regulating the extent to which staff members can undertake outside employment, be associated financially with outside concerns, make public statements, accept honours, gifts and awards, or engage in political activities (other than the normal civic right of voting) which would be inconsistent with their international status.[32]

The most controversial issue which has so far arisen grew out of the allegation made in 1952 by a United States Grand Jury and a subcommittee of the Senate that certain United States nationals, employed as staff members, had engaged in subversive activities directed against the United States Government. Over a score of those staff members called upon to testify before these bodies refused to answer any questions relating to their political activities, claiming their constitutional privilege against self-incrimination embodied in the Fifth Amendment.

The Secretary-General suspended the staff members concerned and established a Commission of Jurists to advise him as to what disciplinary measures might be taken. Their opinion[33] was that conviction of subversive activities, or a refusal to testify about such activities, amounted to "serious misconduct" and a "fundamental

---

[31] See Schwebel in (1971) 65 A.J.I.L., 136 for the allegation of a serious beach of this obligation by the U.S.A. against the D.G. of the ILO.

[32] See generally *Repertory*, Vol. V, pp. 186–196. See U.N.J.Y. (1969), p. 228 for the Legal Counsel's opinion that the Secretary-General cannot agree to appoint nationals of a state subject to its consent.

[33] UN Doc. A/INF/51, Dec. 5, 1952. Convenient text in (1953) 47 A.J.I.L. 97–117.

breach" of the contractual obligations of a staff member. Moreover, the Jurists advised that the Secretary-General should dismiss staff members where he had "reasonable grounds for believing (the staff members) to be engaged or to have been engaged, or to be *likely* to be engaged in any subversive activities against the host country."[34]

In their subsequent actions none of the Secretaries-General have accepted this opinion in its entirety. The Secretaries-General have retained a right to determine for themselves whether the conviction was secured in a fair trial, and Mr. Hammarskjold has rejected the "likelihood" test. So far as the actual refusal to testify is concerned, Mr. Lie accepted the view that this constituted a ground for dismissal, but only where the staff member had been given an opportunity to explain his actions to the Secretary-General and that explanation had failed to remove the unfavourable implication of the refusal to testify. However, certain permanent staff members refused to take the opportunity of explaining their refusal to testify to the Secretary-General and appealed to the United Nations Administrative Tribunal on the issue of whether refusal to testify by claiming the privilege against self-incrimination amounted to "serious misconduct." The Tribunal disagreed with the Commission of Jurists and held that summary dismissal, as opposed to other disciplinary measures, was not permissible.[35] The Secretary-General was therefore obliged either to reinstate these staff members or else pay them damages; he chose to do the latter.

Certain conclusions may be drawn with regard to the experience so far gained in the treatment of this particular problem. They are, first, that there is no necessary contradiction between an "international" and a "national" loyalty; on the contrary, cases of a contradiction will be highly exceptional and should be met either by the assignment of the staff member to other work, or, when this is impossible, by his resignation. The view was once taken that the "loyalty" of an international civil servant precluded strike action. In fact many international organisations have now experienced strikes: the ILO, UNESCO, EEC, OECD, NATO, FAO and the UN have all experienced this phenomenon. In general, the right to

---

[34] *Ibid.* p. 97.
[35] Judgments of the UN Administrative Tribunal Nos. 29–38 (AT/DEC/29–38).

strike is now recognised, and the organisations have also recognised the syndicates or trade unions representing staff for bargaining purposes.[36] Second, the Secretary-General has the duty to satisfy himself that allegations against staff are well-founded and in fact reveal conduct incompatible with the status of an international civil servant; neither a conviction nor a refusal to testify constitute, *ipso facto*, adequate grounds for dismissal. Third, governments possessing information tending to cast doubt on a person's qualifications for a post should submit that information at the time of recruitment and not after appointment. And, fourth, the obligations of the staff member are the same whether he is a national of the host state or of any other member State.

(b) *Recruitment, appointment and conditions of service*
Regulation 4.2 of the Staff Regulations provides:

> "The paramount consideration in the appointment, transfer or promotion of the staff shall be the necessity for securing the highest standards of efficiency, competence and integrity. Due regard shall be paid to the importance of recruiting the staff on as wide a geographical base as possible."

There are, therefore, two main principles guiding recruitment; the first that of the personal qualifications of the applicant, the second that of securing a balanced geographical distribution. This second principle is constantly stressed by the Assembly, through its 5th Committee, whenever questions of recruitment policy arise. It is not *per se* inconsistent with the first and paramount principle but, in practice, it is often relatively more difficult to secure staff of appropriate qualifications from countries which do not have the same general standards of education or the same long-established academic institutions or civil services as, for example, the countries of Western Europe.

Another factor which undoubtedly affects recruitment is the size of a given member State's contribution to the annual budget of the Organisation. In practice the "desirable range of posts," which may range from one to three for countries like Togo and

---

[36] See Pellet, "La grève des fonctionnaires internationaux" (1975), RGDIP 932–971.

Afghanistan to 327–436 for the U.S.A.,[37] is roughly proportionate to their contribution.

Naturally, not all posts are subject to the same principles. For example, recruitment of language staff, such as interpreters or translators, or of manual workers (who are mainly locally recruited) cannot be governed by exactly the same principles as the other staff. Moreover, the higher posts of Under-Secretaries and Directors are distributed in accordance with an understanding which is of a primarily political character.

The appointment of staff members is, under Article 101, vested in the Secretary-General, although in the case of certain special organs this appointment is made by the head of the organ.[38] The letter of appointment, and the letter of acceptance by the appointee, together constitute the contract of employment which is, however, subject to all the provisions of the Staff Regulations, Staff Rules and Administrative Instructions relevant to the particular category of appointment made. The Staff Regulations are adopted by the Assembly itself, the Staff Rules are promulgated by the Secretary-General to implement those Regulations and also figure in the same booklet or handbook. The Administrative Instructions do not find a place in the booklet or handbook and are of a more transitory character; they are, nevertheless, if *intra vires* the Staff Rules, binding on staff members.

Staff Regulation 12.1 provides that "these regulations may be supplemented or amended by the General Assembly, without prejudice to the acquired rights of staff members." The question of the binding effect upon staff members of changes in the Regulations made subsequent to appointment has been raised before the Administrative Tribunal, and the Tribunal has dealt with this question in the following way.[39] The contracts contain both "statutory" and "contractual" elements. The former are

---

[37] See Report of S.G. on Personnel Questions, geographical distribution of staff, etc. Doc. A/C.5/750, Oct. 10, 1958.

[38] *i.e.* Office of High Commissioner for Refugees, UNRWA, UNKRA, UNCTAD and UNIDO. The Staff of the European Communities is appointed under an "act of authority" rather than a contract, and hence the notion of acquired rights is not the basis upon which the staff are protected against retroactive changes in their conditions of employment: see the *Algera Case* 1957 Recueil III, 152–4; the *Elz Case* 1960 Recueil VI, 215.

[39] See Judgments of the Tribunal Nos. 19, 20–25, 27 (AT/DEC/19. 20–25, 27); Baade, "The acquired rights of international public servants" (1966–67) *A. J. Comp. Law* 251.

those provisions which affect in general the organisation of the Secretariat and have no personal reference; the latter are those affecting personal status, *i.e.* nature of contract, grade, salary. The "contractual" elements alone are protected by the doctrine of acquired rights and cannot be changed except by the consent of the staff member.

Appointments are of different kinds, and the rights of the appointee vary accordingly.

(i) *Permanent appointments*. These are intended for career service staff and imply tenure until retirement age, subject to a five-yearly revision on grounds of efficiency, competence and integrity. These appointments can be terminated, under Regulation 9.1 (a), for failure to conform to the standard of integrity required under Article 101 (3), or if facts anterior to the appointment come to light which, had they been known, would have precluded appointment; in both cases a report by the Special Advisory Board must precede termination. A final ground of termination is where it "would be in the interest of the good administration of the Organisation," but this ground exists only when the action is not contested by the staff member.

(ii) *Temporary appointments*. These are of three kinds:

(a) INDEFINITE, *i.e.* with no fixed expiration date and designed for persons recruited for field or mission service. These can be terminated under Regulation 9.1 (c) where "such action would be in the interest of the United Nations." However, the Administrative Tribunal has suggested that if the Secretary-General's discretion were exercised from an improper motive the Tribunal would rescind the decision.[40]

(b) FIXED-TERM, *i.e.* with an expiration date but for a period of less than five years. These are designed for persons seconded from government service or universities and carry no expectations of renewal or permanency.[41] They can be

---

[40] AT/DEC/19, 20 and 22–25. See *post*, p. 323.

[41] Compare, however, the fixed term contracts in UNESCO, of which the I.C.J. has stated: "The fact is that there has developed in this matter a body of practice to the effect that holders of fixed-term contracts, although not assimilated to holders of permanent or indeterminate contracts, have often been treated as entitled to be considered for continued employment consistently with the requirements and the general good of the organisation, in a manner transcending the strict wording of the contract." A.O. on *Judgments of the Administrative Tribunal of the ILO*, (1956) *I.C.J. Reports*, 91.

terminated for the same reasons as permanent appointments.

(c) PROBATIONARY, *i.e.* normally for not more than two years and carrying an expectancy of a permanent appointment as a career staff member. They can be terminated like the temporary indefinite appointments.

(iii) *Regular appointments.* These are designed for locally recruited staff members[42] who have already satisfactorily served under a probationary appointment. They can be terminated for the same reasons as temporary indefinite appointments.

Whatever the category of contract held by the staff member, he will be entitled to the benefits of a children's allowance, language allowance, annual leave, termination indemnity and participation in a social security scheme comprising a pension fund, sick leave, compensation for death, illness, etc., also an educational grant for his children, home leave every two years, and a repatriation grant or "service benefit" on repatriation at the conclusion of his service.

It was originally planned that all staff members should be exempt from their "national" income tax, not, it should be added, so as to make a tax-free privileged class but simply to ensure equality in net income between staff members of different nationalities. Accordingly the Convention on Privileges and Immunities of the United Nations of 1946 provided for such exemption. However, difficulties were encountered when certain States, among them the United States, failed to ratify the Convention and proceeded to tax their nationals in the Secretariat. To meet these difficulties a plan was instituted in 1948 whereby all salaries were increased to a "gross" figure and then, under the Staff Assessment Plan, reduced again to the "net" level by an amount deducted in lieu of tax. The income from Staff Assessment is now, by resolution 973 (X) of the General Assembly, paid into a Tax Equalisation Fund and each member State would be credited with the sums paid into the Fund by its nationals. However, where a State has actually levied tax upon one of its nationals, that State would be debited with the amounts paid by the staff members so taxed and the staff member is paid out of the Fund the amount his

---

[42] But note that UNRWA, which employs some 11,000 locally-recruited staff, has a separate system of Area Staff Regulations and Rules which are *sui generis*.

State has collected in tax. This whole procedure is a poor substitute for adoption of the 1946 Convention by all member States, although it does ensure net equality of salary.

Although the above categories relate to the kind of contract held, another classification, based upon the category of post held, is equally important. There are three main categories[43]: the first includes Directors and Principal Officers, essentially the policy-making staff serving directly under the Secretary-General and his Under-Secretaries. The second is the Professional category, ranging from Grade P.1 to P.5, which includes the main body of internationally recruited career staff, and the third is the General Service category comprising locally recruited staff and clerical staff ranging from G.1 to G.5. Within any given grade there are a number of "steps" which represent the normal within-grade promotion, occurring annually.

The breach of the Staff Rules and Regulations which, as has been pointed out, are incorporated into all contracts with staff members, can give rise to disciplinary action by the Secretary-General. Such action may include a written censure, suspension without pay, demotion or dismissal for misconduct and summary dismissal in case of serious misconduct. It must be noted that the grounds for termination of a staff member's services vary according to the type of contract held,[44] and different grounds may call for different procedure on termination. For example, with the permanent appointment, under Regulation 9.1 (a) "unsatisfactory service" is a ground which does not require from the Secretary-General a statement of the reasons for termination whereas failure to "meet the highest standards of integrity" does. To take another example, summary dismissal is only permissible for "serious misconduct" (Regulation 10.2), whereas "unsatisfactory conduct" calls for disciplinary measures, not summary dismissal. Some indication of the meaning of these terms has been given by the UN Administrative Tribunal. Mention has already been made of Judgments Nos. 29–37, which held that the invoking of the Fifth Amendment did not constitute "serious misconduct" and, in the same judgments, the Tribunal indicated that "service" must relate to the person's professional behaviour within the Organisation,

---

[43] Other categories are the Field Service and Manual Workers.
[44] See *ante*, p. 101. The grounds are set out in Regulation 9.1.

whereas "misconduct" could embrace acts committed outside his professional activities.

The disciplinary action taken by the Secretary-General is hinged about with various safeguards. Except in the case of summary dismissal, the Secretary-General must, prior to taking disciplinary measures, refer the matter to a Joint Disciplinary Committee, composed of three members of whom one is appointed by the Secretary-General, another elected by the Staff, and a chairman selected from a panel established by the Secretary-General in consultation with the Staff Committee. The Secretary-General is not bound by the advice of this Committee and an aggrieved staff member is free to appeal to the Joint Appeals Board, a body of three composed in a representative manner similar to the Joint Disciplinary Committee, which has a procedure of a quasi-judicial character. Again, the Secretary-General is not bound to accept the recommendation of the Board, and the staff member may then further appeal to the United Nations Administrative Tribunal.[45]

[45] See *post*, p. 317.

Bibliography

General Works
BOWETT: U.N. Forces (1964).
CHAUMONT: Les Organisations internationales (1963).
DIMITROV: Documents of International Organisations: A Bibliographic Handbook (1973).
FALK and MENDLOVITZ: The Strategy of World Order, Vol. 3 (1966).
GARDINER: In Pursuit of World Order (1964).
GOODSPEED: The Nature and Function of International Organisation (1967).
GOODRICH: The United Nations in a Changing World (1974).
GOODRICH and HAMBRO: Charter of the United Nations. Commentary and Documents (2nd ed., 1949).
GUTTERIDGE: The UN in a changing world (1969).
HALDERMAN: The UN and the Rule of Law (1966).
HIGGINS: Development of International Law through the political organs of the UN (1963).
HILL: The United Nations System (1978).
KELSEN: The Law of the United Nations (1964).
KHAN: Implied Powers of the UN (1970).
LUARD: The United Nations. How it Works and What it Does (1979).

MANIN: L'ONU et le maintien de la paix (1971).

SOHN: Recent Cases on UN Law (Suppl.) (1963).

SOHN: Basic Documents of the United Nations (1956).

TUNKIN: *"The UN"* (1966) 4 *Soviet Law and Government* (No. 4), 3–12.

UNITED NATIONS: Conference on International Organisation (UNCIO), 15 vols. (1945) (these volumes constitute the *travaux préparatoires*).

UNITED. NATIONS: Repertory of Practice of UN Organs, Vols. 1–5 and Supplements.

VIRALLY: L'Organisation Mondiale (1972).

WATERS: The UN International Organisation and Adminstration (1967).

WEISSBERG: The international status of the UN (1961).

The Security Council

BAILEY: Voting in the Security Council (1969). The Procedure of the Security Council (1975).

HIGGINS: "The place of law in the settlement of disputes by the Security Council", (1970) 64 A.J.I.L., 1–18.

JIMENEZ DE ARECHAGA: Voting and the handling of disputes in the Security Council (1951).

KAHNG: Law, Politics and the Security Council (1964).

KERLEY: *"The Powers of Investigation of the UN Security Council,"* (1961) 55 A.J.I.L. 892.

SCHACHTER: *"Legal Aspects of the UN Action in the Congo,"* (1961) 55 A.J.I.L. 1.

STONE: Legal Controls of International Conflict (1959), Chaps. VII and VIII.

UNITED NATIONS: Repertoire of practice of the Security Council, 1946–51 (1954) and Suppl.1952–55 (ST.PSCA/1/Add.1) (1958).

UNITED NATIONS: Repertory of practice of UN Organs, Vol. II (1955) and Suppl. No. 1, Vol. I (1958).

The General Assembly

ANDRASSI: *"Uniting for Peace,"* (1956) 50 A.J.I.L. 563.

ASAMOAH: The legal significance of the declarations of the General Assembly of the UN (1966).

BAILEY: The General Assembly (1960).

BINDSCHEDLER: *"The delimitation of powers in the UN"* (1963) 108 R.C. 305.

CASTANEDA: Legal Effects of UN Resolutions (1969).

CHAUMONT: *"The respective roles of the UN General Assembly and the Security Council"* (1966) 12 *Review of Contemporary Law* (No. 2) 23.

FINLEY: The Structure of the UN General Assembly (1977), 3 Vols.

JOHNSON: "The effect of resolutions of the General Assembly of the UN" (1955–56) 32 B.Y.B.I.L. 97.

KELSEN: Recent Trends in the Law of the UN (1951), Chap. 4.

LAUTERPACHT: The United Nations Emergency Force. Basic Documents (1960).

STOESSINGER: Financing the UN (1964).
UNITED NATIONS: Repertory of Practice of UN Organs, Vol.I (1955) and Suppl. No. 1 (1960); Vol. II (1958).
VALLAT: *"The Competence of the UN General Assembly,"* (1959) 97 R.C. 203.
YEMIN: Legislative powers in the U.N. and specialised agencies (1969).

The Economic and Social Council
CHEEVER and HAVILAND: Organising for Peace (1954), Chaps. 7 and 8.
FALK and MENDLOVITZ: The Strategy of World Order, Vol. 4 (1966), Chap. 6.
GARDNER and MILLIKAN: *"The Global Partnership: International Agencies and Economic development"* (1968) 22 Int. Org. No. 1.
GODSPEED: *"Political Considerations in the UN Economic and Social Council,"* (1961) Y.B.W.A. 135.
GOODRICH and HAMBRO: Charter of the United Nations (1949), 2nd ed., Chaps. IX and X.
HADWEN and KAUFMANN: How UN decisions are Made (1962).
JENKS: *"Co-ordination in International Organisation: an introductory survey",* (1951) 28 B.Y.B.I.L. 29.
KIRDAR: The Structure of UN Economic Aid to Underdeveloped Countries (1966).
MANGONE: UN Administration of economic and social programs (1966).
SHARP: The UN Economic and Social Council (1969).
UNITED NATIONS: Repertory of Practice of UN Organs, Vol. III (1955) and Suppl. No. 1; Vol. II (1958).

Trusteeship Council
HALL, L. D.: Mandates, Dependencies and Trusteeship (1948).
KUNZ, J. L.: *"Chapter XI of the United Nations Charter in Action,"* (1954) 48 A.J.I.L. 103.
LEAGUE OF NATIONS: The Mandate System: Origins—Principles—Application, L. of N. Doc., 1945, VI.A. I.
PARRY, C.: *"The Legal Status of the Trusteeship Agreements,"* (1950) 27 B.Y.B.I.L. 164.
TOUSSAINT, C. E.: The Trusteeship System of the United Nations (1956).
UNITED NATIONS: Repertory of Practice of UN Organs, Vol. IV (1955) and Suppl. No. 1; Vol. II (1958).
UNITED NATIONS: Yearbook of the United Nations, 1946–.

The Secretariat
AKEHURST: The Law Governing employment in International Organisations (1967).
BAILEY: The Secretariat of the UN (1962).
BEDJAOUI: Fonction publique internationale et influences nationales (1958).

GORDENKER: The U.N. Secretary-General and the maintenance of peace (1967).

HAMMARSKJOLD: The International Civil Servant in Law and in Fact (Oxford: Clarendon Press, 1961).

LANGROD: The International Civil Service (1963).

LIE, TRYGVE: In the cause of Peace (1954).

LOVEDAY: Reflections on International Administration (1956).

MERON: The U.N. Secretariat (1977).

PLANTEY: Droit et Pratique de la Fonction Internationale (1977).

RANSHOFEN-WERTHEIMER: The International Secretariat (1945).

RUZIE: Les fonctionnaires internationaux (1970).

SCHACHTER: "*Dag Hammarskjold and the relation of Law to Politics,*" (1962) 56 A.J.I.L. I.

SCHWEBEL: The Secretary-General of the United Nations (1952).

STEIN: "*Mr. Hammarskjold, the Charter Law and future role of the UN Secretary-General,*" (1962) 56 A.J.I.L. 9.

UNITED NATIONS: Repertory of Practice of UN Organs, Vol. V (1955) and Suppl. No. 1; Vol. II (1958).

VIRALLY: "*Le rôle politique du Secrétaire-Général des Nations Unies,*" Annuaire Français (1958), pp. 369–370.

B. ORGANISATIONS OF LIMITED COMPETENCE

CHAPTER 4

THE SPECIALISED AGENCIES, GATT AND OPEC

1. INTRODUCTION

THE process by which various organisations, some in existence prior to the setting up of the United Nations and some created afterwards, were brought into relationship with the United Nations has already been described.[1] We now turn to the examination of these "specialised agencies" in order to see the varying constitutional forms and techniques which have been adopted; it will soon be apparent that the constitutional form of the United Nations is by no means the only feasible form for a global institution. However, since a good deal of the variation in constitutional form depends upon a variation in function, it will be useful, first, to summarise the aims and functions of each of the agencies.

International Labour Organisation (ILO)

This originally formed part of the League of Nations system, and its constitution was to be found in Part XIII of the Treaty of Versailles; it was, however, an autonomous institution, like the P.C.I.J., yet its links with the League made amendment of its constitution necessary upon the dissolution of the League. The constitution was thus amended by the International Labour Conference at Montreal in October 1946,[2] its aims being widened and a new relationship with the UN anticipated. The principal aim, as set forth in the Preamble, is the improvement of conditions of labour; this is to be achieved, for example, by the regulation of hours of work, regulation of the labour supply and the prevention of unemployment, protection of the worker against sickness and industrial injury, recognition of the principle of equal remuneration for work of equal value, recognition of the principle of

---

[1] *Ante*, p. 65.
[2] And again in 1953, the later amendment entering into force on May 20, 1954: see *U.K. Treaty Series*, No. 59 (1961), Cmnd. 1428.

freedom of association and the organisation of vocational and technical education.

The fact that the Organisation is designed to promote the interests of part of the community *within the State*, as opposed to the interests of the State as such, has led to a form of representation of interests other than the State interest which was unique at its inception, but of this more later.

International Civil Aviation Organisation (ICAO)

This was established by the Chicago Convention of September 7, 1944,[3] which, as amended in 1947, 1954 and 1961, replaced by a more comprehensive institution that which had been set up by the Paris Convention of 1919. Its objectives are to develop the principles and techniques of international air navigation and to foster the planning and development of international air transport so as to ensure the safe and orderly growth of international civil aviation and encourage design and operation for peaceful purposes; to encourage the development of air navigation facilities, to prevent economic waste caused by unreasonable competition, to avoid discrimination and promote safety and the development of all aspects of international civil aeronautics. As one might expect, the "State interest" is more predominant here, but the real interest of States varies enormously and devices are included within the constitution to reflect this variation of real interest.

International Bank for Reconstruction and Development (IBRD)

This resulted from the Bretton Woods Conference in July 1944 and the constitution of the Organisation is to be found in Annex B to the Final Act adopted there. Its purposes are to assist in the reconstruction and development of territories by facilitating the investment of capital,[4] to promote private foreign investment by

---

[3] For the text of this Convention, as amended in 1947 and 1954, and all other constitutions referred to in this chapter, see Peaslee, *International Governmental Organisations*, 2nd ed., Vols. I and II. A description of the various substantive agreements concluded at Chicago can be found in most general textbooks on international law; *e.g.* Oppenheim, *International Law*, 8th ed., Vol. I, pp. 525–530.

[4] Note also the "regional" Banks—the Inter-American Development Bank, the Asian Development Bank and the African Development Bank—which have been established under the auspices of the regional economic commissions of the UN and which co-ordinate their activities with the IBRD.

means of guarantees or participation in loans and other investments made by private investors and otherwise to supplement private investment, to promote the long-range balanced growth of international trade and the maintenance of equilibrium in the balance of payments by encouraging investment designed to develop productivity, to arrange loans so that the more urgent projects will receive priority and generally to assist in bringing about a smooth transition from a wartime to a peacetime economy. In 1979, the Bank's current loans exceeded £37,429 million.

Its operations are of a highly technical character,[5] which is reflected in the constitutional provisions, and, again, the real interest of States varies with the degree of their participation. States participate by making subscriptions to the authorised capital of the Bank, standing at $41,000 million. These subscriptions vary greatly from State to State. This variation of "interest" is reflected in the constitution in various ways, such as weighted voting, membership of organs, etc.

International Development Association (IDA)

This was created in 1960 as an "affiliate" of the Bank, having the same Executive Directors, officers and staff and it is, for operational purposes, one with the Bank. Subscriptions are in proportion to the Bank and in 1980 totalled $12,000 millions; however, whilst the high income countries pay 100 per cent. in convertible currencies, the developing countries pay only 10 per cent. and the rest in their own currencies which may not be used without their consent. The IDA's essential purpose is to offer "soft" loans, that is to say loans which are long-term, have no interest other than a "service charge" and which require no governmental guarantees. By 1979 as compared with the Bank's net loan commitments of $28.4 billion, the IDA had commitments of $16.3 billion.

International Finance Coropration (IFC)

This is the second of the "affiliates" of the Bank, created by the Washington Agreement of May 25, 1955. Its purpose is to further economic development by encouraging the growth of productive

---

[5] For a useful description see successive *Yearbooks* of the UN.

private enterprise in member countries, particularly in the less-developed areas, thus supplementing the activities of the Bank. To this end it aims to assist in the financing of productive private enterprises by making investments, without guarantee of repayment by the member government concerned, in cases where sufficient private capital is not available on reasonable terms; to bring together investment opportunities, domestic and foreign private capital, and experienced management, and to seek to stimulate the flow of private capital into productive investment.

Thus, whereas the Bank is limited in its capacity to lend direct and for the most part acts as guarantor of loans by private foreign investors, the Corporation aims at actually participating in the investment; it is an investing rather than a lending institution. A major development of the IFC's lending powers came in 1966 when, following amendments to the charters of both the Bank and IFC, the Bank was empowered to make loans up to $400 millions to the IFC; this will obviously enable IFC to increase the scope and size of its investments. These investments will not cover more than half the cost of an enterprise and will range from $100,000 to $2 millions; they will carry the right to participation in the growth of the enterprise and will not only encourage private investors initially, but will be sold to private investors as soon as the investment proves attractive to them. The Corporation has a capital stock of $650 million, divided into shares with a par value of $1,000. Members subscribe to a given number of shares, ranging from two in the case of Panama to 35,168 in the case of the U.S.A. This variation in the weight of interest is likewise reflected in the constitution, which is very much modelled on that of the Bank; indeed, virtually the same organs operate for both, as we shall see.

International Monetary Fund (IMF)

This is very much the "partner" of the Bank, originating from the same Bretton Woods Conference. Its purposes are to promote monetary co-operation through a permanent institution providing machinery for consultation and collaboration on monetary problems, to facilitate the expansion and balanced growth of international trade, to promote exchange stability and avoid competitive exchange depreciation, to assist in the establishment of a multilateral payments system and the elimination of foreign exchange restrictions hampering the growth of world trade, to

111

make the Fund's resources available to members so as to enable them to correct maladjustments in their balance of payments and, generally, to shorten the duration of the disequilibrium in the international balance of payments of members.

The Fund is equally technical, and the same preliminary comments made above in relation to the Bank apply; in fact the two constitutions are remarkably similar. Each member has a quota, ranging from $11.25 millions for Panama to $5,160 millions for the U.S.A. The total of the quotas is over $60 billion. The quotas were originally paid as to 25 per cent. in gold and the rest in the member's own currency. The member then has "drawing rights," enabling it to purchase other currencies of which it is in need through the Fund for a small service charge and provided, in general, its requests do not cause the Fund's holding of its own currency to exceed 25 per cent. of its own quota. The "par value" of each currency is fixed for most Fund members and cannot be changed by a member without consultation with the Fund.

The liquidity of the Fund has been greatly helped by the "General Arrangements to Borrow," first concluded in 1962 and extended to 1970 whereby 10 industrial countries agreed to lend the Fund up to $6,000 million if required to forestall an impairment of trade. In addition, in response to an UNCTAD recommendation, a system of compensatory export financing was introduced to permit larger drawing rights for the developing countries dependent upon the export of primary products. Moreover, drawing rights were increased by 50 per cent. of the original quota in 1959, and by a further 25 per cent. in 1966. In June 1968, amendments to the IMF Articles of Agreement were adopted giving "Special Drawing Rights" to enable a member to meet balance of payments difficulties or falls in their reserves: these SDR's are to be additional to the normal drawing rights[6] and by 1980 total quotas of SDR's stood at 21.3 billion.

Food and Agriculture Organisation (FAO)

This organisation, established by the United Nations Conference on Food and Agriculture, which met May-June 1943,[7]

---

[6] Keesing's Contemporary Archives, May 1968, 22691A, 22745. And see Gold, *Special Drawing Rights: the role of language*, I.M.F. (1971).

[7] The Constitution being amended subsequently at the 2nd and 10th Sessions of the Conference in 1947 and 1954 and in 1963 and 1964.

Introduction

assumed the functions and assets of the former International Institute of Agriculture at Rome. Its functions are to collect, analyse, interpret and disseminate information relating to nutrition, food and agriculture; to promote international action with respect to research, the improvement of education and administration relating to nutrition, food and agriculture, the conservation of natural resources, improvements of agricultural production, marketing and distribution, the adoption of policies for credit and agricultural commodity agreements; to furnish technical assistance, to organise expert missions and generally to contribute to the raising of standards of nutrition and of living and ensuring humanity's freedom from hunger. In 1963 a joint UN/FAO programme—the World Food Programme (WFP)—was initiated, operated under the control of a joint Inter-Governmental Committee of 24 States elected half by ECOSOC and half by the FAO Council.

In this organisation the relative interests of States are far less readily measurable and the constitution follows a more orthodox pattern.

United Nations Educational, Scientific and Cultural Organisation (UNESCO)

The UNESCO constitution was drawn up at the London Conference and signed on November 16, 1945. The purpose of the Organisation is "to contribute to peace and security by promoting collaboration among the nations through education, science and culture . . . ." To this end the Organisation will collaborate in the work of advancing the mutual knowledge and understanding of peoples, through all means of mass communication and to that end recommends such international agreements as may be necessary; it will maintain, increase and diffuse knowledge by conserving the world's inheritance of books, works of art, etc., and by encouraging co-operation among the nations in all branches of intellectual activity, and by initiating methods of international co-operation calculated to give to the people of all countries access to the printed and published materials produced by any of them.

As with FAO, the aims are of so general a character as to suggest a "general" participation by States, rather than a clear variation in real interest or participation; hence this organisation, similarly, follows a more orthodox pattern. Its comparative

113

removal from acute political problems moreover enables a much more egalitarian participation by States, so that features like the "veto" are absent from its constitution.

World Health Organisation (WHO)

As was pointed out in the first chapter, international co-operation in the field of health has a long history and the WHO, established by a Constitution dated July 22, 1946,[8] assumed the functions of the International Office of Public Health, which had operated under the League from Paris, and also some of the work of the Health Division of the temporary UN Relief and Rehabilitation Administration (now defunct).

The objective of the Organisation "shall be the attainment by all peoples of the highest possible level of health," and to this end there is a list of 22 functions ranging from rendering assistance to governments, furnishing technical assistance, proposing conventions and agreements, promoting research, developing international standards with respect to pharmaceutical products, to the undertaking of studies and the provision of information.

The same observations as were made on FAO and UNESCO apply to WHO.

Universal Postal Union (UPU)

This, similarly, has distinguished antecedents, and the Constitution signed at Vienna on July 10, 1964,[9] is a direct successor to the Postal Convention of 1874 establishing a General Postal Union, which became known as the Universal Postal Union after the Congress at Paris in 1878. Its functions and powers are briefly stated in Article 7, which describes the members as "a single postal territory for the reciprocal exchange of correspondence" and the aim as being "to secure the organisation and improvement of the various postal services and to promote in this sphere the development of international collaboration." Born out of practical necessity, the Constitution lacks the indicia of the political organisations, such as vested rights for certain members, voting privileges, etc. The 1964 constitutional revision radically altered the legal structure of the Union. There are now four basic Acts: (a) the Constitution of the Union (designed to be of a more

[8] And amended on May 28, 1959.
[9] For text see UNJY (1964), 195.

permanent character and not renewed with each Congress as are the other Acts); (b) the General Regulations, providing for the implementation of the constitution; (c) the Universal Postal Convention, containing the general provisions relating to postal services; and (d) the Detailed Regulations of the Universal Postal Convention.

International Telecommunications Union (ITU)

An International Telegraphic Union had been established in 1865, and, after the Berlin Conference of 1906, this took radio under its wing; the Telecommunication Conference of Madrid in 1932 abrogated the previous conventions and established the International Telecommunications Union, revised in 1947 which, after further amendments in 1952 and 1961, was radically revised in 1965.[10]

Its purposes are to maintain and extend international co-operation in the use of telecommunications of all kinds, and to promote the development of technical facilities and the efficiency of telecommunications services. To do this the Union allocates the radio frequency spectrum and registers radio frequency assignments so as to avoid harmful interference between the radio stations of different countries. It also fosters collaboration with a view to establishing low rates for users and undertakes studies and publishes information. It is remarkably similar to UPU.

World Meteorological Organisation (WMO)

An International Meteorological Organisation was established in 1878, and its statutes revised in 1919, 1923, 1929 and 1935; its activities, resources and obligations were transferred to the World Meteorological Organisation on April 4, 1951, although the Convention of WMO had been opened for signature in Washington on October 11, 1947.

Its purposes are to facilitate worldwide co-operation in the establishment of networks of stations for the making of meteorological observations, to promote the establishment of systems for the rapid exchange of weather information, to further the application of meteorology to aviation, shipping, agriculture, and other human activities, to promote the standardisation of meteorological

---

[10] For text see UNJY (1965), 173.

observations and to ensure the uniform publication of observations and statistics, and to encourage research and training in meteorology.

Intergovernmental Maritime Consultative Organisation (IMCO).
This is one of the later specialised agencies to come into being. A Provisional Maritime Consultative Council was established in 1946, and a UN Maritime Conference in February-March 1948 drew up the IMCO Convention, but delay in securing the necessary 21 ratifications, seven of which had to be nations with one million gross tons of shipping, meant that the Convention did not enter into force until 1957.

Its purposes are to provide machinery for co-operation among governments in the field of governmental regulation and practices relating to technical matters affecting shipping engaged in international trade and to encourage the adoption of the highest possible standards in matters of maritime safety and efficiency in navigation[11]; to encourage the removal of discriminatory action and unnecessary restrictions by governments affecting shipping engaged in international trade; to provide for the consideration by the Organisation of matters concerning unfair restrictive practices by shipping concerns; to provide for the consideration by the Organisation of any matters concerning shipping that may be referred to it by any organ or specialised agency of the United Nations; and to provide for the exchange of information among governments on matters under consideration by the Organisation.

The World Intellectual Property Organisation (WIPO)
Established by a convention of July 14, 1967 this organisation became a specialised agency of the UN by General Assembly resolution 3346 (XXIX) of December 17, 1974.

Its purpose is to promote the protection of intellectual property throughout the world, co-operating with the Paris Union (1883) and the Berne Union (1886). It has an Assembly, meeting triennially, a Conference, and a Co-ordination Committee of 38 members, plus an International Bureau or Secretariat.

---

[11] It was via IMCO that in 1976 Inmarsat was established as a separate organisation to develop the use of satellites as an aid to marine navigation: see (1976) 15 I.L.M. 219.

International Fund for Agricultural Development (IFAD)
The decision to establish such a fund had been taken by the World Food Conference in 1974,[12] and in December 1977 the General Assembly by resolution adopted the relationship agreement, making this a new specialised agency. Its essential task is to mobilise the agricultural production of food throughout the world, by financing agricultural development.

To this end, in 1977 members had pledged resources of $U.S. 1,022,100,000: of this sum $567,300,000 was to come from OECD countries, $435,500,000 from OPEC countries, and $19,300,000 from developing countries, but including Rumania and Yugoslavia. These are the only countries from the Socialist bloc to become members.

The UN Industrial Development Organisation (UNIDO)
The constitution of UNIDO was adopted in April 1979[13] so as to permit this hitherto subsidiary body of the UN General Assembly to become the newest, sixteenth specialised agency of the UN. It will enter into force with the eightieth ratification and will have, as its aim, the promotion of industrial development in developing countries, with a view to assisting in the establishment of a new international economic order.

As organs, it will have a General Conference, meeting every two years, an Industrial Development Board of 53 members (33 from developing countries, 15 from the market-economy countries, 5 from the planned economies), and a Secretariat. The Conference at New Delhi in January/February 1980 began badly, with no agreement reached between the Group of 77, the developing countries, and the developed countries, so that it proved impossible to adopt the proposed "Plan of Action."

General Agreement on Tariffs and Trade (GATT)
This is not a specialised agency and is more an international treaty than an international organisation. As a treaty, it establishes a common code of conduct in international trade, it provides

[12] (1976) 15 I.L.M. 916, 922.
[13] (1979) 18 I.L.M. 667.

machinery for reducing and stabilising tariffs and a forum for regular consultations on international trade. The annual sessions of the Contracting Parties (such as the "Tokyo Round" of 1979) afford an opportunity for multilateral tariff negotiations which produce tariff schedules: these become binding contractual commitments when adopted by the meeting of the Contracting Parties and, by virtue of the Most Favoured Nation Clause, tariff concessions registered with one Party become available to all Parties. Quantitative restrictions on imports are in principle forbidden, but exceptions exist for agriculture and for Parties experiencing balance-of-payments difficulties or desiring to protect infant industries in a developing country.

GATT has failed to fully satisfy the demands of the developing countries, hence their insistence on the need for UNCTAD. Actually in 1964 a new Part IV on Trade and Development was added to the GATT, but no system based on reciprocal concessions and bargaining could prove wholly satisfactory to developing countries whose bargaining power is basically weak. However, they do derive considerable benefit from GATT and constitute over one-half of the membership (totalling 85 States in 1979).

The institutional forms of GATT are extraordinarily elementary. When GATT was drafted it was assumed that the ITO, the International Trade Organisation, would be created and would therefore provide the appropriate institutional machinery. Mainly due to U.S. opposition, this did not occur, so that it has been left for the conferences or "sessions" of members to devise a *de facto* machinery of a Council, Committees, sub-committees and working groups. The Council is open to all Parties, and each party has one vote: most decisions are taken by simple majority. However, decisions emerge by general consensus rather than by vote except for decisions on "waivers" which must be voted on (these relate to requests for exemption from the strict application of the GATT provisions).

II. COMPARATIVE SURVEY OF THE INSTITUTIONAL PROVISIONS

Membership

A broad distinction is discernible between "original" and "admitted" members. The first category will normally include either those States which were members of the organisation to which the new organisation is the successor or those States which were invited to participate in the conference which drafted the constitution of a new organisation. One practice is to list such States by name in an annex to the basic convention or agreement; this is done in the case of the ITU, the WMO and FAO. Otherwise the signatory States are given a period of time within which they may ratify or otherwise accept the convention and thus qualify as original members.

The "admitted" members may well be of different categories. In some cases States which are members of the United Nations are admitted *as of right*, simply by communicating a formal acceptance of the convention to the Secretary-General or Director-General of the organisation concerned, as in the ILO, or to a government which exercises depository functions; with the UPU, for example, the acceptance is to be addressed to the Swiss Government. UNESCO, ICAO, WHO, IMCO, WMO and ITU all have this membership "link" with the UN and the Bank has a similar link with the Fund (and not with the UN), just as the IFC has with the Bank.

Other "admitted" members become members, not as of right, but by virtue of an admissions process within the Organisation itself. This varies from a vote of approval by two-thirds of the existing members (*e.g.* WMO, UPU), or four-fifths (ICAO), or even a simple majority (WHO); and in some cases there is a further prerequisite to admission by the plenary organ in the necessity for a recommendation by an executive organ, such as the Council of IMCO or the Executive Board of UNESCO. In the case of the ILO, the "governmental" interest in admissions is safeguarded by the requirement that the two-thirds vote of the General Conference must include two-thirds of the governmental delegates present and voting. There is a curious provision in Article 93 of ICAO which makes admission subject to "the assent of any State invaded or attacked during the present war by the State seeking admission"; this is the nearest equivalent to the veto possible in admission to the UN under Article 4 of the Charter, and, as the Second World War recedes, becomes more and more an anachronism.

Not all the specialised agencies limit membership to States. WMO embraces "any territory or group of territories maintaining its own meteorological service and listed in Annex II,"[14] ITU has "groups of territories listed in Annex I." There is also a device for "associate" rather than full membership, enabling participation by entities less than fully sovereign States. In the WHO "territories or groups of territories which are not responsible for the conduct of their international relations" may be admitted upon application by the State or other authority having responsibility for those relations; similar provisions exist in IMCO and ITU, both of which specifically anticipate a trusteeship territory administered by the UN as a possible candidate for associate membership. Not unnaturally, such associate membership does not confer quite the same rights as full membership, and in the constitutions of IMCO and ITU such members do not have the right to vote in the Assembly, or, in the case of ITU, in any organ of the Union; nor are they eligible for election to certain bodies (Council or Maritime Safety Committee in IMCO; any organ elected by a plenipotentiary or administrative conference in ITU). WHO has regulated the rights and obligations of associate members by a resolution of the first Health Assembly[15] which deprives them of a vote in the Assembly or main committees and of membership of the Executive Board. These are all useful devices, possible in a "non-political" organisation, for associating with the work of the organisation entities other than sovereign States. Whether "associate membership" will ever be accepted within the UN, as a means of dealing with the "mini-States," is doubtful, although there would be advantage in a form of association entitling them to participation in economic and social activities but excluding them from the political activities. Associate membership is, of course, a quite different solution from the kind of tripartite representation in the ILO, of which the members are States, but from which delegations are not exclusively governmental so as to give representation to non-State interests.

Membership can generally be suspended or terminated. Suspension is action by the organisation in the nature of a sanction, and so is compulsory termination, and both processes will be dealt with later.[16] Voluntary termination of membership is frequently ex-

---

[14] Those not in Annex II may apply for admission only when sponsored by the Member responsible for its international relations.

[15] *Off. Rec.* 13, 100, 337.

[16] *Post*, p. 386.

pressly provided for, unlike in the UN Charter or in the constitution of WHO,[17] by giving a right of withdrawal upon notice which may vary from one to two years, and often only after the organisation has been established for a certain number of years, for example four years in the case of FAO. Whereas IMCO, ICAO, ITU, WMO and UPU contain no further condition to the right to withdraw, organisations like the ILO enable a withdrawal to take effect only upon fulfilment of all financial obligations arising from membership and without prejudice to the validity of any conventions ratified. The withdrawal provisions of the "financial" organisations are, understandably, more complex. Whilst withdrawal can be effective immediately upon notification, withdrawal from any one of the Bank, the Fund or the IFC brings about an automatic withdrawal from the other two, and there are detailed provisions on the settlement of accounts, providing for purchase of the retiring member's shares.

Organs

(a) *Plenary organs*

All the agencies have one or more organs on which all members are represented, although "associate" members may not have a vote. The frequency of their meetings varies very much with the kind of functions which the organisation possesses, and so does the division of powers between the plenary organ and other organs of limited composition.

The General Conference of the ILO is unique in certain respects. Meeting at least annually, it comprises all the member States. Yet each member sends four representatives "of whom two shall be Government delegates and the two others shall be delegates representing respectively the employers and the work-people of each of the Members" (Art. 3). All are designated by the government, but the two non-governmental delegates must be "chosen in agreement with the industrial organisations, if such organisations exist, which are most representative of employers or work-people, as the case may be, in their respective countries." Herein lies the famous "tripartite" character of the ILO, which is

---

[17] Yet the U.S. accepted membership subject to an express reservation as to its right of withdrawal on one year's notice and the Communist States withdrew subsequently.

duplicated in the governing body also; the predominance of the "State-interest" is numerically assured, but the introduction of these new interests represented a revolutionary step. The expenses of the non-governmental delegates are borne by the budget of the ILO. Each delegate is entitled to vote individually on all matters, so that alignments develop which cut right across national alignments. The autonomy of the three distinct groups presupposes a relationship within the national State in which State, employers and employees are independent of each other. This presupposition was seriously challenged with the advent of Socialist States, like the U.S.S.R. (admitted to the ILO in 1935), in which the State is also the employer. The employer's representative thus becomes, virtually, one more government delegate. The opposition of the employer's group to such a representative was such that, in 1937, they demanded, unsuccessfully, an opinion from the P.C.I.J. on the legality of the nomination of the U.S.S.R.'s employer's representative. Post-war, the debate continued, and at one stage proposals were advanced for two government delegates, one of which should represent nationalised industry, one delegate from private enterprise and two workers' delegates, one of which should come from State enterprises, the other from private enterprise; in completely socialist countries there would be two government delegates, one employer from State enterprise and two labour union delegates. The issue became crucial when the U.S.S.R. rejoined in 1954 and the McNair Committee was established to consider the constitutional problem. The majority report, not confined to the case of the U.S.S.R., noted that representatives of private industry no longer enjoyed an exclusive title as defenders of the employers' point of view due to the widespread development of State enterprise, and that it would be a question of fact in each case whether representatives were independent or merely docile instruments of governmental policy. The employers' group have, however, continued to refuse to appoint Communist employers to committees of the Conference and their own proposals for reform of the Constitution were rejected in 1956. In order to find a solution which would permit a working method other than that of "associate membership" of the committees, to which the U.S.S.R. strongly objected, a second committee, the Ago Committee, was established in 1957. The proposals of this committee were endorsed by the 43rd session in

1959 and envisage a procedure whereby every delegate applying to his group for membership of a committee should be placed on the list of members of that committee; it was therefore no longer open to the group to exclude a representative from the list. The Conference itself then decides which members shall have the right to vote, *i.e.* compose the "voting section," and delegates excluded have a right to appeal to a special Appeals Board of independent persons appointed by the governing body, which may add no more than two delegates to the voting section and their decision shall be final and not open to debate. This procedure, which is aimed purely at settling the problem of composition of committees and does not pretend to solve the larger issue of the future of the tripartite system within the ILO, has been accepted by the U.S.S.R., but, when used, the employers' delegates boycotted the committees.[18]

This unhappy history has been recounted in some detail since it illustrates very forcibly the kind of problems which may be encountered once interests are represented, other than State interests, side-by-side with States.

The basic voting rule in the ILO General Conference is simple majority, although, again, in matters which involve responsibility which is essentially governmental, the voting procedure is altered so as to enhance the control of the numerically superior governmental delegates. Budgetary and financial matters require a two-thirds majority, so does the adoption of a Convention or Recommendation,[19] the scrutiny of credentials, amendments of the constitution, change of seat, and, of course, admission of new members; this last requires a two-thirds majority of governmental delegates within the overall two-thirds majority.

The General Conference is the principal organ in that the work of formulating recommendations and conventions takes place there; the governing body, the organ of limited composition, has, as we shall see, a much more subsidiary role.

The plenary organs of FAO, UNESCO and WHO are, like the Conference of the ILO, equally the dominant organs of their

---

[18] For further details see Béguin, "ILO and the tripartite system," (1959) 523, *International Conciliation*; also "The 43rd Session of the International Labour Conference," (1959) 80, *International Labour Review*, pp. 203 *et seq.*

[19] See *post*, p. 141.

respective organisations. They meet usually annually,[20] although in FAO and UNESCO it is biennially, but all have a procedure for extraordinary session on the call of the Executive Board (UNESCO), or on the request of the Board or a majority of the members (WHO). Representation is more orthodox in that only States, or associate members other than States, are represented. Each State has one vote and the basic voting rule is generally a simple majority except where a two-thirds majority is required for matters such as recommendations to members, submission of conventions, admissions, approval of the budget, etc. WHO follows the pattern of Article 18 of the Charter, governing the General Assembly's voting procedure, in that Article 60 of the Constitution lists a number of "important questions" requiring a two-thirds majority, requires two-thirds for the determination of additional categories of "important questions," and otherwise requires a simple majority. In the other organisations the requirement of two-thirds is stated in specific articles throughout the constitution, rather than having the voting procedure grouped into one article.

The dominance of the plenary organ is variously expressed. In UNESCO it is for the General Conference to "determine the policies and the main lines of work of the Organisation" and the Executive Board is to act "under the authority of the General Conference," being responsible for the "execution of the programme adopted by the Conference . . . ." In WHO the function of the Assembly is "to instruct the Board in regard to matters upon which action, study, investigation or report may be considered desirable"; it is the Assembly which is entrusted with the "legislative" process.[21] In FAO it is the Conference which "shall determine the policy and approve the budget of the Organisation," and which may make recommendations to members; the Council shall only have "such powers as the Conference may delegate to it," and there is a list of powers which *cannot* be so delegated. In ICAO the Assembly may "delegate to the Council the powers and authority necessary or desirable for the discharge of the duties of the Organisation and revoke or modify the delegations of authority at any time" (Art. 49 (h)); the Council is

---

[20] As did also the Assembly of ICAO until the amendments of 1954 provided for meetings "not less than once in three years" (Art. 48 (a)).

[21] See *post*, p. 144.

to "carry out the directions of the Assembly" and has to report infractions of the Convention to the Assembly.

This repository of power with the plenary organ, and the comparative subjection of the organ of limited composition, is an important feature of these agencies and is well worth the attention of those who, familiar with the UN, tend to think of the organ of limited composition as the executive, effective organ where real power alone lies.

The IMF, Bank, IDA and IFC form a group with distinct, and similar, characteristics. Their plenary organ is the Board of Governors, consisting of one governor and one alternate, meeting annually or at such times as the Board or the Executive Directors determine; extraordinary meetings can be called by five members or by members having one-quarter of the total voting power. Each governor serves for five years and can be reappointed. The operational link between the Bank and the IFC is so close that Article IV (2) of the latter's constitution provides that the governors or alternates of the Bank shall be, *ex officio,* the governors or alternates of the Corporation; moreover, the annual meeting of the IFC Board is held "in conjunction with the annual meeting of the Board of Governors of the Bank" (Art. 2 (e)). Again, it is these plenary organs which really control the policy of these organisations. In the IFC "all the powers of the Corporation shall be vested in the Board of Governors" (Art. IV (2)); in the Fund "all powers of the Fund shall be vested in the Board of Governors" (Art. 12 (2)); and in the Bank similarly (Art. 5 (2)). The unusual feature of the organs is their system of weighted voting. As mentioned above, the variation in the degree of participation and real interest is easily measured here in terms of the actual subscriptions. Hence in the Fund each governor casts the number of votes allotted to the member appointing him, and in the Bank and the IFC each member has 250 votes plus an additional vote for each share held; except where the constitutions provide otherwise (*e.g.* when the authorised capital of the IFC is increased), the voting rule is simple majority.

The Assembly of IMCO must be treated separately, for it contains features which make it *sui generis.* It meets every two years, although extraordinary sessions can be summoned by the Council or one-third of the members. Its functions consist of the election of its own officers, formulation of its rules of procedure, the voting of the budget, and consideration of the reports of the Council; in fact the normal functions of a plenary organ. But it is apparent that it does not enjoy, *vis-à-vis* the Council, the same dominant role which the plenary organs of the organisations reviewed above enjoy. Whilst it may establish temporary subsidiary bodies, it may only establish *permanent* subsidiary bodies "upon recommendation of the Council" (Art. 16 (c)). Its powers of election of members to the Council and the Maritime Safety Committee are carefully circumscribed by the provisions of Articles 17 and 28 dealing with the composition of those organs.[22] Whilst the Assembly is to "perform the functions of the Organisation," it is expressly provided that:

> " . . . in matters relating to Article 3 (a) and (b), the Assembly shall refer such matters to the Council for formulation by it of any recommendations or instruments thereon, provided further that any recommendations or instruments submitted to the Assembly by the Council and not accepted by the Assembly shall be referred back to the Council for further consideration with such observations as the Assembly may make" (Art. 16 (h)).

Hence in matters connected with the essential purposes of the Organisation, as set out in Article 1, or in the drafting of conventions, agreements or other instruments to be recommended to governments and inter-governmental organisations, or in the convening of conferences, it is for the Council to take the effective action. Formally, it will be the Assembly which recommends to governments, but in practice these recommendations will be those of the Council, for the Assembly has no power to alter the Council's recommendations, only to refer them back to the Council with its comments. Similarly, whilst the Assembly is "to recommend to members for adoption regulations concerning maritime safety, or amendments to such regulations . . . ," these regulations are not the Assembly's own work, but rather the regulations which have been referred to it by the Maritime Safety Committee through the Council (Art. 16 (i)).

The evidence so far suggests that this relationship does work out in practice. Certainly a reading of the constitution conveys the

---

[22] See *post*, pp. 131–133.

impression that the major maritime powers which, as we shall see, are certain of representation on the Council and the Maritime Safety Committee, have so drafted the constitution as to ensure that effective power remains in their hands in the organs of limited composition and does not stray into the unpredictable forum of the Assembly, in which each member has one vote and Ghana is as important as the U.S.A. in the securing of the simple majority or, where a specific article so requires, the two-thirds majority necessary for a decision. In fact one is reminded very much of the General Assembly-Security Council division of power; yet, as has been seen, the years can bring a shift of power which the reading of the constitution can never anticipate. Whether this could happen in this organisation, with a plenary assembly meeting only every two years, and with no power to establish *permanent* subsidiary organs *proprio motu,* is open to doubt.

ITU, UPU and WMO may be dealt with together since they have certain common features which stem from the fact they are very much technical organisations, anticipating the minimum of political problems and concerned with the supervision of and occasional improvement of a working régime established by the constitution and annexes. For this reason the Plenipotentiary Conference of ITU and the Congress of UPU meet not at regular intervals but at dates determined by each Conference or Congress, and the Congress of WMO at "intervals not exceeding four years."

The functions of the ITU Plenipotentiary Conference[23] include the revision of the Convention, determining general policies, establishing the budget, considering the report of the Administrative Council on the activities of the Union, and entering into agreements with other international bodies. The Congress of UPU meets every five years in order to revise or complete the Acts of the previous Congress. Both organisations also provide, in their constitutions, for "Administrative Conferences" which, in the case of ITU, meet concurrently with the Plenipotentiary Conference and, in the case of UPU, as and when requested by two-thirds of the members. The task of these administrative conferences, all plenary conferences, is to deal with "questions of an administrative nature" (UPU) and revision of the regulations or other

---

[23] Only Members and Associate Members participate fully; telecommunications operating services of the UN, permanent organs of the Union, and observers from non-Members may participate as advisers or observers.

matters referred to it by the Plenipotentiary Conference (ITU).[24] To these two levels of plenary conferences, the one general, the other specialised, is added in the case of ITU, because of the variety of forms of telecommunications, yet a third in the form of the "Consultative Committees." These, named as permanent organs of the Union, are the International Telegraph and Telephone Consultative Committee (C.C.I.T.T.), and the International Radio Consultative Committee (C.C.I.R.). These committees carry the specialisation of the work of the Union one stage further. The members of the various committees include not only the administrations of members and associate members, but also "any recognised private operating agency which, with the approval of the Member or associate Member which has recognised it, express a desire to participate in the work of these Committees." Each consultative committee also has its own organisational complex in the form of a plenary assembly, meeting every three years, study groups, a Director and a specialised Secretariat distinct from the General Secretariat of the Union.

The UPU in 1957 created a new Consultative Committee of Postal States (CCPS), with a Management Council of 26 States elected by the Congress: the CCPS has plenary membership and, as a Committee of Congress, meets in between sessions of Congress so as to offset the disadvantage of the long intervals between Congresses. Both the ITU and UPU, under their new constitutions, have established rules of procedure (or Regulations) which apply to each successive plenary conference.

In WMO the plenary organs are but one, the Congress. Its members are to be representatives of members amongst which one "should be the director of its meteorological service, as its principal delegate."

There is also power to establish technical commissions of experts, so that, given the relative homogeneity of meteorological problems, as compared with the rather diffuse character of the telecommunications services, this is considered adequate without

[24] The ITU contemplates both world and regional conferences as well as separate administrative conferences to deal wth different aspects of telecommunications, such as (1) Telegraph and Telephone and (2) Radio. The Radio administrative conference (WRAC) has the special task of electing members of the International Frequency Registration Board and reviewing its activities. In 1979 it reached agreement on the reallocation of radio frequencies between different usages, but deferred dealing with short-wave and fixed satellite broadcasing.

resorting to the different levels of specialised plenary conferences and committees found in ITU. The functions of Congress are, in addition to the normal plenary functions of elections, considering reports from the organs, etc., to adopt technical regulations covering meteorological practices and procedures, to determine general regulations prescribing the constitution and functions of the various other bodies of the Organisation, subject only to the Convention, and to determine general policies; this is clearly "the supreme body of the Organisation" (Art. 6 (a)). Each member has one vote and the predominance of State interests is secured by allowing a vote only to State members (not therefore to "territories or groups of territories") on matters like amendment of the Convention, membership, and relations with other inter-governmental organisations (Art. 10 (a)). Voting is normally by a two-thirds majority, except for election of individuals to serve in one capacity or another (*i.e.* expert commissions) which is by simple majority.

(b) *Organs of limited composition*

Recent years have seen an expansion in size of these organs, largely in recognition of the increase in total membership. In the ILO the governing body is, because of its tripartite character, unique amongst the organs of limited composition in the special-ised agencies. Of the 56 representatives, 28 are representatives of governments, 14 of employers and 14 of workers.[25] Of the 28 government representatives, 10 are to be appointed by the members "of chief industrial importance" (Art. 7 (2)) and the other 18 are elected by the Conference. The task of determining which are the members "of chief industrial importance" is now entrusted to the governing body,[26] which is enjoined to make rules and to ensure that the question is considered by an impartial committee before being decided by the governing body. There is, further, a right of appeal by a member against the decision of the governing body to the Conference. The device is an interesting comparison with that used in the Security Council for determining which States, because of their predominant interest in the matters with which the organisation is concerned, shall have security of tenure on the executive organ. The Charter's solution was to

[25] The numbers were originally 32 (16, 8 and 8).
[26] It formerly lay with the Council of the League.

actually name the "Big Five," thus rendering the choice a final one, bearing in mind the fact that the veto applies to amendments of the Charter. Here, in the ILO, the solution allows for a change of importance in the members; admittedly it may be far easier to adopt statistical criteria of industrial importance than of political power. The governing body as a whole enjoys a period of office of three years; there are no "staggered" elections.

The functions of the governing body are general supervision of the International Labour Office (the Secretariat), formulation of policies and programmes, the settling of the agenda for meetings of the Conference, drafting proposals for the budget, appointment of the Director-General and an important role in situations where a complaint of non-observance of a Convention by a member is made.[27] The "legislative" work of the ILO is a matter for the Conference, not the governing body. Except when the constitution requires a two-thirds majority, voting is by simple majority of the representatives on the governing body; apart from their numerical superiority, there is no voting privilege for the governmental representatives or for those from the States "of chief industrial importance."

The Council of ICAO is a "permanent body responsible to the Assembly" (Art. 50); it therefore has no constitutional provisions about the frequency of its meetings and is left, in practice, to do just what the Governing Body of ILO is constitutionally enjoined to do, namely, "fix its own times of meeting." It consists of 33[28] States elected by the Assembly in elections every three years; there is no system of "staggered" elections. The Assembly's discretion in making these elections is limited by a constitutional formula designed to afford representation to the States most vitally affected, although no precise criteria are provided to determine "chief importance" and "largest contribution," so, to that extent, the formula is an elastic one. Article 50 (b) provides:

"In electing the members of the Council, the Assembly shall give adequate representation to (1) the States of chief importance in air transport; (2) the States not otherwise included which make the largest contribution to the provision of facilities for international civil air navigation; and (3) the

[27] See *post*, p. 152.
[28] As from 1980.

130

States not otherwise included whose designations will insure that all the major geographical areas of the world are represented on the Council."

The Council is clearly subordinate to the Assembly. It "carries out the directions of the Assembly," reports to the Assembly, administers finances, appoints the Secretary-General, collects and publishes information, makes studies and may conduct research. Its more unusual functions are the mandatory functions of appointing and controlling the Air Transport Committee[29] and the Air Navigation Commission,[30] of reporting to States any infractions of the Convention and to the Assembly when a State has failed to remedy such an infraction, and of adopting international standards and practices. Clearly it is to the latter more technical body that the Council will look for advice in pursuing this last function. The Council votes by a majority of its members, but no member may vote in the consideration of a dispute to which it is a party and participation without vote is envisaged for specially affected States not members of the Council.

The ICAO structure is very much a pattern followed in IMCO; obviously co-operation in civil aviation and in shipping will pose somewhat similar problems and call for somewhat similar constitutional techniques. IMCO has a Council of 24 members elected by the Assembly and composed as follows:

> Article 18. "(a) Six shall be Governments of States with the largest interest in providing shipping services;
> (b) Six shall be Governments of other States with the largest interest in international seaborne trade;
> (c) Twelve shall be Governments of States not elected under (a) or (b) above, which shall have special interests in maritime transport or navigation and whose election to the Council will ensure the representation of all major geographic areas of the world.[31]

---

[29] Chosen from among the representatives of the members of the Council (Art. 54 (d)).

[30] This is provided for in Ch. X of the constitution, and is to be composed of 12 members apointed by the Council from persons nominated by member States but of "suitable qualifications and experience in the science and practice of aeronautics."

[31] As amended in 1968.

This formula differs from the previous formula under the original 1948 Constitution. Another significant difference is that, whereas under the original formula it was for the Council to determine which States fell into certain categories (thereby limiting the area of discretion left to the Assembly) the present formula merely prescribes the principles to be applied by the Assembly but otherwise leaves it to the Assembly to conduct the elective process. This is symptomatic of the move away from the dominance of the Council over the Assembly which was a characteristic of the original constitution. It is also symptomatic of the tendency to place more emphasis on equitable geographical distribution of seats and less on "technical" criteria: this, as we shall see, is even more obvious in relation to the changes in the Maritime Safety Committee.

The Council meets at a month's notice "as often as may be necessary," upon the summons of the Chairman or upon the request of four or more members. Its functions are to receive the reports of the Maritime Safety Committee for transmission to the Assembly with its own recommendations, appointment of the Secretary-General, submission to the Assembly of a report on the organisation's activities and of the budget estimates, conclusion of agreements with other organisations subject to the approval of the Assembly, and, between sessions of the Assembly, to "perform all the functions of the Organisation . . . " (Arts. 22–27). The voting procedure is the same as for the Assembly.

The other limited membership organ in IMCO is the Maritime Safety Committee. This, now consisting of 16 members, is elected by the Assembly but by a formula which similarly weights the composition to ensure membership for certain States. Of the 16 all must be "Governments of those States having an important interest in maritime safety, of which:

"(a) Eight members shall be elected from among the ten largest shipowning States.

(b) Four members shall be elected in such manner as to ensure that, under this sub-paragraph, a State in each of the following areas is represented:

(i) Africa.
(ii) The Americas.
(iii) Asia and Oceania.

(iv) Europe.

(c) The remaining four members shall be elected from among States not otherwise represented on the Committee."[32]

It might be thought that such a clause provided sufficiently specific criteria. However, in organisations like ICAO and IMCO, whilst the composition of these limited organs is taken out of the realm of pure discretion, there remains the possibility of dispute on the interpretation or application of these criteria. In IMCO the potentialities for dispute were fully realised when at the very first Assembly the eight "largest ship-owning nations" elected to the Maritime Safety Committee did not include either Liberia or Panama, despite the fact that in a working paper before it the list of member States in descending order of total gross registered tonnage contained Liberia as third State and Panama as eighth. The debate revealed a wide divergence of views on the interpretation of the relevant phrase, and, at least in part, the opposition to the candidature of these two States was part of a wider opposition to "flags of convenience," *i.e.* the practice of certain States in registering vessels which, apart from the fact of registration, had little connection with the States concerned or their nationals. The question was then referred to the I.C.J. for an Advisory Opinion, in this form: "Is the Maritime Safety Committee of the Inter-Governmental Maritime Consultative Committee, which was elected on January 15, 1959, constituted in accordance with the Convention for the establishment of the Organisation?"

In its Opinion of June 8, 1960,[33] the Court rejected the view that the use of the word "elected" gave a discretion to the Assembly, and took the view that these eight were necessarily entitled to be elected. The proper test to be applied in determining those eight was the strength of their registered tonnage, and not only of such tonnage as belonged to nationals of the State; such a test was easily applied, and the facts on which it rested easily ascertained, and it was, moreover, consonant with international practice, maritime

---

[32] Amendment to Art. 28 adopted in 1965; *U.N.J.Y.* (1965), 204.

[33] (1960) *I.C.J. Reports*, 1951. It must be noted that the earlier text on which the Court advised did not allow for an election of eight "from among the ten" but provided simply that the eight should be elected. The 1965 amendment in effect restored the Assembly's freedom of choice which the Court's opinion removed.

usage and other international maritime conventions. The failure to elect Liberia and Panama was consequently a breach of the Convention.

The actual functions of the Maritime Safety Committee are to consider matters concerned with aids to navigation, construction and equipment of vessels, manning from a safety standpoint, rules for the prevention of collisions, etc., and generally matters directly affecting maritime safety. Its proposals are submitted to the Assembly through the Council. It meets annually and votes according to the same procedure as the Assembly and Council, and its members are elected for a four-year term and are eligible for re-election.

FAO, UNESCO and WHO may be taken as a group for, in contrast with the organisations discussed above, their limited membership organs contain no such specific criteria for membership either in whole or in part.

FAO has a Council of 49 members elected by the Conference which also formulates the rules governing their tenure and other conditions of office. This is not the policy-making organ, but rather the Conference is, and the powers of the Council are such as the Conference may delegate to it. The voting procedure is not contained in the constitution but is left to the rules of procedure and is basically a simple majority rule. The technical side of the work is dealt with by a number of technical committees (Program, Finance, Commodity Problems, Constitutional and Legal Matters) and by the regional offices specifically provided for in the constitution (Art. 10) and regional conferences.

UNESCO has an Executive Board of 45 (formerly 24) members elected by the General Conference and meeting twice a year or in special session if convoked by the Chairman or the members. The members are State representatives, but there is a clear attempt to secure a Board of technical competence and to ensure that, in their capacity as members of the Board, they act as representatives of the Conference rather than of their States. This is seen in the provision that, in electing them, the Conference "shall endeavour to include persons competent in the arts, the humanities, the sciences, education and the diffusion of ideas, and qualified by their experience and capacity to fulfil the administrative and executive duties of the Board" (Art. 5 (2)). It is also provided that regard shall be had "to the diversity of cultures and a balanced geographical distribution," and, though eligible to serve two consecutive three-year terms, no member is eligible for a third. Moreover, elections are "staggered," 10 members being elected each year. There is the further provision, only capable of insertion in a "non-political" organisation of global character, that the members "shall exercise the powers delegated to them by the General Conference on behalf of the Conference as a whole and not as representatives of their respective Governments" (Art. 5 (11)). This is something of a compromise between the traditional State representative and the independent expert. The essential function of the Board is to undertake the execution of the programme adopted by the Conference, to which the Board is responsible. Again, the voting procedure is not provided for in the constitution, but in the rules of procedure, and simple majority is the basic rule.

The Executive Board of WHO is very similar; its 30 (formerly 18) member States, elected by the Assembly, and taking into account equitable geographical distribution, are directed to designate "technically qualified" persons. They exercise their powers "on behalf of the whole Health Assembly," so the intention of avoiding a pure representation of State interests is the same as in UNESCO. Elections are for three years and are staggered, ten being elected each year. Voting is governed by the same procedure as in the Assembly (Art. 60 (c)). Its task, as executive organ, is essentially to carry out the decisions and policies of the Assembly although it has a certain independent power of action to deal with epidemics and sudden calamities. As in FAO, there is considerable stress on regional co-operation, so that a quite separate strata of organs is to be discerned, necessarily of limited composition. There are in fact six regions, geographically defined by the Assembly under its powers in Chapter XI, each consisting of a separate regional "organisation" with a regional committee and a regional office (Secretariat); naturally membership of regional committees is confined to members and associate members of that region.

The ITU has an Administrative Council, introduced in 1947 specifically to provide for continuity of administration in the long interval of five years between Plenipotentiary Conferences. It meets yearly, or upon the request of six members, and has a total membership of 36 (formerly 25) members of the Union, elected by the Plenipotentiary Conference. Though representatives of members, the individuals must be "qualified in the field of telecommunication services," and the Council ensures the efficient co-ordination of the work of the Union, approves the annual budget, arranges for the convening of the plenipotentiary and administrative conferences and generally acts in the interval between Conferences "on behalf of the plenipotentiary conference within the limits of the powers delegated to it by the latter" (Art. 9 (9)). The character of the organ is thus similar to the Executive Boards of UNESCO and WHO. The second organ of limited membership in ITU is, however, much more striking in the degree to which its composition is "expert" rather than "governmental": this is the International Frequency Registration Board, an organ of five members elected from candidates sponsored by countries. A new organ in 1947, its task is to "effect an orderly recording of frequency assignments made by the different countries . . . with a view to ensuring formal international recognition thereof," and to advise members with a view to "the operation of the maximum practicable number of radio channels in those portions of the spectrum where harmful interference may occur." For this technical task it is composed of "independent members," elected by each world administrative radio conference, who are not to receive instructions from any government or person, and members must "respect the international character of the Board"; members of the Board cannot participate in any manner in any branch of telecommunications apart from the work of the Board. They thus come very near to assimilation to international civil servants.

UPU has a simpler form with just one organ of limited membership, namely the Executive Council.[34] Its essential task is, like the ITU's Administrative Council's, to "ensure the continuity of the work" (Art. 17 (1)) in between the Congresses; such an organ is well-nigh essential when the plenary conferences meet but once in five years. The 39 member-countries of the Executive Council are appointed by Congress on the basis of equitable geographical distribution. The actual representatives of the members elected by the Congress "carry out their functions in the name and in the interests of the Union" (Art. 17 (2)).

WMO similarly has an Executive Committee, meeting yearly

---

[34] This is apart from the Management Council of the CCPS: see *ante*, p. 128.

and taking decisions by two-thirds majority of the votes cast, rather than a simple majority; each member has one vote. The actual number of members is not specified as such but a "balance" formula, rather like that used in the Trusteeship Council, is used in that membership consists of the President and Vice-Presidents, the Presidents of Regional Associations, Directors of Meteorological Services of members "equal in number to the number of regions, provided that not more than one-third of the members of the Executive Committee . . . shall come from one region" (Art. 13 (c)). Such Directors as are necessary to complete the balance with the regions are elected by Congress. The functions are the customary ones of supervising the execution of the resolutions of the Congress, providing technical information, making studies, preparing the agenda of Congress, administering finances, etc., but there is a somewhat unusual one in its power to "adopt resolutions arising out of recommendations of the Technical Commissions on matters of urgency affecting the technical regulations . . . " (Art. 14 (b))[35]; this "legislative" role is necessary in cases of urgency precisely because Congress meets once in four years. It will be noted that the representatives are presumably technically competent, and are elected in their personal capacities and not as representatives of governments.

WMO also has a strong emphasis on regionalism, and Regional Meteorological Associations, which therefore qualify as organs of limited membership, are provided for in Article 18. These meet "as often as necessary," and so far six regional associations have been formed.

There remain the three "financial" organisations, the Fund, the Bank and IFC. The Executive Directors of the Fund establish the pattern, and it is a pattern quite different from those considered above, for, as the name implies, this is truly an "executive" organ. The Directors are "responsible for the conduct of the general operations of the Fund and for this purpose shall exercise all the powers delegated to them by the Board of Governors" (Art. 12 (3)); in short, the Directors execute the policies and decisions of the plenary Board of Governors. They function in continuous session, necessary in view of the functions of the Fund, and the

---

[35] The Technical Commissions are "plenary" bodies of technical experts, established by Congress to advise Congress and the Executive Committee; there are eight such commissions.

chairman is the Managing Director, the chief executive officer equivalent to the Secretary-General in the UN. The Directors are usually 20^{36} in number, of whom:

> "(i) five shall be appointed by the five members having the largest quotas;
>
> (ii) not more than two shall be appointed when the provisions of (c) below apply[37];
>
> (iii) five shall be elected by the members not entitled to appoint directors other than the American Republics; and
>
> (iv) two shall be elected by the American Republics not entitled to appoint directors" (Art. 12 (3) (b)).

The distinction made between "appointed" and "elected" directors is a proper one, and the elections of the latter are governed by a complicated system set out in Schedule D to the Agreement, and are held every two years. Each appointed director is entitled to cast the number of votes allotted to the member appointing him (250 + 1 for each $100,000 of its quota) and each elected director is entitled to cast the number of votes which counted towards his election, and the general voting rule is a simple majority. This system of "weighted" voting, plus the fact that, in the event of a vacancy during a term the same members who elected the director elect his successor, suggests that the directors are representatives of the countries either appointing them or electing them, and not independent experts. The fact that they are paid a salary from the Fund and hold a contract of service, a quite unusual feature for an executive organ, does not really detract from this, and it is of interest to note that there is no provision comparable to that applying to the Administrative Council of ITU, or the Executive Board of UNESCO and of WHO, whereby functions are exercised on behalf of the entire body of members.

The Bank has virtually identical provisions for its Executive Directors; there are 20 of these, five being appointed by the nations with the largest capital subscription and the remainder

---

[36] In 1966, for example, there were 20.

[37] Thes provisions concern the situation when, at the second regular election and subsequently, the members entitled to appoint under (i) do not include the two members, the holding of whose currencies by the Fund have been, on the average over the preceding two years, reduced below their quotas by the largest absolute amounts in terms of gold as a common denominator.

elected by the Governors but without any specific seats for American Republics. The Bank, however, has an additional "Advisory Council" of not less that seven persons selected by the Board of Governors "including representatives of banking, commercial, industrial, labor and agricultural interests, and with as wide a national representation as possible." This body of independent experts, meeting annually, is purely advisory.

The Board of Directors of the IFC is, in its membership, linked with the Bank in exactly the same way as the Board of Governors of the Fund, for the members are *ex officio* the Executive Directors of the Bank provided they represent at least one country which is a member of IFC, and the chairman is the chairman of the Executive Directors of the Bank (who is the President of the Bank, the administrative head). Its powers are comparable to the Executive Directors of the Fund and Bank and its voting procedure "weighted" just as in the Bank. This identity of membership should not be assumed to mean that the organs are legally identical; Article IV (b) states that the Corporation "shall be an entity separate and distinct from the Bank . . . ."

The Executive Board of IFAD consists of 18 members elected by the Governing Council, the plenary body, by a voting arrangement unique in the United Nations. The members are placed in three Groups: Group I (OECD countries), Group II (OPEC countries) and Group III (developing countries). Each Group has 600 votes, and within each group there is a formula to allocate these votes between the members of the group. In Group III, the votes are distributed equally amongst all the members. In Groups I and II, a certain percentage of the 600 votes is allocated equally (17.5 per cent. in Group I, 25 per cent. in Group II), with the rest being allocated on the basis of the financial contribution. Hence, in Group I, for example, in the result the U.S.A. has 179 votes, West Germany and Japan 53 each, the Netherlands 45, the United Kingdom 34 and so on. In Group II, Iran was allocated 154 votes, Saudi Arabia 133, Venezuela 89 and so on.

(c) *The Secretariats*

Provision for a Secretariat or "Bureau" is found in the constitution of every specialised agency. Basically they do not differ in conception from that of the UN (although not all are graced with the title "principal organ") and for this reason a detailed account of individual secretariats of the agencies will not be attempted.[38] Reference to the privileges and immunities attaching to the members of the various secretariats will be made at a later stage,[39] and so will reference to the ILO Administrative Tribunal which acts as the body with jurisdiction over disputes between staff and organisation not only for the ILO but for various of the specialised agencies.[40]

The idea has been mooted of having one single international civil service, of which the secretariat of each organisation forms a part. This has not even begun to be implemented, and probably gives rise to more problems than it solves. In practice the executive heads of each organisation meet in the ACC (Administrative Committee on Co-ordination) and a good deal has been done, via this body and otherwise, to standardise conditions of employment for the staff of the various organisations.

A point worth noting at this juncture is the variations in the functions of the administrative head of the various organisations. Called "Secretary-General," "Director-General," "Managing Director" (Fund) and even "President" (Bank and IFC), he is not always appointed jointly by two organs as in the UN. In all three of the "financial" organisations he is selected by the Executive Directors, and within these organisations he has a considerable executive role in conducting the ordinary operations of the organisation; hence he is automatically the chairman of the Executive Directors and as such he has a deciding vote in case of an equal division of the directors. There is, of course, no comparable role for the Secretary-General of the UN.

III. The "Legislative" Processes of the Specialised Agencies

The use of inverted commas around the word "legislative" is intended to prevent the word being taken literally. As seen above in Chapter 3, within the United Nations the Security Council can take specific decisions, binding on members by virtue of Article 25 of the Charter. And the General Assembly has what may be described as a "quasi-legislative" role. By way of contrast, the European Communities, described later in Chapter 6, have true legislative powers, being empowered to adopt decisions, regula-

---

[38] See Giraud, "Le secrétariat des institutions internationales," (1959) 79 R.C. 373.
[39] *Post*, p. 355.   [40] *Post*, p. 318.

tions and directives with direct legal effect within the legal systems of the members. The specialised agencies have powers more akin to the United Nations for, like the UN, they lack the "supra-national" character of the European Communities. Nevertheless, they have developed techniques which allow their acts to become binding obligations for Members rather more effectively than is the case within the UN. All the specialised agencies are, clearly, organisations through which the members, co-operate; there is no real supra-national element in them and no decisions become, *ipso facto*, law for the members. What must be considered, therefore, is the process whereby the decisions or other acts of the organisations can become law, can create legal obligations, for the members.

The process adopted by the ILO is unique because of the peculiar "tripartite" character of the representation of members in its organs, but at the same time it formed a model upon which the newer organisations based their own procedures. It therefore merits attention in some detail.[41]

The Conference as a whole, not merely the government delegates, adopts proposals in the form of either an international Convention or a Recommendation; the vote in either case being a two-thirds majority. Upon adoption these are signed by the President of the Conference and the Director-General for purposes of authentication; they are not signed by delegates.

In the case of a Convention, this is then communicated to *all* members for ratification, not merely to those whose government delegates voted for the proposal. Thereupon, *all* members are bound to submit the Convention to the appropriate authorities within the State for the enactment of legislation or other action necessary to give the Convention application within the State[42]; and this submission must be within one year or, when this is impossible owing to exceptional circumstances, within 18 months. This is not an obligation to ratify, but an obligation to submit to

---

[41] See generally Jenks, *The International Protection of Trade Union Freedom*, (1957), Chap. 5. And for more general studies, not confined to the ILO, see Detter, *Law Making by International Organisations* (1965); Saba, "Quasi-legislative activities of the specialised agencies of the UN," (1964) 111 R.C. 607–690.

[42] Where power to implement rests with some body other than the legislature, the Convention should nevertheless also be submitted to the legislature for the purpose of informing public opinion: see Report of the Committee on the Application of Conventions and Recommendations, ILO 53rd Sess. 1969.

the appropriate authorities who can give consent to ratification. Moreover each member must inform the Director-General of the measures taken in pursuance of this obligation, and of which authorities are competent and of the action taken by them. When the competent or appropriate authorities give their consent to the Convention, the member State then communicates a formal "ratification" of the Convention to the Director-General and is then bound to take such action as is necessary to make the Convention effective. Even thus far, this process has features which distinguish it from the normal process with a multilateral treaty. First, the "parties" which draft the text are not entirely State representatives, and it is not signed by them; to this extent "ratification" is an unfortunate term to use to describe the final act of acceptance, for it is not an act whereby the State ratifies the previous signature of its representatives. Secondly, whereas with the normal multilateral treaty a State which does not vote for or accept the text cannot be regarded as having any further obligations in respect of it, in the ILO *all* members are bound notwithstanding any negative vote to submit the Convention to their legislature or other competent authority for approval and consent. Thirdly, a State actually ratifying cannot in so doing make a reservation; since 1921 the doctrine has been firmly established that, because the adoption of the text the Convention is the act of the entire General Conference consisting of delegates other than State delegates, it is not competent for a member State to ratify subject to a reservation which constitutes an alteration of the obligations as set out in the agreed text. Further consequences of the adoption of the Convention by a "tripartite" Conference are that the States parties to a Convention cannot agree *inter se* on an interpretation of the Convention; this, as we shall see, is governed by a fixed procedure.[43] Nor can the States parties to a Convention revise it by their own action *inter se*; the ILO Conventions contain clauses enabling this to be done by a revising Convention in which the Conference as a "tripartite" body expresses its will.[44]

---

[43] *Post*, p. 150.
[44] For further details see Jenks, "Some characteristics of international labour conventions," (1935) 33 Can. B.R. 448–462; "The significance for international law of the tripartite character of the I.L.O.," (1936) 22 *Trans. Grotius Soc.* 45–86; "The revision of international labour conventions," (1933) 14 B.Y.B.I.L. 43–64; also Dillon, *International Labour Conventions,* (1941), especially Chaps. III and IV.

For the member ratifying a Convention there is a continuing process of supervision, through reports submitted annually to the organisation and a "complaints procedure" which will be discussed later.[45] For the member not ratifying there is also a continuing process of inquiry in that, upon the request of the governing body, such a member must at intervals report the position of its law and practice in regard to the matters dealt with in the Conventions, showing the extent to which compliance in fact exists, and stating the difficulties which prevent or delay ratification. This is indeed an advance on normal treaty practice; its whole purpose is to maximise the ratifications secured by the ILO Conventions.[46]

With a Recommendation it is otherwise. It is communicated to all members with a view to effect being given to it by legislation or otherwise. Here again the member has the obligation within the same period of time to bring it before the competent authorities within the State and to inform the organisation of the steps taken and of action taken by the competent authorities. Beyond this no further obligation rests on the members other than that of reporting the position in the law and practice of their countries and of any progress made in implementing the recommendation or any modifications found necessary.

In Federal States, where sovereign power is divided between the federal and the state authorities, the actual implementation of conventions or recommendations may well require action by the component States jointly with the federal authorities, or even exclusively by them. The ILO Constitution, Article 19 (7), therefore provides that in such cases the federal government is required to make arrangements for the reference of the conventions and recommendations to the appropriate State, provincial or cantonal authorities within eighteen months, to arrange for periodical consultations between the federal and State, provincial or cantonal authorities with a view to co-ordinating the action necessary to give the conventions or recommendations effect; and then the further obligations apply of reporting to the organisation on steps taken, on which are the appropriate state, provincial or cantonal authorities, on the position in law and practice and on the extent of implementation and modification in the case of Recom-

---

[45] *Post*, p. 152.
[46] By June 1967, 3,292 ratifications had been received to 126 Conventions.

mendations, just as in the case of a unitary State. All this procedure relates to the pre-ratification position of the Federal States; once it ratifies, it is bound exactly in the same way as a unitary State that has ratified. The procedure was introduced in 1946 as a replacement for the previous procedure under which Federal States were, in certain circumstances, entitled to treat conventions as if they were recommendations.

This, then, is the detailed procedure adopted by the ILO.[47] Its influence on the practice of other organisations is evident, although, in the case of other specialised agencies, the delegations to the organisation are entirely governmental and, therefore, the procedure is less revolutionary. UNESCO adopts conventions and recommendations, the former by a two-thirds majority and the latter by a simple majority, and each member State is bound to submit these to its competent authorities[48] within one year (Art. 4 (4)); the member States are then bound to report periodically to the organisation on their laws, regulations and statistics and on the action taken with regard to conventions and recommendations (Art. 8). WHO has a similar procedure, except that the period for taking "action relative to the acceptance of such convention or agreement" as the Health Assembly adopts is 18 months and, if not accepted, the member is bound to furnish a statement of reasons for non-acceptance (Art. 20). Moreover, each member is bound to report annually on action taken with regard to conventions, recommendations and regulations (Art. 62). These regulations, a lesser order of "legislation," are adopted by the Assembly on matters like sanitary and quarantine procedures, nomenclatures for diseases and pharmaceutical standards, and on adoption become binding on all members unless they "opt out" by communicating to the organisation their rejection or reservations.[49] FAO also contemplates the submission to members of recommendations and conventions adopted by the Conference;

---

[47] For an account of its effectiveness see Landy, "The Effective Application of International Labour Standards," (1953) 68 *International Labour Review* 346.
[48] "Competent" means competent to legislate, not just to study: see UNESCO Memorandum in *U.N.J.Y.* (1965), 137.
[49] Reservations are, under the International Sanitary Regulations adopted in 1951, not valid unless accepted by the Assembly, and Regulations do not enter into force for a State entering a reservation until so accepted.|The Regulations also bind new members three months after their admission, subject to their right to reject them or enter reservations. *Off. Rec. of W.H.O.*, No. 37, pp. 335–353.

although there is no constitutional obligation to submit these to the appropriate authorities, there is an obligation to report to the organisation periodically on the action taken on the basis of these, and these reports are then analysed by the Director-General and submitted to the Conference. Members are also bound, on request, to communicate all laws and regulations concerning nutrition, food and agriculture (Art. XI). Neither these conventions and recommendations, nor the regulations and supplementary agreements approved by the Council, come into force for any member unless they are expressly accepted by the member in accordance with its own constitutional procedure (Art. XIV). In ICAO, although it does not contemplate specifically the adoption of conventions[50] or recommendations which impose obligations on members, the Council may adopt international standards and recommended practices to supplement the Convention itself in the form of Annexes. These Annexes become effective within three months *unless* a majority of the members register their disapproval with the Council. The Annexes distinguish between "standards," which in general consist of specifications the uniform application of which is *necessary* for the safety or regularity of international air navigation, and "recommended practices" of which the uniform applicability is considered *desirable*. Members are bound to conform to the former and must notify the Council if they find it impossible to comply with them. With the "recommended practices" the obligation is a lesser one, namely to "endeavour" to conform to them. WMO has a weaker kind of obligation, for there members agree to "do their utmost to implement the decisions of the Congress," which may under Article 7 adopt technical regulations or make recommendations to members, and the members are bound to state the reasons why they find implementation impracticable.

In the UPU the various agreements bind only members acceding to them, and the detailed regulations to implement both the Convention and these supplementary agreements are drawn up "by common consent" (Article 22). There is thus no question of legislating so as to bind the minority. The unusual feature is the procedure for dealing with proposals to amend any "Act of

[50] Yet in 1971 three different Conventions were in fact adopted, two dealing with "hijacking" and one with the revision of the Warsaw Rules on Carrier's Liability: see (1971) 10 I.L.M. 133, 613, 1151. These bind only ratifying States.

Union" in the long intervals between Congresses.[51] This, set forth in Chapter III, involves the circulation of such proposals by the international bureau (Secretariat) and the recording of replies. Whether, on the basis of these replies, the amendment becomes effective, depends on whether a sufficient number of affirmative replies is received, and this number varies according to the nature of the proposal (Art. 30): amendments to the Constitution require a two-thirds majority. In order to preserve the uniform application of the Acts of the Union, reservations are only allowed at the time of signature and with the consent of Congress.

The IMF has, in recent years, demonstrated what can be achieved via an organ's regulatory powers. Exchange rate stability was fundamental to the Articles of Agreement and the Fund's code of conduct. By 1971, however, the system of exchange rate stability had been virtually destroyed and the Fund was forced to adapt to the new system of floating currencies. The Fund does not adopt conventions, like the ILO, and revision of the Articles was at that stage premature. So, in 1974, the Executive directors adopted "guidelines," of an experimental character, to keep the floating of currencies within manageable limits.[52] Although strictly not binding, these guidelines served as, in effect, regulations until formal amendment of Article IV of the Agreement was achieved in 1976.[53] And even under the amended Article IV, the need for flexibility dictated that the Executive directors could adopt "principles"[54] for its implementation, these principles being in effect binding on the Members. It provides an example of delegated legislative power.

What emerges from this brief survey of "legislative" techniques is not that there has occurred any dramatic change in the basic rule of international law that States assume new legal obligations only with their consent, but rather a pattern of procedure for improving the chances of a decision of the majority (be it simple or two-thirds) of a "legislative" character securing general consent.

---

[51] There is the same problem in ITU. This led the UK to propose in 1965 that amendments of minor matters in the Radio Regulations might be made by postal vote.

[52] Decision No. 4232 (74/67), June 13, 1974.

[53] (1976) 15 I.L.M. 499.

[54] IMF Executive Directors decision on Surveillance over Exchange Rate Policies, (1977) 6 *IMF Survey* 131.

Quite apart from the special features of the ILO procedure which stem from the tripartite character of the organs, other features have proved adaptable generally. Thus, the obligation on *all* members to submit conventions or recommendations to the appropriate authorities is adopted by UNESCO and WHO; the further stage of reporting back to the organisation what has been done is seen to be adopted in these organisations and in FAO. Thereafter, the members which do not proceed to ratify or implement the majority proposals are exposed to the political pressure of the ratifying members within the organs of the organisation and the reasons for hesitancy possibly exposed as spurious or even shown by other States, on the basis of their own experience, to be groundless. This pressure is designed to promote acceptance on as wide a basis as possible. It is quite distinct from the procedure to ensure compliance by a member that has accepted the obligations but which does not appear to be observing them.[55]

It is also clear that, at a lower level in the form of "regulations," in some organisations it is possible to accept the principle that a majority in a particular organ can actually create obligations for all members unless they take positive action by "opting out"; this is the remarkable feature of the WHO technique. In ICAO the "standards" adopted by the Council do not even give members this option, although a member would be entitled to withdraw entirely from the organisation.

IV. INTERPRETATION OF CONSTITUTIONAL TEXTS

The constitutional texts of the agencies are clearly capable of giving rise to diputes concerning their interpretation.[56] Whilst the UN Charter contains no specific compromissory clause providing for the settlement of disputes with regard to the interpretation of the Charter,[57] such a clause is common in the constitutions of the

[55] See *post*, p. 151.
[56] See Hexner, "Interpretation by Public International Organisations of their basic instruments," (1959) 53 A.J.I.L. 341, a useful article but limited to the "financial" organisations. Also Mann, (1970) 43 B.Y.B.I.L. 1–19.
[57] See A.O. of July 20, 1962, on *Certain Expenses of the UN*, in which the Court, having noted the absence from the Charter of any procedure enabling the Court to determine the validity of acts of the organs, concluded that each organ must, in the first place at least, determine its own jurisdiction and the presumption of validity would apply to such determination: (1962) *I.C.J. Reports*, 168.

specialised agencies. Such disputes can be either between the members or between members and the Organisation; the latter situation will commonly arise when a member disputes an interpretation adopted by an organ of the Organisation. The difference between these two types of disputes becomes extremely relevant when one considers the feasibility of recourse to the I.C.J.; for, whereas in a dispute between members (assuming they are States), this can be referred to the Court as a contentious dispute on which the decision of the Court will be binding, when the Organisation as such is a party the possibility of a binding decision is ruled out by Article 34 of the Statute of the Court (which provides that "only States" can be parties to a decision) and the only recourse is to the advisory jurisdiction of the Court.

Both the ITU and the UPU contemplate, in their constitutions, only this first class of disputes. ITU, in Article 28, contemplates the solution of such disputes through ordinary diplomatic channels or by virtue of existing treaties between the members concerned for pacific settlement of disputes; failing that, recourse *may* (not must) be had to arbitration in accordance with a procedure set forth in Annexe 3. UPU provides directly for arbitration in Article 32 (although this clearly does not exclude diplomatic settlement) and, in stating that a disagreement "shall be settled by arbitration," would seem to envisage compulsory arbitration. The arbitral body is to be composed of disinterested members, one being appointed by each member in dispute (with a third selected by the arbitrators if the vote is equal), or a single arbitrator if the parties can agree on one.

However, since the ITU (but not the UPU) is authorised by the General Assembly of the UN to request advisory opinions from the I.C.J., it also possesses this means of settling any dispute to which the Organisation itself is a "party," although not in binding form.

These apart, most of the specialised agencies contemplate the settlement of disputes on interpretation by organs of the Organisation. This is a sensible and entirely expected procedure. The differences appear when one asks whether the decisions of these organs are regarded as final or are subject to some form of appeal.

The three "financial" organisations, the Bank, Fund and IFC, all give their organs a right of *final* decision. The procedure is for a dispute, whether between members or between members and the

Organisation, to be submitted to the Executive Directors (Board of Directors in IFC) with a right of appeal to the Board of Governors whose decision shall be final. The only disputes to which this does not apply are those with members who have withdrawn or are permanently suspended, and these go outside the organisation to an independent arbitral tribunal of three members, one appointed by the member, one by the organisation, and an umpire appointed by the President of the I.C.J. unless the parties can agree on one themselves.

Other agencies entrust disputes to their own organs but subject to a right of appeal to an outside body. The organ is the plenary organ in FAO, WHO and WMO, and the Council, the organ of 27 States, in the case of ICAO.[58] From these two organs an appeal lies either to the I.C.J. or to some other arbitral body agreed upon by the parties, although WMO makes no mention of the I.C.J. and refers simply to "an independent arbitrator appointed by the president of the International Court of Justice, unless the parties concerned agree on another mode of settlement" (Art. 29). The ICAO Council has now become an important disputes-settlement organ, with its own Rules for the Settlement of Differences.

IMCO is slightly different. In the first case, whilst the Assembly is named as the organ to settle disputes arising from the interpretation or application of the Convention, there is a special clause providing that "Nothing in this article shall preclude the Council or the Maritime Safety Committee from settling such question or dispute that may arise during the exercise of their functions." It has been pointed out before that, in this organisation, the plenary organ is not given as much power *vis-à-vis* the organs of limited composition as in other organisations. The second feature to be noted about IMCO is that legal questions not so settled may be referred for an advisory opinion to the I.C.J.; there is no express provision by way of a compromissory clause to give the Court contentious jurisdiction between the member States as there is in other organisations. Reference has already been made to IMCO's use of the power to request an advisory opinion

---

[58] See *Appeal relating to the Jurisdiction of the ICAO Council (India v. Pakistan)* (1972) *I.C.J. Reports*, 46. And note that the ICAO Council may also hear complaints under the numerous bilateral Air Transport Agreements.

in order to determine the proper composition of the Maritime Safety Committee.[59]

Other organisations do not specifically mention the powers of their own organs to interpret the convention in the event of a dispute, but provide that such disputes shall be referred directly to arbitration, as in the UPU, or to the I.C.J. or a tribunal specially appointed, as in the ILO or UNESCO.[60] It cannot seriously be contended that this *excludes* the organs of the organisation from attempting to settle such disputes; indeed, if, through an organ, the question can be settled there will be no dispute remaining to be submitted to the outside body. Moreover, in general it will be better for such disputes to be settled internally. However, the ultimate recourse is there, if needs be.

It must finally be observed that all the specialised agencies bar the UPU have now been authorised by the General Assembly to request advisory opinions from the I.C.J.[61] This, as we have mentioned, is the only way in which the organisation as such can appeal to the Court for an interpretation of its constitution. The disadvantage is that the advisory opinion is not, *per se*, binding; to get a binding decision the organisation would have to have power to submit the dispute to some other arbitral body. The desirability of constant reference to the Court is questionable, and it may be noted that the Assembly always excludes from its grant power to request an advisory opinion on questions affecting the relationships of the specialised agencies *inter se*, or with the UN itself. This is a clear indication that certain constitutional issues are not thought suitable for independent judicial settlement.

The disputes procedure of GATT is of special interest. Complaints of non-observance of the Treaty or that the benefits of the Treaty are "nullified or impaired" are circulated to all members and a "consultation" occurs in which not only the "plaintiff" and "defendant" Parties participate but any other Party having an interest in the issue. Failing a satisfactory solution by

---

[59] *Ante*, p. 133.
[60] Hence the reference, under Art. 14 (2), to an ad hoc tribunal of the question whether members of the Executive Board who cease to be members of the delegation of their State are eligible for re-election: the *UNESCO (Constitution) Case*, (1949) A.D., Case 113.
[61] See generally *post*, p. 277.

these means a panel of conciliation is appointed by the Contracting Parties which makes recommendations. If these are not accepted by the "defendant," the Contracting Parties can authorise the "plaintiff" to retaliate by way of withdrawing concessions from the "defendant." This has rarely proved necessary and this points to the efficacy of this form of consultation under the pressure of the opinion of the membership as a whole. There is no further appeal from this adjudication by the Contracting Parties: a dissatisfied Party is left with the possibility of withdrawing from GATT.

V. Sanctions and Enforcement Procedures

The notion that an international organisation may undertake sanctions or enforcement measures against a Member is not confined to the United Nations.[62] However, the decision to embark on sanctions presupposes two prior stages:

(i) the acquisition of evidence to prove a breach of obligation, whether under the constitution or some other convention. Such evidence can be provided by reports, by inspection,[63] or by complaints or petitions.[64]

(ii) the determination by a competent organ that a breach has occurred.

The potential range of sanctions then available is very wide: military or economic sanctions (as under Chapter VII of the Charter), suspension of voting rights,[65] suspension of representation, suspension of the services of the organisation, suspension of the rights and privileges of membership, expulsion from particular organs or the organisation as a whole,[66] fines or other financial

---

[62] As to the UN, see *ante*, p. 37.

[63] As in the Trusteeship system, or in the IAEA or ENEA where inspectors visit nuclear installations.

[64] As in the petitions to the Trusteeship Council, or complaints to the UN or European Commissions on Human Rights, or to the I.L.O., or to the Committee of 24.

[65] *Post*, p. 386.

[66] *Post*, p. 392.

penalties.[67] And the sanction can be imposed either by a political or a judicial organ. Although the specialised agencies do not possess this whole range of sanctions it will be useful to deal with the enforcement procedures adopted by the specialised agencies at this stage, since they demonstrate a remarkable venture by the ILO, and its adaption by other specialised agencies.

Under this head it is proposed to deal with the procedures by which the obligations assumed by members under conventions or other acts concluded within the organisation are enforced. Reference has already been made to the "legislative" role of organisations like the ILO, UNESCO, WHO, UPU, ITU, WMO, FAO and ICAO, all of which envisage the adoption of rules which may exceptionally become binding on members upon adoption by an organ, or, more often, which become binding when embodied in the traditional form of a convention and are accepted by members by ratification or otherwise.

The supervision and enforcement procedures designed to ensure compliance with the obligations thus assumed are seen, in the most "sophisticated" form, in the ILO. It will be recalled that *all* members are bound to report to the Organisation on the position in their law and practice with regard to matters dealt with in conventions or recommendations, and that members who are parties to particular conventions are bound to report on the measures taken to give effect to such conventions. With the influence brought to bear within the organisation on members not *legally* bound (either because not parties to the convention, or because a recommendation only is in question) we are not here concerned; it is with the means of enforcing the legal obligations assumed by parties to conventions that we must now deal.

Complaints of non-observance may be made against a member by any other ratifying member or by a delegate to the Conference or by the governing body itself, and these may be referred by the governing body under Article 26 of the Constitution to a Commission of Enquiry either directly or after prior communication to the government concerned. This commission, an independent body, is empowered to ascertain the facts and to make *recommendations* in a report which is published. Each government must, within three months, inform the Director-General whether

---

[67] *Post*, p. 210.

it accepts these recommendations or wishes to refer the complaint to the I.C.J.[68] The Court may affirm, vary or reverse any of the findings or recommendations of the Commission of Enquiry and its decision on the matter or complaint is final. In the event that a member fails to carry out the recommendations of the Commission, or the decision of the Court, the governing body "may recommend to the Conference such action as it may deem wise and expedient to secure compliance therewith" (Art. 33). The ultimate sanction therefore rests with the Conference, and, in view of the fact that originally neither suspension nor expulsion were provided for in the constitution, this seemed a rather tame ending to what appears a very impressive machinery of enforcement. Legally that may be true; in practice it has never proved necessary to resort to such lengths, and, indeed, in practice this entire "complaints procedure" has proved to be something kept in reserve rather than something for habitual use. The "reports procedure" mentioned earlier, by which the annual reports of members are examined first by an independent Committee of Experts and then by a tripartite Committee on the Application of Conventions and Recommendations, has rendered use of the "enforcement procedure" a course of last resort.

It should also be noted that there is a special procedure under Article 24 for dealing with complaints by industrial associations of employers or workers. These are transmitted to the government concerned by the governing body for its observations, and, if no reply is received or the reply is unsatisfactory, the governing body may publish both the complaint and the reply, if any. The sanction is then a political one within and without the organisation. There is also, since 1950, a special procedure for complaints of the infringement of trade union rights,[69] referred to the ILO either

[68] A course not open to delegates as such because they have no *locus standi* before the Court in a contentious matter. This procedure under Art. 26 has been used rarely: in 1962 Ghana brought a complaint against Portugal, in 1963 Portugal brought a complaint against Liberia and in 1971 a Commission of Inquiry into alleged breaches of conventions by Greece was appointed. In 1975 the Governing Body itself referred to a Commission of Inquiry complaints against Chile.

[69] There are three important conventions on this matter: the Freedom of Association and Protection of the Right to Organise Convention, 1948; the Right to Organise and Collective Bargaining Convention, 1949; and the Right of Association (Non-Metropolitan Territories) Convention, 1947. See generally, Jenks, (1951) 28 B.Y.B.I.L. 348.

directly or through the Economic and Social Council of the UN. These are submitted to an independent fact-finding Commission of nine persons, working in panels of three to five members, and reference to the Commission is only by consent of the government concerned. This procedure is supplementary to those envisaged in the actual constitution and is, in contrast to them, more frequently used. When, because consent is not forthcoming, the Commission cannot act, the inquiry nevertheless proceeds within the Committee on Freedom of Association.[70]

We have previously seen that several of the agencies have adopted, to a greater or lesser degree, the "legislative" process of the ILO; so also with the "enforcement procedure," but to a much less impressive extent.

UNESCO, FAO, WHO, WMO and ICAO all have a form of "reports procedure"; UPU and ITU alone of the agencies with what we have described above as a "legislative function" do not. But, on the basis of these reports, the supervision and enforcement procedures are almost entirely political, in the sense that it is then for the members to bring criticism to bear on the non-compliant member within the Conference, Assembly or other plenary organ. Failing satisfaction, ICAO has no power of suspension or expulsion,[71] nor has UNESCO or FAO; WHO has the possible sanction of suspension, since this can be done "in exceptional circumstances" (Art. 7) which are not confined to non-fulfilment of budgetary commitments. WMO has power of suspension for breach of obligations "under the present Convention," so this sanction would not apply to the technical regulations, adopted by the Congress, which constitute that agency's "legislative role." The IMF can declare a member failing to fulfil its obligations ineligible to use the Fund's resources under Art. XV, though this extreme sanction has never been used.[72]

---

[70] This Committee has become a substitute, quasi-judicial hearing, avoiding the need for consent. It has heard over 800 cases and now assumes that freedom of association is a customary law right. Although possibly an extra-constitutional development, it now seems acepted in practice.

[71] Despite this, in 1973 the Afro-Asian bloc forced through a resolution denying Portugal an invitation to ICAO meetings until it complied with UN resolutions on decolonisation.

[72] See Gold, "The sanctions of the IMF" (1972) 66 A.J.I.L. 737. The IMF relies, essentially, on the pressures exerted during informal consultations with a Member and the threat to report to the Executive Board.

Moreover, when one looks at the provisions for settlement of disputes, it will be seen that there is rarely anything comparable to the very comprehensive system of settlement which plays so large a part in the ILO enforcement system. In ICAO a dispute between two or more members concerning either the interpretation or *application* of the Convention or its Annexes shall be referred to the Council, with an appeal either to an ad hoc arbitral tribunal or the I.C.J. (Art. 18); there is, therefore, a means for the judicial settlement of the question whether these legislative texts are being applied by a State bound by them.[73] Similarly in UPU the issue of "responsibility imposed upon a postal Administration" by the application of the Acts of the Union appears to be subject to compulsory artbitration; not so in ITU, where arbitration is optional.[74] In WMO there can be arbitration of disputes relating to either the interpretation or application "of the present Convention" (Art. 29), so that the application of the technical regulations adopted by decision of Congress is not subject to judicial review; WHO is similarly limited in its reference to the I.C.J. on the questions of interpretation or application of the Convention only (Art. 75). In UNESCO and FAO the reference of disputes to arbitration or to the I.C.J. is confined to questions of *interpretation* of the Convention.[75]

One is left with some doubt on whether the exclusion of the question of the *application* of legislative texts from a disputes provision which refers only to *interpretation* is intentional. Whilst there appears to be no direct decision on this, it may be contended that to refer the *interpretation* of a provision to a court is to ask for a decision as to its meaning; whereas the question of its *application* raises before the court the question of whether a member is applying the provision, as a question of fact as well as of law, in a manner consistent with its obligations. Hence the advantage of clauses which provide for the "application" issue to be put to a court, in this particular context of the machinery for enforcement of the obligations assumed under this kind of "legislation."

---

[73] See *ante*, n. 58.

[74] The contrast is between a clear "may" in Art. 25 of ITU, and the phrase "shall be settled by arbitration" in Art. 32 of UPU.

[75] Note, however, the UNESCO Special Protocol to the Convention against discrimination in Education of 1962 which establishes a Commission of Conciliation and Good Offices.

VI. THE ORGANISATION OF THE PETROLEUM EXPORTING COUNTRIES (OPEC)

The Statute of this organisation was adopted at the Caracas Conference in 1961[76] in order to establish an inter-governmental organisation of which the primary aim is "the co-ordination and unification of the petroleum policies of Member Countries and the determination of the best means of safeguarding their interests, individually and collectively" (Art. 2).

The membership includes the Founder Members (Iran, Iraq, Kuwait, Saudi Arabia and Venezuela), Full Members ("any other country with a substantial net export of crude petroleum, which has fundamentally similar interests to those of Member Countries": Art. 7 (c)) and Associate Members (a "net petroleum-exporting country" which does not qualify for full membership: Art. 7 (d)). Admission to either category is by a three-fourths vote of the Conference, including the concurrent vote of all the Full Members.

The Organisation has a simple structure of three organs. The Conference is the "supreme authority," a plenary organ ordinarily meeting twice-yearly and, except on procedural questions, deciding by unanimous vote. This permits the resolutions of the Conference to be treated, prima facie, as binding. Under Article 11 (c), resolutions become effective after 30 days unless a Member notifies the Secretariat of its non-acceptance of the resolution. The role of the Conference is to formulate general policy, but it may give specific directions to the Board of Governors and take decisions on the basis of reports or recommendations submitted by the Board. In practice, the decisions of the Conference which take the public eye are those fixing the price of oil.[77]

The Board of Governors has, under Article 20, the management of the affairs of the organisation, including such matters as

---

[76] Text in UNTS, Vol. 443, 247. The Organisation of Arab Petroleum Exporting Countries (OAPEC) is different from OPEC, being formed in January 1968 by Saudi Arabia, Kuwait and Libya, primarily to serve the cause of Arab unity: see Mikdashi, *The Community of Oil Exporting Countries* (1972), Chs. 3 and 4.

[77] See Rouhani, *A History of OPEC* (1971), Ch. 13. Less spectacular, but equally important, is the activity of the OPEC Special Fund, established in 1976; (1976) 15 I.L.M. 1357. In 1978 OPEC made grants to developing countries in excess of $5.7 billion, and made loans of $210 million. And in 1980 the OPEC Fund for International Development was given new legal status by the Agreement of May 27, 1980 with funds of $4 billion: (1980) 19 I.L.M. 879.

drawing up the budget for adoption by the Conference, preparing for the Conference and implementing its decisions. For this purpose the Board meetings are held not less than twice a year, and the Governors are individuals nominated by the members, and confirmed by the Conference, to serve a two-year term.

The third organ is the Secretariat, headed by the Secretary-General, and conforming to the normal pattern of international secretariats.[78]

Although not named as organs, the Statute also makes provision for Consultative Meetings, comprising the Heads of delegations, to be convened on the request of the President of the Conference when the Conference itself is not in session. In addition, the Conference can establish so-called "specialised organs" as occasion requires.

The budgetary provisions are somewhat unusual. Each Associate member is asked by the Conference to pay a fixed annual subscription, and, in addition, budget appropriations between Members are apportioned "on equal basis," taking into account the annual subscriptions of the Associate Members (Art. 38).

[78] The Statute is unusual in the detail with which it sets out the qualifications for the Secretary-Generalship and the structure of the Secretariat.

Bibliography

ADAM: Les organisations internationaux spécialisés (1965), 2 vols.
ALEXANDROVICZ: World Economic Agencies (1962).
AUFRIGHT: The IMF: legal bases structure, functions (1964).
BUERGENTHAL: Law-Making in ICAO (1969).
CHAUBERT: L'Union postale universelle (1970).
CODDING: The UPU (1964).
CODDING: The International Telecommunications Union—an experiment in international co-operation (1952).
DAM: The GATT law and international economic organisation (1970).
FAWCETT: *"The IMF and International Law"* (1964) 40 B.Y.B.I.L. 32.
FRIEDMANN, KALMANOFF, MEAGHER: International Financial Aid (1966).
GOLD: The IMF and International Law (1966).
ICAO: Memorandum on ICAO; the story of International Civil Aviation Organisation (1951).
ILO: The impact of International Labour Conventions and Recommendations (1976).

JOHNSON: The ILO (1970).
KUBBAH: OPEC Past and Present (1974).
LANDY: The Effectiveness of International Supervision (1966).
LAURENT: "*Les institutions spécialisées de l'O.N.U.*," Juris Classeur, Fasc. 130, 135, 140.
MACMAHON: "*The ILO*" in LUARD: The Evolution of International Organisations (1966), 177.
MANIN: L'Organisation de l'Aviation Civile Internationale (1970).
MENON: "*The UPU*" (1965) Int. Council No. 552.
MORRIS: La Banque Mondiale (1965).
PEASLEE: International Governmental Organisations. Constitutional Documents, 2nd revised ed. (1971), 2 vols. (This reproduces the basic constitutional texts and the texts of the agreements with the UN.)
SABA: "*Quasi-legislative activities of the specialised agencies,*" (1964) 3 R.C. 607.
SCAMMELL: "*The IMF*" in LUARD: The Evolution of International Organisations (1966), 200.
SHONFIELD: "*The World Bank*" in LUARD: *op. cit.*, 231.
SZASZ: The law and practice of the IAEA (1970).
UNITED NATIONS: Agreements between the UN and the specialised agencies (1952).
UNITED NATIONS: Inter-Agency Agreements and Agreements between specialised agencies and other intergovernmental organisations (1953).

PART TWO

Regional Institutions

CHAPTER 5

INTRODUCTION—"REGIONALISM" WITHIN THE UNIVERSAL SYSTEM

EVEN prior to the League "regionalism," in the sense of a grouping of States by a common bond of policy, existed; the Monroe doctrine or the British Empire are obvious examples. Article 21 of the League Covenant recognised that the new global organisation must co-exist with such regional groupings by providing that "Nothing in this Covenant shall be deemed to affect the validity of international engagements such as treaties of arbitration or regional understandings like the Monroe doctrine for securing the maintenance of peace." The League therefore saw the creation of the Balkan Entente, the Locarno Agreements, and the Briand proposal for a European Union. When, at San Francisco, the same problem of reconciling the new global organisation with regional understanding arose, there was already in existence a fairly comprehensive Inter-American system (Pan-American Union), which in 1948 was to become the "Organisation of American States," and also the newly-formed League of Arab States, inaugurated by the Pact of March 22, 1945. In order to meet the fears of the American States, in particular, provision was expressly made to ensure that the new arrangements for collective security in the Charter, operating under the Security Council, should not stultify the arrangements already in being on a regional basis. Article 52 (1) of the Charter therefore provides that:

"Nothing in the present Charter precludes the existence of regional arrangements or agencies for dealing with such matters relating to the maintenance of international peace and security as are appropriate for regional action provided that such arrangements or agencies and their activities are consistent with the Purposes and Principles of the United Nations."

Clearly, the concern here is to avoid a conflict between the respective security systems of the United Nations and the "regional arrangements."

However, the attempt at San Francisco to reconcile the conflicting claims of regionalism and universalism produced a compromise which had within it two areas of latent difficulty.

The first area of difficulty was that of pacific settlement of disputes. Article 33 included resort to regional arrangements as a method which the parties must use "first of all," before having recourse to the Security Council. Article 52 (2) and (3) imposed upon the parties and the Security Council the obligation to utilise regional procedures for settlement. However, Article 52 (4) specifically stated that "this Article in no way impairs the application of Articles 34 and 35," so that the Council's own right to investigate a dispute or situation, and the member State's right to appeal to the Council seemed to be preserved: the inherent contradictions are obvious.

Thus, in the practice of the OAS, the Arab League and the OAU there has been advanced the thesis that regional procedures have a "priority" over the Security Council's procedures for settlement and even, in its extreme form in the U.S. argument in the Guatemalan case in 1954, an "exclusive" competence over inter-regional disputes so as to deny a State the right to appeal to the Security Council.[1] This argument over jurisdictional competence was politically motivated, especially in an OAS practice where the U.S.A. feared that reference to the Security Council would bring a Soviet veto and where the Soviet Union feared that the OAS procedures would be dominated by U.S. influence.

The Security Council, after a somewhat questionable abdication of jurisdiction in the Guatemalan case, has more recently shifted towards a more pragmatic approach in which, whilst supporting the use of regional procedures, it nevertheless retains a "supervisory" jurisdiction by maintaining the question on its own agenda (as in the Haitian and Panama Cases in 1963 and 1964) and even, in the case of the Dominican Republic in 1965, despatching its own observer mission.

Any attempt to rationalise the competing claims to jurisdiction

---

[1] See, on the OAS practice, Claude, "The OAS, the UN and the United States" (1964) *Int. Concil.* No. 547; Thomas and Thomas, *The Organisation of American States* (1963), Chaps. 16, 17; Macdonald, "The Developing relationship between Superior and Subordinate Political Bodies at the International Level," (1964) 2 Can. Y.B.I.L. 41. On the Arab League see Macdonald, *The League of Arab States* (1965), Chap.X.

over a dispute must take account of three basically different categories of "disputes."

(i) Disputes involving no actual or potential threat to international peace—here the priority of the regional procedures is undisputed, and the matter ought not to be referred to the Security Council.

(ii) Disputes involving a potential threat to international peace—here, the matter seems to fall squarely under Chapter VI of the Charter, so that the rights of the Council under Article 34, and of States under Article 35, are clear. Reference to a regional organisation's procedures becomes a matter of convenience, not of obligation, and much depends on the willingness of the parties to accept such a reference.

(iii) "Disputes" which involve an actual threat to peace—here the situation properly belongs in Chapter VII, not Chapter VI, and the "primary responsibility" of the Security Council to deal with the matter is clear: there can be no question of "priority" for regional procedures. Equally clearly, there is nothing to prevent the Security Council utilising regional procedures to assist in any measures taken under Chapter VII, but they do this subject to the Council's primary responsibility.

This last category brings us into the second area of difficulty, namely that of "enforcement" action which, under Article 53, cannot be taken except under the authorisation of the Security Council. The practice of the OAS has shown a tendency to minimise this restriction on the scope of regional collective action of a coercive character in three ways. First, the OAS (and the US in particular) has argued that the concept of "enforcement action" subject to prior authorisation by the Security Council does *not* embrace measures falling short of the use of armed force[2] or taken

---

[2] Hence the partial economic santions against the Dominican Republic (1960), Cuba (1962) and full economic sanctions against Cuba (1964) would not require S.C. authorisation. See the U.S. and U.K. arguments in the Security Council in the Dominican case, 1960. It is difficult to reconcile this view with the concept of intervention embodied in the G.A. resol. 2131 (XX), or Art. 15 of the OAS Charter, or the I.C.J.'s definition of enforcement action in the *Expenses Case* (1962).

pursuant to a recommendation as opposed to a decision[3] and, moreover, that the Security Council's "authorisation" can lie in an *ex post facto* approval or even failure to disapprove the action.[4] Secondly, the OAS has taken a broad definition of the notion of "collective self-defence" which, under Article 51 of the Charter, is clearly distinct from enforcement action and does not require prior authorisation.[5] Thus the view that has been taken would not confine self-defence to "armed attack" but would embrace indirect aggression or subversion: this view is reflected in the 1962 Punte del Este Declaration. This view was long criticised by the Soviet Union, although the intervention by Warsaw Pact countries in Czechoslovakia in 1968 seems to have marked a reversal of policy. Thirdly, the OAS in the Dominican case in 1965, and the Arab League in Kuwait in 1961 and in the Lebanon in 1976, have developed a concept of "regional peace-keeping" involving the use of armed forces but not for "enforcement action."

The difficulty about these developments is that they expand the role of regional arrangements in the vital area of the regulation of coercion without necessarily offering any real guarantee that this role will be subject to the safeguards of world opinion which, whatever the weaknesses of the UN, do find reflection in UN organs. The regional arrangements are *not* microcosms of the UN: in general they have a professed bias—against "communism," "capitalism," "colonialism," etc.—and do not guarantee the objectivity desirable in any authorisation of the use of coercion against another State. Nor can one region develop a role which can be denied to another region, so that whatever the OAS can do under the UN Charter, so can the OAU, etc. It is not therefore desirable for regional autonomy to develop too far in this area.

Not all organisations with membership limited to States in a given area are regarded as "regional arrangements" within the sense of Chapter VIII. The relative subordination of the regional

---

[3] Meeker, "Defensive Quarantine and the Law" (1963) 57 A.J.I.L. 521: this is a misunderstanding of the I.C.J. opinion in the *Expenses Case* (1962).

[4] Chayes, "Law and the Quarantine of Cuba" (1963) 41 *Foreign Affairs*. This must be nonsense both in terms of the plain meaning of "authorisation" and the fact that a U.S. veto would thus always ensure "authorisation" of OAS action. Nor does the S.C. practice in the Dominican case support it.

[5] See *The Inter-American System: Its Development and Strengthening* (1966), 105–154, a publication of the Inter-American Institute of International Legal Studies.

arrangement to the Security Council became politically embarrassing once the "cold war" developed; the Western powers wished to create an organisation for security against the Soviet Union, yet any "regional arrangement" they contrived would be virtually under the control of an organ of the United Nations in which the Soviet Union held a veto. Hence the North Atlantic Treaty Organisation, formed in 1949, made no mention of any relationship to the Security Council as a "regional arrangement," nor did it contain any provision providing for action only upon the authorisation of the Council or for reporting activities "in contemplation." Instead, the treaty expressed the organisation to be one for "collective self-defence," under Article 51 of the Charter, and, correspondingly, embodied only the obligation to report "measures taken" to the Council. The question whether all regional security arrangements must necessarily be "regional arrangements" under the Charter is complicated by the fact that no definition of a regional arrangement is given in the Charter; various attempts to insert one at San Francisco were rejected on the ground of incompleteness. Sir Eric Beckett[6] argued that "regional arrangements" were essentially different from organisations for collective self-defence. His contention was that Article 53 envisages the use of regional arrangements for "enforcement action," and this term, as evidenced by Articles 2(5) and 50, means "action ordered or authorised by the proper organ of the United Nations."[7] Such action, he contended, is essentially different from action in self-defence which the Charter recognises does not require any prior authorisation from the Security Council. Kelsen[8] has denied that "enforcement action" has so restricted a meaning. Beckett's further argument was that whereas Chapter VIII of the Charter indicates a number of matters with which regional arrangements may appropriately deal, collective self-defence is not amongst them. To this Kelsen replied that such express mention would have been superfluous in view of the previous Article 51, and "such matters relating to the maintenance of international peace and security as are appropriate for regional action" is in any event perfectly apt to include collective

---

[6] *The North Atlantic Treaty* (1950).
[7] *Ibid.* p. 7.
[8] "Is the North Atlantic Treaty a Regional Arrangement?" (1951) 45 A.J.I.L. 162; and also in *Recent Trends in the Law of the UN* (1951), pp. 918 *et seq.*

self-defence. Beckett's final argument was that regional arrangements contemplate the case of action against a member State of the arrangement, whereas collective self-defence contemplates attack from a State outside the organisation; Kelsen maintains this has "no basis in the Charter."

The present writer has suggested elsewhere[9] that, in this form, the problem posed is a sterile one. The question is not whether a given organisation is a regional arrangement or not, but rather whether particular action is taken as a regional arrangement or not. No one doubts the capacity of the Organisation of American States, which is expressly stated to be a "regional arrangement" in Article 1 of the Treaty of Bogota, 1948, to take collective self-defence, and in so doing it would be subject to the obligations of Article 51; Chapter VIII would be irrelevant to that situation. But assume a situation where the action contemplated is coercive action directed against a State and authorised by a competent UN organ (here we accept the *Expenses Case* definition of "enforcement action") and, clearly, the regional organisation must act only under the authority of that organ.

We shall see, therefore, that certain of the regional security arrangements purport to be "regional arrangements" under Chapter VII of the Charter, whereas others do not. We shall also see that the scope of regional organisations is much wider than either that of "regional arrangements" or even regional collective security organisations.

Whilst it is true that, because of the outbreak of the "cold war" and the consequent breakdown of the UN collective security system, regionalism has developed most in the form of organisations for collective security, it has never been contended that collective security was the *only* domain in which the principle of regionalism could operate. It was self-evident that, in the political and economic fields, greater progress might be made on a regional basis, between States whose fundamental similarity of political and economic institutions lessened the barriers to progress and co-operation. The United Nations itself recognised this fact by establishing the regional economic commissions, like ECA, ECE, ESCAP, ECLA.[10] Hence, nothing in the UN Charter has, equally,

---

[9] *Self-defence in International Law* (1957), pp. 222 *et seq.*
[10] See *ante*, p. 71.

prevented the growth of regional organisations in these other fields, and many of the organisations to be dealt with will be seen to have no connection with the "regional arrangements" mentioned in Article 52, or, indeed, with collective security as such.

By and large, and setting aside the development of the regional blocs for military purposes, the development of these strong regional tendencies has been a beneficial one in terms of the co-operation achieved between States. There is, however, a certain danger which is most obvious in the collective security field but which is also of a general character, namely that States may so concentrate on their regional associations as to minimise their efforts to co-operate on a global or universal basis through the United Nations and the specialised agencies. Trygve Lie once said "regional arrangements can never be a substitute for world organisation"; indeed, these developments should be regarded as complementary to, and not in substitution for, those embraced by the UN and its agencies.

The organisations treated in the following chapters are dealt with by regions, and then grouped according to whether their competence is general or limited. It has been thought preferable to adopt this method of presentation, rather than to attempt a classification according to function which cuts right across any regional grouping. The fact is that within one region the different organisations may form part of one comprehensive system, and become explicable only by reference to that system: this will be seen to be particularly so in Europe.

CHAPTER 6

EUROPEAN ORGANISATIONS

THE European scene has been remarkable for the growth and development of international institutions in the post-World War II era; indeed, it has been in Europe, the traditional centre of nationalism and State sovereignty, that experiments in co-operation have been set afoot which involve restrictions on national sovereignty seen nowhere else in the world. The sources of this dynamism are in themselves a complex study, but, at the risk of over-simplification, they may be said to be four: first, the need for co-operation on the practical level brought about by the fact of increased inter-relationships; secondly, the feeling that the rapid economic reconstruction necessary to make the European economy viable and competitive once more could only be achieved by concerted action; thirdly, the ideological appeal of "European Unity," a kind of "United States of Europe" which would emerge to replace the independent, sovereign States; and fourthly, the fear of Soviet aggression against Western Europe which has manifested itself in the formation of Western military alliances. The order in which these sources are put should not be taken as indicating the relative importance which they have had in promoting co-operation.

The institutions which have developed can be broadly grouped according to whether the primary aims are of a general political character, or are limited to matters of defence, or economics. The first covers the Council of Europe and institutions under its aegis; the second NATO, Western European Union, the Balkan Alliance, OECD, and the European Communities. As will soon be apparent, these organisations can only be said to be political, military or economic by reference to their *principal* competence or purpose; many of their activities overlap into other fields, thus making the classification one of convenience for the purposes of presentation rather than one of descriptive accuracy.

I. ORGANISATIONS OF GENERAL COMPETENCE

1. The Council of Europe

The idea of the political unification of Europe is by no means of recent origin, but in the immediate past it manifested itself in numerous national and international organisations sponsoring European unity, such as the United Europe Movement, the European Union of Federalists and the Economic League for European Co-operation. These combined in 1947 to form the "International Committee of the Movements for European Unity" which then organised a "Congress of Europe" at The Hague in May 1948. This whole development was non-governmental; that is to say, whilst many prominent statesmen participated in it, they did so as private individuals, not as State representatives. However, the resolution of the Hague Congress, expressing a desire for a "united Europe," stimulated the governments into action and the Consultative Council of the Brussels Treaty Organisation, an organisation set up in March 1948, established a committee to study proposals for European unity and it was here that the basic features of the new political organisation were worked out before being submitted to a conference of ambassadors which included not only representatives of the Brussels Treaty Powers but also representatives from Ireland, Italy, Denmark, Norway and Sweden. A draft Statute of the Council of Europe emerged, to be signed by ten countries on May 5, 1949.[1] The Statute represented a victory for those States which favoured a "functional" approach to unity as opposed to outright federation, namely, an approach based upon voluntary co-operation between States retaining their full, sovereign powers. Such co-operation would, however, extend into various sectors of their economy and of their social and cultural policies. This is not the place to examine the political, economic and even psychological factors which produced this caution in countries like the U.K., Denmark and Norway; time alone will justify or condemn this policy of caution which prevented the creation of a "United States of Europe."

The aims of the Council, as set out in Article 1 of the Statute, are to achieve a "greater unity between its Members for the purposes of safeguarding and realising the ideals and principles which are their common heritage and facilitating their economic and social progress." This aim is to be pursued through the organs of the Council "by discussion of questions of common concern and by agreements and common action in economic, social, cultural,

[1] *European Yearbook*, p. 275.

THE COUNCIL OF EUROPE

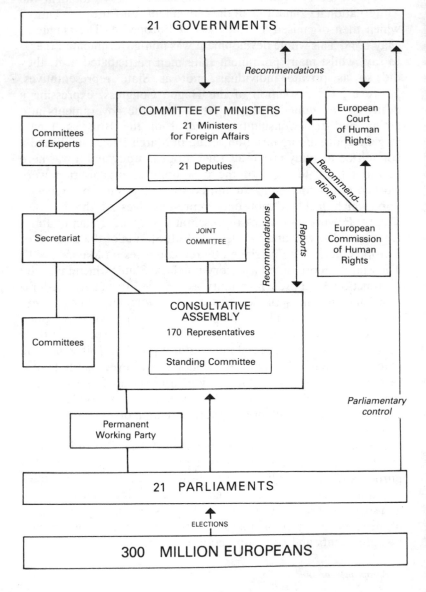

scientific, legal and administrative matters and in the maintenance and further education of human rights and fundamental freedoms." The aims are thus very broadly phrased, but it will be noted that the medium of pursuit is *discussion* and *agreement*; as we shall see when the organs are examined, the powers for the achievement of these aims are extremely limited. There is one specific exclusion from these aims, namely, under Article 1 (d) "matters relating to National Defence do not fall within the scope of the Council of Europe." The exclusion is accounted for partly by the pre-existence of NATO, and partly by the fact that some of the "neutral" members like Ireland, Austria[2] and Sweden were not willing to participate in any military bloc.

Membership is either "original," *i.e.* the first 10 signatories, or "admitted" or "associate." Article 4 provides that "any European State which is deemed to be able and willing to fulfil the provisions of Article 33" (these relate to acceptance of the rule of law and human rights and collaboration in the realisation of the aims of the Council) may be invited to become a Member by the Committee of Ministers. Article 5 provides for "associate Membership," also by invitation of the Committee,[3] but with representation only in the Assembly, not the Committee. So far as termination of membership is concerned, any Member may, under Article 7, withdraw at the end of a given financial year as did Greece in 1969. There is also a right in the Committee to suspend a Member from its right of representation for a serious violation of Article 3 and to request the Member's withdrawal. There is a separate right of suspension for non-fulfilment of a Member's financial obligations.

The Organs of the Council are remarkable not so much for their powers but for their composition; the one, the Committee of Ministers, is the typical organ of governmental representatives; the other, the Assembly, introduced a quite novel form whereby representation was of the Parliaments of the Members. It will be noted that these are the only two named organs; provision is made for a Secretariat to serve both, and this is very much modelled on the UN Secretariat, although the Council's Secretariat is not a

---

[2] Austria was merely an "observer" from 1952–56 and only thereafter became a full member following the Austrian State Treaty.

[3] W. Germany and the Saar were associate members until West Germany became a full member in 1951 and the Saar became integrated into W. Germany in 1955. There are now 21 members, the last being Lichtenstein (1978).

"principal organ" and, surprisingly, the Statute says nothing of the powers of the Secretary-General.

(a) *The Committee of Ministers*

This is the organ of traditional character, that is to say, it is governmental; each Member has one representative and one vote, the representatives being the respective Ministers for Foreign Affairs or alternates who shall be, wherever possible, members of their governments (Art. 14). The provision is somewhat optimistic about the importance which the Members attach to the Council, for in practice their Foreign Ministers are pre-occupied with more important tasks than attendance at the Committee's meetings, even though these take place twice yearly only (only once yearly as a matter of obligation under the statute). From 1952 onwards the practice has developed, without any express authority in the statute, of appointing "Deputies" who are able to take decisions of the same force and effect as the Ministers themselves *except* on important questions of policy.[4]

Decisions of the Committee are in the main taken by the unanimous vote of representatives casting a vote, and a majority of those entitled to sit. However, procedural questions are decided by simple majority and certain matters by a two-thirds majority; this last category includes admission of new Members, adoption of the budget, recommendations for amendment of the statute,[5] and decisions on questions arising from the findings of the Commission on Human Rights. Article 20, which governs voting, adopts the technique of specifying which matters fall into which category of vote (unlike the broad dichotomy of procedural and non-procedural matters in the Security Council); it also provides for the settlement of any dispute as to which vote governs a particular matter by a two-thirds vote, and by the use of the phrase "casting a vote" avoids problems of absence and abstention: all in all, a more comprehensive formula than the Security Council's.

The operation of the unanimity rule caused considerable

---

[4] These "deputies" are often the Permanent Representatives which Members have accredited to the Council of Europe, similar to those accredited to the UN and fulfilling the role of an ambassador accredited to a foreign State in so far as they maintain permanent contact and liaison.

[5] But not amendment of the voting article, Art. 20, for which unanimity is required.

difficulty, for it virtually granted a power of veto and retarded the work of the Committee. In 1951 the Committee therefore agreed to a system whereby "Partial Agreements" could be reached,[6] thus allowing Members in favour of a particular proposal to proceed with it without the participation of non-assenting Members. However, this system was not used until April 1956, on the adoption of the European Settlement Fund; it was not used by the "Six" who, in establishing the European Coal and Steel Community in 1951, preferred to act right outside the framework of the Council of Europe.

The scope of the functions of the Committee is very wide indeed. Under Article 15:

> "(a) On the recommendation of the Consultative Assembly or on its own initiative, the Committee of Ministers shall consider the action required to further the aim of the Council of Europe, including the conclusion of conventions or agreements and the adoption by Governments of a common policy with regard to particular matters. Its conclusions shall be communicated to Members by the Secretary-General.
>
> (b) In appropriate cases, the conclusions of the Committee may take the form of recommendations to the Governments of Members, and the Committee shall request the Governments of Members to inform it of the action taken by them with regard to such recommendations."

It is readily apparent, therefore, that the Committee cannot take decisions binding upon Governments; its only power is to recommend matters to Governments, so that it is in no sense an *executive* organ. Wide functions are combined here with extremely limited powers and the only power to take binding decisions relates solely to questions of internal organisation (Art. 16). It is also true that in practice the initiative for such action as has been taken has come from the Assembly rather than from the Committee, evidencing a lack of common political will amongst the Members which would seem to suggest that there is little to be gained in granting more extensive powers to the Committee at this stage.

The Committee has an elaborate structure of committees and

---

[6] A similar possibility was provided for in Article 14 of the OEEC Convention.

subsidiary bodies of governmental experts, mostly established on a permanent basis and meeting fairly regularly.

(b) *The Consultative Assembly*

The composition of the Assembly is remarkably unusual. The Assembly consists of 170 representatives, each Member being represented by a number corresponding to its population size. Thus France, Germany, Italy and the United Kingdom have 18, Spain and Turkey 12, Belgium, Netherlands, Greece and Portugal 7, and so on to 3 for Iceland, Luxembourg, Cyprus and Malta, and 2 for Lichtenstein. Since May 1951 these representatives have been elected by parliaments of Members, not by the governments, and under Article 25 (a) of the statute a Parliament could decide on some other manner of appointment, thus opening up a possibility of direct suffrage—election by the national electorate of their own representatives at Strasbourg. Representatives must be nationals of the Member they represent, though not necessarily parliamentarians. In practice, however, they invariably are, and it is the intention that a given national delegation should represent the political balance of the parties within the national parliament. Thus, in the United Kingdom, with the Conservatives in the majority, the delegation, decided upon in consultation with the Party whips, is 9 Conservative, 8 Labour and 1 Liberal. Representatives sit in alphabetical order, not in delegations, and the whole tendency is for alignments to develop which are based upon a common political view rather than on nationality. There is, at Strasbourg, the genesis of "European" conservative, socialist, Christian democrat and liberal parties. The ability to vote as an individual, without in any way committing his government, gives to a representative a remarkable freedom which needs considerable discipline and restraint unless it is to become irresponsible in the sense of being detached from practical realities.

The function of the Assembly is a *deliberative* one; Article 22 describes it as the "deliberative" organ, with power to make recommendations to the Committee of Ministers. The scope of its deliberations is limited only by the scope of the statute itself, and, even then, the Assembly has tended to take a liberal view of its powers. As we have seen, "matters of national defence" are excluded from the statute under Article 1 (d), and when the Assembly in 1950 called for the creation of a unified European

Army, the Committee of Ministers, in taking note of the recommendations, reminded the Assembly of this fact.

The conclusions of the Assembly are presented to the Committee in the form of "recommendations," requiring a two-thirds majority vote, or of "resolutions" or "opinions" requiring a simple majority; "resolutions" can also be addressed directly to governments. The difference is largely one of terminology, although in general recommendations call for action by the Committee and resolutions do not, and opinions are given on questions referred to it by the Committee. The essential point is that they are all of a purely persuasive character; the Assembly cannot bind the Committee or any State by its actions, and thus, whilst its composition is reminiscent of a parliamentary body, it is very far indeed from being a true European Parliament with real legislative power.

Under Article 32 the Assembly is to meet annually for not more than a month at a time; usually, however, this annual session is divided into three parts, meeting in the New Year, the spring and the autumn. The tendency is exactly that which developed in the General Assembly of the UN, though the reason here is perhaps more to fit in with the sessions of the national parliaments than to acquire increased political power by more permanent repesentation. There is, under Article 34, power to convene an extraordinary session with the agreement of the Committee of Ministers.

The Assembly has its own elastic committee structure. The Standing Committee meets in between and during sessions, preparing the agenda and co-ordinating the work of other committees. There are also general (or permanent) committees with a membership varying from 26 to 30 and covering matters such as Political Affairs, Economic Affairs and Development, Social and Health Questions, Legal Affairs, Culture and Education, Science and Technology, etc.; then there are ad hoc committees for special problems. These may all meet between sessions and thus provide continuity and preparation for the work of the Assembly.

The Assembly's relationship with the Committee of Ministers has been a somewhat uneasy one, for whilst the former demonstrated considerable initiative, the latter, whose recommendations to governments are essential for further progress of a given scheme, demonstrated conservatism and even apathy. The Statute contained little formal procedure for liaison between the two organs: Article 19 demanded only an annual written report from the Committee to the Assembly containing a statement of its activities. The Committee accepted a proposal by the Assembly in 1950 to refer matters not acceptable to the Committee back to the Assembly with a statement of reasons, but these have rarely been fully explanatory. Understanding has, however, been improved by the adoption of a further Assembly proposal that members of the Committee should appear in person before the Assembly, speaking either on their own behalf or on behalf of the entire Committee. Most important, however, was the creation in 1950 of the Joint Committee of up to 14 members, seven of them from the Assembly, in order to examine problems common to both organs; it is essentially a liaison committee. Even in this the Ministers showed little interest, and the Joint Committee now works most effectively at the "Deputy" level, with the Assembly putting written questions to the deputies for answer.

Undoubtedly a considerable feeling of frustration exists in the Assembly. This is manifest in various proposals for reform, all aiming at increased powers. Of these, two merit attention; the "La Malfa Proposals" whereby the Member governments would inform the Council of all projects with European implications and receive guidance on them, and the even more ambitious "Mackay Protocol" which aimed at entrusting the Council with the functions of OEEC and the Brussels Treaty Organisation[7] and to give to the Council effective legislative and executive powers with two parliamentary houses and power to legislate directly for Member States. This proposal really aimed at a degree of federation; it goes far beyond the kind of co-operation on which the Council is presently based and, like all other proposals for a general European Political Authority, seems beyond any prospect of realisation in the immediate future. Indeed, in a report on "The Function and Future of the Council of Europe" published by the Assembly in 1967 it is obvious that the Assembly desires the Council to move away from its earlier preoccupation with political unity and to concentrate on the social and technological fields, integrating much more closely with the technical Ministerial Conferences referred to below.

[7] See *post*, p. 178, for further proposals for rationalisation of European organisations.

This is not to minimise the value of the work already achieved by the Council of Europe. Quite apart from the production of a habit of co-operation and greater mutual understanding between the Member States, work of a more tangible nature had been accomplished. This work is seen in the conclusion of various conventions and, secondly, the sponsoring of "specialised conferences."

(c) *The European Conventions*

Over 100 conventions, agreements and protocols[8] have come into being, having successfully run the gamut of the Committee. Most important is the European Convention for the Protection of Human Rights and Fundamental Freedoms, concluded on November 4, 1950 and five Protocols. This really attempts to amplify the conditions of membership set out in Article 3 of the statute. It sets out a number of individual rights, establishes a Commission, to which there is a right of individual petition when a "defendant" State has accepted this optional clause, and a Court. This machinery will be considered in greater detail later.[9]

There are a number of conventions of a social character, including a "Social Charter."[10] There is a Cultural Convention[11] and various Conventions dealing with educational matters such as the equivalence of diplomas leading to admission to Universities, the Convention on Equivalence of Periods of Study and the Convention on the Academic Recognition of University Qualifications.[12] There are three patent conventions,[13] standardising the formalities for patent applications and providing a uniform system for their classification. There is a Convention on Establishment of December 13, 1955,[14] which attempts to secure general equality of treatment in matters like entry, residence, work and ownership of property in the signatory States for nationals of any

[8] Most texts are given in the successive *European Yearbooks.* For an up-to-date list see Council of Europe *Report on the Activities of the Council of Europe,* 1979–80, App. G.
[9] *Post,* Chap. 9, s. 1.
[10] See Ganshof van der Meersch, *Organisations Européennes* (1966), 377–381.
[11] *Ibid.* 394.
[12] December 11, 1953, December 19, 1954, December 15, 1956, and December 14, 1959; *European Treaty Series,* Nos. 15, 18 and 21.
[13] *Ibid.* Nos. 16 and 17.
[14] *Ibid.* No. 19.

other signatory State. There is also the Convention on the Peaceful Settlement of Disputes of April 25, 1957,[15] the Convention on Extradition of December 13, 1957 and on the Suppression of Terrorism, 1977.[16] There is the Agreement on the Movement of Persons of December 13, 1957,[17] which attempts to eliminate passports. There are also conventions dealing with the exchange of blood plasma, television films, compulsory insurance against civil liability in respect of motor vehicles, mutual assistance in crime detection, and the abolition of visas for refugees.[18]

(d) *The Specialised Conferences*

The Council of Europe, established as an organisation for co-operation merely, and having none of the powers of a federal or quasi-federal organisation, failed to satisfy certain States which were prepared to co-operate or possibly integrate in specified fields to an extent which meant the creation of an authority with greater powers. The acceptance of the Schuman Plan by the "Six" (France, W. Germany, Italy, Belgium, Netherlands, Luxembourg), and the consequent establishment of the European Coal and Steel Community,[19] whilst it did not take place as a "specialised authority" under the aegis of the Council of Europe, inspired the Assembly to propose a number of similar organisations with real powers in specific sectors of the European economy. During the years 1950 to 1952 proposals were made in various fields. In agriculture such proposals led to the creation of the Committee of Ministers of Agriculture in 1955, originally as a body of limited powers and within the framework of OECD rather than the Council of Europe in order to facilitate the participation of countries like Portugal and Switzerland which at that time belonged to OECD and not the Council. A European Conference of Ministers of Transport was established in 1953, independent of the Council but due to its initiative; similarly with the European Civil Aviation Conference, established in 1954 and linked with ICAO, and the 1963 Conference of Ministers of Science under

---

[15] *Ibid.* No. 23.
[16] *Ibid.* No. 24.
[17] *Ibid.* No. 25.
[18] For a useful summary of all the Conventions, see Ganshof van der Meersch, *op. cit.*, 245–403.
[19] See *post*, p. 199.

OECD auspices. There is also a European Space Agency (ESA) established in 1955, with its ministerial Council and committee structure.

However, five "conferences" directly under the aegis of the Council of Europe have been established: the Conference of Local and Regional Authorities, the European Parliamentary and Scientific Conference, the Conference of Ministers of Education, the Conference of European Ministers of Justice and the Ministerial Conference on the Environment.[20]

(e) *Relationships with other bodies*

The Council has no system of "specialised agencies" attached to it as does the UN. It does, however, have relationships with other international organisations with a view to co-ordination of their activities.

Agreements have been concluded with the UN,[21] the ILO, WHO, UNESCO, FAO and several European organisations, providing for reciprocal communication of matters of common interest, consultation, and attendance at meetings by observers; certain of the specialised agencies transmit their annual reports to the Council. Not unnaturally, relationships with the European organisations tend to be closer. With OECD the arrangements provided for permanent liaison committees and the economic reports of OECD provide the basis for the Council's debates on economic affairs. With Western-European Union, the Council has virtually taken over much of its cultural work and the Assembly of the Union is, by the treaty establishing the Union, to be composed of two-thirds of the members of the Consultative Assembly; thus the principle of *identity of membership* is adhered to and provides an effective safeguard against unnecessary overlapping.

The Council's relationship with ECSC was a problem of great importance, for some foresaw a danger of the Six breaking away

---

[20] These meet at irregular intervals, except for the first which is more formalised and has a "Charter" and permanent status under Art. 17 of the Council's Statute.

[21] See (1955) *Documents,* Dec. 337, Appendix III; the agreements are effected by exchange of letters between the respective Secretaries-General. Although no formal relationship exists between the Council of Europe and ICAO, the European Civil Aviation Conference stemmed from their joint initiative. See generally Golsong and Kiss, "Les accords entre le Conseil de l'Europe et d'autres organisations internationales," (1958) *Annuaire Français,* 477.

entirely from the Council in their march towards a more effective integration and, possibly, political federation. In order to prevent such a rift the Eden Plan of 1952 proposed that the Council should be remodelled so that its organs could serve as the institutions of the ECSC, the proposed EDC and any future, similar organisations; naturally, the organs would in such case be limited to the Six. The relationship eventually agreed to in the Protocol to the Treaty on Relations with the Council of Europe[22] was far less close; the organs remain distinct but the principle of identity of membership is adopted as a *desideratum* (not, therefore, obligatory), and provision was made for the transmission of reports to the Consultative Assembly, for joint meetings of the two Assemblies, of the High Authority and the Committee of Ministers, and the appearance of members of the High Authority before the Economic Committee of the Consultative Assembly.

No doubt the failure of the EDC plan and the consequent set-back to the idea of a European Political Community of the Six alleviated the problem of the relationship between the Six and the rest of the Council of Europe. The signature of the Rome Treaties in March 1957, establishing the European Economic Community (Common Market) and Euratom, posed the same kind of problem as did ECSC originally. What has so far been agreed is the partial identity of membership of the various parliamentary bodies. Moreover, the Consultative Assembly urged the creation of EFTA, the European Free Trade Area, as a counterpart to the Common Market and, therefore, a means of holding the entire body of States together.

II. ORGANISATIONS OF LIMITED COMPETENCE

1. The North Atlantic Treaty Organisation (NATO)
By 1948 concern in the West over the security of Western Europe had developed to the extent that the Brussels Treaty Organisation, established on March 17, 1948, by the United Kingdom, France, Belgium, Netherlands and Luxembourg, and purporting to be an organisation for collective self-defence under Article 51 of the Charter, was realised to be inadequate for the defence of Western Europe almost as soon as it was formed.

---

[22] 1 *European Yearbook*, 451.

Moreover its purpose of preventing a "renewal by Germany of an aggressive policy" was not the purpose for which effective defence was needed; eyes were on the Soviet Union, not Germany. The Berlin blockade and the Communist coup in Czechoslovakia in February 1948 increased the alarm and by June 1948 the Vandenberg Resolution was adopted by the U.S. Senate, authorising the government to associate the U.S.A. with alliances for defensive purposes. It had been clear for some time that security could not be guaranteed by the collective security machinery of the Security Council, and thus, in signing the North Atlantic Treaty on April 4, 1949,[23] the Western powers determined to create a regional security organisation capable of defending Western Europe and North America.

The treaty was originally signed by 12 States, including the U.S.A., Canada and Iceland; it lay open to other European States by invitation, and in 1952 Greece and Turkey also joined. The number was brought up to 15 in 1955 with the accession of W. Germany. The Organisation is not, therefore, strictly European; but it is so much the organisation for the security of Western Europe that the only sensible course is to treat it in the group of European institutions. Certain European States are not members because their adherence to a neutralist policy prevents their association with this alliance of the Western powers; Sweden, Switzerland, Finland and Austria are the obvious examples. Following a period of substantial disagreement between France and the remaining members, particularly over the United States/ United Kingdom control of the nuclear deterrent capacity of NATO, in March 1966 General de Gaulle notified the NATO members of France's decision to withdraw all French military personnel from the integrated commands, to require the removal from French territory of these commands and to refuse the common use of joint infrastructure undertakings on its territory. France has not, however, ceased to be a party to the NATO Treaty, so that the Treaty is unaffected.[23a]

Under the Treaty the Parties agree to "consult together, whenever, in the opinion of any of them, the territorial integrity, political independence or security of any of the Parties is

---

[23] (1949) 43 A.J.I.L. Supplement, 159.
[23a] See Stein and Carreau, "Law and Peaceful Change in a Subsystem: 'withdrawal' of France from NATO" (1968) 62 A.J.I.L. 577.

threatened" (Art. IV); as we shall see, the institutional forms are designed to bring about almost continuous consultation. The essence of the treaty, however, lies in Article V, in which the Parties agree that "an armed attack against one or more of them in Europe or North America shall be considered an attack against them all . . . ."; Europe and North America are more closely specified in Article VI, so that a geographical area is defined and, after the accession of Turkey and Greece, this was extended by a Protocol of October 17, 1951, to cover their territories. The obligation of each Party in the event of an armed attack on a Member within the area is to take forthwith, individually and in concert with the other Parties, "such action as it deems necessary." Technically, therefore, the commitment is a weak one,[24] for it is for each Party to decide on the form of assistance it will give. In practice, as we shall see, the system is far more centralised.

The brevity of the treaty on its institutional forms is extraordinary, for it mentions only a Council and a Defence Committee. This may have been a happy fault, because considerable constitutional changes occurred in 1951 and 1952 and organs have had to be created very much in the light of experience.

(a) *The Council*

This is the supreme organ, a political organ on which each Member (including France) is represented; it is to be so organised as to be able to meet "promptly at any time." In fact the task in hand called for almost continuous session, and, since Foreign Ministers are busy people, in 1950 Council Deputies were appointed to represent them. These were abolished in 1952 and now Members appoint permanent representatives to the NATO Council who have the same powers as Foreign Ministers. The Council has even met "at the summit," for example at the meetings of heads of government in December 1957.

The procedures of the Council are somewhat unusual. It has no voting procedure and in fact never takes a decision by a vote. Its aim is to secure unanimous agreement, and this illustrates the essential character of the Council as a forum for negotiation. Its meetings also bring out this same character, for they can be either

---

[24] The absence of a more concrete obligation is due to the difficulty of obligating the U.S.A. to take armed action when, constitutionally, a declaration of war is a matter for the Senate.

"normal" or "restricted" (with only one or two advisers present besides the representative) or even "informal" (only the permanent representatives, and with no agenda or records). Another unusual feature is that the Secretary-General is now the permanent Chairman of the Council.

The entirety of the other bodies is subject to the Council. These other bodies are part of either the "civil" organisation or the "military" organisation. It is best to treat the two separately, taking into account the reorganisation and relocation consequent upon the French partial withdrawal.

(b) *The "Civil" Organisation*

The Defence Committee, intended as a Committee of Defence Ministers to advise the Council on the implementation of Articles 3 and 5 of the Treaty, was absorbed into the Council itself in 1951. There being no other committees named in the Treaty, the Council simply uses the general power to create committees in Article 9; some of these are highly technical, but others are of wider competence and cover problems which are adequately indicated by their titles, such as the Committee of Political Advisers, the Committee of Economic Advisers, the Defence Planning Committee, the Defence Production Committee, the Civil Defence Committee, the Nuclear Defence Affairs Committee and, under it, the Nuclear Planning Group. All committees are purely advisory.

The Secretariat may also be included on the "civil" side.

(c) *The "Military" Organisation*

This, too, operates under the authority of the Council. It is headed by the Military Committee, as the supreme military authority of NATO and containing the Chiefs of Staff of all the Members (except France). They, like Foreign Ministers, are busy people and a Military Committee meets almost continuously in Washington on their behalf. The Military Committee's primary task is to give strategic direction to NATO.

Beneath the Military Committee, and responsible to it, are the Supreme Allied Commander in Europe (SACEUR), with his headquarters in Belgium and known as SHAPE. Since the Korean War there has been a great deal more centralisation, and the appointment of SACEUR dates from that time. Under his own immediate command is a vast network of air, sea and land commands, split into different regions for N. Europe, Central Europe, S. Europe, plus the separate naval commands of SACLANT (Atlantic) and CINCHAN (the English Channel). Details of this network can be studied in the official NATO publications.[25]

The extent to which co-operation has progressed, with joint training staff colleges, standardisation of weapons, the construction of NATO installations, pipelines, depots, airfields (the infrastructure programme) and the like now means that a Party is much more involved than the rather loose obligation in Article 5 suggests. Its defence programme and expenditure are examined yearly in the Annual Review, based on a searching questionnaire, and the Supreme Allied Commander makes recommendations directly to governments. Admittedly, there is no *legal* hindrance to a Party cutting down its defence programme or even withdrawing its forces from their NATO commitments, and this has been done by France; but it is now difficult for one Party to act in a way to which the rest are opposed. The "sanction" is political, not legal, and the forum for its application is the Council, not an international court.

There is little doubt of the success of NATO as a military alliance; the NATO powers have, in peacetime, co-operated to a degree which has never previously been attained by allies in wartime. This success has led to a movement to extend and expand the field of co-operation into a non-military side, in order to progress towards an "Atlantic Community." The prospects for this are uncertain, for, particularly since the French reversion to an acutely "sovereignty-conscious" policy, it may be doubted whether there are the political, economic, cultural and social ties to bind the Members in a more comprehensive organisation. It would always lack the "neutrals," and then OECD has handled most of the economic co-operation and, for many of the Members, the Council of Europe is a sufficient general political bond (as opposed to a pure alliance). However, the Suez adventure of 1956 proved a need for closer political consultation, and, after a report by the "Three Wise Men," the Council established a Committee of

---

[25] See *The North Atlantic Treaty Organisation*: Facts and Figures (1978). And note the creation in 1967 of the Standing Naval Force Atlantic, a multinational naval task force.

Political Advisers. There is, moreover, the rather extraordinary development of the NATO Parliamentary Conference, which first met in 1955 and now meets annually. This is a conference of parliamentarians from NATO countries, which makes recommendations to the Council; but it is quite "unofficial" and is nowhere mentioned in the constitutional texts. The Parliamentary Conference is nevertheless now well established as a consultative assembly and clearly indicates that NATO is something more than a military alliance.

2. Western European Union (WEU)[26]

The inadequacy of the Brussels Treaty Organisation for the defence of Western Europe has already been referred to; with the development of NATO the Brussels Treaty Organisation became virtually redundant. During the years 1949–54 it did attempt to develop activities in the social and cultural fields, although even these could well have been handled by the Council of Europe. In 1954, however, events transpired which brought the Brussels Treaty Organisation a new lease of life, albeit with an enlarged membership and a different title—Western European Union.

The French refusal to ratify EDC, combined with the NATO Council's decision that W.Germany should be re-armed and take her place in the Western system of collective security, brought about a need for some machinery to permit, but at the same time control, that participation. Thus a series of Protocols to the Brussels Treaty were signed in Paris on October 23, 1954,[27] transforming the Brussels Treaty Organisation so as to meet that need. Italy and W. Germany are added to the previous Brussels Members, and W. Germany also joins NATO and becomes free of the occupation régime. The WEU is expressed to last until at least 1998, unlike NATO which permits a Member to withdraw with one year's notice from 1969 onwards. It is, like NATO, an organisation for collective self-defence, based on the idea that an attack on one is an attack on all. However, the obligation to assist the immediate victim is, under Article 5, much stronger, for it contains no clause such as "such action as it deems necessary."

The first Protocol modified the treaty by deleting all reference to

[26] Members are Belgium, France, W. Germany, Italy, Luxembourg, Netherlands, and U.K.
[27] II *European Yearbook*, 313 *et seq.*

"renewal by Germany of a policy of aggression" and substituted the broader aim of "promoting the unity and encouraging the progressive integration of Europe." It went on to provide for close co-operation with NATO, for a Council of WEU and an Assembly.

The second Protocol set upper limits to the sizes of the forces which WEU Members can maintain on the Continent and provided for their command by the Supreme Allied Commander (SACEUR); in this lay the limitation on German re-armament. The third Protocol and its four Annexes bound W. Germany not to undertake the manufacture of certain weapons (atomic, chemical or biological, warships and strategic bombers, etc.). And the fourth Protocol set up an Agency for the Control of Armaments to ensure that the commitments in the third Protocol are observed. With this outline in mind, the institutions can now be examined.

(a) *The Council*

This consists of the Foreign Ministers of the Member States and is the executive body of the organisation; it is to be "so organised as to be able to exercise its functions continuously," hence it meets more frequently as a meeting of ambassadors resident in London, with an under-secretary from the U.K. Foreign Office and under the chairmanship of the Secretary-General and is then called the "Permanent Council." Its basic voting rule is unanimity, although for certain matters specified in the Protocols either a qualified or even a simple majority suffices: the simple majority rule is not confined to procedural matters and includes, for example, decisions on breaches of the agreements restricting the manufacture of certain armaments. The power to take decisions binding on governments, often by a majority, thus makes the Council a more powerful organ than the Council of OECD (which proceeds by unanimity) or the Committee of Ministers of the Council of Europe (which only makes recommendations to governments). The Council relies on NATO for information and advice of a military character. It reports annually to the Assembly but is not in any way controlled by it.

The Agency for the Control of Armaments is responsible to the Council, although subject to the general administrative control of the Secretary-General. This Agency receives reports from the

Members on their armaments position, and can carry out inspections and test checks to verify them[28]; although originally limited to government-owned defence establishments, by a convention of December 14, 1957, the system of inspection was extended to privately-owned establishments manufacturing arms. This convention not only defines the measures to be taken by Member States to enable the control system to operate effectively, it also provides for a Tribunal to protect private interests against unwarranted interference by the Agency.

Also under the Council is the Standing Armaments Committee, with the general task of co-ordinating the supply and standardisation of equipment to the national forces; it sits in Paris to enable liaison with NATO.

(b) *The Assembly*

This was established by Article 5 of Protocol I, providing merely that the Council shall report to it annually and that it shall consist of the representatives of the Members to the Consultative Assembly of the Council of Europe. Thus the "identity of membership" principle is established. Otherwise the treaty is silent, and it has been left to the Assembly itself to deal with practical matters like finance, privileges and immunities, procedure, committee structure, etc. It has now adopted a Charter and Rules of Procedure; the former provides:

"Art. I (a) The Assembly carries out the parliamentary functions arising from the application of the Brussels Treaty. In particular, the Assembly may proceed on any matters arising out of the Brussels Treaty and upon any matter submitted to the Assembly for an opinion by the Council.

(b) The Assembly shall determine its own Agenda in conformity with the provisions of paragraph (a) above and having due regard to the activities of other European organisations."

In one sense, therefore, its terms of reference exceed those of the Assembly of the Council of Europe, since defence matters are not excluded, although, presumably, the proviso will keep the

---

[28] The United Kingdom is excluded from the inspection system.

Assembly clear of matters such as human rights which are not specifically mentioned in the treaty and which the Council of Europe does deal with.

The Assembly meets twice yearly, mostly takes decisions by majority vote, and has its own committee structure[29]; it also holds ad hoc joint meetings with the Council to promote co-operation between the two bodies. It possesses its own Secretariat, distinct from that of the Council, and has a separate budget which can, however, be amended by the Council; if an amendment is more than 20 per cent. of any one subhead there is a provision for a joint meeting between the two organs. Provision is made for Ministers to be present at Assembly sittings as of right—and a Ministerial bench is provided—and these can be heard at their own request or that of the Assembly and there is also a right to submit written or oral questions to the Ministers; but these are the trappings of an "accountability" of the Ministers to the Assembly which does not in fact exist. A further "parliamentary" feature, with rather more substance, is the official recognition of political parties, such as one finds in Parliament of the European Communities.

Essentially this is a consultative organ, with no kind of control over the executive organ such as the European Parliamentary Assembly possesses over the Commission. Yet it can record its disagreement with the substance of the annual report by the Council. Moreover it can transmit resolutions directly to governments and it has an independent power of investigation—both powers lacking in the Consultative Assembly of the Council of Europe.

The chief importance of the Assembly lies in the fact that it is the only official parliamentary body with power to discuss the defence of Western Europe. One important sphere of activity disappeared with the abandonment of the proposal for an international régime for the Saar, an abandonment brought about by the vote of the plebiscite in 1955 for return to Germany. In its other activities there is considerable danger of overlap with the Council of Europe or OECD, and one might say that WEU is not necessary if the control activities could be handed over to NATO and the Council of Europe's Consultative Assembly entrusted with

[29] Committees include those on Defence Questions and Armaments; General Affairs; Budgetary Affairs and Administration; Rules of Procedure and Privileges. The number of representatives varies with each country.

the parliamentary functions in matters of defence.[30] However, the partial French withdrawal from NATO has tended to strengthen the arguments for retaining WEU. Moreover, WEU served the U.K. well in affording a forum which bridged the gap between Britain and the Communities of the Six. Yet the need for the bridge disappeared when the U.K. joined the EEC.

3. The Organisation for Economic Co-operation and Development (OECD)

It may be recalled that by a Convention of April 16, 1948,[31] OEEC was established to administer Marshal Aid, in conjunction with the Economic Co-operation Administration (ECA) established by the United States; the organisation was open to "any signatory European country" (Art. 25), although in fact it became very much a Western European Organisation since the U.S.S.R., Poland and Czechoslovakia declined to participate. Twelve years later, with the economic recovery of Europe virtually completed, the decision was taken to reconstitute the organisation as the Organisation for Economic Co-operation and Development. This reconstitution was accomplished by the treaty of December 14, 1960.[32]

The membership of OECD is wider than in OEEC; in Article 16 it is open of "any Government" by unanimous invitation of the Council, and Australia, New Zealand, Canada, Japan and the U.S.A. have become Members of OECD whereas they were only associate Members of OEEC.[33] To that extent it becomes

---

[30] On the problem of rationalisation of European institutions generally, see Robertson, *European Institutions* (1959), Chap. 10; Ball, *NATO and the European Movement* (1959), Chap. 12.

[31] 1 *European Yearbook*, 231.

[32] U.K. Treaty Series No. 21 (1962), Cmnd. 1646. For an excellent general commentary see Hahn, "Die Organisation für wirtschaftliche Zusammenarbeit und Entwicklung," (1962) 22 Z.f.a.ö.r.u.V. 49.

[33] The OEEC Convention made no reference to the possibility of associate membership, yet this became an established status. Moreover, Spain became a full member of OEEC only for agricultural questions from 1955 onwards, although gradually from 1958 it began to participate in other activities; Yugoslavia, originally an "observer," had full participation in the European Productivity Agency from 1957 onwards, as did Finland in the Maritime Transport Committee. The laxity of this practice on membership is probably unprecedented, and the relationship with Yugoslavia and Finland is being continued.

189

somewhat artificial to treat OECD within the "European Orga-nisations," but its links with OEEC and its predominantly European character justify this course. One striking feature of OECD is the provision for representation (though clearly not as a "Member") in the work of the Organisation of the European Communities. This is provided for in Article 13 of the Convention and in Supplementary Protocol No. 1, and the Commission of the three European Communities will be represented in the Council and subsidiary organs but, presumably, without the right to vote.

The aims of the new organisation are necessarily changed to reflect the change in purpose from one of restoration of the European economy to maintenance of economic growth and the promotion of economic development both within and without the territories of the Members themselves. As now defined they are "to achieve the highest sustainable economic growth and employ-ment and a rising standard of living, in Member countries . . . and thus to contribute to the development of the world economy"; to "contribute to sound economic expansion in Member as well as non-member countries . . . "; and "to contribute to the expansion of world trade on a multilateral, non-discriminatory basis" (Art.1). The aims are therefore no longer European, but worldwide. To this end the Members undertake joint and several obligations with regard to efficient use of economic resources, development of these resources and research, the pursuit of policies to achieve growth and stability without endangering the economy of others, the pursuit of efforts to minimise trade barriers and payments difficulties, and contribution to general economic development in Member and non-Member countries.

The organisational structure established for these purposes is essentially a medium for co-operation between Members; the French desire in 1948 for a "stronger" institution was opposed by the United Kingdom and, thus, there was, and still is, nothing of a "supra-national"element and action rests with the Members on a voluntary basis.

(a) *The Council*
This, the principal organ, comprises all the Members and is "the body from which all acts of the Organisation derive" (Art. 7). Representatives meet at the level of Ministers or of Permanent

Representatives, the latter being the more frequent, and the powers of the Council do not vary. Under Article 6 decisions and recommendations are by unanimity,[34] unless otherwise agreed for special cases, and it is expressly provided that the abstention of any Member will not invalidate decisions or prevent them from becoming binding on other Members; for this reason the unanimity rule has never developed into a "veto," for States in opposition to a resolution have simply abstained. Each State has but one vote.

The expressions of will take the form of "decisions" which are binding upon those voting for them, once they have complied with their own constitutional procedures[35] and "recommendations" (Arts. 5 and 6). The fact that no Member can be bound *against* his will deprives the Council of any "supra-national" character. It would be a mistake, however, to underestimate the power the Council had under OEEC or probably now actually possesses. For example, in connection with its programme for the liberalisation of trade, the Council adopted on August 18, 1950, a Code of Liberalisation[36] containing the obligations of Members with respect to the elimination of discrimination in intra-European trade. Admittedly no Member was bound to concur in this decision of the Council, but, once adopted, it gave to the Council considerable powers to decide whether a particular Member's actions were consistent with its obligations under the code and the Member was bound to comply with that decision. The revised code of 1962 on Liberalisation of Capital Movements does, however, appear to be somewhat weaker in the obligations it imposes.[37]

---

[34] Art. 6 is a general voting article for the Organisation, not merely the Council. However, there will be certain exceptions; the Council and Board of Management of the European Monetary Agreement and the Committee on Invisible Transactions and other Technical Committees will not use the unanimity rule (see *post*, p. 192).

[35] Art. 6 (3).

[36] III *European Yearbook,* 255. The Preparatory Committee charged with examining the problems of transition from OEEC to OECD recommended that both the Code of Liberalisation and the Capital Movements Code would have to be re-drafted because of U.S.A. and Canadian participation (*The Organisation for Economic Co-operation and Development* (Bluebook) published by OECD, 1960, Chap. 4). The new edition of the Code of Liberalisation of Capital Movements was published in May 1962, following the decision of the Council of December 12, 1961.

[37] Art. 15 (e) of the Code.

(b) *The Executive Committee*

This organ was specifically provided for under OEEC, but under OECD Article 9 merely provided that the Council "may" establish an Executive Committee together with such other subsidiary organs as may be required. In fact it has been so established by Council resolution of October 30, 1961, with a membership of 14, for a period of two years in the first instance. Under OEEC its practice was to meet weekly, as opposed to three or four times a month for the Council at the Permanent Representative level and two or three times a year at the Ministerial level. It thus carries on the day-to-day business of the Organisation and acts under the instructions of the Council. It acts as a clearing-agency for Council business in that it pre-examines questions to be submitted to the Council and may make suggestions to it. It has power of decision only when such power is expressly delegated to it by the Council.

(c) *The Committees*

Under OEEC the Committees were generally plenary (except for the Overseas Territory Committee) and fell into two categories: the "horizontal" committees were engaged in the general study of economic and financial problems common to all Members, whilst the "vertical" committees dealt with specific products or services such as Coal, Iron and Steel, or Maritime Transport; the "vertical" committees tended to be staffed by experts from industry or internal government departments as opposed to personnel drawn from the permanent delegations to OEEC established in Paris.

The Preparatory Committee of OECD made detailed, but not exhaustive, recommendations[38] on the desirable committee structure of OECD. Those to be established were the Economic Policy Committee (which looks like being the "main body of the Organisation in matters of economic policy," attended by senior officials), the Economic and Development Review Committee, the Development Assistance Committee (with power to make recommendations to Members direct), the Technical Co-operation Committee, Trade Committee, Payments Committee, Committee on Agriculture and Fisheries, Committee for Invisible Transactions,[39] and other committees dealing with Insurance,

[38] See "Bluebook," Part I.
[39] With a composition to be defined in the Code of Liberalisation.

Energy and Industry, Tourism, Maritime Transport, Manpower, Fiscal Matters, Scientific and Technical Personnel and Scientific Research, Consumer Policies, Environment, Restrictive Business Practices, and Multinational Enterprises. To some extent, therefore, the "horizontal" and "vertical" distinction is still discernable although it appears that there will be less expert representation than before; the only committee which is clearly designed as a committee of experts is the Group of Experts on Restrictive Business Practices. OECD has in fact over 200 specialised committees and working groups, so that it is pre-eminently a functional organisation which collects and collates data and studies questions of common concern to the members which, by and large, adhere to similar economic and social systems.

(d) *The Secretariat*

OECD has its own Secretariat at the headquarters in Paris, essentially similar to the UN Secretariat. It tends to employ, because of the rather specialised, economic character of the work, more personnel on secondment from industry, the universities and government departments. It is headed by a Secretary-General with somewhat lesser powers than those of the UN Secretary-General,[40] but with the important power of submitting his own proposals to the Council or any other body of the Organisation. OECD also has its own administrative tribunal for disputes between the staff of the Secretariat and the Organisation; this same tribunal has competence over disputes between the European Organisation for Nuclear Research and its Staff.[41]

(e) *De-centralisation of the functions of the Organisation*

The variety of the economic problems with which OEEC concerned itself meant that considerable de-centralisation was essential, involving the setting up of a number of operating agencies, distinct from the OEEC's own organs but related to them in varying degree.

---

[40] However, the former restriction in the old Art. 18 (a) that senior staff appointments require approval by the Council is omitted in the new Art. 11. Moreover, the S.G. has an increased status since he will now preside over the Council when it meets as Permanent Representatives.
[41] See *post*, p. 318.

One of the objectives of OEEC was to achieve a "multilateral system of payments." In October 1948 the Council accepted an Agreement for Intra-European Payments and Compensation giving limited drawing rights and using the Bank for International Settlements (B.I.S.) in Basle as a clearing agency; a second agreement in September 1949 put these drawing rights on a multilateral, as opposed to a bilateral, basis. However, these schemes were still too rigid and tended to induce an artificial level of trade between debtor and creditor countries. Therefore, in September 1950, the Council agreed on the terms of a European Payments Union. This was to be a mechanism for the regionally multilateral settlements of accounts, so that all debts and credits were cancelled out until, at the end of each month, each country was left with a single credit or debit towards EPU; total immediate settlement was not necessary provided the country remained within its allocated "quota." The whole system was managed by a Managing Board of seven experts appointed by the Council; it took decisions by a majority. Clearly the *raison d'être* of the system was the absence of free convertibility of European currencies, so that the EPU was always envisaged as a temporary device to liberalise trade until such time as free convertibility was achieved. Hence, when a majority of OEEC countries declared their currencies convertible, the EPU was wound up and replaced by the European Monetary Agreement, on December 29, 1958.[42] Under this agreement payments are made on a fully convertible basis and credit (which was automatic under EPU within quota limits) has to be obtained by application to the Managing Board—identical to the EPU Managing Board—whose decisions are binding. This system, as we have seen, is retained in OECD.

A second operating agency called the European Productivity Agency was set up by the Council of OEEC in June 1953[43] in order to further the aim of developing production, stated in Article 2 of the OEEC Convention. Under OECD the European Productivity

---

[42] Text in vII *European Yearbook*, 267. For a useful description of the structure and working of the Agreement, see Elkin, "The European Monetary Agreement: its structure and working," vII *European Yearbook,* 148. For the texts of Supplementary Protocol No. 3 of January 15, 1960, and the amendments made by decision of the Council of OEEC on July 20, 1959, and December 18, 1959, see Command Papers, Miscellaneous No. 2 (1960), Cmnd. 959, or "Bluebook," paras. 38–40.

[43] For text of decision of Council, see 3 *European Yearbook*, 205.

Agency has been discontinued and its functions assigned to the Technical Assistance Committee or, when a research project is concerned, to the Committee for Scientific Research.

A third agency was the Ministerial Committee on Agriculture and Food,[44] established within the framework of OEEC in January 1955. This could take action within the competence of the Ministers of Agriculture represented on the Committee and, on matters outside their competence, make recommendations to the Council of OEEC. It operated in a field which is one of the most difficult in which to secure agreement on really effective co-ordination—as the negotiations on the EFTA treaty and on Britain's entry into the European Economic Community testify. The Preparatory Committee of OECD recommended a Ministerial Committee on Agriculture which will continue the Organisation's activities.[45]

A fourth agency is the Nuclear Energy Agency,[46] first established in December 1957 by the Council of OEEC and equipped with similar functions to Euratom which the Six had set up in the previous March. Obviously the creation of this agency was a direct response to this move by the Six, an attempt, as it were, to provide on a general OEEC level the same facilities as the Six were providing for themselves, although, admittedly, OEEC had been anxious about co-operation in this field since at least 1954. The Agency is operated by the Council's own Steering Committee for Nuclear Energy, which had been created in 1956. The Preparatory Committee of OECD recommended that ENEA should be retained within the organisation in its existing form.[47] The Council also approved a Convention on the Establishment of a Security Control in the Field of Nuclear Energy, which was signed on December 20, 1957,[48] in order to ensure the restriction of the joint

[44] This replaced the European Conference on the Organisation of Agricultural Markets which met first in 1953 and from which certain countries had hoped a "Green Pool" would emerge comparable to the Coal and Steel Pool (ECSC).
[45] "Bluebook," paras. 21–26.
[46] Not to be confused with the European Organisation for Nuclear Research (CERN), established by treaty of July 1, 1953, for the purpose of collaboration in research and consisting of a Council and Director; this is linked very loosely with UNESCO. The statute of the Agency can be found in IV *European Yearbook,* 273. The 1957 Treaty was replaced by a Treaty of 1972 on the adhesion of Japan.
[47] "Bluebook," para. 28.
[48] V *European Yearbook,* 283; and see *post,* p. 203, for contrast with Euratom.

enterprises envisaged, and their products, to non-military purposes. The Convention gives considerable powers of inspection and control to a Control Bureau, composed of one representative from each State, and establishes a Tribunal to adjudicate on questions of default. Another unusual venture in this field, which is worthy of mention, was the formation under a treaty[49] of an international company, Eurochemic, by 12 OEEC countries in the same month; this company built and operated a plant processing irradiated fuel until it ceased operations in 1974.

A further offshoot from OEEC, in the sense that it began from the initiative of the OEEC Council, is the European Conference of Ministers of Transport, created by a Protocol signed at Brussels on October 17, 1953. The relationship between OEEC and this body is being continued by OECD.[50] Its chief aim is the rationalisation of the European transport system, and it possesses a Council, consisting of the Ministers and a Committee of Deputies to represent them more frequently. Many of the decisions reached are left to be put into effect by the individual action of the Ministers (Art. 9); in such cases as require a formal international agreement, the Ministers have to equip themselves with the necessary "full powers." It is something of a counterpart to the European Civil Aviation Conference set up by the Council of Europe's initiative.

Another autonomous body, the International Energy Agency (IEA) was set up by the Council in 1974[51] to develop co-operation on energy questions following the oil crisis of 1973. Its programme commits the 20 members to sharing oil in emergencies, reducing their dependency on oil imports and developing relations with oil-producing countries.

An assessment of the work of OEEC, and even a proper description of its activities, is more a task for the economist than for the lawyer. By and large, general opinion seems to regard its career as a successful one. Without pretending that this success has been directly attributable to its institutional form, it is apparent that certain institutional techniques have developed which in fact made the organisation more effective than a literal reading of its

---

[49] *Ibid.* 303.
[50] "Bluebook," para. 131.
[51] Agreement of November 18, 1974: 14 I.L.M. (1975).

powers would suggest it could be. It was an organisation based wholly on voluntary co-operation by States, yet, by the use of small groups of technical experts, by the technique of question- naire, analysis of the replies of States and "confrontation" within the committees, that is to say cross-examination of State repre- sentatives on those replies, the Organisation was able to impose a general standard of concurrence in its activities which is indeed impressive. It was a bold Member State which pursued an economic policy at odds with the rest.

It is clearly apparent that OECD will continue the "confronta- tion" technique, particularly in the main Trade Committee,[52] so that OECD will remain technically an organisation for voluntary co-operation but practically much stronger.

4. The European Free Trade Association[53] (EFTA)

The essential characteristic of a Free Trade Area is that, whilst it aims at a gradual elimination of protective customs duties and quota restrictions between the Members, it permits each Member to fix its own external tariff *vis-à-vis* non-Member States: the degree of sovereignty surrendered is therefore minimised. In contrast, a Customs Union—or "Common Market"—envisages a common external tariff and, correspondingly, a need to develop a common commercial policy towards the outside world. This difference produces many consequences, for a Customs Union will tend to induce by regulation free movement of goods, labour and capital and to attempt a harmonisation of social and economic policies so as to bring about an equalisation of the cost elements in production. The Customs Union is therefore moving towards complete economic integration, involving a far more substantial surrender of sovereignty.

EFTA was established by the Convention of January 4, 1960[54] as a counterpart to the EEC. Its essential objective is the promotion of a sustained expansion of economic activity, fair competition in trade and the avoidance of significant disparity between Members in the conditions of supply of raw materials

---

[52] "Bluebook," para. 62.
[53] A good, non-technical, account is given in *The European Free Trade Association* (1980) published by the EFTA Secretariat. Members are Austria, Iceland, Norway, Portugal, Sweden, Switzerland and, as associate member, Finland.
[54] U.K. *Treaty Series* No. 30 (1960) Cmnd. 1026.

within the Area (Art. 2). Tariff and quota restrictions in practice apply largely to manufactured goods. Agricultural goods, fish and other marine products are largely excluded and, in these spheres, it is anticipated that the countries exporting these products will find compensation in bilateral agreements on agricultural products (Art. 27) or that an expansion of trade in fish and other marine products will occur so as to offset the loss of tariffs on imported manufactures (Art. 28). The EFTA members each have bilateral free trade agreements with the EEC, and a free trade system for industrial products between the EEC and EFTA was achieved in 1977.

The organisational structure of EFTA is extremely simple. The Council is the plenary supreme organ on which all Members[55] have one vote: discussions or recommendations usually require unanimity although an abstention does not act as a veto. The Council may "legislate" to the extent that it can by decision amend the Convention in many particulars or enact new treaty-law in furtherance of EFTA's objectives. The Council can, by a majority vote of four, regulate in detail such matters as are provided for in general terms by the Convention. Thus, any member can veto new, substantive obligations but not mere decisions implementing the existing obligations. The Council also adjudicates on disputes between Members, but may (and, if a State requests must) refer the matter to the Examining Committees provided for in Article 33: these are "ad hoc" and lend a certain objectivity to proceedings in which some members of the Council will be interested parties. The Council adopts a recommendation by majority and, if not accepted and the Council finds there is a breach of obligation, may ultimately authorise any Member State to suspend obligations under the Convention owed to the recalcitrant Member.[56] In broad outline, the procedure follows the GATT procedure.[57] A further feature of the Council is that it operates at two levels: the Ministerial level (infrequently) and the Heads of Permanent Delegations level (frequently). This "lower"

---

[55] Originally 7 Members and 1 Associate Member (Finland). Note that Portugal, the least developed, has a special treatment prescribed in Annex G to the Treaty.

[56] For detailed discussion of the complaints procedure see Lambrinidis, *The Structure, Function and Law of a Free Trade Area* (1965) Chap. XI.

[57] *Ante*, p. 150. But note that the GATT "sanction" is not confined to cases where there has been a breach of the GATT provisions.

level thus substitutes for what in other organisations might be termed an "Executive Board."

The Council has set up various subsidiary committees under its general power to establish subsidiary organs (Art. 32 (3)): to date there are committees on Customs, Budget, Economic Development, Economics, Agriculture and Fisheries and also a Committee of Trade Experts and a Consultative Committee.

There is also a permanent Secretariat, based on no more than the Council's power "to make arrangements for the secretariat services" (Art. 34 (b)), but consisting of persons on loan from Governments rather than career international civil servants.

5. THE EUROPEAN COMMUNITIES: the European Coal and Steel Community (ECSC), the European Economic Community (EEC) and the European Atomic Energy Community (Euratom)

(a) *The Aims of the Communities*

The six States of Europe—France, Germany, Italy, Netherlands, Belgium and Luxembourg—to whom neither the Council of Europe nor OEEC seemed ambitious enough sought means whereby a closer economic (and possibly, at a later stage, political) integration might be achieved. The first positive step was achieved by the creation of ECSC by the Treaty of April 18, 1951.[58] This had as its objective the creation of a single market for coal, iron and steel, involving the elimination of all barriers to free, competitive trading such as tariff barriers, quota systems, all forms of price discrimination (including those in transport), restrictive agreements and cartels. ECSC has virtually achieved its objective of creating a single market: its current problems relate to the diminishing use of coal as a source of power, growing State intervention in support of coal, problems of investment, and the need for revision of the 1951 Treaty. A second, but abortive, step was the attempt to create a European Defence Community (EDC).[59] A third step was successfully taken, however, by the conclusion of the Rome Treaties in March 1957, for these created two new institutions—EEC and Euratom.

---

[58] I *European Yearbook*, 359.
[59] *Ante*, p. 185.

The essential aim of EEC was to establish by three stages, over a transitional 12 to 15-year period, a "common market" in which all internal tariffs, quota restrictions, etc., were to be eliminated and a uniform external tariff created. Incidental to this main aim was the promotion of the free movement of labour and capital, the adoption of a common transport policy, control of cartels, the establishment of a European Investment Bank[60] and a European Social Fund; this last was to contribute to the raising of the standard of living of workers and to assist in the retraining and resettlement of workers made unemployed by conversion of their industries. Agricultural commodities were included in the scheme, but under a special régime envisaging price control and the gradual evolution of a common agricultural policy. In practice, achievements have fallen short of aims. A customs union for all *industrial* products, and therefore a common external tariff, came into effect on July 1, 1968. On the same date free trade for nearly all agricultural products came into effect. But the Council has so far only decided upon a programme of measures moving towards a common transport policy and there is as yet very little progress on a common commercial policy and very little on the establishment of a true European capital market. Free movement of persons, and freedom of establishment, has made much greater progress.[61]

Overseas territories were associated with EEC by decision of the Council, thus enabling any Member to invest in and trade in such territories on the same conditions as the parent country. With the advent of independence for many of these overseas territories a more formal Association Agreement was concluded at Yaoundé in 1963 and revised in 1969 with 18 African States, presumably under Article 238 of the Rome Treaty. The Arusha Agreement with East African States was concluded in 1969. The Yaoundé Convention and the Arusha Agreement were replaced by the Lomé Convention of 1975 between the European Communities and 46 African, Caribbean and Pacific States (the ACP States). It accommodates the States newly-associated with the Communities as a result of the U.K.'s accession and has since been extended

---

[60] This has a capital of $2,025 million, its own Board of Governors, Board of Directors and Management Committee; it will give or guarantee loans to members or to public or private enterprises to assist investment projects.
[61] For a useful summary of progress see *Tenth General Report on the Activities of the Community,* June 1967.

even wider, applying to 58 developing countries. A new Lomé II Convention of October 31, 1979[62] provides for tariff-free entry into the Community of ACP exports, without reciprocity, and a scheme to stabilise export earnings from commodities produced by the ACP States called STABEX. Both the associated territories and the Associated States benefit from the first and second Development Funds.[63] Protocol 22 of the Act of Accession of 1973 offers some 20 independent Commonwealth countries an opportunity of association with the Community.

Although the creation of a customs union lay at the root of the ideas behind the Rome Treaty, it was apparent that it did not create such a union. The French, particularly, regarded it as premature to take that step at that stage. However, the treaty did not prevent particular Members from establishing a customs union *inter se*, and this has in fact been done in the treaty instituting the Benelux Economic Union of February 3, 1958.[64] This treaty also set up a Committee of Ministers, a Consultative Interparliamentary Council, a Council of the Economic Union, a College of Arbitrators, an Economic and Social Advisory Council, and various committees. A Court of Justice was added in 1965, consisting of nine judges, whose task is to promote uniformity in the application of legal rules specified either in conventions or in decisions of the Committee of Ministers. The Court has both a contentious and an advisory jurisdiction. The College of Arbitrators must suspend its own function of settling differences in any case where a matter of interpretation of such rules arises, pending a decision of the Court.[65] The real executive power here lies with the Committee of Ministers, which takes decisions by unanimity, so that, whilst economically more advanced, the Economic Union is constitutionally not so advanced as EEC or the ECSC.

The European Atomic Energy Community is very much the twin of the EEC, although confined to a narrower field of operation. The aim of the Community, as defined in Article 1 of the treaty signed on March 25, 1957,[66] is to contribute to the

---

[62] See 16 C.M.L. Rev. (1976) 315–334; 17 C.M.L. Rev. (1980) 415–436.
[63] At January 1, 1968 the First and Second Funds had expended $581,250,000 and $461,887,000 respectively.
[64] v *European Yearbook,* 167. A description of Benelux can be found in Van der Meersch, *Organisations Européennes* (1966), 419–451.
[65] xiii *European Yearbook,* 259.
[66] v *European Yearbook,* 455.

raising of the standard of living in the Member States and to the development of commercial exchanges with other countries by creating the conditions necessary for the speedy establishment and growth of nuclear industries. Its functions (Art. 2) include the creation within one year of a common market for specialised materials and equipment, investment, development of research and dissemination of information, establishing standards for the protection of public health, the supply of ores and nuclear fuels, ownership of special fissionable materials,[67] co-operation with other countries and organisations for the peaceful use of nuclear energy, and security control.

Certain of the powers may be mentioned by way of illustration of the extent to which the Community has gone beyond mere co-operation and adopted measures unknown in international organisation outside the European Community. The Community has a right of access to installations, it may discuss investment programmes directly with individuals or firms, it has the exclusive right to purchase nuclear materials from outside the Community and an option to purchase all materials produced within it, and has an exclusive right to export such materials. The Council of the Community may, by unanimous vote, fix prices. Special fissile materials, whether produced in or imported by Member States, automatically become the property of the Community. The Council may adopt basic standards for health protection by a qualified majority, which become binding on all the States whose duty it is to enact the legislation necessary to enforce them; in cases of urgency, the Commission may issue directives to the States, requiring them to take all measures necessary to protect these basic health standards.

The control system, designed to ensure that nuclear materials are used for the intended purpose and not, for example, for military purposes, is a good example of the extent of the powers given to the Community. This system is set out in Chapter VIII of the treaty, not in a separate convention as is the case with the European Nuclear Energy Agency; and it has obviously formed a model from which the ENEA convention is drawn. The actual

---

[67] An idea harking back to the proposal for international ownership in the Baruch plan placed before the UN Atomic Energy Commission in 1946 by the U.S.A.; this had proved unacceptable on a world-wide basis. The special materials are defined in the treaty as plutonium, U-233 and U-235.

ownership of the special fissionable materials (Art. 86), and the right of option over other nuclear materials produced within or imported into the Community, are powers which ENEA does not have and clearly enhance the degree of control. Otherwise the two systems compare closely. There is a right in the Commission to demand the production of operating records and the deposit of any excess of special fissionable materials with the Agency (the supply organ of Euratom). The Commission may also send inspectors into the territories of the States, and these shall have access at all times "to all places and data and to any person who by reason of his occupation deals with materials, equipment or facilities . . . " (Art. 81). Not that these are to be random, surprise visits, for the Commission is obliged to enter into consultation with the State, prior to the first visit of any inspector, in order to arrange for all future visits. However, any opposition to a visit by the State may be met by an application to the President of the Court of Justice of Euratom for a warrant ordering the inspection, or the Commission may itself issue such a direction. The penalties for infringements of the treaty or of the conditions under which supplies or facilities are authorised range from a warning to the suspension of supplies and withdrawal of materials already delivered; there is also, in Euratom, but not in the ENEA, power in the Commission to take over, jointly with the State, the actual administration of a defaulting enterprise.

The overlap with the ENEA convention, to which most of the Euratom States are parties, is obvious; it is met by a provision in the ENEA convention that the control functions of ENEA will be carried out in the territories of those States who are Members of Euratom by the agencies of Euratom, by delegation from the ENEA Control Bureau.

These two control systems illustrate the point made at the beginning of this Second Part, namely that co-operation to a greater degree can often be achieved on a regional basis where it has proved impossible on a universal basis. It will be recalled that the United Nations has not so far been able to introduce a control system for disarmament and the control of atomic energy which is acceptable to East and West. The future of co-operation via Euratom is not, however, a matter of complete certainty. French proposals in 1968 looked towards a reduction rather than an expansion of its activities.

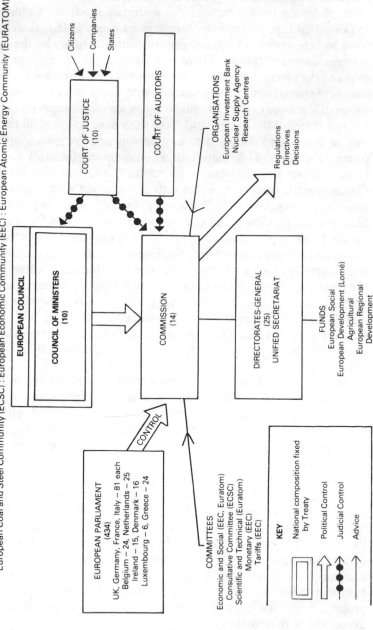

THE EUROPEAN COMMUNITIES

European Coal and Steel Community (ECSC) : European Economic Community (EEC) : European Atomic Energy Community (EURATOM)

EUROPEAN COUNCIL

COUNCIL OF MINISTERS
(10)

COURT OF JUSTICE
(10)

COURT OF AUDITORS

Citizens
Companies
States

ORGANISATIONS
European Investment Bank
Nuclear Supply Agency
Research Centres

COMMISSION
(14)

Regulations
Directives
Decisions

DIRECTORATES-GENERAL
(25)
UNIFIED SECRETARIAT

FUNDS
European Social
European Development (Lomé)
Agricultural
European Regional
Development

EUROPEAN PARLIAMENT
(434)
UK, Germany, France, Italy – 81 each
Belgium – 24, Netherlands – 25
Ireland – 15, Denmark – 16
Luxembourg – 6, Greece – 24

CONTROL

COMMITTEES
Economic and Social (EEC, Euratom)
Consultative Committee (ECSC)
Scientific and Technical (Euratom)
Monetary (EEC)
Tariffs (EEC)

KEY

National composition fixed
by Treaty

Political Control

Judicial Control

Advice

204

Euratom is, therefore, entrusted with far wider powers than the European Nuclear Energy Agency established by the Council of OEEC in December 1957[68]; the latter is, true to the OECD pattern, essentially an organisation for voluntary co-operation with no kind of "supra-national" element. Euratom must also be distinguished from CERN, the European Organisation for Nuclear Research which originated from UNESCO's initiative and is based on a treaty of July 1, 1953.[69] This is, equally, an organisation through which a number of European States, including all but Luxembourg of the Six, have collaborated to conduct research of a kind which is too costly for individual States to contemplate; its research programme is based on two big machines called a "synchro-cyclotron" and a "proton-synchroton."

(a) *The Institutions of the Communities*
Although the three communities were established as separate organisations, based upon separate treaties, their institutional structure was almost uniform and this, together with the obvious need to co-ordinate the overall economic planning of the three, suggested the desirability of common organs.

Accordingly, simultaneously with the conclusion of the Rome Treaties establishing EEC and Euratom, a "Convention relating to certain Institutions common to the European Communities"[70] was concluded providing a single Court to replace the ECSC Court. The same Convention also provided for one Assembly for all three organisations, to be called the European Parliamentary Assembly. However, it was not until July 1, 1967 that it became possible to merge the executive organs of the three communities, namely the three Councils into one Council and the three Commissions (actually called "High Authority" in ECSC) into one Commission.[71] The Treaty of Accession of January 22, 1972 whereby the U.K., Ireland and Denmark became members caused

---

[68] See *ante*, p. 195.
[69] 1 *European Yearbook*, 487–507.
[70] *European Yearbook*, 587.
[71] See Treaty establishing a single Council and a single Commission of the European Communities, XIII *European Yearbook*, 461: the Treaty is dated April 8, 1965. For commentary see Houben, "The Merger of the European Communities," 3 *C.M.L. Rev.* (1965–66), 37; Weil, "The Merger of the Institutions of the European Communities," (1967) 61 A.J.I.L. 57.

the various bodies to be enlarged. So, too, with the accession of Greece by Treaty of May 28, 1979.

The European Parliament. This is now the one parliamentary organ for the ECSC, the EEC and Euratom, and meets in ordinary session a dozen times a year in Luxembourg or Strasbourg. It is, naturally, modelled on the previous Common Assembly of the ECSC, but there are two important differences. First, the number of representatives has been increased. The numbers now stand at 81 for Italy, West Germany, United Kingdom and France, 24 for Belgium and Greece, 25 for the Netherlands, 15 for Ireland and 16 for Denmark and 6 for Luxembourg, giving a total of 434. Alignments of the representatives are less and less on a national basis. There are in fact several officially recognised political parties in the Assembly which cut across national alignments: the Christian Democrats, Socialists, Liberals, European Democrats, Progressive Democrats, Communists and a few independents.

The second notable difference is that, whereas in the ECSC treaty direct universal suffrage as a means of election of the Assembly was an alternative to appointment by national parliaments which governments could adopt at their option, Article 138 of the new treaty provides that "The Assembly shall draw up proposals for elections by direct universal suffrage in accordance with a uniform procedure in all Member States." Accordingly, on May 7, 1960, the Assembly approved a proposed Convention[72] whereby 165 million people of the Six will elect their representatives to the Assembly by direct universal suffrage. But it was not until 1978 that arrangements for direct elections were finally concluded[73]; the first elections took place in 1979.

Although the Parliament has no legislative powers, it does, however, possess a power of control over the Commission which is unique in international organisations and is reminiscent of the power of a national parliament to force the resignation of a government. This lies in the right of the Parliament to force the resignation of the entire Commission by a vote of censure, passed in open ballot by two-thirds of the members voting and a simple majority of the total membership of the Parliament. So far, this right has never been used, and control is exercised by less dramatic methods.

[72] (1960) *Journal Officiel des Communautés Européennes*, 834.
[73] *Ibid.*, (1976), No. L. 278.

The fact that the Commission is answerable to Parliament is crucial, for this helps to maintain the independence of the Commission from the Council. The Commission's obligation to reply to written or oral questions from members of Parliament is part of the technique of control. Another part is the requirement that the Commission should consult Parliament on the more important of the Commission's proposals before the Council takes its decision.

There are also signs that the Parliament is striving for even greater powers. When it was decided to give the Community financial resources of its own, the Member States agreed to increase Parliament's budgetary powers. Parliament now has the last word on all expenditure that is not the automatic or virtually automatic result of the Treaty or Community legislation. Parliament's budgetary powers therefore cover the institutions' administrative costs and most operational expenditure, representing some 21 per cent. of the budget. The remainder of the budget is made up of "necessary" expenditure which the Treaty or the previous acts of the Community make unavoidable. Basically, this is expenditure on the Common Agricultural Policy, most of it for price support. Parliament can propose modifications to this category. Provided they do not increase the total amount of expenditure such modifications are deemed to be accepted unless the Council rejects them by a qualified majority. Lastly, Parliament has the right to reject the budget as a whole.

The shift to direct elections has re-inforced the Assembly's claim to wider powers. The argument is, however, more complex. It lies, essentially, in the proposition that, as the Communities exercise more power, so the national governments necessarily exercise less: there occurs a "transfer" of powers. From this it would follow, or so the argument goes, that the democratically-elected representatives of the people must exercise the same control over these governmental powers via the European Parliament as they did in national Parliaments when the powers lay with national governments.

The Council of Ministers. This common organ consists of representatives of each Member State, with equality of representation—one representative each: the Minister attending will change according to whether the meeting is discussing EEC, ECSC or Euratom business. Meetings, to be held on the initiative of the

President (an office rotating among the members at six-monthly intervals) or upon the request of a member or of the Commission, will normally be preceded by a preparatory meeting of the Committee of Permanent Representatives to prepare the work of the Council.

The voting procedure of the Council depends upon the Treaty under which it acts and on the specific procedure required for the specific action taken. The voting procedure of the Council under the ECSC Treaty was always complex. Its most important decisions require unanimity, but many important decisions, particularly those reached in the later stages of the transitional period,[74] were to be made by a qualified majority, with the votes weighted as follows: Italy, Germany, United Kingdom and France, 10 each; Netherlands, Greece and Belgium, five each; Denmark and Ireland, three each; Luxembourg, two. A "qualified majority" is constituted by 45 votes, and, in the case of a decision on a proposal by the Commission, any 45 will suffice. In other cases the 45 votes must include those of at least six Members. A decision which constitutes an amendment of a proposal by the Commission must be taken unanimously, otherwise the proposal must be referred back to the Commission; it is in this provision that considerable power lies for the Commission, for its views will prevail unless there is unanimity in the Council, or the Council is prepared to leave the problem unsolved. In all cases when the Treaty does not require either unanimity or a qualified majority, a simple majority suffices.

A special problem posed by the merger was that the concepts of "unanimous vote" and "qualified majority" as used in Article 78 of the ECSC Treaty (relating to the budget) did not correspond to the analogous provisions of the Rome Treaties. Therefore, the merger Treaty has amended Article 28 of the ESCC Treaty which deals with voting procedures, so as to produce conformity. Abstention is no bar to a decision requiring unanimity and the term "qualified majority" is now uniform.

It must also be noted that, under the EEC treaty, as part of the transition from the second to the third stage on January 1, 1966 the changes in voting in the Council gave rise to serious disputes

---

[74] For example, the reduction of internal tariffs in the third stage (Art. 14 (2) (c)); the decision on a common agricultural policy after the second stage (Art. 43 (2)).

between France and the other five Members. A French six-months boycott of the Council ended after a compromise was reached in the following terms:

> "Where, in the case of decisions which may be taken by majority vote on a proposal of the Commission, very important interests of one or more partners are at stake, the members of the Council will endeavour, within a reasonable time, to reach solutions which can be adopted by all the members of the Council while respecting their mutual interests and those of the Community, in accordance with Article 2 of the Treaty."[75]

The Six agreed to disagree on what would happen in the event of a failure to reach agreement. However, the chances of a real impasse were lessened by the adoption of seven points under the heading "Co-operation between the Council and the Commission," all of which are designed to minimise the risk of the Commission presenting a proposal to which one Member has violent objections. The whole controversy was symptomatic of the growing French emphasis on sovereignty and a distrust of a powerful Commission.

So far as the actual powers of the Council are concerned, these of course vary with each Treaty, but in effect the Council expresses the political will of the Members and exercises the legislative or regulatory function. In general terms, the Council has lesser powers (and the Commission correspondingly more) under the ECSC Treaty.[76] However, even under this Treaty certain decisions of the Commission require the concurrence of the Council, for example the restriction of exports when a serious shortage of certain products occurs[77]; the Council is itself empowered to take decisions on a number of matters, for example the amendment of the powers of the Commission or of the Treaty generally.[78] It is also the Council which instructs the Commission on negotiations

---

[75] Text of official Communiqué in 3 *C.M.L. Rev.* (1965–66), 469.

[76] But see the suggestion by Reuter that in practice the powers of the High Authority proved less, and those of the Council of Ministers more, than the treaty envisaged: *Law and Contemporary Problems: European Regional Communities* (1961) 26, No. 3, "Juridical and Institutional Aspects of the European Regional Communities," 381 at 387.

[77] Art. 59 (5); see further examples in Arts. 55 (2), 56 (b), 58 (i), 68 (5), 74.

[78] Arts. 95, 96; see further examples in Arts. 9, 29, 32, 58 (3), 78 (b), 81.

with third States relating to economic relations with the Community.

The functions of the Council under the EEC Treaty are "to ensure the co-ordination of the general economic policies of the Member States" and "to have power to take decisions" (Art. 145). Hence the subordinate position of the Commission to the Council, and the contrast with the ECSC Treaty is clear. The matters to which these decisions relate are scattered throughout the Treaty, and it is usual for such decisions to be based upon proposals made by the Commission.

The Commission. The new unified Commission is to be composed of 14 members "chosen on the grounds of their general competence and whose independence is beyond doubt" (Art. 10 of the Merger Treaty). Though nationals of the Members (although not more than two from any one State), they retain their essential character as individuals acting only in the interest of the Communities as such. They are to be chosen "by mutual agreement" between the Members and hold office for four years, although this period is renewable.

The Commission acts by simple majority vote. Its functions vary from treaty to treaty.

Under the ECSC treaty the Commission takes three kinds of decisions: "decisions" which shall be binding in all their details; "recommendations" which shall be binding so far as the objectives they specify are concerned, but which leave the States or enterprises to which they are directed free to choose the appropriate means for attaining these objectives; and "opinions" which are merely persuasive. It is in the decision-making powers, which directly bind the enterprises without any need for intervention by governments, that the core of the Commission's "supranational"[79] character is to be found.

Moreover, the Commission has power to enforce its decisions by the imposition of fines and penalties on enterprises (Arts. 50, 54, 59) and, if these are not paid, the Commission may withhold sums which it is itself due to pay to the enterprises (Art. 9), and this power has already been frequently used. Apart from this right of withholding sums, the Commission must rely on enforcement of its

[79] This term, used in the ECSC Treaty, no longer figures in the 1965 Merger Treaty, presumably due to French sensitivity on this point.

decisions via the executive agencies of the Member States, for it possesses no executive arm of its own. Hence, under Article 92, "decisions . . . imposing financial obligations on enterprises are executory. They shall be enforced on the territory of Member States through the legal procedures in effect in each of these States . . . ." The Member States are themselves bound "to take all general and specific measures which will assure the execution of their obligations under the decisions and recommendations of the institutions of the Community . . . " (Art. 86). The Commission is, therefore, not a federal authority equipped with its own powers of direct enforcement; but the ability to take decisions binding on States, and on enterprises within these States without the intervention of the States, is clearly a hall-mark of a "supranational" authority.

Not surprisingly, checks have been provided against a misuse or abuse of these considerable powers by the Commission. The Commission is answerable for its action to the Parliament which, in the last resort, can bring about the collective resignation of the Commission by a vote of censure. There is also the Court of the Communities, which has power to adjudicate on the legality of the action of the Commission under the treaty. Less stringent, but more often used in practice, are the checks involved in the role of the Council as a "harmoniser" of the action of the Commission and of the Member governments; and also in the existence of the Consultative Committee of ECSC[80] which the Commission may consult.

A final point, worth mentioning because it is a feature rarely seen in international organisations, is that the financing of the ESCC Community is not by subscriptions to a budget by the governments, but by the Commission, which has the power to borrow or to place a levy on the production of coal and steel which is paid by enterprises direct to the Commission (Arts. 49, 78). The revenues of the EEC and Euratom stem from national contribu-

---

[80] This is not a main organ or "institution," but an advisory body designated to assist the Commission. The members, which number between 60 and 84, are appointed by the Council and shall include producers, workers, consumers and dealers in equal numbers. They act in a purely individual capacity and are intended to present the Commission with a sounding-board of general opinion through the Community. It appears, however, that the experiment is not very successful and only the trade unionists meet systematically in a group which cuts across national loyalties.

tions although in 1970 the Council decided that as from 1975 the budget should be financed entirely from the Communities' own resources. These resources consist of import levies on agricultural produce and customs duties and, in addition, a fraction of the VAT charged in each Member State. The Merger Treaty, of course, has rationalised the financial provisions of the three treaties.[81] There will be a common budget, but *excluding* the operational expenditures (and the corresponding revenues from levies) of ECSC because of this "self-financing" feature.

Under the EEC and Euratom treaties the powers of the Commission are more limited than those under the ECSC treaty, and responsibility for achieving the aims of the treaty is in fact shared with other organs of the Community, particularly the Council. The Commission will more frequently be called upon to "formulate recommendations or opinions" and "participate in the preparation of acts of the Council and of the Assembly" (Art. 155). The Commission does have a limited power of decision, by simple majority, in certain matters delegated to it by the Treaty; but, all in all, the more important decisions rest with the Council and it is for the Commission to assist in carrying them out. Robertson concludes that "the supranational element is therefore lacking from the powers of the Commission."[82]

The Commission reports annually on the work of the Community to the Assembly, and the same principle of parliamentary control is seen in the power of the Parliament to force the collective resignation of the Commission by a vote of censure, requiring a two-thirds majority.

Under the EEC and Euratom Treaties there exists an advisory body to the Commission, the Economic and Social Committee. This is a consultative committee which, rather like the Consultative Committee of the ECSC, is to represent professional, trade union and similar interests. The 156 members (Big Four 24 each, Belgium, Greece and the Netherlands 12 each, Denmark and Ireland 9, Luxembourg 6) are appointed by the Council, acting unanimously and after consultation with the Commission. Con-

---

[81] Note, in particular, that the EEC budget procedure now applies to all three communities. It is the Council which adopts the budget after consultation with the Assembly. Previously, under ECSC, this power rested with the Committee of Presidents, a body somewhat independent of the Member States.

[82] *European Institutions*, p. 158.

sultation with the Committee is obligatory in certain matters, such as formulating rules for the free movement of workers (Art. 49), otherwise optional. Whether this Committee, twice the size of its fellow in the ECSC, has proved more effective than its fellow is doubtful.

The Commission will also have under its direction some 25 General Directorates, covering all the functions of the three executives, and embracing a common administration or civil service. This has required uniform staff regulations and uniformity of privileges and immunities: the latter has already been provided for in a new Protocol annexed to the Merger Treaty.

The ultimate benefits from the merger should be considerable and the Commission's primary task will be to prepare a single Treaty effecting a real merger of the three communities. What is somewhat in doubt is how far, given the present French attitudes which oppose the "supra-national" tendencies inherent in the Community treaties and the present call by the U.K. for renegotiation of the terms of accession, the Communities will develop in the dynamic manner anticipated in the pre-Gaullist era. Whatever else may be said, the European Communities will not lack interest.

The European Council. The strengthening of the Communities, their enlargement and the extension of political co-operation made the reinforcing of existing structures imperative.

The personal intervention of the Heads of Government in the Community process became a major development. Their so-called summit meetings were often required to take decisions which came to be regarded as the major guidelines for the development of the Community. In answer to the evident need for more frequent consultation at the highest level, it was decided at the summit meeting in Paris in December 1974 to institutionalize the meetings.[83] The *European Council* brings together Heads of State or Government, the Foreign Ministers and the President and a Vice-President of the Commission. They meet three times a year, generally in the capital of the member state which currently exercises the presidency of the Council of Ministers. They provide an opportunity for dialogue in an informal atmosphere.

The Court of Auditors. The Court of Auditors was set up by the

---

[83] See R.H. Lauwaars, *The European Council,* 14 CML Rev. 25–44 (1977).

second Budget Treaty of 1975[84] and held its constituent meeting in Luxembourg on October 25, 1977. The Court takes over from the EEC and Euratom Audit Board and from the ECSC Auditor as the body in charge of external auditing of the Community's budget and the ECSC's operational budget; the internal audit is still a matter for the financial controller of each institution. The members of the Court, one from each state, are appointed for a term of six years by the Council acting unanimously after consulting Parliament.

The Court examines the accounts of all revenue and expenditure of the Community and any body created by the Community, and draws up a report on its work at the end of each financial year. The Court has the right to submit observations on specific questions on its own initiative, and may deliver opinions at the request of an institution.

The Court has more authority than its predecessors. Not only is it a permanent institution with its own staff, but Parliament has shown its intent to make the most of the opportunities offered by the Court in order to re-inforce its own control over the Community budget.

The Court of Justice. This will be dealt with in greater detail in a later chapter.[85] It may be noted at this juncture, however, that rather than have separate courts for each of the three organisations of the Community of the Six, it was decided to have a single court to replace the ECSC Court and also serve the EEC and Euratom. The "Convention relating to certain Institutions common to the European Communities,"[86] concluded at the same time as the EEC and Euratom treaties, provides for this and introduces certain amendments to the ECSC treaty to make this possible.

[84] Treaty amending certain financial provisions of the treaties establishing the EEC and of the treaty establishing a single council and a single commission of the EC, Brussels, July 22, 1975, article 28.
[85] *Post*, Chap. 9, s. II.
[86] v *European Yearbook*, 587.

CHAPTER 7

THE AMERICAS, THE MIDDLE-EAST, ASIA AND THE FAR EAST, EASTERN EUROPE AND AFRICA

1. THE AMERICAS

1. The Organisation of American States (OAS)

(a) *Origins*

THE historical development of the OAS is in itself a sufficiently good illustration of varying kinds of co-operation between States to be worth a brief outline. The International Union of American Republics, formed in 1890, was not an organisation in the modern sense of the term at all, but simply a series of conferences designed to promote commerce and peaceful settlement of disputes; it was assisted by a Commercial Bureau which came to be called the "Pan-American Union."

By 1906 wider aims were accepted, and policies were determined by a plenary governing board, but these aims still remained non-military and largely non-political. Even after the First World War, whilst the series of Inter-American Conferences continued, the unilateral character of the Monroe Doctrine, by which the U.S.A. had established a hegemony over the Western Hemisphere, prevented any real political co-operation from developing. With the change to a "good neighbour policy," the U.S.A. at the Montevideo Conference of 1933 accepted the principle of non-intervention in the affairs of other American States and at Buenos Aires in 1936[1] accepted the principle of consultation between the American States as an alternative to unilateral United States action on matters affecting the peace of the continent.[2] Thus the principle of equality, and consequently, prospects for co-operation, began to emerge. In 1938, at the Lima Conference, a Meeting of Foreign Ministers was established as a procedure for such consultation, and use was made of this organ to make various

---

[1] Convention on Rights and Duties of States, Art. 8; (1934) 28 A.J.I.L., Suppl. 75.
[2] Convention for the Maintenance, Preservation and Re-establishment of Peace; (1937) 31 A.J.I.L., Suppl. 53.

215

affirmations of common policy during the early stages of the Second World War.

After the War, at the Mexico City Conference in 1945, the Act of Chapultepec reaffirmed the basic postulate upon which the security system had developed, namely, that an attack against any one of the American States constituted aggression against all, and resolved to give the Inter-American system a permanent charter or constitution. Since the Act of Chapultepec was in the form of a "declaration," it was subsequently incorporated in treaty form (so far as the security system was concerned) in the Rio Treaty of 1947, properly termed the Inter-American Treaty of Reciprocal Assistance,[3] a treaty which gave definitive form to the security system and established an Organ of Consultation, a consultative organ of Foreign Ministers. The charter or constitution came in the following year, in 1948, with the Pack of Bogotá,[4] establishing the Organisation of American States.

Meanwhile, at the San Francisco Conference the American States had combined to introduce alterations to the Dumbarton Oaks proposals, so that the UN Charter as it finally emerged contained not only the present Article 51, which was designed to ensure that the security system envisaged in the Act of Chapultepec could operate, but also a comprehensive Chapter VIII on Regional Arrangements which catered for the regional pacific settlement procedures which had for long been an essential part of the inter-American system.

The present decade has seen significant development of the Organisation. In 1961 the Charter of Punta del Este created the "Alliance for Progress," intended to give economic activities greater emphasis. Progress under this programme has not been striking. Indeed, general dissatisfaction with the structure and functioning of the OAS led to a series of Special Inter-American Conferences in 1964, 1965 and 1967 which produced significant amendments to the OAS Charter.[5] Dissatisfaction has continued and, in 1973, the Assembly called for a complete re-structuring of the organisation.

---

[3] *Ibid.* (1949) 43 A.J.I.L., Suppl. 53 and see 1975 amendments in (1975) 14 I.L.M. 1122.
[4] *Ibid.* (1952) 46 A.J.I.L., Suppl. 43. It came into effect on December 13, 1951.
[5] (1967) 6 I.L.M. 310: Protocol of Buenos Aires, February 27, 1967.

STRUCTURE OF THE
ORGANIZATION OF AMERICAN STATES

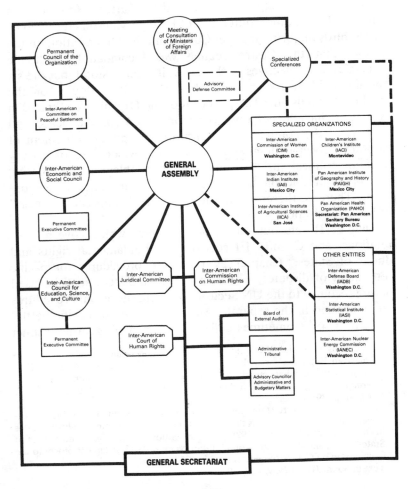

(b) *Aims and purposes*

The Bogotá Charter describes the Organisation of American States as a "regional agency" within the United Nations (Art. 1), membership of which is open to all American States.[6] However, the Act of Washington of 1964 established a procedure for admission requiring a two-thirds vote of the Council and excluding from membership any political entity whose territory is subject to litigation with an extracontinental country until the dispute is ended: this procedure has been subsequently embodied in the 1967 Protocol of Amendment. Whilst Members can withdraw, there is no provision for expulsion under the Charter. However, on January 31, 1962, the Conference of Foreign Ministers resolved by a two-thirds majority to expel Cuba from the Organisation on the ground that the Castro régime was incompatible with the principles and objectives of the OAS; it is understood that the six abstaining Members abstained because of their doubts on the legality of expulsion.[7] The purposes of the Organisation, stated in Article 4, include not only common action for the peace and security of the continent, and ensuring the pacific settlement of disputes between Members, but also the wider ones of solving common political, juridical and economic problems and promoting by co-operative action their economic, social and cultural development. There is, therefore, no doubt of the "comprehensiveness" of the Organisation.

Chapter II sets out the basic principles which govern their relations, and Chapter III sets out the fundamental rights and duties of States.[8] Chapter IV relates to procedures for pacific settlement of disputes, which, it is contemplated, shall be used before recourse to the UN Security Council; the actual procedures are contained in the separate American Treaty of Pacific Settlement of 1948[9] (sometimes called the Pact of Bogotá as distinct

---

[6] Canada has never joined, although the term "American States" rather than "American Republics" was chosen to allow for its joining. See Anglin, "U.S. opposition to Canadian membership in the Pan-American Union," (1961) 15 *International Organisation*, 1. Trinidad and Tobago were admitted in 1967.

[7] See *post*, p. 393.

[8] To some extent a re-statement of principles embodied in previous inter-American agreements such as the Convention on the Duties and Rights of States in the Event of Civil Strife, 1928; the Convention on the Rights and Duties of States, 1933; and the Protocol on Non-intervention 1936. A later Protocol to the Convention on Civil Strife was signed in 1957.

[9] Text in Sohn, *World Law*, p. 1059.

from the Charter of Bogotá). This provides for good offices and mediation, investigation and conciliation, arbitration, and judicial settlement by the International Court of Justice. However, this treaty has never entered into force and the Council has in practice developed its own techniques of peaceful settlement, using the Inter-American Peace Committee. Significantly, under the 1967 amendments, a considerable emphasis is placed on pacific settlement and it becomes a major function of the proposed Permanent Council.

Chapter V, on collective security, consists of but two brief articles which virtually incorporate the Rio Treaty, so it is to that treaty that one must turn for a more detailed appreciation of the system of collective security. The treaty is based upon the premiss that "an armed attack by any State against a State Party shall be considered as an attack against all the State Parties,"[10] thus giving rise to the right of individual and collective self-defence under Article 51 of the UN Charter. When such an attack occurs either within the region described in Article 4 or within the territory of an American State, the obligation on all Members to assist the victim arises automatically; in all other cases, as where the attack is outside that area or the aggression[11] does not take the form of an armed attack, the obligation is merely one of consultation. In all cases there is no obligation on a Member to use armed force except with its consent (Art. 23). For characterising action as aggression and for consultation and agreement on measures to be taken an Organ of Consultation was established, a consultative body of all the Foreign Ministers; these functions are now formally assumed under the Bogotá Charter by the Meeting of Consultation of Foreign Ministers.

Chapters VI, VII and VIII deal respectively with Economic, Social and Cultural standards.

(c) *Organs*

(i)*The General Assembly.* This is nominally the "supreme organ," a plenary body on which each State has one vote and which meets infrequently, although "Special" Conferences have

---

[10] Art. 3. For further detail see Kunz, "The Inter-American Treaty of Reciprocal Assistance," (1948) 42 A.J.I.L. 117.

[11] Article 9, as amended in 1975, adopts the General Assembly's definition of aggression in resol. 3314 (XXIX).

been called frequently in recent years. "It decides the general action and policy of the Organisation and determines the structure and function of its Organs, and has the authority to consider any matter relating to friendly relations among the American States" (Art. 33). Its terms of reference could, therefore, scarcely be wider.

(ii) *The Meeting of Consultation of Ministers of Foreign Affairs.* This serves as the Organ of Consultation under the Rio Treaty, so that, as one might expect, its task is to "consider problems of an urgent nature" (Art. 39). But, in addition, it has tended to serve as the "supreme organ," exercising broad powers more properly ascribed to the Conference. A meeting can be convened by a majority of the Council (see below) at the request of any one Member. However, a meeting is obligatory, and without delay, in the event of an armed attack within the territory of an American State or the region defined in Article 4. The convening of the Meeting of Consultation in its capacity as the Organ of Consultation has occurred less frequently than might be supposed, due to the way in which the Council has solved most of the disputes without finding it necessary to convene the Organ of Consultation. However, when in 1960 the Foreign Ministers were convened by the Council to deal with the Venezuelan complaint against the Dominican Republic, this was the sixth time it had been so convened; it was also the first time sanctions had ever been decided on, in this case taking the form of calling for a severance of diplomatic relations with the Dominican Republic by all OAS Members, the imposition of an arms embargo and further economic sanctions as necessary. A seventh meeting in 1960 virtually condemned Cuba for accepting the promise of Soviet military protection against a possible U.S. attack, and, as already mentioned, in January 1962 the Meeting voted to suspend Cuba from membership and to both establish an arms embargo and consider the desirability of extending the embargo to other items of strategic importance. In 1964 these sanctions against Cuba were extended to cover a severance of diplomatic and consular relations, a general trade boycott and sea transportation; in June 1967 the twelfth meeting of Ministers of Foreign Affairs recommended members to blackball vessels trading with Cuba. As discussed earlier, these "sanctions" raise a difficult problem of relationship with the Security Council. However, the new Article 8 as revised in 1975 explicitly allows the Organ of Consultation to adopt sanctions, including the use of armed force.

There is an Advisory Defence Committee to advise on problems of military co-operation, meeting concurrently with the Meetings of Foreign Ministers when defence against aggression is involved, or at other times when requested by the Meeting of Foreign Ministers or two-thirds of the Member governments. The only permanent defence organ is the Inter-American Defence Board, established in 1942, which has been continued and acts as the organ of preparation for collective self-defence and also serves as the secretariat for the Committee.

There is no kind of joint command and, compared with the NATO system, the collective defence machinery is extremely rudimentary. One suspects that the Latin-American Members are not so far convinced of the necessity for development of this military side of the OAS. Indeed, whilst an Inter-American Peace Force was created in 1965 during the Dominican crisis, the discussion on constitutional amendment between 1965–1967 saw strong opposition to the idea of giving any permanence to such an institution, and none was established.

(iii) *The Permanent Council.* This, too, is a plenary body, at ambassadorial level, which is subordinate to the previous two organs. It is, in effect, the continuation of the old governing board. It supervises the secretariat, the Pan-American Union, co-ordinates the activities of the American specialised conferences and organisations and concludes agreements with them, promotes collaboration with the UN and other international organisations, fixes the budget quotas and formulates the statutes of its own subsidiary organs, the Inter-American Economic and Social Council,[12] the Inter-American Council of Jurists[13] and the Inter-American Cultural Council, all plenary bodies.[14] In June 1949 the Council established a permanent mixed commission of six members, three from the Council and three from the Economic and Social Council to ensure close collaboration, a step which

---

[12] This is the only one of the three subsidiary organs meeting continuously; it has its own technical assistance programme and co-ordinates with ECLA.

[13] A kind of regional International Law Commission; its counterpart is the Afro-Asian Legal Consultative Committee.

[14] But they are in turn select committees which are of limited composition, such as the Juridical Committee and the Committee for Cultural Action.

suggests that these subsidiary organs have more autonomy than is usually the case.

In addition to these named organs of a semi-autonomous character, the Council has the power to create its own committees; examples have been the General Committee, Permanent Committee on Inter-American Conferences, Permanent Committee on Inter-American Organisations, Committee on the Organs of the Council and their Statutes, Committee on Finances, and the Committee on Dependent Territories (concerned with expediting the disappearance of the last traces of "colonialism" in the Americas).

The Council also has important political functions. These consist of functions assigned to it under the Rio Treaty, whereby it "shall serve provisionally as the Organ of Consultation when the circumstances contemplated in Article 43 of this Charter arise" (Art. 52, Bogotá Charter). In practice this gives it considerable powers except in those situations where a meeting of the Meeting of Foreign Ministers is obligatory; in all other situations it may virtually constitute itself the provisional organ of consultation when a request for consultation is made (under Article 6 of the Rio Treaty, for example). In practice it has often been able itself to settle disputes without even summoning the actual Meeting of Foreign Ministers; for example, during the Dominican crisis in 1965 it was the Council which assumed a continuing responsibility, with the Meeting of Ministers of Foreign Affairs convening only intermittently, and in 1964 the Council dealt with the Panama/ U.S. dispute exclusively. The Council's work in the area of political settlement is of great importance. In matters of fact-finding and investigation it has frequently relied upon the Inter-American Peace Committee, first established in 1940, with the same composition as the Council. Under its earlier Statutes the powers of investigation of this Committee did not even require the consent of both parties. However, an amendment in 1956 introduced the requirement of consent and much reduced the Committee's powers.[15] On occasions the Council has set up ad hoc conciliation missions, such as the 5-man peace mission sent to the Dominican Republic in 1965.

[15] For a survey of the Inter-American Peace Committee's activities see *The Inter-American System* (1966), 82–104.

The Council has also placed increasing importance on its economic work. The Inter-American Economic and Social Council (IA-ECOSOC) is a subsidiary organ of the Council and became the central organ of the Alliance for Progress. However, a detailed sub-structure was required and a Committee of eight Members (CIAP) was established to function between the annual IA-ECOSOC meetings. Unhappily, this was never given any executive role of *deciding* upon the allocation of funds under the Alliance, due to United States opposition, and its power is limited to recommendations. The Alliance has its own Special Fund and there is also the Inter-American Development Bank (1959), a separate institution. The IDB, the OAS and ECLA all participate in a Tripartite Committee on Co-ordination. This complex of economic institutions under, or related to, the OAS has failed to satisfy the economic aspiration of the OAS. The decision of the Chiefs of State at the Punta del Este meeting in April 1967 to establish a Latin-American Common Market by 1970[16] will have far-reaching effects upon both structures and policies within the OAS.

Under the 1967 Amendments, this single Council was replaced by three Councils: The Permanent Council, as a standing political organ and with the new Inter-American Committee on Peaceful Settlement subordinate to it; the IA-ECOSOC with its own permanent executive committee; and a new Council for Education, Science and Culture, also with a permanent executive committee. The three Councils will be plenary and equal in status, although the Permanent Council, as the political body and serving as preparatory organ to the meetings of the new Assembly, will be *primus inter pares.*

(iv)*The General Secretariat.* This is described as "the central and permanent organ of the Organisation of American States and the General Secretariat of the Organisation" (Art. 78). This is located in Washington and headed by a Secretary-General who is elected by the Council and who may participate in any of the organs, but without the right to vote.

The role of the Union is the customary role of any international secretariat, and Articles 89 and 90 safeguard its independence by

[16] Text in Dept. State Bull. No. 1453, May 1967, 712. This decision is not yet implemented.

223

imposing obligations on personnel not to seek or receive outside instructions and on States not to give them.

(v) *The Specialised Conferences.* These are envisaged for "special technical matters or to develop specific aspects of inter-American co-operation" (Art. 93); they can be convened by the Conference, the Meeting of Consultation, or the Council. The programme and regulations for the conferences will be prepared either by the organs of the Council or by the "Specialised Organisations." They have been held on a variety of matters such as Copyright, Travel, Cartography, and Highways, Education and Agriculture.

(vi) *The Specialised Organisations.* In an attempt to co-ordinate the activities of the various intergovernmental, technical organisations operating in the western hemisphere, the Bogotá Charter envisaged a kind of relationship between the Organisation of American States and these "specialised organisations" roughly comparable to that between the UN and the specialised agencies. The specialised organisations enjoy the fullest technical autonomy (Art. 97), but submit to the Council reports on their work and on their budgets. Agreements can be made between the Council and the specialised organisations for transmission of budgets for approval and even the collection of contributions by the Pan-American Union (Arts. 53, 99).

The organisations now brought into relationship with the OAS are: the Pan-American Institute of Geography and History; the Pan-American Health Organisation (whose bureau is the regional office for WHO); the Inter-American Indian Institute; the Inter-American Institute of Agricultural Sciences; the Inter-American Childrens Institute; and the Inter-American Commission of Women.

The Organisation of American States thus appears as the most comprehensive of the regional organisations outside Europe. It is perhaps more impressive structurally than in practice, for its achievements do not really compare with those in the European sphere. The frequent internal conflicts between the various Members of OAS have done little to demonstrate the political unity necessary for further political integration, and, whilst most of these conflicts have been satisfactorily dealt with under the settlement procedures of the Meeting of Consultation of Foreign Ministers, the Council (and the Inter-American Peace Committee), the Guatemalan and Cuban cases show a far less satisfactory outcome. Yet, currently, though there is no trace of "supra-nationalism," steps are being taken which mirror the European experiment.

The Inter-American Commission on Human Rights has existed since 1959, and its Statute was strengthened in 1966 and 1967. Then, in 1969, the Convention on Human Rights was adopted and the IACHR became a principal organ of the OAS, with power to receive individual complaints about violations of human rights, to make recommendations to member States, and also to make reports to the Conference or the Meeting of Consultation on the situation in particular countries. It has seven members, elected in a purely personal capacity.

A further development occurred in 1979, when a Court of Human Rights was established, comprising seven judges.[17] But, unlike its European counterpart, this Court does not make binding decisions. Moreover, its relations with the Commission are different, for there is no appeal from the Commission to the Court.

2. The Organisation of Central American States (ODECA)

This is, in a sense, a regional organisation within a regional organisation. Established under a Charter signed in 1951,[18] the organisation embraced the five States of Costa Rica, El Salvador, Guatemala, Honduras and Nicaragua.[19] Its early history was not impressive but in December 1962 the new San Salvador Charter was signed,[20] entering into effect in March 1965. This attempted to revitalise the organisation and, whilst it is in no real sense a "supra-national" organisation,[21] it has been re-structured to give increased effectiveness.

The "supreme organ" remains the Meeting of Heads of State, meeting irregularly, just as the Conference of Ministers of Foreign

---

[17] (1980) 19 I.L.M. 1458. The American Convention on Human Rights is given in (1970) 9 I.L.M. 673: it is in force but not for the U.S.A.

[18] (1952) 4 *Annals of the OAS,* 352–355.

[19] Panama, though not a member, is an Observer and by a Protocol of 1966 secured an actual right of participation in certain organs.

[20] Text in *The Inter-American System* (1966), 480.

[21] Although certain provisions give the Executive Council and the Economic Council limited law-making and "decision-taking" powers reminiscent of the European Communities.

Affairs, meeting annually or extraordinarily, remains the "principle organ": voting on substantive questions is by unanimity. However, a new Executive Council has been established as a "permanent organ," with weekly meetings at the seat in Salvador attended by Ministers of Foreign Affairs or their representatives: this is the core of the attempts to revitalise the organisation and the Executive Council "is to direct and co-ordinate the policy of the Organisation" (Art. 9).

There is also a Legislative Council comprising three representatives from each national legislature and designed to advise on legislative matters and to study possibilities for the unification of municipal law: it meets annually, votes by majority and obviously reflects the European experiment with legislative assemblies in the Council of Europe and the European Community. It may well become the embryonic parliament of a true Central American federation.

There is also a new Central American Court of Justice. It will be recalled that its predecessor, founded in 1907 with compulsory jurisdiction and procedural capacity for individuals, ended in 1918. The new Court is far less ambitious. It meets when necessary and includes the "Presidents of the Judicial Power" of each Member and it has the two limited functions of deciding disputes between States (with jurisdiction based on consent) and rendering opinions on projects for unification of law when asked by the Conference of Foreign Ministers or the Executive Council. There are also a Central American Economic Council, a Cultural and Educational Council and a Council for Central American Defense; all these are "Ministerial" Councils.

The new Charter also has a specific "non-interference" in matters of domestic jurisdiction clause (Art. 24) and, in the same article, a clause safeguarding the rights of each State as a member of the UN and of the OAS.

3. The Central American Common Market (CACM)

The Treaty of Managua of December 13, 1960[22]—The General Treaty for Central American Economic Integration—was to a large extent born out of frustration with ODECA and the belief that by concentrating on the economic sphere more impressive

---

[22] Text in *Instruments Relating to the Economic Integration of Latin-America* (1968), 23.

progress could be made. The experience is not uncommon: the emergence of the European Communities out of frustration with the Council of Europe and OEEC, or of the African regional "Common Markets" out of frustration with the OAU is a comparable development.

The CACM aimed at a fully established Common Market in five years as well as a customs union. The Organisation was, however, virtually wrecked by the hostilities between El Salvador and Honduras in 1969, and no longer functions, but negotiations to re-activate it are pending.

4. The Latin-American Integration Association (ALADI)

This new organisation, created by Treaty of 12 August 1980,[23] has replaced LAFTA, the Latin-American Free Trade Association, with the long-range objective of establishing a Latin-American Common Market. Its novel feature is that it envisages differential treatment amongst the members to accomodate their differing levels of economic development.

It has a Council of Foreign Ministers as a supreme organ, taking decisions on broad policy. Yet, since the crucial commitments of members will derive from the agreements to be freely negotiated between members, the Council is not a "supra-national" body. There is a Conference, meeting every three years, and a permanent body in the form of a Committee of Representatives, plus a Secretariat. The Council, Conference and Committee take decisions by a two-thirds majority vote *provided* no member country casts a negative vote on certain defined, important questions (Article 43).

5. The Latin-American Economic System (SELA)

This was established by the Agreement of Panama of October 1975,[24] as a regional entity for joint consultation in economic and

---

[23] (1981) 20 I.L.M. 672. Mexico is the only member from Central America, but many of the members are also members of SELA. LAFTA had aimed at the elimination of tariff barriers between all members by 1972, and in this it failed, in part due to the differences in economic development of the members. The new organisation classifies members into three groups, according to development, and provides for tariff concessions to be granted individually rather than collectively, but with preferences being given to the poorer countries.

[24] This embraces countries from both Central and South America: text in (1976) 15 I.L.M. 1081.

social matters. It has a permanent Secretariat and two other organs. One is the Latin-American Council, meeting annually at Ministerial level and voting either by consensus or by two-thirds majority, according to the nature of the matter in question. The other organ, or set of organs, is the Action Committees, designed to carry out specific studies or programs. So far three such committees have been established to deal with the establishment of multinational enterprises; the manufacture of fertilisers; and the manufacture of low-income housing units.

6. The Andean Pact

This organisation began as a sub-regional agreement within LAFTA. Under the Treaty of Bogotá of 26 May 1969,[25] the States of Bolivia, Chile, Ecuador, Peru and Venezuela[26] moved towards closer integration than was possible within LAFTA itself, and the sub-regional grouping was approved by the LAFTA Permanent Executive Committee.

The organs are the Commission, which is the supreme organ, the Board or "Junta" (a technical organ of three members somewhat akin to the Commission of the European Communities), the Committees which advise the Board and the Court of Justice.[27] The Andean Development Corporation[28] is a separate institution, but one with which the Commission and the Board maintain contact. The Commission exercises the real power, usually by a two-thirds majority vote, but the negative vote of any member will defeat a proposal. However, its decisions once adopted are directly applicable within the member countries.

The present signs indicate progress because in 1979 the decision was taken to establish a Parliament[29] and a Council of Foreign Ministers.[30]

---

[25] (1969) 8 I.L.M., 910.
[26] Venezuela adhered by a separate instrument: *ibid.*, 939. Chile subsequently withdrew in 1976.
[27] For the Agreement of 1968 establishing the Corporation see *ibid.*, 940.
[28] (1979) 18 I.L.M. 1203.
[29] (1980) 19 I.L.M. 269. This is to be directly elected, but pending arrangements for this, each Member sends five representatives from the National Parliament.
[30] (1980) 19 I.L.M. 612. The Council will act by consensus.

7. The Caribbean Community (CARICOM)

This organisation has replaced CARIFTA, the Caribbean Free Trade Area since May 1974. The Treaty of Chaguaramas of 1973[31] established a closer form of economic integration, with a Conference of Heads of State as the supreme organ, a Council of Ministers and a Secretariat. Progress has been hindered by the failure to agree on development policy, and Trinidad and Tobago reached an agreement in May 1979 to form a separate Organisation of East Caribbean States (OECS).

8. The Treaty for Amazonian Co-operation

This Treaty, signed on July 3, 1978[32] between Bolivia, Brazil, Colombia, Ecuador, Guyana, Peru, Surinam and Venezuela, is designed to ensure co-operation in the development of the Amazon basin. It is for the most part a statement of aims, and these will be fulfilled via periodic meetings within a modest organisational structure. This structure provides for Meetings of Ministers of Foreign Affairs, an Amazonian Co-operation Council, meeting yearly at ambassadorial level, and a Secretariat to be provided by the host country for the meeting. Decisions of any meeting require a unanimous vote.

II. THE MIDDLE EAST

1. The Arab League

The Arab League is a regional, political organisation of comprehensive aims. Although, in the exploratory discussions in September 1944 between delegates of Arab States, the possibility of federal union was discussed, the organisation which eventually emerged in the pact signed on March 22, 1944,[33] is one for co-operation between sovereign States and nothing more; the comparison with the history of the Council of Europe is an interesting one.

Membership, under Article I of the Pact, is open to independent

---

[31] See Instruments of Economic Integration in Latin-America and the Caribbean (1975), 2 vols., published by the Inter-American Institute of International Legal Studies, p. 645. See also the Caribbean Investment Corporation established earlier in 1973 under CARIFTA, and still in being, *ibid.*, p. 617.

[32] 17 I.L.M. (1978), 1045.

[33] Convenient text in (1945) 39 A.J.I.L. 266.

Arab States which "shall have the right to adhere to the League." However, the subsequent membership of Libya, Sudan, Morocco, Tunisia, Bahrein, Qatar, Oman, Mauritania and the United Arab Emirates was by application, and "acceptance" of the application by the Council of the League, so that membership does not in practice seem to be as of right. Withdrawal is provided for in Article XVIII, and so is expulsion on the ground that the State is not fulfilling its obligations under the Pact. No other form of membership is provided for, but in practice there is an "observer" status, and in 1959 representatives of the Algerian Nationalists were admitted in this capacity.

The aims of the League are very widely phrased. The main aim is to co-ordinate the political programme of Members "in such a way as to effect real collaboration between them, to preserve their independence and sovereignty . . . " and, as an incident to this main aim, co-operation is envisaged specifically in economic and financial affairs, commercial relations, customs, currency, agriculture and industry, communications, cultural affairs, nationality questions, social and health affairs (Art. III). Indeed, by an agreement of 1964 the aim of removing all customs and trade restrictions by 1974 was adopted, but this has not been achieved.

Under Article V the League Members renounce recourse to force to resolve disputes between them and, whilst they do not accept the jurisdiction of the Council of the League to mediate or arbitrate as compulsory over such disputes, if they do have recourse to the Council its decision is binding. In practice the League Council has used the more informal processes of conciliation on many occasions in dealing with inter-regional disputes, without any formal acceptance of the Council's jurisdiction under Article V. Indeed, in the Kuwait crisis in 1961, the Council established an Inter-Arab Force as a "peace-keeping" operation in view of the dispute between Kuwait and Iraq. The Council did the same in June 1976 in the Lebanon.[34]

Under Article VI each Member has a right to summon the Council immediately in the event of aggression, whether by another League Member or an outside State. The Council may then, by unanimous vote (excepting the aggressor State), decide upon measures to check the aggression. This collective security

---

[34] Feuer, "Le force arabe de sécurité au Liban" (1976) 22 Ann. F.D.I. 51–62.

function is further specified in a separate collective security pact, based upon Article 51 of the UN Charter and on the notion that aggression against any League Member is aggression against all; the pact entered into force on August 23, 1952, and established a Permanent Joint Defence Council and Permanent Military Commission. On the occasion of the Anglo-French aggression against Egypt in 1956, involving the landing of troops in Suez, the collective security machinery failed to bring assistance to Egypt. Prior to the Arab/Israeli war of June 1967, Egypt, Jordan and the PLA (Palestine Liberation Army) instituted a joint military command, although it is clear that no integration of armed forces comparable to that which has occurred in NATO and the Warsaw Pact has yet happened.

It will thus be seen that the Arab League qualifies as a "regional arrangement" within the meaning of Chapter VIII of the UN Charter.[35] It also plans to operate as an organisation for collective self-defence, akin to NATO in the West.

The organisational structure established to carry out these aims and functions is comparatively simple. The Council is the supreme organ, meeting twice yearly and composed of representatives of each participating State, each with one vote. Under Article VII unanimity is the basic rule and decisions taken unanimously are obligatory on all the participating States, which are bound to execute these decisions in accordance with their own constitutions; decisions on measures to check aggression require unanimity under Article VI. Other decisions, such as decisions consequent upon arbitration or mediation under Article V or on the matters specified in Article XVI (personnel, budget, decisions to adjourn), can be taken by majority vote. The Council normally meets twice a year but has provision for extraordinary sessions convened at the request of two Members.

Apart from the Council, Article IV calls for committees of plenary composition on each of the matters specially mentioned in Article II (economic affairs, communications, cultural affairs, etc.). The voting rule is simple majority and they meet annually. The League has also set up an Arab Telecommunications Union, an Arab Postal Union, an Arab Defence Council, an Arab

---

[35] See Khadduri, "The Arab League as a Regional Arrangement," (1946) 40 A.J.I.L. 756; also Boutros-Ghali, "The Arab League 1945–1955," 498, *International Conciliation.*

Development Bank (1959) in which the Members hold percentages of the stock, just as in the International Bank, and various conferences have been sponsored, such as the Inter-Arab Economic Conference of 1951 or the "Arab Oil" Congress of 1959. The cultural and economic activities of the League have developed considerably over the years and the Economic Council of the League has initiated studies on the possibility of an Arab common market. It may finally be noted that the League had its permanent seat in Cairo, with a permanent Secretariat headed by a Secretary-General. The Secretary-General has developed a political role similar to the UN Secretary-General and is far more than a mere administrative head. The League Secretariat also exercises control over the League Boycott Office, subject to guidance from the League Council and the Economic Council. The League Boycott against Israel, which first originated in 1945, involves the trading activities of States and companies throughout the world.

The overall impression is, therefore, of a useful organisation which is of a rather rudimentary form. It may lack the necessary political cohesion to advance very rapidly to a greater degree of co-ordination or even integration at the present stage. The disputes between Egypt and Jordan, the complaints of domination of the League by Egypt (for example, by Tunisia in 1958), and the breakdown of the brief union between Syria and Egypt suggest the absence, at present, of sufficient political unity to make a more integrated form feasible. Indeed, at the meeting of the Council in Beirut on August 28, 1962, the Egyptian delegation threatened withdrawal from the League if the Council pursued its hearings of complaints against Egypt by Syria. The area in which the co-operation has been most effective is that of co-ordinating policies in relation to third States. On issues such as the complaints against France over the Tunisian, Moroccan and Algerian questions, or against the United Kingdom over the Yemen and Oman, or in relation to the blockade against Israel, the League acts as a forum in which common policy can be formulated. The effectiveness of this can also be seen in the United Nations, for there it is quite evident that, *via* the League, the Arab States have unified their policies well in advance of the UN meetings and act as a "bloc." Above all, on the Israeli question the League maintained a general unity which was effective until President Sadat's independent peace initiative with Israel in 1978. The Arab Peoples

Conference in Tripoli in December 1978 called for Egypt's expulsion from the League. In March 1979 the Baghdad Conference of the League suspended Egypt's membership of the League with effect from the date of Egypt's signature of the peace treaty with Israel and transferred the League's headquarters from Cairo to Tunisia.

III. ASIA AND THE FAR EAST

The principal organisations in this region were for many years the two organisations for collective self-defence, SEATO and ANZUS, the Afro-Asian Solidarity Conference (a political organisation of hybrid form) and the Colombo Plan in the economic field.

With the dissolution of SEATO in June 1977, only ANZUS remains as a defence pact and there is no comprehensive military organisation embracing the majority of States within the region.

In the broader political field there is the Afro-Asian Solidarity Conference. As will be seen, this has the beginnings of a permanent structure, but it is an organisation which straddles Africa and Asia and which, since Cairo in 1958, has purported to represent "peoples" rather than governments. It is, therefore, with some difficulty that one includes this within a treatment purporting to be confined to governmental organisations. One should perhaps remember that the UN itself offers to the Afro-Asian States a valuable forum for discussion of their common problems; the Afro-Asian States, which meet regularly as a "bloc" in private meetings connected with the UN and its conferences, in fact now form a majority of the UN Members. However, two limited, regional organisations have come into being, both concerned with political and economic matters. The first is the Asian and Pacific Council (ASPAC), established by 9 non-Communist countries in June 1966.[36] The second is the Association of South-East Asian Nations (ASEAN), formed in August 1967[37] between Indonesia, Malaysia, Thailand, Philippines and Singapore (the last three also belonging to ASPAC). Both envisage annual ministerial meetings with a permanent standing committee.

[36] (1966) 5 I.L.M. 985.
[37] (1967) 7 I.L.M. 1233.

In the economic field the Colombo Plan is the most important regional forum for consultation, supplementing the work of the UN agencies such as the International Bank, UNDP, ECAFE, and the newer International Finance Corporation. In 1966 the Asian Development Bank was initiated.[38]

There are various other inter-governmental organisations in this region which space will not permit to be treated: the Asian Legal Consultative Committee (a kind of regional International Law Commission); the Asia-Pacific Forestry Commission, the Indo-Pacific Fisheries Council; the South Pacific Commission, a consultative body formed by six governments with dependent territories in the area; and the UNESCO research centre on the social implications of industrialisation in Southern Asia.[39]

1. The ANZUS Council

By Article VII of the tripartite security pact between Australia, New Zealand and the U.S.A. (whose initials give rise to the term "Anzus") a Council was established "to consider matters concerning the implementation of this Treaty"; the treaty entered into force on April 29, 1952.[40]

This organisation is, like SEATO, on the NATO pattern as an organisation for collective self-defence. It antedated SEATO and, since SEATO, has lost a good deal of its *raison d'être*. However, the two differ in the areas covered and in their definition of the *casus foederis*. The obligations of assistance in the event of aggression are not automatic, as in NATO, but of the much weaker kind which was in due course adopted for SEATO.

Apart from the Council, a consultative organ of Foreign Ministers meeting annually, there have been established a Council of Deputies to meet in between sessions of the main Council,[41] and a Military Committee of military representatives meeting as the governments decide. Any decisions are by unanimity. In recent years the Council has dealt with the possibilities of co-operation in

---

[38] (1966) 5 I.L.M. 262: and see (1965) 4 *Philippine L.J.* Spec. Supp.
[39] Details on all these organisations can be obtained from the *Yearbook of International Organisations.*
[40] Text in (1951) 13 *Foreign Relations,* Chap. V: Starke, *The ANZUS Treaty Alliance* (1965), 243.
[41] Though no formal meeting has ever taken place.

the peaceful uses of atomic energy, so that the organisation is not exclusively of a military character. ANZUS has no formal or informal relationship with NATO, and none is likely so long as the United States opposes United Kingdom participation in ANZUS.

2. The Association of South East Asian Nations (ASEAN)

Asean developed from the Declaration of 8 August 1967 of the foreign Ministers of Indonesia, Thailand, Malaysia, Singapore and the Philippines. Its aims are both economic and political, for they include not only the promotion of economic collaboration but also the promotion of regional peace and stability.

Its structure is extremely simple, involving an annual Ministerial meeting, supported by a Standing Committee, and a variety of permanent committees dealing with particular areas of concern— science and technology, food and agriculture, shipping, air transport, finance, communications, commerce and industry, etc. The meetings were to be serviced, not by a central Secretariat, but by national secretariats in the various capitols, acting whenever a meeting was convened there.

The political aims were furthered by the 1976 proposal for a Treaty of Amity and Co-operation in S.E. Asia and, in the following year, by the withdrawal of the controversial Philippine claim to Sabah.

3. The Afro-Asian Solidarity Conference

The Conference of Afro-Asian States, held at Bandung in 1955, was an ad hoc conference for the discussion of common problems and, in its final communiqué, put forward resolutions on matters such as economic co-operation, cultural co-operation, human rights and self-determination, problems of dependent peoples, and world peace.[42] Twenty-nine governments were represented at that conference.

Subsequently, at Cairo in 1958, the second Afro-Asian Solidarity Conference was held and set up a Permanent Council, to meet annually and composed of one representative from each national committee, and a permanent Secretariat headed by a Secretary-

---

[42] See R.I.I.A. *Survey,* 1955–56, and *Documents,* 1955, Part IV; the text of the final communiqué is given in the latter at p.429.

General. It is financed by the governments, but at the Cairo Conference "peoples" rather than States were represented, there being 400 representatives from 46 peoples of Asia and Africa. The organisation thus appears to be something of a hybrid, for it cannot be regarded as a strictly inter-governmental organisation since 1958.

4. Colombo Plan for Co-operative Economic Development in South and South-East Asia[43]

At the first meeting of the Foreign Ministers of the British Commonwealth of Nations in Colombo in January 1950, Australia proposed a programme of economic assistance to South and South-East Asia. Following on this proposal a Commonwealth Consultative Committee was established, a committee with no administrative authority or power of decision but purely an organ for consultation. From this organ, in turn, sprang the Commonwealth Technical Assistance Scheme, for the administration of which there was set up a Council for Technical Co-operation, holding annual meetings and composed of all participating States, and a Technical Assistance Bureau which is continually functioning and acts as a clearing-house for requests for technical assistance. The Council has a regular liaison with the UNDP.

Both the Consultative Committee, which is concerned with economic development in general, and the Council for Technical Co-operation, which is concerned with the narrower field of technical assistance, are consultative conferences of governments. These governments are now no longer confined to Members of the Commonwealth, but include States like the U.S.A., Philippines, Japan, Indonesia, etc. The organs are simply a forum for discussion of common problems and even the aid supplied is by means of bilateral agreements; there is no "common pool" such as was created under OEEC. It therefore represents an example of governmental co-operation at the most elementary level from the organisational point of view.

[43] Basch, "The Colombo Plan: A case of regional economic co-operation," (1955) 9 *International Organisation*, 1–18; Waugh, "The Colombo Plan: Origins and Progress," (1954) *Dept. State Bull.*, 640–644.

IV. Eastern Europe

1. Communist Information Bureau (Cominform)

The Warsaw manifesto of October 5, 1947,[44] which emanated from a conference of representatives of various Communist Parties in Eastern, and to a lesser extent Western, Europe resolved to set up an Information Bureau consisting of representatives of the Communist Parties of Yugoslavia, Bulgaria, Roumania, Hungary, Poland, Soviet Union, Czechoslovakia, France and Italy. Its function was to organise interchange of experiences and co-ordination of the activities of the Communist Parties on the basis of mutual agreement, and it was to consist of two representatives from each Central Committee and to be located in Belgrade.

It will be seen that the Cominform is not, really, a governmental organisation, but rather an organ of consultation between Communist Parties; however, in the main, the identification between the Communist Parties and the governments in these countries is so close as to justify treating the Cominform as an organisation whereby, indirectly, the various governments can consult on common problems, especially those of a political nature. Of course, France and Italy stand out as the anomalies; they can neither be treated as part of Eastern Europe, nor can the same identification of policy between Communist Party and Government be said to exist in these countries. As was said at the beginning of this book, classifications have to be made as a matter of convenience which cannot stand the test of scientific accuracy.

2. The Warsaw Treaty Organisation

This Organisation began with the signature of a Treaty of Friendship, Co-operation and Mutual Assistance at Warsaw on May 4, 1955,[45] a treaty initially of 20 years' duration, to which there are now seven parties, Bulgaria, Czechoslovakia, German Democratic Republic, Hungary, Poland, Roumania and the U.S.S.R.; China, Mongolia, North Korea and North Vietnam at one time sent observers to the Political Consultative Committee

---

[44] R.I.I.A., *Documents on Regional Organisations outside W. Europe*, 1941–49, 80–84.
[45] Text in R.I.I.A., (1955) *Documents on International Affairs*, 193; (1955) 49 A.I.I.L., Supp. 194.

but ceased to do so in 1962 and Albania withdrew from membership in 1968 after the Soviet invasion of Czechoslovakia.

The Organisation is a direct counterpart of NATO, and, as the preamble recites, was prompted by the re-armament of Western Germany and its inclusion in NATO consequent upon the formation of WEU. The treaty reaffirms the obligations of Article 2 (4) of the UN Charter, and contains an undertaking to work for general disarmament and to consult on all international questions relating to the common interests of the Members; membership is open to all other States "irrespective of their social and state systems" ready to assist in preserving peace. It is, therefore, in practice only and not by its terms confined to Eastern Europe; this is consistent with the repeated invitation by the U.S.S.R. to the Western Powers to join in a general European security treaty.

The crux of the security system lies in Article 4 whereby, on the basis of Article 51 of the UN Charter, an armed attack in Europe on any Member gives rise to the individual and collective obligation to render "immediate assistance . . . by all the means it may consider necessary, including the use of armed force." Whereas, originally, the Treaty was interpreted to apply only to aggression by an *external* Power, the Soviet intervention in Hungary in 1956 and the combined invasion of Czechoslovakia by the Soviet Union and other Warsaw Pact members in 1968, which was justified on the basis of the Treaty, has clearly demonstrated that the Treaty is not so limited in practice.

The organisational structure established to achieve this consists of a Political Consultative Committee, a plenary committee meeting once or twice a year, and with equality of voting power for all Members and voting by unanimity. This has power to set up auxiliary organs, and in fact a Permanent Commission has been established to give continuity to the work between sessions.

The establishment of a joint command for the armed forces of the Members was specifically envisaged in the treaty,[46] and this has been achieved: the armies of the member countries are in effect

---

[46] Art. 5; and see the accompanying statement, *ibid,* p.198. The status of Soviet forces on the territory of other Members is governed by a series of bilateral agreements, according to principles broadly similar to the NATO Status of Forces Agreement; see U.S.S.R./German Democratic Republic Agreement of March 12, 1957, U.S.S.R./Hungary, May 27, 1957, U.S.S.R./Poland, December 17, 1956; texts in (1958) 52 A.J.I.L., Documents, 210–221.

treated as an organic whole and there is a Staff of the Joint Armed Forces.

So far as can be ascertained from the available material, which is very sparse in comparison to that on NATO, the Warsaw Treaty Organisation is nothing like so developed as NATO, constitutionally speaking. It is essentially a defensive alliance, with organs for consultation and co-operation, and does not purport to attain the wider economic and political aims of NATO, nor does it have the very comprehensive structure of organs which NATO possesses.

3. Council for Mutual Economic Aid (Comecon or CMEA)

This was established at an economic conference in Moscow in January 1949,[47] obviously as a counterpart to OEEC which had been established in Western Europe in the previous year. The nine Member States are Bulgaria, Cuba, Czechoslovakia, German Democratic Republic, Hungary, Mongolia, Poland, Roumania and U.S.S.R.[48] In addition China, Vietnam and the Peoples' Republic of Korea have observer status, although China ceased attending in 1962 and Yugoslavia has accepted associate member status since 1965.

The Council is described as "an open organisation which can be entered by other European States which agree with the principles" (of Comecon), and Members participate on the basis of equal representation, decisions affecting any Member being made "only with the agreement of the interested country." There is considerable emphasis on the retention of full sovereignty by all members and Soviet writers emphasise that the organisation contains no "supranational" element. The Council meets in regular sessions in rotation in the capitals of the participating Members. It is, in principle, simply an organ for consultation between governments in the economic field. Until 1956 it operated largely on the technical level but from 1956 onwards (East Berlin meeting) it

---

[47] R.I.I.A., *Documents on Regional Organisations outside W. Europe*, 1941–49, 85–87. For a general description of the Council see (1961) *International Law*, 374–375, a publication of the Academy of Sciences of the U.S.S.R.; Agoston, *Le marché commun communiste* (1964); Grzybowski, *The Socialist Commonwealth of Nations* (1964), Chaps. 3, 4.
[48] Albania was expelled in December 1961.

drew up more comprehensive five-year plans for economic co-ordination, plans which were further extended at the Moscow meeting in 1958 at which China, Outer Mongolia, Korea and Vietnam Peoples' Republics were represented. The Council has established seven permanent subsidiary organs or "meetings" dealing with such matters as legal questions, State Labour Agencies, Water Agencies, Internal Trade and so forth. In 1962 a new Charter for the Council was adopted, deleting the clause confining membership to European States and a new body, the Executive Committee, added. This Committee, assisted by a permanent Secretariat, meets every three months and is given policy-making and executive powers. In practice, whilst no member is bound to comply with decisions to which it has not consented, the national economic policies are strongly influenced by decisions of the Committee and of the Council.

There are, in addition, over 20 standing Commissions, each dealing with specified areas of industrial or economic activity. A 1963 agreement on multilateral payments operates with an International Bank for Economic Co-operation, also established in 1963, acting as the clearing house. In close liaison with Comecon are a Railway Organisation (1957), a Postal and Communications Organisation (1957), a Joint Institute for Nuclear Research (1956), a Common Pool of Freight Cars (1963), an Organisation for the Co-operation in the Ball-bearing Industry (1964), an Organisation for Co-operation in Ferrous Metallurgy (1964), an International Centre for Scientific and Technical Information (1969), an Organisation for Co-operation in Small-Tonnage Chemical Production (1969), an International Investment Bank (1970), an Organisation for Space Communication (1971) called Intersputnik and an International Bank for Economic Co-operation (1964), with a capital of 300 million roubles.

V. AFRICA

Until 1963 the African States were divided into three main political groups—the Casablanca, Monrovia and Brazzaville groups—thus apparently blocking the way to a unified, African political organisation. However, in May 1963, there convened in Addis Ababa the Summit Conference of Heads of State and

Governments, from which emerged the Charter of the Organisation of African Unity. Although Article 4 provides that "each independent sovereign African and Malagasy State shall be entitled to become a Member of the Organisation," South Africa and, even more so, Rhodesia were not likely to fall within the Organisation's view of what constitutes an "independent, sovereign African State." This issue has never been posed, and an application for membership is unlikely from South Africa, but the Organisation's answer would surely be that no entity is qualified for admission unless governed by a Government which is truly representative of the indigenous, African people.

1. The Organisation of African Unity

(a) *Purposes and principles*

These are contained in the Preamble and in Articles II and III of the Charter. Being based on the "sovereign equality of all Member States" (Art. III (1)) it is clear that the OAU falls far short of the true organic, federal union for which Nkrumah had argued: it is a loose organisation for co-operation with no kind of supra-national element. The intended scope of activity is very wide, embracing "political and diplomatic co-operation," "economic co-operation, including transport and communications," "health, sanitation and nutritional co-operation," "scientific and technical co-operation," and "co-operation for defence and security," (Art. II (2)). The principles established to guide these activities correspond in their language to the language of the UN Charter except possibly in two respects. The first is the emphasis on "absolute dedication to the total emancipation of the African territories which are still dependent": there can be no question but that the elimination of colonialism and the struggle against apartheid (which for African States constitutes simply another aspect of colonialism) have been given primary emphasis. Indeed, as we shall see, this aspect of the work of the Organisation has attracted more effort on the part of Member States than any other. The second is the "affirmation of a policy of non-alignment with regard to all blocs." In none of the other regional organisations has there been this express, constitutional dedication to the policy of non-alignment.

241

(b) *Institutions*

The principal institutions named in Article VII[49] are the following:

(i)*Assembly of Heads of State and Government.* This is the "supreme" organ, a plenary body on which each State has one vote and which meets annually or in extraordinary session with the approval of a two-thirds majority. Its resolutions are passed by a two-thirds majority, except on questions of procedure which require a simple majority. Apart from resolutions or decisions having an effect internal to the Organisation, such as the adoption of the budget or appointment of Committees, the Assembly's decisions are in effect no more than recommendations to Member States.

The Assembly is empowered by Article XX to establish "such Specialised Commissions as it may deem necessary, including the following:

(1) Economic and Social Commission.
(2) Educational and Cultural Commission.
(3) Health, Sanitation and Nutrition Commission.
(4) Defence Commission.
(5) Scientific, Technical and Research Commission."

To these the Assembly in 1964 added a sixth, the Commission of Jurists and a seventh, the Transport and Communications Commission. The Commissions are plenary and are intended to be composed of the appropriate Ministers from each Government. For this reason they have taken the view that, whilst they are clearly subordinate to the Assembly, they are not subordinate to their equals and counterparts in the Council. Duplication of competence and activities both between the Specialised Commissions themselves and with the United Nations bodies active in Africa[50] led to considerable dissatisfaction with their work and in 1966 the Assembly reduced the number of Commissions to three; Economic and Social, Education and Culture, and Defence.

---

[49] Note also Article VIII envisaging the creation of "specialised agencies": the distinction between these and the specialised commissions is not clear, but to date none have been established.

[50] For the Agreement on Co-operation between the OAU and ECA see UN Doc. A/6174 of December 16, 1965.

However, ad hoc Commissions can be established and a Commission on Refugees was established in 1965.

The other body established by the Addis Ababa Summit Conference in 1963, and subordinate to the Assembly, was the "Liberation Committee," originally composed of nine Member States but now expanded to 21. This Committee, with a Headquarters in Dar-es-Salaam, was charged by the Resolution on Decolonisation with the task of harmonising the assistance given by African States to the national liberation movements within the colonial territories and, to this end, administered the Special Fund to be financed by voluntary contributions.

The Committee came under considerable criticism over its administration of this Fund and over the political decisions implicit in its decisions on which liberation movements were to be recognised and financially supported. Moreover, the Committee sought a somewhat autonomous role, free from the control of the Secretariat in Addis Ababa. In 1966 the Council of Ministers resolved certain of these difficulties by re-affirming the overall control of the OAU Secretariat, by denying to the Committee the power to engage in "policy-making" and by giving every OAU Member State a right to be present (but not to vote) at its meetings.

(ii)*Council of Ministers.* This body consists of Ministers (normally Foreign Ministers) of the member States and meets twice-yearly or in extraordinary session. It meets immediately prior to the Assembly and is "entrusted with the responsibility of preparing conferences of the Assembly" (Art. XIII). It also implements the decisions of the Assembly and has a general responsibility for co-ordinating inter-African co-operation. It also considers and approves the Regulations of the Specialised Commissions and the budget of the Organisation. Its voting procedures are the same as those of the Assembly and it is, as a body, responsible to the Assembly.

The Rules of Procedure of the Council, adopted in August 1963, provide that meetings shall be held in private but leave it possible for the Council to decide, by simple majority, upon public meetings.

(iii)*General Secretariat.* This is headed by an "Administrative Secretary-General" appointed by the Assembly and the very name discloses the determination *not* to create an office with indepen-

243

dent political powers comparable to those of the Secretary-General of the United Nations.

This determination is also evident in the fact that he has no explicit right of participation in the meetings of the Assembly, the Council or the Specialised Commissions unless their own rules of procedure so provide. In practice, however, Diallo Telli had made his attendance the normal rule and, so long as the same impartiality and authority is made manifest, the Administrative Secretary-General can be expected to maintain the role which the constitutional texts do not provide for.

Article 18 is almost identical to Article 100 of the UN Charter and attempts to ensure the complete independence of the staff. Also, the Protocol on Privileges and Immunities, adopted in 1964, follows closely the 1946 Convention on the Privileges and Immunities of the United Nations.

(iv)*Commission of Mediation, Conciliation and Arbitration.* The creation of a separate, principal institution for the peaceful settlement of disputes is indicative of the decision to treat inter-African disputes as exclusively African affairs and to exclude, so far as possible, the over-riding authority of the Security Council.[51]

Article XIX envisages a "separate treaty" establishing the Commission and it was not until 1964 that the separate Protocol on Mediation, Conciliation and Arbitration was approved by the Assembly as an integral part of the Charter.[52] The Commission is essentially a "panel" of 21 members, elected by the Assembly, of whom three members only (President and two Vice-Presidents) are full-time and constitute the Bureau of the Commission. The Commission has so far been little used.

2. Organisation Commune Africaine et Malagache (OCAM)

The basic assumption at the 1963 Summit Meeting in Addis Ababa was that the different political groupings would merge into the new OAU. The French speaking Brazzaville group, formally linked in the Union of African States and Malagasy (UAM) initially showed some disinclination to accept their own demise. In a resolution of August 10, 1963 the OAU Council of Ministers

---

[51] *Ante*, p. 34.
[52] (1964) 3 I.L.M. 1116: for discussion of the working of the Commission see *post*, pp. 279–282.

accepted the feasibility of regional groupings continuing within the OAU subject to the following criteria:

"*(a)* Geographical realities and economic, social and cultural factors common to the States:

(b) Co-ordination of economic, social and cultural activities peculiar to the States concerned."[53]

The deliberate omission of reference to *political* activities made the essential point that the OAU was to be the sole political organisation. Hence, at Dakar in March 1964 the UAM transformed itself into the Union Africain et Malagache de Co-operation Economique (UAMCE), with exclusively economical, technical and cultural objectives. This, in turn, was replaced by the Organisation commune Africaine et Malgache (OCAM) in February 1965, and this new organisation's Charter was finally signed at Tananarive in June 1966.[54] Whether this new Organisation will respect the OAU's exclusive competence in political activities is at least doubtful, and a number of withdrawals from membership in 1972 and 1973 indicate that this organisation faces considerable uncertainty.

The Organisation's purpose "is to strengthen co-operation and solidarity between the African and Malagasy States in order to accelerate their economic, social, technical and cultural development" (Art. 2). Its institutions comprise a Conference of Chiefs of State and of Government, the supreme organ meeting annually, which has the somewhat novel feature of allowing one State to vote for another by proxy. The Conference's voting procedure, prescribed by Internal Regulations, requires a simple majority for procedural decisions, a two-thirds for other resolutions, but unanimity for "recommendations of a political nature" (Art. 24). There is no provision for determining whether the recommendation is political—the familiar "preliminary question"[55]—so that difficulty may be anticipated on this score. There is a Council of Ministers meeting annually as a preparatory conference for the

---

[53] CM/Res. 5 (1).

[54] (1967) 6 I.L.M. 53. At the Tananarive meeting President Senghor of Senegal raised the proposal for a more closely-integrated French-speaking Union (to include other countries such as Canada and Cambodia): the proposal has no immediate prospect of realisation.

[55] Ante, p. 30.

Conference of Chiefs of State and Government and with responsibility for supervising execution of the "directives" of the Conference: the Council also has the "proxy vote" provision and votes by two-thirds majority on matters other than procedure. And there is an Administrative General Secretariat which is also given supervision over the multinational airline, Air-Afrique, and the Union Africaine et Malagache des Postes et Télécommunications. The Convention providing Regulations governing the Personnel of the Organisation[56] is quite unlike the UN pattern of Staff Regulations and Rules.

3. Other African Economic Organisations

The fact that it has not so far proved possible to establish more than a loose political organisation for co-operation between States, coupled with the fact that rapid advance seems more likely in a regional grouping than on a broad pan-African basis, has led to the formation of several economic organisations of limited participation.[57] The parallel with Europe is marked, and just as the Council of Europe fell short of the expectations of many States, and led to the initiation of the European Communities of the Six, so the comparative ineffectiveness of the OAU has led to these new regional groupings in Africa.

Central African Economic and Customs Union (UDEAC)

Signed in 1964,[58] the treaty became effective in 1966 and embraces the five States of Cameroon, the Central African Republic, Chad, Congo (Brazzaville) and Gabon. It envisages a Council of Heads of State with powers of decision which must be taken unanimously but are legally enforcible in each State; it also has a Management Committee and a General Secretariat.

West African Economic Community (ECOWAS)

Under Articles of Association signed in May 1967,[59] this was designed as a Common Market for Dahomey, Ghana, Ivory

[56] (1967) 6 I.L.M. 70.
[57] Of course the African Development Bank has wide participation, including 29 Member States, but this was initiated by the ECA, so that it more properly forms part of the UN's economic apparatus than part of any OAU or OCAM system.
[58] (1965) 4 I.L.M. 699.
[59] (1967) 6 I.L.M. 776. There was an earlier agreement on an interim organisation dated February 17, 1965: (1965) 4 I.L.M. 916.

Coast, Liberia, Mali, Mauretania, Benin, Nigeria, Senegal and Sierra Leone. The treaty established an Interim Council of Ministers with the primary task of preparing a treaty governing the Community, for submission to Member States.

The new Treaty of 28 March 1975, signed at Lagos, is designed to place the organisation on a more permanent footing. The Interim Council is replaced and there is to be the Assembly of Heads of State and Government, the Council of Ministers, an Executive Secretariat, the Tribunal of the Community, and four technical commissions.

Economic Community of East Africa (ECEA)

Under terms of association signed on May 5, 1966,[60] this organisation came into being on December 1, 1967, embracing Kenya, Tanzania and Uganda but it had applications for admission from Ethiopia, Zambia and Somalia. It was intended to take over the common services previously operated by the East African Common Services Organisation (except for the self-accounting services of railways, ports, airways, posts and communications). Its structure is now well-developed. There is an East African Authority, which is the principal executive organ comprising the Heads of State: although, inevitably, they delegate much of the work to the Ministers and the Council. Then there is an East African Legislative Assembly comprising three Ministers (one from each State), three Deputy-Ministers, and twenty-seven appointed members (nine from each State). This Assembly can legislate for the member States provided its laws are signed by all three Heads of State. The East African Ministers constitutes yet another organ of three, appointed jointly for an indefinite term to assume responsibility for the day-to-day running of the Community. There are also five Councils dealing with the Common Market, Communications, Economic and Planning Consultations, Finance, Research and Social Affairs. There is a Common Market Tribunal, consisting of a Chairman and four members, with a role somewhat akin to that of the Court of the European Communities. In addition there is the Court of Appeal for East Africa, rather like the Privy Council of old, although it has no competence over the interpretation of the national constitutions. There is a Tax

[60] (1966) 5 I.L.M. 633.

Board, to advise on the harmonisation of the tax systems. Various Corporations have been established to run Railways, Harbours, Posts and Telegraphs, and Airways. And, finally, there is a Secretariat.

There are in addition various Committees or Commissions of States, organised under treaty to deal with specific problems of common interest such as the Senegal River Committee, the Niger River Commission, the Chad Basin Commission, the Mano River Union, the Trans-Sahara Liaison Committee and the West African Rice Development Association[61]; these tend to operate in close co-operation with ECA and with UNDP financial support.

[61] (1971) 10 I.L.M. 648.

Bibliography

General Works

BEBR: *"Regional Organisations: a United Nations Problem"* (1955) 49 A.J.I.L. 166.

HAGUE ACADEMY: 1971 Colloquium on "Les aspects juridiques de l'intégration économique" (1972).

OBERN: Selected regional international organisations; a comparative study (1955).

SABA: *"Regional Arrangements in the UN Charter"* (1952) 80 R.C. 635.

STEIN and HAY: Law and Institutions in the Atlantic Area (1967), 2 vols.

THARP: Regional international organisations (1971).

WILCOX: *"Regionalism and the UN"* (1965) 18 Int. Org. 789.

YAKEMITCHOUK: *"Le régionalisme et l'ONU"* (1955) R.G.D.I.P. 406.

YALEM: Regionalism and World Order (1965).

European Organisations

General

——, *"European Regional Communities"* (1961) 26 Law and Contemporary Problems, No. 3.

BALL: NATO and the European Union Movement (1959).

CARTOU: Organisations Européennes (1975).

IMBERT: L'Union de l'Europe occidentale (1968).

PINTO: Les Organisations Européennes (1965).

POLITICAL AND ECONOMIC PLANNING (PEP): European Organisations (1959).

REUTER: Organisations Européennes (1965).

ROBERTSON: European Institutions (1973).
VAN DER MEERSCH: Droit des Communautés Européennes (1969).

The Council of Europe
THE COUNCIL OF EUROPE: Concise Handbook of the Council of Europe (1954).
THE COUNCIL OF EUROPE: Ten Years of the Council of Europe (1961).
ROBERTSON: The Council of Europe. Its Structure, Functions and Achievements, 2nd ed. (1961).
VASAK: Le Conseil de l'Europe (1965).

NATO
BRITISH INFORMATION SERVICE: Western Co-operation. A reference handbook (1955).
BUCHAN: *"The Reform of NATO"* (1962) 40 Foreign Affairs, 165.
ISMAY: NATO, The First Five Years, 1949–1954 (1955).
NATO INFORMATION SERVICE: NATO: Facts and Figures.
SALVIN: *"The North Atlantic Pact"* (1949) International Conciliation 373.

OECD
HAHN: *"Die Organisation für wirtschaftliche Zusammenarbeit und Entwicklung (OECD),"* (1962) 22 Z.f.a.o.r.u.V. 49.
MILLER: *"The OECD"* (1963) Y.B.W.A. 80–95.
SZULDRYNSKI: *"Legal aspects of OEEC"* (1953) 2 I.C.L.Q. 579.
The OECD: History, Aims and Structure (1971).

EFTA
FIGGURES: *"Legal Aspects of EFTA"* (1965) 14 I.C.L.Q. 1079.
LANBRINIDIS: The Structure, function and law of a free trade area (1965).
MEYER: The EFTA (1960).

The European Communities
BRINKHORST AND MITCHELL: European Law and Institutions (1969).
EFRON and NANES: *"The Common Market and Euratom Treaties: Supernationality and the Integration of Europe"* (1957) 6 I.C.L.Q. 670.
HAHN: *"Constitutional Limitations in the law of the European organisations"* (1963) 108 R.C. 195–300.
HALLSTEIN: *"The EEC Commissions: a new factor in International Life"* (1965) 14 I.C.L.Q. 727.
HURTIG: *"The European Common Market"* (1958) 517 International Conciliation.
KITZINGER: The Challenge of the Common Market (1966).
LASOK and BRIDGE: Introduction to the Law and Institutions of the European Communities (1976).
PARRY and HARDY: EEC Law (1981).
PESCATORE: The Law of Integration (1974).
POLACH: Euratom (1964).

Other Organisations

REUTER: La Communauté Européenne du Charbon et de l'Acier (1953).
SCHERMERS: Judicial Protection in the European Communities (1979).
STEIN, HAY, WAELBROECK: European Community Law and Institutions in Perspective (1976).

The Americas

AQUILAR: El Panamericanismo (1965).
BALL: The OAS in Transition (1969).
CANYES: The Organisation of American States and the UN (1960).
CONNELL-SMITH: The Inter-American System (1966).
DELL: Latin-American Common Market? (1966).
DREIER: The OAS and the Hemisphere Crisis (1962).
GARCIA-AMADOR: *"Institutional Development in Central American Integration"* (1967) P.A.S.I.L. 167–174.
GARCIA-AMADOR: The Andean Legal Order (1978).
GEISER, ALLEYNE and GAJRAJ: Legal Problems of Caribbean Integration (1976).
INSTITUTO INTERAMERICANO: Instrumentos Relativos a la Integracion economica en America Latina (1964).
INSTITUTO INTERAMERICANO: Problematica Juridica e Institucional de la integracion de America Latina (1967).
INTER-AMERICAN INSTITUTE OF INTERNATIONAL LEGAL STUDIES: The Inter-American System, its development and strengthening (1966).
Instruments of Economic Integration in Latin-America and the Caribbean (1975), 2 Vols.
MANGER: The Alliance for Progress: a critical appraisal (1963).
NYE: Central American Regional Integration (1967) *Int. Concil.* No. 562, 1–66.
SIMMONDS: "The Caribbean Economic Community" (1974) 23 I.C.L.Q. 453–8.

The Middle East

BEYSSADA: La Ligne Arabe (1968).
BOUTROS-GHALI: "La Ligue des Etats Arabes" (1972) 137 R.C. 1.
HASSOUNA: The League of Arab States and Regional Disputes (1975).
MACDONALD: The League of Arab States (1965).
SAAB: *"The League of Arab States: an innovation in Arab institutional history"* (1966) 7 World Justice 449.

Asia and Far East

ASEAN: The Asean Report (1979), 2 Vols.
BURNS: *"The Colombo Plan,"* (1960) Y.B.W.A. 176.
HAAS: Basic Documents of Asian Regional Organisations (1974), 8 Vols.
KENNEDY: The Security of Southern Asia (1965).
MODELSKI: SEATO: Six Studies (1962).
SOLIDUM: Towards a South-East Asian Community (1974).
STARKE: The ANZUS Treaty Alliance (1965).

Eastern Europe
BUTLER: A Source-Book on Socialist International Organisations (1978).
COMECON: Progress and Prospects, Colloquium (1977) NATO publication.
FOSCANEANU: *"La Banque internationale de cooperation économique"* (1965) 92 Journal du D.I., 591.
GINSBURGS: "The Constitutional Foundations of the Socialist Commonwealth" (1973) Y.B.W.A. 173.
LACHS: *"The Warsaw Agreement and the question of collective security in Europe"* (1955) International Affairs.
MARKOWSKI: "Money in International Communist Economics" (1973) Y.B.W.A. 257.
SKUBISZEWSKI: L'Organisation du Traité de Varsovie" (1967) Revue Belge de D. Int., 82.
SZAWLOWSKI: The System of International Organisations of the Communist Countries (1976).
UN: *Economic integration and industrial specialisation among the member countries of the Council for Mutual Economic Assistance* (1966).

Africa
AKINTAU: The Law of International Economic Institutions in Africa (1977).
AGORO: *"The Establishment of the Chad Basin Commission"* (1966) 15 I.C.L.Q. 542.
CERVENKA: The OAU and its Charter (1968); The Unfinished Quest for Unity (1977).
EL-AYOUTY: The OAU after Ten Years (1975).
ELIAS: *"The Commission of Mediation, Conciliation and Arbitration of the OAU"* (1964) 40 B.Y.B.I.L. 336.
ELIAS: *"The Charter of the OAU"* (1965) 59 A.J.I.L. 243.
OAU: Basic Documents and Resolutions (1963).
SOHN: Documents of African Regional Organisations (1971), 4 Vols.

PART THREE

Judicial Institutions

CHAPTER 8

THE TREND FROM AD HOC TRIBUNALS TO
PERMANENT INSTITUTIONS

THE problem of solving disputes between States has led to the
creation of a wide range of procedures including negotiation,
good-offices, inquiry, mediation, conciliation, arbitration and
judicial settlement. In one sense they can all be regarded as
"institutions," yet we propose to restrict this term to bodies set up
for the specific purpose of carrying out these procedures for
settlement and, moreover, to concentrate on the "judicial"
procedures such as arbitration and judicial settlement in which, in
general, one finds an adjudication according to the law and
resulting in an award binding on the parties.

It may first be observed, however, that conciliation, as a process
for settling disputes not deemed immediately susceptible to
settlement by a judicial process—hence often termed "political"
disputes—has become equally institutionalised. Developing from
the International Commission of Inquiry provided for in the
Hague Conventions for the Pacific Settlement of Disputes of 1899
and 1907, and utilised in the celebrated Bryan "cooling-off"
treaties of 1914 and the Locarno Pacts of 1925, the conciliation
commissions of the General Act for the Pacific Settlement of
International Disputes of 1928 were charged "to elucidate the
questions in dispute, to collect with that object all necessary
information by means of inquiry or otherwise, and to endeavour to
bring the parties to an agreement" (Art. 15). The commissions
could be rendered permanent at the request of one party.[1] Yet the
real future of conciliation lay with the permanent political
organisations which were being established; the Locarno Pact had
virtually accepted this in providing for reference of the dispute to
the Council of the League in the event of failure by the permanent
conciliation commissions to settle the dispute. The General Act
for the Pacific Settlement of Disputes of 1928 likewise linked the
permanent and special conciliation commissions envisaged by the

---

[1] And see Chap. II of the European Convention for the Peaceful Settlement of
Disputes of 1957, providing for conciliation of disputes other than legal disputes
by permanent conciliation commissions: v *European Yearbook* 34.

Act to the League Council's conciliation functions by excluding the former where a dispute had been referred to the Council (unless the Council itself referred the dispute to conciliation). The Council of the League, and now the Security Council of the United Nations, are themselves perfectly good examples of permanent conciliation commissions; admittedly they have (or had) other functions, and in relation to conciliation the League Council's jurisdiction was limited to disputes likely to lead to a rupture and the Security Council's to those "likely to endanger international peace and security," if we use the terms of Chapter VI of the Charter. The Security Council moreover now has the advantage over the traditional conciliation commission that neglect to comply with its "recommendations" under Chapter VI will be one factor to be considered in the event that the situation deteriorates so as to become a "threat to the peace, breach of the peace, or act of aggression" under Article 39 and thus, possibly, occasions enforcement action. The defect of the Security Council's practice with regard to conciliation in the relatively little use made of its fact-finding powers. Fact-finding is a necessary stage of the process of conciliation and yet, in practice, the Council has used its fact-finding powers under Article 34 far more in relation to "peace-keeping" than peaceful settlement.[2] Happily, the UN has begun serious study of ways in which to improve its machinery for fact-finding.[3]

Conciliation is also well-developed in the political organs of regional organisations. The Councils of NATO, the Arab League, the OAU and the OAS have all assumed this role. The OAU has, of course, established the Commission of Mediation, Conciliation and Arbitration but in addition to this the OAU has undertaken conciliation in the Algerian/Moroccan dispute, in the Congo and in Nigeria. The OAS has the most highly-developed practice of all, of which a special feature is the Inter-American Peace Committee which has undertaken both fact-finding and conciliation (although the revised statutes of 1956 limited its role to disputes where both

---

[2] *International Disputes: the legal aspects* (1972), paras. 18, 19.
[3] S.G.'s Report on Methods of Fact-Finding (A/5694) and see G.A. Resol. 2326 (XXII) of December 18, 1967 which encourages States to utilise the fact-finding facilities of international organisations and asks the S.G. to establish a register of experts for this purpose. This is minimal progress. What is needed is a more effective machinery available for use by the S.C. and G.A., preferably with a right of access to any State's territory.

parties consented to its acting). Indeed, as a general observation, it may be true to say that the immediate future holds better hope for improvement of peaceful settlement via political organs— whether of the UN or of regional organisations—than it does for improvement of the more strictly legal techniques.

Returning to the procedures of arbitration and judicial settlement, which are our primary concern in this chapter, it is apparent that the distinction between the procedures lies in the nature of the adjudicating body and not in the nature of the procedures: they are both procedures for the settlement of disputes over the legal rights of the parties, on the basis of established law (unless the parties agree otherwise) and resulting in an award binding on the parties. Hence in 1958 the International Law Commission defined arbitration as "the procedure for the settlement of disputes between States by a binding award on the basis of law and as the result of an undertaking voluntarily accepted."[4] With arbitration the initial undertaking to arbitrate, whether in the form of an ad hoc agreement or of a pre-existing general arbitration treaty, is essentially a *pactum de contrahendo*, an imperfect obligation which becomes effective only when the further stage of agreeing on the setting up of a tribunal and its terms of reference is completed. Hence, as Johnson has said "the constitution of the tribunal is, on the whole, the *fundamental* problem of arbitration, because without a tribunal there can be no arbitration and the failure of this particular method of settling international disputes is a *total failure*."[5]

To leave this question to negotiation on each occasion a dispute arose was to invite frustration of the undertaking to arbitrate, for the *compromis d'arbitrage* which would supplement the original undertaking by specifying not only the composition of the tribunal but also the issue to be decided by it[6] and the procedure to be

---

[4] Report of the I.L.C. concerning the Work of its Tenth Session, 1958, G.A.O.R., Thirteenth Session, Suppl. No. 9 (A/3859). The Argentinian refusal to accept the Beagle Channel Award led to an agreement with Chile in January 1979 to accept Papal mediation (1979) 18 I.L.M. 1.

[5] Johnson, "The Constitution of an Arbitral Tribunal" (1953) 30 B.Y.B.I.L. 152.

[6] Clearly the problem of whether the particular dispute lies within the scope of the original undertaking to arbitrate is also a considerable one. The solution of it may be facilitated where that issue can itself be referred for settlement to the I.C.J. under its compulsory jurisdiction: see the *Ambatielos Case*, (1953) *I.C.J. Reports*.

followed would not be concluded when one party was reluctant to abide by its original undertaking. Moreover, even where a *compromis* emerged, or matters like the composition of the tribunal were already covered by agreement, there remained the possibility of disagreement on the actual persons to be appointed as arbitrators. Hence one can treat the trend from ad hoc to permanent institutions as, very largely, the history of attempts to make an undertaking to arbitrate effective by ensuring that a tribunal, capable of adjudicating upon the dispute, shall exist.

Whilst, it is true, arbitration has a respectable lineage going back to the ancient Greeks, it is generally conceded that modern arbitration began with the 1794 Jay Treaty between Great Britain and the United States. Since that time ad hoc arbitral bodies have been, basically, of three types: the single arbitrator, the joint commission and the "mixed" commission. The single arbitrator, chosen by mutual agreement between the parties, would frequently be a foreign sovereign or head of State, or a collegiate chief of State like the Senate of Hamburg or the Swiss Federal Council, or even a Chief Justice of a neutral State.[7] The primary difficulty, obviously, was to secure agreement on the arbitrator. It could normally be expected that the heads of State appointed would delegate the task of deciding to an independent expert, whose name would not necessarily be divulged; a reasoned judgment would not necessaily be given.[8]

With the joint commissions the tribunal would consist of a plurality of persons, as opposed to a single arbitrator, but they would all be of a highly "representative" character. In some, each party would appoint an equal number of commissioners; the Alaskan Boundary tribunal established in 1903 by the United States and Great Britain had six members, three appointed by

[7] For example, *The Clipperton Island Case* (1931) Mexico/France decided by the King of Italy; the *Delagoa Bay Arbitration* of 1872, submitted to the King of France (who appointed five eminent Frenchmen); the *Costa Rica Packet* (1895) referred to a jurist selected by the Czar of Russia; the *Croft Case* (1856) G.B./Portugal and *White Case* (1864) G.B./Peru, decided by the Senate of Hamburg; the *Tinoco Arbitration* (1923) G.B./Costa Rica, decided by Taft, C.J. of the United States.
[8] *e.g.* the awards of President Cleveland in the *Cerruti Case* (1912) Italy/Colombia, of President Loubet in the Panama-Costa Rica Boundary arbitration (1911), and of King Edward VII in the U.S./Chile *Alsop Case* (1909). A neglect to give a reasoned judgment is treated by many writers and by Art. 35 of the I.L.C. Model Rules as a reason for nullity of the award.

each Party. Here the process becomes almost one of negotiation of a compromise, and the risk of a failure to reach agreement is high. This risk is lessened by the practice adopted in the 1794 Jay Treaty of choosing an "odd" member by agreement or by lot; there were three commissions established and each was to consist of either three or five members, the third or fifth being the "odd" member. Whilst the chances of a decision are obviously greater here, the "odd" member was also a national or one or other party so that it is not possible to regard this as the introduction of a "neutral" element. An alternative, which achieved the same end, was to refer the dispute to an umpire in the event of the failure of the commissioners to agree; the U.S./G.B. treaty of 1853 adopted this technique, the umpire being a citizen of the United States, agreed upon by the commissioners.

A substantial advance is seen in the "mixed" commissions which contain a "neutral" element; that is to say a member or members with the decisive vote and not nationals of either party. The chances of a decision being reached, and, moreover, a decision likely to be based on an impartial view of the legal rights of the parties are obviously much higher than with the joint commission. In the celebrated *Alabama Claims* of 1872, the United States and Great Britain as parties each appointed one member only; the King of Italy, the President of the Swiss Confederation and the Emperor of Brazil each appointed one further member, producing a kind of collegiate international court. The precedent was successfully followed in the *Behring Sea Fur Seals Arbitration* of 1893. There was an even further advance with the *Venezuelan Preferential Claims Case* of 1904, in which none of the interested parties had its nationals on the tribunal; all were "neutral" and were selected by the Emperor of Russia, the selection being from the panel of the Permanent Court of Arbitration. The mixed arbitral tribunals established under Article 304 of the Treaty of Versailles, or the similar provision of the treaties of St. Germain, Trianon, Neuilly, Sèvres and Lausanne, for the purpose of settling claims by nationals of the Allied and Associated Powers against Germany and the other Central Powers were of a similar kind. The three-man tribunal appointed to arbitrate the Rann of Kutch dispute between India and Pakistan in 1966 is a more recent example.[9]

[9] See Award in (1968) 7 I.L.M. 633–704.

A recent, and novel, feature is to be found in the Convention on the Settlement of Investment disputes between States and nationals of other States, concluded in 1965 under the auspices of the International Bank.[10] This envisages the use of Conciliation Commissions and Arbitral Tribunals, constituted from a Panel of arbitrators: its novelty lies in the use of arbitration in disputes between States and individuals.

This brief survey of types of arbitral bodies, with a few random examples, will perhaps serve to illustrate the problems inherent in the task of settling the composition of the tribunal afresh, for each new arbitration. Moreover, the ideal of a "neutral" arbitral body was far from being realised as a necessary part of impartial adjudication. The idea of facilitating the solution of these problems by providing for the constitution of a tribunal *in advance* of particular disputes was given partial expression in the Permanent Court of Arbitration, established by the Hague Convention for the Pacific Settlement of International Disputes of 1899 and 1907.[11]

1. THE PERMANENT COURT OF ARBITRATION

The Hague Convention of 1899 and 1907 established the Permanent Court of Arbitration which was, in fact, neither permanent nor a court. It consisted, essentially, of a "panel" of arbitrators. Each party to the Conventions could appoint four individuals of recognised competence in international law. In the event of the States parties to a dispute agreeing to go to arbitration (for there was no question of the Conventions imposing compulsory arbitration) they were able to utilise this "panel" so as to compose their tribunal. Under Article 45 of the 1907 Convention the parties could by agreement choose any number of arbitrators from the panel, but in default of agreement each party would appoint two arbitrators, of whom one only could be its national or chosen from amongst the persons selected by it as members of the panel. These

[10] (1966) 60 A.J.L. 892. See *post*, p. 282.
[11] Note that this was not the first attempt. The Union for International Transport by Rail had by a convention of 1890 empowered the Central Office, organised by the Swiss Government, to decide disputes; the Swiss Government established a permanent tribunal consisting of the Director of the Office and two judges appointed by the Swiss Federal Council. Even earlier, in 1862, Great Britain had by treaty with other States established permanent mixed courts at Sierra Leone to adjudicate on seizures of vessels suspected of engaging in the slave trade.

arbitrators would then choose an umpire, or, where their votes were evenly divided, a third State selected by the parties would choose him, or, if no agreement on a third State was reached. each party would choose a different State and these two States would then choose the umpire, or, failing agreement, would draw lots from amongst members of the panel not being those members appointed by the parties or nationals of the powers. Thus, in the last resort, a tribunal could be constituted, and it would include an "odd" member who would be truly independent.

This, then, was the significant advance. It fell far short of a permanent tribunal in the accepted sense. The only really permanent organ was the International Bureau, the registry of the "Court," which had custody of the archives, acted as intermediary for communications relating to the Court and dealt with administrative questions, subject to control by the Permanent Council consisting of the diplomatic envoys of the contracting Powers accredited to The Hague.

Admittedly the Conventions of 1899 and 1907 had other useful features. They dealt with good offices and mediation, international commissions of inquiry and, in relation to arbitration, not only provided for this "panel" of arbitrators but set out a code of rules of procedure for adoption by tribunals if the parties failed to adopt rules themselves by agreement and even provided a special summary procedure for arbitration. Another ambitious (though never used) provision was Article 53 of the 1907 Convention allowing the Permanent Court to settle the *compromis* if the parties agreed. But these scarcely affected the institutional weaknesses of the system established with the Permanent Court of Arbitration. The proposal in 1907 for a Court of Arbitral Justice, a truly permanent court, failed because no agreement could be reached on the method of selecting the judges, each State wishing to ensure that it had a judge of its own nationality on the Court.

The process of arbitration, quite apart from the desirability of a permanent judicial tribunal, remained a useful process to which improvements could be made and, indeed, there will always remain a category of disputes which the parties may prefer to refer to arbitration by a small body based essentially on their own choice rather than an international court. Thus, the establishment of the Permanent Court of International Justice in 1920 did not lead to the abolition of the Permanent Court of Arbitration; and the

General Act for the Pacific Settlement of International Disputes of 1928[12] dealt in detail with arbitration, containing in Chapter III elaborate provisions to ensure the appointment of both "neutral" and "national" members of the tribunal and specifying the categories of reservations which could be entered to the general obligation to arbitrate. It was, however, a document "free neither from inconsistencies nor from a substantial degree of unreality"[13]; the chief inconsistency was the notion that arbitration was appropriate to disputes other than those as to the legal rights of the parties, and even though the arbitral tribunal was directed to apply the law as derived from the sources specified in Article 38 of the Statute of the P.C.I.J. in all cases where the parties did not themselves specify the rules to be applied. The General Act clearly embodied a confusion between arbitration and conciliation.

Since the Second World War the utility of the arbitral process has been seen in the creation of numerous tribunals[14]: most of the peace treaties used a form of "mixed" commission to decide claims, with a neutral umpire in the event of disagreement between the national commissioners, appointed by the governments or, failing their agreement, by the Secretary-General of the UN. We have also noted earlier, in the chapter on the specialised agencies, how arbitration is envisaged in the compromissory clauses providing for interpretation of their constitutional texts. The Bonn Convention of 1955 provided for an ad hoc arbitral tribunal of nine members, three from each party and three "neutral" members appointed by the parties. Other important arbitrations between governments have been the Ambatielos arbitration,[15] the abortive Buraimi arbitration,[16] the United Kingdom/France Continental Shelf Arbitration of 1977, the Beagle Channel Arbitration of 1977, and the Sharjah/Dubai Boundary Arbitration of 1980. The European Convention for the Peaceful Settlement of Disputes of April 29, 1957,[17] concluded

---

[12] See now the Revised General Act, adopted by the General Assembly on April 28, 1949, substituting references to the I.C.J. and the UN organs for those to the P.C.I.J. and organs of the League.

[13] Oppenheim-Lauterpacht, *International Law,* Vol. II 7th ed., p.94.

[14] See *International Disputes: the legal aspects* (1972), pp. 113–116.

[15] *United Kingdom Treaty Series,* No. 20 (1955), Cmd. 9425.

[16] *Ibid.* No. 65 (1954), Cmd. 9272. The tribunal broke up after the U.K. member alleged the corruption of the Saudi Arabian member.

[17] Simpson and Fox, *International Arbitration* (1959), Chap. III.

within the Council of Europe, provides for compulsory arbitration of disputes not settled by conciliation before a tribunal of five members of which three shall be "neutrals" chosen, in the absence of agreement, by a third State which is itself chosen, in the absence of agreement by the President of the I.C.J.[18] An even more striking testimony to the continued usefulness of the arbitral process is the set of Model Rules on Arbitral Procedure adopted by the International Law Commission in 1958.[19] This sets out a body of rules which parties may adopt in order to implement an agreement to arbitrate; their scope is extremely wide, for they refer the question of "arbitrability" to the I.C.J., they define the essential contents of a *compris*, the powers of a tribunal and model rules of procedure, the essentials of an award, grounds for annulment, etc. On the crucial question of composition they provide for recourse, in final analysis, to the President of the I.C.J.[20]

The continuing value of arbitration did not, however, affect the desirability of a permanent judicial tribunal. If we may revert to the position in 1907, it was clearly the selection of the judges which constituted the main hindrance to agreement on the establishment of such a tribunal. Somewhat surprisingly, this problem of selection of judges was solved in connection with the Convention for an International Prize Court of 1907 which the Conference adopted, but which, not so surprisingly, never entered into force. That court would indeed have been a permanent court, in that there would have been fifteen judges appointed for six-year terms; eight States would have had an automatic right to appoint a

[18] The tribunal decides "ex aequo et bono, having regard to the general principles of international law, while respecting the contractual obligations and the final decisions of international tribunals which are binding on the parties" (Art. 26); this "quasi-legal" basis for the decisions is explicable by reason of the fact that, under Art. 1, *legal* disputes are to be submitted to the I.C.J. This Convention is not yet in force, a disappointing result considering that the European States generally regard themselves as the most progressive in the field of pacific settlement.

[19] A/3859.

[20] The wisdom of this has been questioned by Johnson, *loc. cit.*, pp. 153–158, who (using the refusal of the President or Vice-President of the I.C.J. to appoint an arbitrator in the dispute between the Anglo-Iranian Oil Company and Iran under the Concession Agreement of 1933 as an example), points out that Art. 37 of the Statute of the I.C.J. did not cover the succession to such powers conferred on the President or Vice-President of the P.C.I.J. and, moreover, that the President or Vice-President may decline on the ground that it would prejudice the Court's decision on "arbitrability" in a dispute between two States.

member, other States' appointees would have sat according to a scheme of rotation. The function of the court would have been to hear appeals from the prize decisions of national courts.

The problem of election of judges naturally decreased when the number of participating States decreased. Hence in 1907 the five Central American States of Costa Rica, Guatemala, Honduras, Nicaragua and El Salvador were able to establish the Central American Court of Justice, with each State having its own judge on the Court (and paying him); this Court functioned until 1918, and during its brief history decided 10 cases. One may safely say, therefore, that at this stage States were in principle in favour of a permanent judicial body,[21] subject to a system of election of judges being found which would be equitable without resorting to the absurdity of every State having a judge on the court. This difficulty of electing the judges in a way acceptable to States acutely conscious of their "sovereign equality" was only removed when the establishment of the League came about, for the successful Root-Phillimore plan was able to utilise the League's own organs in the election process.

II. The Permanent Court of International Justice

The Covenant of the League of Nations in Article 14 placed upon the Council of the League the duty to "formulate and submit to the Members of the League for adoption plans for the establishment of a Permanent Court of International Justice . . . ." The Council appointed an advisory committee of jurists, and it was within this committee that the Root-Phillimore plan emerged to solve this crucial question of the election of judges.

The plan, as embodied in the Statute of the Court, involved two stages—nomination and election—with the first being entrusted to the "national groups" in the Permanent Court of Arbitration; these provided existing, responsible bodies able to make suitable nominations. A State which wished to become a party to the Statute of the Court, but was not a member of the P.C.A., was required to establish a national group on the same conditions as those prescribed in Article 44 of the 1907 Convention (Art. 4).

---

[21] Note the Permanent International Joint Commission of 1909 established by U.S. and Canada to solve boundary problems and invested with judicial and quasi-judicial powers.

Before proceeding to nomination each national group was moreover requested to consult its highest courts, law faculties and national academies devoted to the study of international law (Art. 6). Each national group was permitted to nominate not more than four persons, not more than two of whom were to be of the nationality of the group (or for periodic elections not more than double the number of vacancies) (Art. 5 (2)).

From the list of nominees thus secured the Assembly and Council of the League would "proceed independently of one another to elect the members of the Court" (Art. 8), of which there were to be 15.[22] Any nominee securing an absolute majority in both organs was considered as elected, and, if places remained unfilled, a second or third meeting[23] would be held to try to secure this absolute majority in both organs. If places still remained unfilled, a joint conference of the organs (three members only from each organ) would attempt to choose one name for each vacancy by an absolute majority, and would recommend such names to both organs. If the joint conference failed to secure the necessary majority to agree on a nominee, then the members of the Court already elected would proceed to fill the vacancies from among those candidates who obtained votes in either the Assembly or the Council, and, in the event of an equality of votes, the eldest judge had a casting vote.

This, then, was the solution. It remains the system of election for the present I.C.J., subject to certain changes. The references to the Assembly and Council of the League were changed to read General Assembly and Security Council of the UN and, in the voting on elections within the Security Council, there is a specific provision (Art. 10 (2)) to exclude the veto. Moreover Article 13 of the new Statute embodies a scheme for the "staggering" of the elections, so that five are elected every three years to serve a nine-year term, and any judge is capable of re-election. The advantage of "staggering" is, of course, that it ensures a certain continuity of experience on the Court at any one time. The three-yearly election is quite distinct from the occasional elections to fill vacancies caused by death or resignation.

[22] Originally 11, with four deputy judges, but alteration was effected by resolution of the Assembly in 1930, although formal amendment came only in 1936.
[23] Since 1946 the General Assembly and Security Council have interpreted "meeting" to mean "ballot."

The other questions of parties, jurisdiction, etc., can all be dealt with under the International Court of Justice in the following section, where any salient changes between the two Statutes will be pointed out.

III. THE INTERNATIONAL COURT OF JUSTICE[24]

1. Composition
The system of election has already been described.[25] Mention must be made of the two criteria which govern the election. The one, in Article 2, is personal to the judges in that they are to be persons "of high moral character, who possess the qualifications required in their respective countries for appointment to the highest judicial offices, or are juriconsults of recognised competence in international law". The other criterion, in Article 9, is that the body of judges as a whole should represent "the main forms of civilisation and . . . the principal legal systems of the world . . . ." There has developed a tendency to insist on the kind of "equitable geographical distribution" which has characterised the composition of so many of the UN organs or bodies of limited composition, possibly to the neglect of the first criterion which is personal to the judges.

Whereas, with the ad hoc tribunal, the "representative" character of the judges was all too prominent, the essential aim of both the P.C.I.J. and the I.C.J. was to secure a body of independent judges. Article 2 therefore provides for election "regardless of their nationality"; in practice, however, the permanent members of the Security Council always have usually had a judge of their nationality on the Court. Consistently with the intent to disregard nationality in the election, a judge is not debarred from sitting on a particular case to which the State of his nationality is a party; yet, somewhat inconsistently, Article 31 entitles the other party who does not have a judge of its nationality on the Court to nominate a judge ad hoc; and, if neither party has

---

[24] We shall not here be concerned with the substantive law evolved by either the Permanent Court or the I.C.J.: as to this see Lauterpacht, *The Development of International Law by the International Court* (1958); Hambro, *The Case-law of the International Court,* 1952–60, 2 vols.; *Fontes Iuris Gentium,* Series A, Section I, Vol. 1 (1922–30), Vol. 3 (1931–34).

[25] For a critical evaluation of the electoral system see Rosenne, *The International Court of Justice* (1957), pp. 136 *et seq.*

a judge of its nationality on the Court, entitles *both* parties to nominate judges ad hoc. The political desirability of allowing the ad hoc judge as an inducement to States to use the Court is one thing; but it is scarcely consistent with the notion of the Court as an independent body and it is not without significance that no ad hoc judge has ever voted against his own State. One justification, often advanced, is the need to ensure that the views of the State appointing the judge are fully explained to the Court; this argument seems to ignore the availability of the agents and the counsel of the State concerned.

The independence of the judges is further reinforced by their security of tenure; there is no retiring age and dismissal can be brought about only by the unanimous decision of the other members of the Court (Art. 18). Moreover Article 16 forbids the judges to exercise "any political or administrative function or engage in any other occupation of a professional nature," and Article 17 excludes from a particular case any judge who acts or has acted in that case as agent, counsel, etc. This attempt to ensure independence in the sense of an absence of any incompatible occupation necessarily means that the judges must be adequately paid as judges. They are in fact paid a tax-free salary subject to a pensions scheme,[26] and even ad hoc judges are paid out of the funds of the Court and not by the parties as was the practice in ad hoc tribunals.

2. Access to the Court.

(a) *In contentious cases*

Under Article 34 (1) "only States may be parties in cases before the Court." The States which can thus appear are from one of three categories. The first includes all UN Members who, under Article 93 (1) of the UN Charter, are *ipso facto* parties to the Statute of the Court. The second includes non-UN Members who desire a permanent association with the Court, and, under Article 93 (2) become parties to the Statute on conditions to be determined in each case by the General Assembly on the

---

[26] See General Assembly Resol. 86 (1) of December 11, 1946. By reason of the gap occurring between the demise of the League and the establishment of the UN, the I.L.O. assumed the task of administering the pensions scheme of the judges of the P.C.I.J.

recommendation of the Security Council. These conditions, imposed on Switzerland in 1947 and Liechtenstein in 1950, involved acceptance of the Statute, of the obligations of UN Members under Article 94 of the Charter, and of an undertaking to contribute an equitable amount to the expenses of the Court. The third category includes non-UN Members who wish to appear before the Court as parties in a particular dispute or class of disputes but without becoming parties to the Statute. This is possible under Article 35 (2) of the Statute, and the Security Council by a resolution of October 15, 1946, imposed the conditions that such States should undertake to comply with the decision of the Court and accept the obligations of Article 94 of the Charter; the Court itself fixes the amount due towards the expenses of the particular case. The salient difference between the second and third categories is that, whilst the second can participate fully in the scheme for compulsory jurisdiction under Article 36 (2)—the "Optional Clause"—the third category can sign the Optional Clause but cannot rely on it as against States who are parties to the Statute (*i.e.* in categories 1 or 2) unless they specifically agree.

It thus appears[27] that international organisations have no *locus standi* as parties in a contentious case before the Court. With their rights to present information to the Court and to request advisory opinion from the Court we shall deal at a later stage.

(b) *In respect of its advisory jurisdiction*

Article 65 of the Statute provides that the Court may give an advisory opinion on any legal question at the request of whatever body may be authorised by or in accordance with the Charter of the United Nations to make such a request.[28] The constitutional significance of this procedure for the organs of the United Nations and the other intergovernmental organisations so authorised will be discussed later. Suffice it to point out at this stage that individual States have no power to request an advisory opinion.

---

[27] But see the argument by Weissberg, *The International Status of the UN* (1961), p. 195, that the UN may be regarded as a "State" for the purposes of Art. 34; the present author does not accept this view.

[28] Contrast Art. 14 of the League Covenant which referred to opinions requested by the Assembly or the Council "upon any dispute or question."

Their rights are limited to furnishing information under Article 66; the situation is thus in a sense the reverse of the contentious jurisdiction where the States are parties and international organisations are limited to presenting information.

3. The Jurisdiction of the Court

The jurisdiction of the Court rests on the consent of the parties. As Article 36 (1) states, it comprises "all cases *which the parties refer to it* . . . ." Thus, as in the traditional arbitration, a form of *compromis* might be agreed upon where jurisdiction rests essentially on an ad hoc agreement. Yet this is not the only means of expressing consent to the jurisdiction of the Court, and, indeed, no special form is required, so that in the *Corfu Channel Case*[29] a letter to the Registrar written by the Albanian Deputy Minister for Foreign Affairs was considered to be a sufficient expression of consent by Albania. Moreover, since nothing in the Statute requires consent to be given by both parties *before* an application to the Court can be made, it is possible for a prorogated jurisdiction to exist. In such a case the Court is seised with a unilateral application to which the other party pleads on the merits, without contesting the jurisdiction; this is treated as an acceptance of the jurisdiction, rather like an estoppel by conduct.[30] Consent can thus be express or tacit, and can be deduced from one act or a series of successive acts.[31]

However, such consent may well have been given in advance, and Article 36 (1) continues with the phrase " . . . and all matters specially provided for in the Charter of the United Nations or in treaties and conventions in force." In fact the Charter does not contain any provision for an agreed jurisdiction; the power of the Security Council to recommend to Members that they refer their legal disputes to the Court, contained in Article 36 (3), was not regarded by the majority of the judges in the *Corfu Channel Case* as involving an obligation on the parties to do so (although this view was *obiter* since the Court decided there was jurisdiction on the basis of the Albanian letter). There are, however, many "treaties or conventions in force" which provide for reference to

---

[29] *Preliminary Objection* (1948) *I.C.J. Reports* 28.
[30] See the *Minorities Schools Case,* P.C.I.J. Ser. A, No. 15.
[31] As in the *Monetary Gold Case* (1954) *I.C.J. Reports* 19 so far as U.K., U.S.A., France and Italy were concerned.

the Court.[32] It may be recalled that a primary purpose of the 1928 General Act was to establish the jurisdiction of the Permanent Court by this means, and we have already referred to the similar purpose of the European Convention for the Pacific Settlement of Disputes of 1957. We have seen earlier how some of the specialised agencies have in their constitutions a "compromissory clause" to cover disputes between Member States which is in effect a conventional title to jurisdiction. The Court publishes annually in its Yearbook the texts of such compromissory clauses in treaties in force. Special provision is made in Article 37 for the succession by the I.C.J. to jurisdiction conferred by pre-1945 treaties on the P.C.I.J.[33] Lastly, jurisdiction may be accepted under Article 36 (2), the "Optional Clause," whereby the "States parties to the present Statute may at any time declare that they recongise as compulsory *ipso facto* and without special agreement, in relation to any other State accepting the same obligation, the jurisdiction of the Court in all legal disputes concerning:

(a) the interpretation of a treaty;

(b) any question of international law;

(c) the existence of any fact which, if established, would constitute a breach of an international obligation;

(d) the nature or extent of the reparation to be made for the breach of an international obligation."

This marked the extent to which the States were prepared to accept compulsory jurisdiction in 1945; as we have seen, it is compulsory *once it is voluntarily accepted.* There is no obligation to make a declaration under Article 36 (2)[33a] and, in effect, it is only different from the jurisdiction existing under 36 (1) in the degree of consent.

These declarations may be made for "a certain time" (Art. 36

---

[32] Note the reluctance of the Court to allow a party to argue that such a treaty is void or terminated and its obligation to submit to the jurisdiction therefore ended: *Fisheries Jurisdiction Case,* Judgment of February 2, 1973.

[33] Hence in the *S.W. Africa Case* (1950) *I.C.J. Reports* 133, the Court noted that Art. 7 of the Mandate was still in force and South Africa therefore under an obligation to accept the compulsory jurisdiction of the I.C.J. However, in the extraordinary Judgment of 1966, virtually reversing the earlier 1962 Judgment on the preliminary objection, the Court held that the applicant States Ethiopia and Liberia had no *locus standi* in proceedings against South Africa: see *ante,* p. 74.

[33a] By 1972 only 46 States out of 135 had done so.

(3)) and are, in fact, often limited to a period of years. The extent to which they effectively confer a compulsory jurisdiction is limited by three factors. First, the declarations are effective "in relation to any other State *accepting the same obligation"* and, under 36 (3), may be made "on condition of reciprocity." Hence the subject-matter of the dispute must fall within the terms of the acceptances of both parties; either can rely on a reservation made by the other and impose a limitation on jurisdiction *ratione materiae.* Second, both declarations must be currently valid so that either party may rely on the other's limitation *ratione temporis.*[34] It will suffice, however, if both parties' declarations are valid and subsisting at the time of the application; the Court will not become disseised because of the expiry of a declaration during the proceedings.[35] The better view is that, once the declaration is made for a fixed period, it cannot be unilaterally terminated prior to the conclusion of the period, for this would undermine the whole purpose of the Optional Clause. However, a practice has begun whereby certain States have made declarations terminable upon notice, and such declarations, if used to prevent a particular dispute from reaching the Court, make nonsense of the acceptance of compulsory jurisdiction and may well make the whole acceptance of doubtful validity.

The third, and common, limitation arises from the appending of reservations to the declaration; these may exclude from the acceptance of compulsory jurisdiction a particular dispute or whole classes of disputes. Some of these, such as the United States reservation of matters within the domestic jurisdiction of the United States "as determined by the United States" challenge the basic principle of Article 36 (6) that the Court shall decide whether or not it has jurisdiction in the event of a dispute. The validity and effect of such reservations has not yet been decided by the Court. However, in the *Norwegian Loans Case* and the *Interhandel Case* (1959) several Judges thought them invalid. Judge Lauterpacht believed them to be so fundamentally invalid that they rendered the entire acceptance of the Optional Clause invalid. Other judges believed the invalid reservation could be severed from the

---

[34] See the *Electricity Company of Sofia Case*, P.C.I.J. Ser. A/B, Nos. 77, 79, 80, where Bulgaria as defendant relied on the Belgian limitation *ratione temporis.*
[35] *Nottebohm Case* (1953) *I.C.J. Reports* 111.

remaining, valid acceptance, and the Court's Order of June 22, 1973 in the *Nuclear Tests Case* gives some support to this view. Another highly questionable reservation is that of the right to exclude any given category of disputes by notifying the Secretary-General, with immediate effect upon notification.[36] In fact recent years have seen a "decline in the Optional Clause"[37] of such dimensions as to lead to scepticism about the possibility of compulsory jurisdiction ever being established in the foreseeable future. As presently working, the Optional Clause places in the most favourable position the "opportunist" State which is a party to the Statute but which makes an ad hoc acceptance under Article 36 (2) when self-interest favours judicial settlement of its disputes and which rescinds when it does not.

Article 36 (5) provides for succession by the I.C.J. to jurisdiction conferred upon the P.C.I.J. by declarations under the old Article 36 (2), just as Article 37 provides for succession to the "conventional jurisdiction." It is only necessary to point out that where a State did not become a party to the Statute of the I.C.J. until some time *after* that Statute came into force its declaration under the old Statute will have lapsed with the extinction of the P.C.I.J. and will therefore not be a declaration "still in force" to which Article 36 (5) applies.[38]

Apart from the jurisdiction over the main issue, the Court has an incidental jurisdiction to deal with three matters, by way of interlocutory proceedings. The first is the "preliminary objection." Where a party disputes the Court's jurisdiction, this is dealt with by the Court as incidental to the merits and without prejudice to the decision on the merits. The second is an application to intervene. Under Article 63 of the Statute there is a right to intervene for a State party to a treaty the construction of which is in issue in a case. All other applications to intervene are granted or not at the descretion of the Court under Article 62 of the Statute. The Court must be satisfied that the State has an interest of a legal natue which may be affected by the decision. Such applications to intervene have been few, and Malta's application to intervene in

---

[36] See the Portuguese declaration of December 19, 1955.

[37] See the extremely important article by Waldock in (1955–56) 32 B.Y.B.I.L. 244. The texts of all acceptances under Art. 36 (2) are given in the current *Yearbook* of the I.C.J.

[38] *Aerial Incident of July 27, 1955* (Preliminary Objection), (1959) *I.C.J. Reports.*

the Libyan/Tunisian dispute in 1981 was rejected because Malta failed to meet that test. It remains an open question whether, in addition, there must be a jurisdictional link between the actual parties and the would-be intervener.

The third type of interlocutory proceeding is the application for an order of interim measures of protection under Article 41 of the Statute. Here the jurisprudence shows that the Court's decision will depend on two, interrelated factors. One is the likelihood that the Court has jurisdiction on the merits, the other is the degree of urgency and risk of irreparable damage if an order of protection is not made. There must be prima facie evidence of a good basis for jurisdiction, and there must be a risk of real damage to a State's interests which any eventual judgment will not repair.[39]

Although much thought and discussion have been given to the problem of encouraging the use of the Court and extending its jurisdiction,[40] there seems to be little immediate prospect of increased activity by the Court. In the first twenty years after 1945, the Court gave thirteen Judgments and twelve Advisory Opinions only. It can hardly be hoped that the extraordinary decision in the *S.W. Africa Case* will have enhanced the reputation of the Court or given the confidence necessary to encourage its use by the newer nations. However, in 1972 the Court amended its rules in three respects in order to encourage States to make greater use of its jurisdiction. The recourse to Chambers of the Court is facilitated by conceding to the parties considerable influence over the composition of ad hoc Chambers. The procedures for both contentious and advisory proceedings have been accelerated. And the Court can now regulate preliminary objections so as to settle the issues at an early stage, thus avoiding a double discussion of the same issues at both the preliminary stage and at the stage of the merits.[41]

4. The law applicable

This is set out in Article 38 and constitutes a statement of the primary sources of international law. It may be noted that Article

---

[39] See Mendelson, (1972–3) *B.Y.B.I.L.* 46, 259; Goldsworthy, (1974) *A.J.I.L.* 68, 258 and subsequently the Order of September 11, 1976 (the Aegean Case) and December 15, 1979 (the Hostages Case).

[40] Jenks, *The Prospects for International Adjudication* (1964) gives a comprehensive account of these endeavours.

[41] For texts see (1973) 67 A.J.I.L. 195 and for commentary Arechaga, *ibid.*, p. 1.

38 (c)—"the general principles of law recognised by civilised nations"—constitutes a refutation of the notion that *lacuna* exist in the law which may make a dispute "non-justiciable." The reference in Article 38 (2) to "judicial decisions" as "subsidiary means for the determination of rules of law" is also worthy of note in that, despite Article 59 which prevents any rigid doctrine of *stare decisis* from developing, it enables the Court to utilise the advantage of its own permanence by looking to its own previous decisions as evidence of what the law is. It is, of course, not limited to looking at its own decisions, but a certain consistency of special respect for them can, not unnaturally, be discerned in its judgments. The power to decide *ex aequo et bono* (which in any event rests on the special agreement of the parties), whilst of theoretical interest, ought perhaps not to detain us here, for it is a power which has so far never been entrusted to the Court.

5. The institutional role of the Court

(a) *Its relationship to the UN*

Whereas the Statute of the P.C.I.J. was completely independent of the League Covenant, the present Statute is an "integral part" of the Charter and the I.C.J. is itself the "principal judicial organ of the United Nations" (Art. 92). Membership of the UN gives automatic participation in the Statute (Art. 93 (1)), unlike the League, but, like the League, judicial settlement by the Court forms an essential part of the general procedures for settlement envisaged in the constitution of the general political organisation, without, however, giving to any organ of the latter the power to *impose* compulsory judicial settlement.[42]

The General Assembly and Security Council have assumed the same role in the election process as did the Assembly and Council of the League, and the Security Council has assumed a similar role to the League Council in respect of the enforcement of decisions given by the Court. This power of enforcement, which is in all legal systems essentially one for the executive branch of government to wield in the last resort, rather than the judicial branch itself, is, of course, crucial to the effectiveness of the process for

[42] *Ante*, p. 147.

judicial settlement.[43] Under the Covenant the Council was empowered to "propose what steps should be taken to give effect" to the decisions of the Court (Art. 13 (4)). Under the Charter, Article 94 (2) provides:

> "If any party to a case fails to perform the obligations incumbent upon it under a judgment rendered by the Court, the other party may have recourse to the Security Council, which may, if it deems necessary, make recommendations or decide upon measures to be taken to give effect to the judgment."

This should, therefore, permit the use, in the last resort, of the enforcement measures of Chapter VII although the Council is not compelled to do so. The factors, largely of a political nature, which tend to stultify Chapter VII have already been noted[44]; in this particular connection one has to add the reluctance of the Soviet Union to utilise the Court and a probable opposition to any attempt to use Article 94 in the way in which it was intended. Fortunately, States rarely refuse to abide by or execute decisions of the Court; the refusal of Albania to pay damages awarded in the *Corfu Channel Case* and of Iceland to comply with the judgment in the *Fisheries Jurisdiction Cases* are the exceptions (to which must now be added Iran's refusal to comply with the Court's order for the release of the U.S. hostages).[45] It must be noted, nevertheless, that institutional enforcement is more unlikely than likely, and a successful litigant will be left with such measures of self-help as are consistent with its obligations under the Charter, especially Article 2 (4).

No specific procedure for amendment of the Statute of the P.C.I.J. was envisaged, hence a special conference of all the signatories had to be convened in 1929, which then reported on

---

[43] See generally Schachter, "Enforcement of International Judicial and Arbitral Decisions," (1960) 54 A.J.I.L. 1; Reisman, "The role of economic agencies in the enforcement of international judgments and awards" (1965) 19 *Int. Orgs.* 929.

[44] *Ante*, pp. 30, 41.

[45] Discussion of enforcement of the Court's order for provisional measures in the *Anglo-Iranian Oil Case,* or of the *A.O. on S.W. Africa* does not directly concern Art. 94, since no "judgment" had been given. Refusal of States like Iceland, France and Iran to even appear before the Court to defend cases is as disturbing as refusal to comply with a judgment.

various amendments to the League Assembly which "adopted" them in the form of a Protocol opened for signature. It was not until 1936 that the Protocol was able to enter into force, due to the tardiness of some of the ratifications; and even then, it entered into force lacking three ratifications but with the Council being satisfied that there were no objections by the three States concerned. With the I.C.J. the institutional link is so close as to have justified Article 69 of the Statute providing for amendment of the Statute in the same way, or rather by the same process, as the Charter itself, subject to provisions being made for participation by States parties to the Statute but not Members of the UN. Article 70 empowers the Court itself to propose amendments.

In budgetary matters the links with the UN are as close as they were with the League. Article 33 of the Statute provides for the expenses of the Court to be borne by the UN "in such a manner as shall be decided by the General Assembly." The Court's budget is, therefore, a part of the overall UN budget which is approved by the General Assembly under Article 18 of the Charter. The estimates are prepared by the Registry in close co-operation with the Secretary-General, leaving the Registry administratively free in its use of the moneys once allocated. For non-UN Members who are parties to the Statute, the Assembly fixes an annual, percentage contribution acting under Article 93 (2) of the Charter; the Court itself fixes the amount due towards its expenses from States appearing before it under Article 35 (3) of the Statute.

The relationship between the Court and the UN is thus seen to be very close. The Court is, however, the "judicial organ," so that the relationship has to be one in which the judicial independence of the Court is recognised. Hence the Court, alone of the principal organs, does not itself submit annual reports on its activities which then form the basis of discussion, and possibly criticism, within the General Assembly. Fears that this close relationship might prejudice the independence and integrity of the Court are largely misplaced for this is to ignore the highly political role which the Court plays[46] and the growing importance of its role in the constitutional development of the UN and specialised agencies, as

---

[46] This is the central thesis of Rosenne, *The International Court of Justice*; no better book on the Court as an institution has yet been written and the extent of the present writer's indebtedness to it is readily and gratefully expressed.

compared with its role as an adjudicator on disputes between States. It is to this "constitutional" role that we now turn.

(b) *Advisory opinions*

We have seen that no international organisation has any *locus standi* before the Court as a *party* in a contentious case; this results directly from the "only States" provision in Article 34 (1). The only participation in such cases envisaged for international organisations is that of presenting information relevant to cases before the Court[47]—which public international organisations may do as of right under the Article 34 (2)—and of being notified "whenever the construction of the constituent instrument (of the particular organisation) . . . or of an international convention adopted thereunder is in question in a case before the Court . . ." (Art. 34 (3)).

Conversely, the advisory jurisdiction of the Court is available to organisations but not to States. In contrast to a judgment in a contentious case, however, an advisory opinion has of itself no binding force; it cannot create a *res judicata*[48] and there are strictly no parties. It is, therefore, a far "weaker" statement of the law than a judgment, in strictly legal terms; its moral and political effectiveness is another matter, and the judges themselves have spoken of "all the moral consequences which are inherent in the dignity of the organ delivering the opinion . . . "[49] or "the legal position as ascertained by the Court."[50]

The right to request an advisory opinion is an *original* right under Article 96 (1) of the Charter for the General Assembly and the Security Council[51], it is a *derivative* right (in the sense of being

[47] It was requested by the Court in the Advisory Opinions on *Reservations, UN Administrative Tribunal* and *ILO Administrative Tribunal* cases, but has never been used in a contentious case.
[48] Hence the I.L.C.'s criticism in its work on the Law of Treaties of the *A.O. on Reservations to the Genocide Convention* was bold but not improper. And, even though the G.A. "accepted" the A.O. on *Certain Expenses etc.*, the U.S.S.R. was technically within its rights in refusing to be bound by the legal opinions of the Court.
[49] Judge Azevedo in the *A.O. on the Peace Treaties* (1950) *I.C.J. Reports* 80.
[50] Judge Lauterpacht in the *A.O. on the S.W. Africa Committee, ibid.* (1956), p. 47.
[51] The vote by which such a request can be made is not entirely clear; the S.C. has never made such a request, and, whilst the Assembly has, it is to be noted that in 1949 the President of the Assembly ruled that it was a procedural matter, G.A.O.R. (IV) Plenary, p. 536.

conferred by the Assembly under Article 96 (2)) for ECOSOC, the Trusteeship Council, the Interim Committee and the Committee on Applications for Review of UN Administrative Tribunal Judgments—all organs of the UN—and all the specialised agencies except the UPU (which has no power to request advisory opinions). With the Assembly and Security Council the advisory opinion may be requested "on any legal question"; hence on occasions doubts have been expressed over whether a given question was "legal" or "political," on the view that political questions were outside the jurisdiction of the Assembly to request and of the Court to grant.[52] The Court is never under a *duty* to give an opinion upon request, so that it could well refuse on grounds of propriety. However, refusal to give an opinion ought never to be based on the ground that the question at issue is a "political" one: the distinction between "legal" and "political" questions has many meanings and should not be used as a *jurisdictional* criterion. A more proper response for the Court is that the jurisdiction to make the decision requested has been allocated elsewhere (for example, to the Security Council or General Assembly) and is not reviewable by the Court.[53] It might also be argued that it is equally for the requesting organ to exercise propriety and that to involve the Court in an opinion when the issue has given rise to substantial disputes betwen Member States affecting their own obligations, or when the political opposition to an opinion is likely to be so severe that the opinion will not be accepted by all the Members, only harms the reputation of the Court and aggravates the difficulties of finding an eventual solution to the disputes. The unhappy experience of the Advisory Opinion on *Certain Expenses* lends support to this view. Equally, however, if both the requesting organ and the Court are satisfied on the propriety of giving an opinion, it would be harmful to the Court's reputation if the Court

[52] See the doubts of Krylov and Zoričic in the *A.O. on Admissions,* (1948) *I.C.J. Reports;* similar objections were made in the Assembly in connection with the request on the *Reservations Case.* An excellent discussion of the problem is to be found in Rosenne, *op. cit.* pp. 454–68. The Court recently rejected this argument against its giving an opinion on *Certain Expenses of the UN* on July 20, 1962, (1962) *I.C.J. Reports* 155, and again in its opinion on the interpretation of the W.H.O./Egypt Agreement, (1980) *I.C.J. Reports,* 1.

[53] See Greig, "The Advisory Jurisdiction of the ICJ and the settlement of disputes between States" (1966) 15 I.C.L.Q. 325 and Higgins, "Policy Considerations and the international judicial process" (1968) 17 I.C.L.Q. 58 for valuable discussion of this point.

declines to consider the "political" antecedents and implications of the issue before it. An opinion based on purely legal reasoning and abstracted from the political context in which it has been requested is unlikely to serve any useful purpose.

With the specialised agencies a fairly standard clause, adopted first in the relationship agreement with the ILO, is to be found limiting much more rigidly the scope of opinions to be requested; the clause is "on legal questions arising within the scope of its activities other than questions concerning the mutual relationships of the Organisation and the United Nations or the specialised agencies"[54]; there is also an obligation to notify ECOSOC of the request.

There is, finally, the limitation, which is now firmly established in the jurisprudence of the Court that an advisory opinion will not be given when in effect it would be tantamount to giving a decision on a dispute between parties, one of whom refuses to participate in the proceedings.[55] However, the effect of this limitation has to be considered in the light of the Court's opinions in the *Peace Treaties* case[56] and the *Namibia* case.[57] In the former the Court emphasised that its opinions are given to the requesting organ, not to the States, that they are not legally binding, and that the principle in the *E. Carelia Case* would not apply where, as in the present case, the opinion related to a purely procedural matter and not the substantive issue involved. In the latter case the Court found that there was no dispute pending between States (as it was bound to do following its decision in 1966 rejecting the *locus standi* of Ethiopia and Liberia) and the *E. Carelia* principle could not therefore apply. The phrase used by the Court, that "the reply of the Court, itself an 'organ of the United Nations,' represents its participation in the activities of the Organisation, and, in principle, should not be refused"[58] suggests that refusal will come very reluctantly: there is no case in which a refusal has been given by the I.C.J.

However, since there are limits to the jurisdiction to give

---

[54] Relationship Agreement, Art 11.
[55] The *Eastern Carelia Case,* P.C.I.J. Ser. B, No. 5, an opinion requested by the Council of the League.
[56] (1950) *I.C.J. Reports.*
[57] (1971) *I.C.J. Reports* paras. 30–35.
[58] (1950) *I.C.J. Reports* p. 71.

opinions, and to the power to request them, a "preliminary question" of jurisdictional competence can arise. It must be noted, however, that although by Article 68 of the Statute "in the exercise of its advisory functions the Court shall further be guided by the provisions . . . which apply in contentious cases to the extent to which it recognises them to be applicable," there is no separate stage of the "preliminary objection"; the jurisdictional question is treated as part and parcel of the main opinion.

Before turning to the typical constitutional problems on which opinions have been sought it is necessary to distinguish the so-called "compulsive" opinions from the normal advisory opinions. Lacking direct access to the Court as parties, organisations have resorted to a device whereby disagreements *with States* can, by a prior agreement which provides both for recourse to an advisory opinion and for the acceptance of the opinion as binding, be referred to the Court. The General Convention on Privileges and Immunities of 1946 and the Headquarters Agreement between the UN and the U.S.A. of 1947 both use this device. Needless to say, the binding force of the opinion derives from the prior agreement and not from the opinion as such.

This apart, the normal advisory opinion has been used for three main purposes. First, it has been used as a means of securing an authoritative interpretation of the Charter provisions, or of the provisions of the constitutional documents of the specialised agencies: the *Admissions and Competence* cases[59] the *IMCO* case,[60] or the *Expenses Case* of July 20, 1962, are obvious examples. It must be added, however, that these interpretations are "authoritative" and not strictly binding. The Charter has, of course, no specific provision regarding settlement of disputes over interpretation—no "compromissory clause" so-called—nor has the Court been entrusted with any power of judicial review over the legality of the actions of the organs of the UN at the request of a Member State (other than the recourse from the UN Administrative Tribunal dealt with below).

Secondly, it has been used to secure guidance for various organs

---

[59] (1948) *I.C.J. Reports* 57; (1950), p. 4. For a discussion of these opinions see *ante*, p. 43.
[60] (1960) *I.C.J. Reports* 150. See *ante*, p. 147 for a discussion of the various compromissory clauses in the constitutions of the specialised agencies.

in the carrying out of their functions; the *Peace Treaties*,[61] *Reservations*,[62] *Reparations*,[63] *S. W. Africa (Voting)*,[64] *UN Administrative Tribunal*,[65] *ILO Administrative Tribunal (UNESCO)*[66] and the *Namibia*[67] cases are all opinions of this kind. It is particularly in relation to these two purposes that the Secretary-General fulfils a role of *amicus curiae*, presenting information both by way of written statements and documentation and/or oral argument through counsel to the Court. Third, it has been used as a means of introducing a form of recourse from judgments of administrative tribunals. The details of the procedures under Article XII of the Statute of the ILO Administrative Tribunal and Article XI of the UN Administrative Tribunal will be described in a later chapter. The grounds upon which a request for an advisory opinion can be made vary somewhat between the two Statutes, and, moreover, whereas it is for the Governing Body and the Administrative Board of the Pensions Fund to challenge the ILO Tribunal's decision, in the case of the UN Tribunal this challenge can be made by a Member State, the Secretary-General or the individual affected by the decision. Thus the UN Tribunal's Statute places the individual staff member on a footing of comparative equality at this stage, which the ILO Tribunal's Statute does not. The further difficulty is to ensure some kind of equality before the I.C.J. once the advisory proceedings are initiated, for the individual is not mentioned in the Court's own Statute as having any *locus standi* whatsoever. This difficulty is met in Article XI of the UN Tribunal's Statute by requiring the Secretary-General "to transmit to the Court the views of the person referred to . . . " and by the recommendation that States and the Secretary-General confine themselves to written statements, foregoing their rights to make oral statements. But in the case of the ILO Tribunal, its Statute contains no provisions for the representation of the individual's views before the Court. Hence in the *ILO Administrative Tribunal (UNESCO) Case*[68] in 1956 the

---

[61] *Ibid.* (1950), p. 221.
[62] *Ibid.* (1951), p. 15.
[63] *Ibid.* (1949), p. 174.
[64] *Ibid.* (1955), p. 67.
[65] *Ibid.* (1954), p. 47.
[66] *Ibid.* (1956), p. 77.
[67] *Ibid.* (1971), p. 16.
[68] *Ibid.* (1956), p. 77.

I.C.J. refused to allow counsel for the staff members involved to submit a written memorandum or participate in oral argument, and UNESCO itself forwarded to the Court a written statement made by counsel for the staff members. The Court itself dispensed with oral proceedings but noted the absence of equality between the parties; however, recognising that the régime of the Tribunal's Statute was essentially for the protection of the officials, it added that "any seeming or nominal absence of equality ought not to be allowed to obscure or to defeat that primary object."[69] The I.C.J. refused to answer the questions put for an opinion, other than the first relating to the competence of the Tribunal, on the ground that they did not raise an issue of "jurisdiction" or "fundamental fault" which are the only issues upon which, under Article XII, an opinion can be asked. In *Application for review of Judgment No. 158 of the U.N.A.T.*[70] the I.C.J. re-affirmed that equality was satisfied by the opportunity to submit written statements and, in the event, upheld the judgment of the UN Administrative Tribunal. The opinions, once given, are binding on the Tribunals and the Organisations in question as a whole.

This particular problem has been dealt with at some length, not solely because of its rather complicated history, but because it shows an extraordinary development whereby the interests of individuals are being put to the I.C.J. for adjudication by way of an opinion, and it brings out the difficulties inherent in using for this purpose a Court before which, basically, "only States" can be parties.[71] We shall meet a similar problem in relation to the European Court of Human Rights.

IV. The International Centre for Settlement of Investment Disputes (ICSID)

This institution was established by the Convention on the Settlement of Investment Disputes between States and Nationals of other States, sponsored by the World Bank and entering into force in 1966.[72] Its essential aim is to foster private foreign

---

[69] *Ibid.* p. 86. See Gross, "Participation of Individuals in Advisory Proceedings before the I.C.J." (1958) 52 A.J.I.L. 16.

[70] A.O. of July 12, 1973, (1973) *I.C.J. Reports* 167.

[71] Judge Morozov dissented largely on the ground that the whole procedure is contrary to the Court's statute: *ibid.*

[72] 575 UNTS 159. At June 1980 there were 79 Contracting States.

investment by providing a mechanism for settlement of investment disputes, but without elevating such disputes to an inter-State confrontation. This necessarily means that the private investor is directly a party to the dispute with a State, litigating on the international plane.[73]

The Centre does not settle disputes itself. It has a fairly minimal structure of an Administrative Council (a plenary body, under the Chairmanship of the President of the World Bank) and a Secretary-General. However, the Centre maintains separate Panels of conciliators and arbitrators, nominated by the contracting parties, and settlement is by these persons, acting in their individual capacity.

As with the I.C.J., consent is the basis of the jurisdiction. The consent must be in writing, but it can be expressed in a contract, or in a compromis concluded after a dispute has arisen, or even in separate submissions to the Centre: and, once given, it cannot be withdrawn unilaterally (Article 25). It can, however, be subject to qualifications or "reservations," such as requiring the prior exhaustion of domestic remedies.

The Parties are, on the one hand, the State (or a subdivision or agency designated by the State) and, on the other, the private investor who must be a national of another Contracting State, whether an individual or a corporate entity (Article 25 (2)). The dispute must be a "legal dispute arising directly out of an investment" between the parties.

The process of settlement is initiated by a request filed with the Secretary-General who registers the request unless he finds it to be "manifestly outside the jurisdiction of the Centre" (Article 36 (3)). This screening role is designed to avoid inflicting on States proceedings that are manifestly beyond the scope of what they intended.

The request will, of course, indicate whether conciliation or arbitration is required. In either event, the parties are free to select the Conciliation Commission[74] or Arbitration Tribunal,[75]

---

[73] For this reason the investor not only does not need the intervention or diplomatic protection of his own State, but his State is debarred from so intervening unless the arbitral award is not complied with (Article 27).

[74] So far conciliation has not been used, which raises the interesting question of why it is regarded as less attractive than arbitration.

[75] Arbitration has been used, although not with great frequency. In 1980 there were only 3 cases, although a number of treaties make reference to ICSID.

and they are not confined to choosing persons from the two Panels. However, they must have an odd number, and Article 39 imposes certain restrictions on the number of nationals that may be chosen. The failure of the parties to agree on the choice of conciliators or arbitrators does not produce an impasse, for the Chairman of the Administrative Council may then appoint.

Once constituted, the Commission or Tribunal will automatically apply the Rules of the Centre, unless the parties have agreed on other rules. They are each judge of their own competence, and are not bound by the Secretary-General's view on receivability in registering the request. Their functions are those traditionally associated with conciliation and arbitration. The Conciliation Commission will clarify the issues and attempt to bring about an agreement, though its recommendations are not binding on the parties: and its work culminates in a report. In contrast, the Arbitration Tribunal produces a binding award, applying such rules of law as may be agreed between the parties, or, in the absence of such agreement, the law of the Contracting State and any applicable rules of international law.[76] The award must be enforced[77] in the territory of the Contracting States as if it were a final judgment of a court of the State (Article 54).

There are limited grounds upon which annulment of an award may be sought: improper constitution of the Tribunal, excess of power, corruption, a serious departure from a fundamental rule of procedure, and failure to give reasons. The nullity hearing is before an ad hoc committee of three new persons, nominated from the Panel by the Chairman (Article 52). There is, under Article 64, a separate provision for reference to the I.C.J. of any dispute between Contracting States regarding the interpretation or application of the Convention, but this would not allow the I.C.J. to be used to challenge the validity of an award, or the appeal to an ad hoc committee for nullification of an award.[78]

There are signs that the ICSID model may be followed

---

[76] It is the application of international law, rather than the Contracting State's law exclusively which accounts for the fact that few Latin-American States are parties to the Convention.

[77] Enforcement may be stayed if there is a request for interpretation (Article 50), or revision (Article 51) or annulment (Article 52) of the award. Interpretation or revision is effected by the original tribunal, annulment by a new ad hoc body.

[78] Report of the Executive Directors, Doc. LCSID/2, Annex (1966), Para. 45.

elsewhere. In 1980 the International Energy Agency (IEA) established its own dispute Settlement Centre to deal with disputes between buyers and sellers of oil or parties to an exchange of oil.[79]

---

[79] (1981) 20 I.L.M. 241.

CHAPTER 9

REGIONAL COURTS

THE creation of permanent judicial institutions, on a regional basis, is prima facie an easier task than on a universal basis, not least because it facilitates the problem of selecting the judges. Hence, as we have already mentioned,[1] the Central American Court of Justice was established by the Washington Convention of December 20, 1907,[2] before the advent of the League made the P.C.I.J. possible. This Central American Court, which functioned between 1908 and 1918, was really the first instance of States accepting the principle of compulsory judicial settlement in advance of the existence of any dispute and establishing a permanent institution for that purpose. No reservations were admitted to this acceptance of compulsory jurisdiction, a feature all the more significant because that jurisdiction comprised not only disputes between States, but also cases brought against States by individuals (arising out of a violation of treaties or having an international character), even if the State of the nationality of the individual did not support the claim. The only restrictions on this right of the individual to claim were that he must have been a national of one of the States members of the Court and he must have first exhausted all local remedies. Five such claims were made before the Court, though none were successful; one was disallowed and four were declared inadmissible. The constitution of the Court itself provided little difficulty, for each Member State had a judge of its nationality on the Court, five in all, and these were paid regular salaries from the Treasury of the Court.[3] Judicial independence was marginal; in one instance a judge was dismissed from office during the tenure of his five-year term by the State appointing him.

Having received its quietus in 1918, due largely to the influence of the United States in the Nicaraguan affair, no regional court

---

[1] *Ante*, p. 264. Space does not permit discussion of national courts of international composition, such as the Mixed Courts of Egypt, Tangiers and Shanghai.

[2] For text of Convention see (1908) A.J.I.L. Suppl., 231.

[3] But *semble*, the Treasury acted as intermediary and each State virtually paid its own judge, sometimes in arrears.

was instituted to replace it until the new Charter of the Organisation of Central American States (ODECA) came into force in 1965[4] and provided for a new Central American Court of Justice. But this is a much less ambitious venture. It has no compulsory jurisdiction over inter-State disputes and its members are the "Presidents of the Judicial Powers" of each of the Member States who meet only when necessary or when convoked by the Executive Council. There is no right of access for individuals and the only innovation is the power given to the Court to render opinions on projects for the unification of Central American legislation. The OAS has established a new Inter-American Court of Human Rights in 1980, though this, too does not provide for access for individuals. Then, too, in the Andean Pact, a Court of Justice has been established in 1979, to function within that Pact rather like the Court of the European Communities.

It may be noted that the Arab League has also promoted the study of the question of establishing an Arab Court of Justice, and a three-man commission prepared a draft statute in 1950[5]; there, too, no further progress by the Member States of the League is apparent.

As early as 1950 the Council of Europe evinced some interest in regional judicial machinery, and in 1951 the Assembly recommended the establishment of a European Court of Justice. The subsequent work of the Assembly's Committee on Legal and Administrative Questions and of the Committee of Experts appointed in 1953 by the Committee of Ministers would suggest, however, the rejection of this idea. The European Convention for the Peaceful Settlement of Disputes of 1957[6] makes no attempt to establish such a court, but instead provides for conciliation, arbitration or the compulsory jurisdiction of the I.C.J.

The OAU has, of course, introduced its own regional machinery for settlement of disputes in the form of the Commission of Mediation, Conciliation and Arbitration, but this has yet to function. Similarly, one has yet to see whether the Tribunals

---

[4] *Ante*, p. 225.
[5] See generally Foda, *The Projected Arab Court of Justice* (1957); Appendix B is the draft statute.
[6] *Ante*, p. 178. See Robertson, *International Institutions in Europe* (1961), pp. 81–86 for a discussion of this idea.

established within the economic communities of West Africa (ECOWAS) and East Africa (ECEA) will actually function.

Whilst, therefore, the creation of regional, permanent judicial institutions is a problem of the future rather than of the present, it is of interest to note that certain fundamental questions will necessarily arise regarding the relationship of any such institutions to the I.C.J. There is first the danger of "regional" systems of international law developing in the "jurisprudence" of regional courts to the detriment of the unity of international law. The notion of an "international law of the Americas" is by no means new, and, indeed, there is scope for some regional rules which can exist without detriment to the universality of the general rules of international law: the *uti possidetis* doctrine relating to sovereignty over territory in the former Spanish territories in the Americas is a case in point. It may also be recalled that in the *Asylum Case*[7] Colombia had invoked "American international law" to support an alleged regional or local custom peculiar to Latin-American States. The Court did not, significantly, reject out of hand the notion that there could be rules of law of this character, but rather regarded Colombia as having failed to discharge the burden of proving such a custom. Foda, in his book on the projected Arab Court of Justice, devotes a special chapter to "Islamic International Principles," clearly suggesting that there is a body of international legal rules peculiar to that region. The danger of serious rifts developing between general and regional international law would, of course, be lessened if a right of appeal lay from any regional courts to the I.C.J.[8] However, in the draft statute of the Arab Court of Justice, no such right of appeal is envisaged, for its decisions are to be final (Art. 53).

The other serious danger is that conflicting jurisdictions might arise, *i.e.* one State might refer the matter to the I.C.J. and the other to the regional court. One solution would be to equip the I.C.J. with powers to order the suspension of such regional proceedings when the matter falls within the jurisdiction of the I.C.J., or to compel the regional court to refer some special point by way of case stated.[9] Another, the one adopted both in Article

---

[7] (1950) *I.C.J. Reports*, 276.
[8] See Jenks, "Regionalism in International Judicial Organisations" (1943) 37 A.J.I.L. 315.
[9] *Ibid.* And see Foda, *op. cit.* pp. 208–211.

62 of the European Convention on Human Rights, and in the Court of the European Communities (see *post*, p. 303), is to include an undertaking *not* to go to the I.C.J. (or for that matter any other means of settlement) in cases arising out of the interpretation or application of the Convention establishing the regional court. Certainly the existence of regional courts will pose problems for both the regional and the International Court.

To date the only existing regional courts are to be found in South and Central America, in Europe, namely the European Court of Human Rights (which will be treated together with the Commission of Human Rights) and the Court of the European Communities and in Africa (the OAU Commission and the ECOWAS and ECEA Tribunals). The following discussion is confined to those actually functioning.

I. THE EUROPEAN COMMISSION AND COURT OF HUMAN RIGHTS

The European Convention for the Protection of Human Rights and Fundamental Freedoms, signed at Rome on November 4, 1950,[10] constitutes one of the most important achievements of the Council of Europe.[11] It contains an enumeration of these rights and freedoms, derived in part from the UN's Universal Declaration of Human Rights of 1948, but (in contrast to the purely moral value of that Declaration) in the form of a binding treaty (to which, admittedly, reservations are permitted and which also permits denunciation). Under Article 1 of the Convention the parties "shall secure to everyone within their jurisdiction the rights and freedoms defined in section I of this Convention." Hence, by way of a radical departure from the traditional refusal of international law to concern itself with the relations between a State and its own nationals,[12] the Covention governs the relations between a State and *all* persons within the jurisdiction of a party so

---

[10] *European Treaty Series* No. 5; 1 *European Yearbook,* 317. There are now five additional Protocols, all of which are now in force. All the texts are reproduced in successive *European Yearbooks* or in *The European Convention on Human Rights* (1968), Council of Europe.

[11] *Ante,* p. 177.

[12] There have been occasional exceptions: *e.g.* the Minorities Treaties concluded after the First World War, or the recognition of "crimes against humanity" in Art. 6 of the Charter of the Nuremberg Tribunal, or the Genocide Convention of 1948. The UN Covenants on Civil and Political Rights and Economic, Social and Cultural Rights will, now adopted, provide exceptions.

far as they fall within the scope of the Convention. By Article 63 a State may declare that the Convention shall apply to "any of the territories for whose international relations it is responsible," so that, whilst the parties must be Members of the Council of Europe, the application of the Convention is not restricted geographically to Europe. Apart from the territories of Member States in Europe, the Convention applies to many overseas territories of the U.K. (21 in January 1968) and to the Netherlands Antilles. Within these territories the States must ensure that their legislation and their judicial and executive decisions comply with their obligations assumed under the Convention, and, under Article 57, each State shall, upon request, supply to the Secretary-General of the Council of Europe "an explanation of the manner in which its internal law ensures the effective implementation of any of the provisions of the Convention." Certain of the contracting States have expressly incorporated the Convention into their municipal law so that the rights secured to individuals thereby become directly enforceable as part of municipal law.[13] It is, however, with the machinery for the supervision and enforcement of this far-reaching obligation assumed by the parties that we are here immediately concerned. That machinery consists of two organs, a Commission and a Court.

1. The European Commission on Human Rights

The Commission is composed of a number of members equal to the number of contracting States, but no two members may be nationals of the same State (Art. 20). They are elected by the Committee of Ministers of the Council of Europe, by an absolute majority of votes, from a list of names drawn up by the Bureau of the Assembly and, in order to give the Committee a real choice, each group of representatives of the States is obliged to put forward three candidates of whom two at least shall be nationals of that State. There are, oddly enough, no criteria for election stated in the Convention and in practice reference has been made by way of analogy to Article 39 (3) which sets out the qualifications required in members of the Court. Elections are for six years, with

---

[13] F.R. of Germany, Belgium, Italy, Luxembourg, Netherlands and Turkey; but not Denmark, Ireland, Norway, Sweden or the U.K. Greece was in the former category but in 1969 denounced the Convention and withdrew from the Council of Europe, rejoining in 1974.

the possibility of re-election, and are "staggered" so as to renew half of the members every three years. Most important, the members are to sit "in their individual capacity" (Art. 23); they are not representatives of the States. The independence of the members is reinforced by the grant of the privileges and immunities envisaged in Article 40 of the Statute of the Council of Europe. Nothing is specified in the Convention about salaries, for the volume of work to be expected was a matter for speculation. In fact the Commission is not in permanent session, and when it meets (usually in Strasbourg) the members are paid a *per diem* allowance which is a charge on the budget of the Council of Europe.

The function of the Commission is, basically, one of the conciliation; hence the fact that it sits in private. On the basis of application or petitions received alleging non-compliance with the Convention, it undertakes an examination of the petition and, if needs be, an investigation (Art. 28 (a)); it then proceeds to "place itself at the disposal of the parties concerned with a view to securing a friendly settlement of the matter on the basis of respect for Human Rights as defined in this Convention" (Art. 28 (b)). The actual performance of this function is at present vested, not in the entire Commission, but in a Sub-Commission of seven members on which each of the parties concerned may appoint one person of its own choice, with the remainder being chosen by lot (Art. 29). However, the Third Protocol of 1963 envisages the deletion of the Sub-Commission and the transfer of this function to the full Commission.

The right to petition the Commission is vested in each contracting State, and there is no "rule of nationality of claims" to limit the States to protecting their own nationals.[14] In addition, in relation to any State accepting this specifically,[15] the Commission has the right to receive petitions from "any person, non-governmental organisation or group of individuals claiming to be

[14] Hence, for example, the Greek Government's complaint against the U.K. over the treatment of Cypriots in 1957.

[15] So far only 15 of the 20 States which are parties have accepted the right of individual petition: Austria, Belgium, Denmark, France, Fed. Rep. of Germany, Ireland, Iceland, Italy, Luxembourg, Netherlands, Norway, Sweden, United Kingdom and Switzerland. Cyprus, Greece, Malta and Turkey have not made declarations under Article 25; and Spain and Liechtenstein are not parties at all.

the victims of a violation . . . of the rights set forth in this Convention" (Art. 25). The acceptance of the principle that individuals may directly petition the Commission is perhaps the most striking of all the innovations of the Convention. There have been instances of individuals having a *locus standi* before international tribunals before,[16] but never on so grand a scale and so as to secure compliance by States with obligations assumed by treaty towards individuals as such. It is, of course, a perfectly logical step to take once one grasps the fact that, under this Convention, it will normally be against their own State that they wish to petition; hence the inappropriateness of the traditional method whereby the State takes up the claim of its nationals against another State.

There are two conditions precedent to the Commisison's jurisdiction; first, all domestic remedies must first be exhausted, and, second, the Commission must then be seised of the petition within six months of the final decision by the State authorities (Art. 26). These two conditions apply to all petitions, whether by States or individuals; in addition, in relation to individual petitions the Commission is forbidden to deal with any which are anonymous, or have already been examined in substance (or referred to another mode of international investigation or settlement) and contain no new information, or are incompatible with the Convention, manifestly ill-founded, or an abuse of the right of petition (Art. 27).[17] The competence of the Commission is thus limited territorially; it is also limited to petitions by States, unless a particular "defendant" State has accepted the right of individuals to petition; it is limited in subject-matter, namely to those rights specified in the Convention; and, finally, it is limited in point of time to petitions based on facts subsequent to the entry into force of the Convention for the particular "defendant" State.

The question of the "admissibility" of the request is obviously an important one, and it is dealt with by a procedure which varies according to whether the petition is by a State[18] or an individual.[19] In the first case the petition is immediately communicated to the

---

[16] See Lauterpacht, *International Law and Human Rights* (1950), Chap. 3.
[17] For a brief résumé of the Commission's jurisprudence on these conditions, see *Juris-Classeur*, Fasc. 155 F, §§ 95–99.
[18] By the end of 1977 there had been 11 inter-State applications.
[19] And over 8,000 individual applications.

other State (against which the complaint is made) for its observations on admissibility. When, however, the petition is from an individual it is first "screened" by a group of three members; if they are unanimous that it should be admitted the petition is communicated to the "defendant" State forthwith. If they are not, the whole Commission will either declare it admissible or refer it to the "defendant" State for its observations before reaching a decision. The decision of the Commission on admissibility is always a reasoned decision, and, naturally, is communicated to both parties. This entire procedure is based on the Rules of Procedure and not on the Convention itself. Assuming the petition is declared admissible, the procedure then enters its second phase of ascertaining the facts and attempting to bring about a friendly settlement of the matter. The fact-finding itself comprises two stages, the first on the basis of written pleadings, the second on the basis of oral pleadings, which may include examination of witnesses or even a visit by the Commission or some of its members to the *locus in quo*. If the "friendly settlement" is then reached, a report is adopted by the full Commission and transmitted to the parties, the Committee of Ministers and the Secretary-General of the Council of Europe and is published.[20] If no settlement is reached, a report is drawn up, stating the facts and whether, in the view of the Commission, they disclose a breach of the Convention,[21] and this is submitted to the States concerned[22] (who may not publish it) and to the Committee of Ministers to whom, in addition, the Commission may make any proposals they think fit (Art. 31). It thus has the character of an "opinion"and not a "judgment."

From this stage on the procedure depends entirely upon whether or not the matter is referred to the Court either by a contracting State or the Commission itself under Article 48. If it is not so referred within three months of the transmission of the report, then under Article 32 the Committee itself, by a two-thirds

---

[20] See the two cases against Belgium and Germany (the *Böckmans* and *Pörschke* applications) in *Yearbook of the European Convention on Human Rights* (1965), p. 410; (1966), p. 632.

[21] Dissenting or individual opinions may be included.

[22] There is no provision enabling publication to the individual petitioner, except, under Art. 76 of the Rules of Procedure, where the matter is subsequently referred to the Court.

majority vote, decides whether there has been a violation of the Convention. Quite how this political organ, otherwise than by simply adopting the opinion of the Commission, can make an independent *legal* decision is not clear. If the Committee decides affirmatively it then prescribes a period of time within which the State must take the measures required by the Committee; if the State fails to comply the Committee, by a two-thirds vote, "shall . . . decide . . . what effect shall be given to its original decision and shall publish the Report" (Art. 32 (3)). Under Article 32 (4) members agree to regard as binding upon them any decision taken under this Article by the Committee.[23]

So far, the Committee has not yet been placed in the position of having to deal with a recalcitrant Member State in breach of the Convention. Greece avoided this situation by withdrawing from the Council of Europe. In the *Belgian Linguistics Case,* where eventually the Court held that on one of the six points the Belgian legislation was not in conformity with the Convention, Belgium altered its legislation in 1972 rather than defy the Committee.

It may be added, finally, that, whilst it is beyond the scope of this book to consider the "jurisprudence" or "case-law" developed by the Commission, except in so far as it bears on the institutional aspects of the Convention, the existence of such a body of jurisprudence is worthy of the student's notice. Part II of the annual *Yearbook of the European Convention on Human Rights* gives the texts of selected decisions and summaries of all the decisions. In Part III, students will find lists of the decisions of domestic courts of the parties referring to the European Convention.

2. The European Court of Human Rights

The establishment of the Court was not simultaneous with the entry into force of the Convention but, since acceptance of its jurisdiction is optional for the contracting parties, awaited such acceptance by eight of the parties to the Convention; this came about only on September 3, 1958. The constitutional provisions relating to the Court are mainly within Part IV of the Convention,

---

[23] This is an exception to the general rule that the Committee can only make recommendations to States; see *ante*, p. 173.

together with the Rules of Procedure adopted by the Court under Article 55 on September 18, 1959.[24]

(a) *Composition*

The Court is to consist of "a number of judges equal to that of the Members of the Council of Europe" (Art. 38), hence Spain, whilst not a party to the Convention, still has a right to have a judge on the Court (though not a member on the Commission). No two judges may be nationals of the same State. They are elected by a majority vote[25] of the Consultative Assembly from a list of nominees of the Member States, each nominating not more than three candidates of whom two at least are to be nationals. Candidates must be of "high moral character and must either possess the qualifications required for appointment to high judicial office or be juriconsults of recognised competence" (Art. 39 (3)); they are elected for nine years, but the elections are staggered so as to elect a third of the Court every three years and thus provide continuity of experience. Elections to fill casual vacancies, or when new Member States are admitted, are by "the same procedure."[26]

There is no specific affirmation of the independence of the judges, but the work of the judges presupposes independence, and privileges and immunities are accorded under Article 59. Similarly there is nothing in the Convention on incompatibility of other professions with the office of judge; it is left to the rules of procedure to exclude from office members of governments or holders of posts or professions "likely to affect confidence in his independence" (Rule 4) and from a particular case any judge who has a personal interest in it or has participated in the case in one capacity or another (Rule 24 (2)). Salary also bears on independence but, such is the uncertainty over the work likely to be involved the judges receive a *per diem* allowance fixed by the Committee of Ministers and not a salary; this also links up with the fact that they are free to carry on with their professions, subject to Rule 4. There is no autonomy over the Court's budget for, like the Commission, it forms part of the general budget of the Council of Europe (Art. 58).

[24] (1958–59) *Yearbook of the European Convention*, 2.
[25] *Semble* an absolute rather than simple majority; the vote is by secret ballot.
[26] Does this mean that all the Member States can propose candidates or only the new Member or the State whose judge has vacated the seat? Presumably the latter is the correct interpretation.

The Court sits in Strasbourg normally, but can sit elsewhere (Rule 15) and must meet in plenary session once a year (Rule 16); unlike the Commission, its hearings are normally public although the actual deliberations prior to judgment and after conclusion of the arguments by the parties are, of course, private. The States are represented by agents and the Commission by delegates who are members of the Commission; there is, as we shall see later, no direct representation of individuals before the Court. As with the Commission, the procedure is in two stages, written and oral.

(b) *Jurisdiction*

Turning to the competence and jurisdiction of the Court, it will be seen that it comprises "all cases concerning the interpretation and application of the present Convention which the High Contracting Parties or the Commission shall refer to it in accordance with Article 48" (Art. 45). The Convention is, therefore, the basis of its competence, and its jurisdiction is limited *ratione materiae*. Suggestions have been made for extending the Court's jurisdiction to cover the interpretation of *all* Conventions concluded under the auspices of the Council of Europe, and also to give it power to give advisory opinions, but these are still mere proposals. There is a limitation *ratione temporis*, for the case must arise out of facts subsequent to the entry into force of the Convention in relation to the particular "defendant" State. There is also the limitation *ratione loci, i.e.* the territorial limitation of the Convention. Jurisdiction is also limited *ratione personae*, for its jurisdiction rests essentially on the consent of States and, in a way strongly reminiscent of Article 36 of the Statute of the I.C.J., this consent may be given ad hoc in a particular case or may be given in advance by way of a declaration that the State "recognises as compulsory *ipso facto* and without special agreement the jurisdiction of the Court . . . " (Art. 46 (1)). Without such consent no State can be made to appear as defendant, and consent may also be made "unconditionally, or on a condition of reciprocity on the part of several or certain other High Contracting Parties or for a specified period" (Art. 46 (2)).[27]

The further question is, who are the possible "plaintiffs," or, more precisely, who can bring a case before the Court? Article 44

[27] See Part 1 of the current *Yearbook of the European Convention* for the list of declarations recognising compulsory jurisdiction.

limits this to the Contracting Parties and the Commission; moreover, under Article 48 it is not any Contracting Party, but only one "whose national is alleged to be a victim" (48 (b)) or "which referred the case to the Commission" (48 (c)). The "defendant" State can also, under Article 48 (d), bring the case before the Court, a proposition not nearly so startling when one considers that the Commission may have made a report finding that State to be in breach of its obligations under the Convention—so that for the State in question the recourse to the Court is almost like an appeal.

Finally it should be noted that the jurisdiction of the Court presupposes that the matter has first been referred to the Commission and that not more than three months has elapsed from the transmission of the Report of the Commission to the Committee of Ministers.

Once the Court is seised of the case, either by the Commission or one of the Contracting Parties entitled to do so, a Chamber of seven judges is then established to consider the case (Art. 43). The entire Court (now 20 judges) is to that extent a "panel" from which the seven are drawn. Yet, the seven are not entirely chosen by lot by the President, for the "national judges," *i.e.* judges of the nationality of any of the States concerned, are entitled to sit *ex officio*; moreover, in the absence of a national, any such State can nominate a judge ad hoc (Art. 43 and Rule 21). Again the similarity to the I.C.J. is striking. The Chamber is thus the normal adjudicating body, and it may have referred to it by the President any new case between the same Parties and relating to the same article or articles of the Convention (Rule 21 (5)); the procedure is really one for the "joinder" of cases.

Exceptionally, under Rule 48, the Chamber may relinquish its jurisdiction in favour of the plenary Court; this arises where the case "raises a serious question affecting the interpretation of the Convention." Such relinquishment is obligatory "where the resolution of such question might have a result inconsistent with a judgment previously delivered by a Chamber or by a plenary Court"; this is clearly desirable if consistency of interpretation is to be achieved. The plenary Court may then deal with the whole case or, alternatively, decide the question of interpretation and refer the case back to the Chamber.

The Chamber may disseise itself (and presumably the Court)

297

under Rule 47 (3) where the Commission informs it that a friendly
settlement has been reached which satisfies Article 28 of the
Convention. Jurisdiction can also be ended when the Party
bringing the case notifies its intention to discontinue, provided the
other parties agree and the Chamber, after consultation with the
Commission, approves. Approval is accompanied by a reasoned
decision communicated to the Committee of Ministers in order to
enable them to supervise the execution of any undertakings by the
parties (Rule 47 (1)). Approval is necessary; the "plaintiff" alone
cannot end the jurisdiction of the Chamber.[28]

The Second Protocol, concluded in 1963, and in force in 1970,
envisages a new kind of jurisdiction for the Court, namely to give
advisory opinions at the request of the Committee of Ministers
"on legal questions concerning the interpretation of the Convention and the Protocols thereto." However, there is an important
limitation on this jurisdiction in that:

> "Such opinions shall not deal with any questions relating to
> the content or scope of the rights or freedoms defined in
> Section 1 of the Convention and in the Protocols thereto, or
> with any other question which the Commission, the Court or
> the Committee of Ministers might have to consider in
> consequence of any such proceedings as could be instituted in
> accordance with the Convention."

(c) *The role of the Commission before the Court*

The system whereby one judicial body can seise another with
jurisdiction and actually participate in the proceedings before that
other is somewhat extraordinary. Its justification lies essentially in
the fact that the purpose of the Convention is to protect the rights
of individuals, and, *since these individuals have no right of access to
the Court,* the Commission must intervene so as to assist the Court
in having the case for the individual put before the Court. The

---

[28] Thus in the *De Becker Case* which the Commission took to the Court, the
proceedings did not cease when, in 1961, De Becker notified the Commission
that he withdrew his complaint as a result of Belgium's amendment of the law
originally alleged by him to be in contravention of the Convention. The Court
itself struck the case off the list on March 27, 1962, after noting De Becker's
withdrawal and Belgium's objection to the continuation of proceedings. Judge
Alf Ross dissented on the ground that the Court should have decided the
question whether the law prior to its amendment was in breach of the
Convention; *Yearbook of the Convention* (1962), 321.

Commission itself has taken the view that it does not appear as *advocate* for the individual, for so to do would be detrimental to the objectivity and impartiality which it must retain if, in the earlier stages when the matter is before the Commission, it is to be able to act as conciliator in trying to effect an amicable settlement.[29] Its role is therefore that of an *amicus curiae* or "ministère public" more than a "party," though this is to be deduced from practice so far, rather than from specific provisions in either the Convention or the Rules of the Court.[30]

The very first case brought before the Court by the Commission, the *Lawless Case*,[31] raised forcibly the difficult problem of the Commission's role. The Commission had received an application from Lawless in November 1957 and in its report transmitted to the Committee of Ministers on February 1, 1960, had concluded that the facts did not disclose a breach of the Convention by the Republic of Ireland. However, since the minority vote had been a substantial one (9–5 and 8–6 on the two main questions) and since the case raised issues of fundamental importance to the application of the Convention, the Commission decided to refer the matter to the Court.

It was quite clear that the Commission's report should be before the Court and that the Court must take this report into consideration (Rule 29 (2)) and that the Commission, via its delegate(s), should take part in the proceedings (Rule 29 (1)). The more difficult question was the manner in which the Commission should ensure that the individual's view should be presented to the Court. Rule 38 (1) of the Court provided that a Chamber may "hear as a witness or expert or in any other capacity any person whose evidence or statements seem likely to assist it in the carrying

---

[29] See the Commission's President's (Professor Sir Humphrey Waldock) opening address to the Court in the *Lawless Case*.

[30] But Rule 71 of the Commission's Rules states that it shall *assist* the Court. So did the Court in the *Lawless Case* judgment of November 14, 1960, (1960) *Yearbook*, 506.

[31] Judgment of November 14, 1960; (1960) *Yearbook*, 493. The case arose from the detention without trial of Lawless, an Irish citizen, by the Irish Government under statutory powers intended to deal with a state of emergency; he had been denied habeas corpus by the Irish Supreme Court. The Commission and the Court upheld the action of the Irish Government as being within Art. 15 of the Convention, and therefore not in breach of it. It is the preliminary objection, not the main judgment, with which we are concerned here.

out of its task." But this provision was scarcely a justification for allowing the individual to appear in order to argue his case, bearing in mind the quite specific terms of Articles 44 and 48 of the Convention.[32]

Anticipating this problem, the Commission on March 30, 1960, adopted a new Rule 76 of its Rules of Procedure, providing for the communication of the report to the individual applicant, and notifying him of his right to submit written observations thereon, in cases referred to the Court. Pursuant to this rule the Commission transmitted its report to Lawless, pointing out that it must be kept secret, secured the written observations of Lawless and communicated them, together with its own report, to the Court. The Republic of Ireland objected (by way of preliminary objection under Rule 46) to this procedure on, basically, two grounds. The first was that, under Article 31 of the Convention, publication of the report was to be confined to the Committee of Ministers and the States concerned "who shall not be at liberty to publish it," and therefore Rule 76 was *ultra vires*. The Court declined to assume a competence to delete a rule from the Commission's Rules of Procedure[33] and went on to point out that the requirement of secrecy was relevant more to the earlier stage when the proceedings of the Commission and the Committee of Ministers were in private; thus, at the later stage of public hearings before the Court, this was a more relative requirement and, hence, "the Commission is enabled under the Convention to communicate to the Applicant, with the proviso that it must not be published, the whole or part of its Report . . . ."[34] The second ground was that the Commission had no right to communicate the individual's comments on the report to the Court, for this was giving him indirectly a *locus standi* which the Convention did not permit. The Court likewise rejected this argument, noting that "it is in the interests of the proper administration of justice that the Court should have knowledge of and, if need be, take into consideration the applicant's point of view" and continued that the

---

[32] And see Rule 41 which allows objections to a "witness or expert," thus suggesting the individuals are summoned to give evidence rather than arguments.

[33] p. 506.

[34] p. 512.

Commission "as the defender of the public interest, is entitled of its own accord to make known the applicant's views to the Court . . . ."[35]

In 1970, in the *Vagrancy Case* against Belgium the delegates of the Commission before the Court asked the Court to allow the lawyer of the applicants to make a short statement of a factual nature; this the Court allowed, despite Belgium's objection that the applicants were not parties before the Court.

Here, then, is the procedure which, stopping short of allowing the individual direct access to the Court, ensures some measure of equality of the parties (in the true sense) before the Court. It compares with the procedure followed in the *ILO Administrative Tribunal (UNESCO) Case*[36] and has been dealt with in some detail in order to illustrate the problems inherent in the submission to an international tribunal before which individuals have no direct *locus standi* of legal questions affecting rights conferred upon the individuals directly.

Apart from the kind of problems raised in the *Lawless Case*, there is the further problem of the extent to which the Court will rely on the Commission's report. Clearly it will not do so as far as propositions of *law* are concerned (save, possibly, for propositions made about the Commission's own procedure); but one may assume that, certainly where the interested States do not contest the facts as set out in the report, the Court will normally proceed on the basis of facts as stated therein. The Chamber does, of course, have its own fact-finding powers: powers to call witnesses, etc. (Rule 38 (1)) and even power to conduct an enquiry or investigation on the spot through its own members (38 (2)) or through another body (38 (3)).

(d) *The judgments*

As we have seen in the *Lawless Case,* preliminary objections can be dealt with prior to the judgment on the merits. The Convention makes no mention of a power to order interim measures of protection, but Rule 34 allows the President, prior to the constitution of the Chamber, and the Chamber once constituted,

---

[35] p. 516.
[36] See *ante*, p. 101. The Court itself referred to the practice of the I.C.J., obviously with this case in mind for the Commission had invoked this case as a precedent.

power to "bring to the attention of the Parties any interim measures the adoption of which seems desirable"; this seems to be by way of recommendations rather than orders.

The main judgment must be reasoned, and it is taken by a simple majority vote, with members having the right to append either individual or dissenting opinions, as in the I.C.J. Judgment can also be given in default of the appearance of a Party (assuming the Party has accepted the jurisdiction). The judgment is final and binding on the parties to the case (Arts. 52, 53),[37] subject to the right to request an interpretation of it within three years (Rule 53) and to request revision of it upon the discovery of a fact which might have a "decisive influence" within three months of the discovery (Rule 54). There is no process for an appeal and, as we have seen, no recourse to the I.C.J.

The judgments are not directly executory in the sense that they annul the national decision found incompatible with the Convention; it is for the State concerned to take such action and if the internal law of the State allows only "partial reparation," the Court may itself "afford just satisfaction to the injured party" (Rule 50); this may include damages and in 1972 in the *Ringeisen Case* against Austria the Court awarded DM 20,000 damages to be paid without attachment.[38]

The execution of the Court's judgment is, as is normally the case, an "executive" function rather than a judicial one and the Committee of Ministers "shall supervise its execution" (Art. 54). It is here that the system may have its weakest link, bearing in mind the nature of the Committee.[39]

The success of the system of the Convention as a whole is difficult to assess at this stage. Broadly speaking, cases seem to have arisen not so much from deliberate violations of the Convention but more from inadvertence, or from out-moded legislation, or from Governments adopting an interpretation of the Convention with which the Court has disagreed. It is clear that

---

[37] Hence it does not constitute a binding precedent to which, as a matter of law, other States must, comply or even which the Court itself must necessarily follow.
[38] Austria had initially deposited the sum with an Austrian court to enable creditors of Ringeisen to attach the money.
[39] See *ante*, p. 173, and see Higgins, "The execution of the decisions of organs under the European Convention on Human Rights" (1978) *Rev. Hell*, D.I. 1–39.

before the Commission it is the right of individual petition which has really brought a great deal of business. By May 1980 there had been 33 cases before the Court and two of them against the United Kingdom had considerable political repercussions (*Ireland* v. *U.K.* (1978)[40] and the *Sunday Times Case* (1979)).[41] It is probable that the most substantial effect of the Convention lies in its inducement to States to bring their law and practice into conformity, and thus avoid the ignominy of being cited before the Commission or the Court. Moreover, the Secretary-General of the Council of Europe has power under Article 57 to require an explanation on the compatibility of a Member's law with the Convention (and used this power in 1964). There is clear evidence of its impact upon the law and the judicial decisions of some of the parties.[42] There is also evidence of its effect on the world at large. Certain States, like Nigeria, Sierra Leone and Cyprus, have adapted the Convention's statement of human rights to form part of their own constitutions. The African Conference on the Rule of Law in January 1961 proposed the conclusion of an African Convention on Human Rights. The Organisation of American States in 1969 adopted a Convention on Human Rights, providing for a Commission and a Court, closely modelled on the European Convention, and both bodies are now in existence.[43] The potentialities of this movement are enormous, and much will depend upon the efficacy of the machinery established for the enforcement of these rights which, without such machinery, may simply remain an expression of idealism.

II. The Court of Justice of the European Communities

This Court, established by Article 4 of the 1957 Rome Treaty establishing the European Economic Community,[44] has assumed the functions of the Court of Justice of the European Coal and Steel Community (ECSC) which had been in existence since 1953 and has become a common Court for the three European Communities: ECSC, the European Economic Community (EEC)

---

[40] This case involved allegations of torture against H.M. Forces in N. Ireland.
[41] The so-called 'Contempt' Case.
[42] See Part III of the succesive *Yearbooks of the European Convention*.
[43] See *ante*, p. 225.
[44] IV *European Yearbook* 413.

and Euratom.[45] The three Treaties were modified by the Convention relating to certain institutions common to the European Communities of 1957[46] so as to ensure an identity of the texts governing the organisation of the Court; its powers vary according to whether it is acting as the Court of one or other of the three communities.

1. Composition

The Court consists of 10 judges appointed by the unanimous agreement of the Member States for a six-year term from among "persons whose independence is beyond doubt and who possess the qualifications required for appointment to the highest judicial office in their respective countries or who are jurists of recognised competence" (Treaty, Art. 167). The Court is partially renewed every three years, five and five judges being appointed in alternate elections, and all are eligible for re-election.

The Court is assisted by four advocates-general, appointed in a similar way and according to the same qualifications. Their duty is "acting with complete impartiality and independence, to make, in open court, reasoned submissions on cases brought before the Court of Justice" (Treaty, Art. 166). These officers represent something quite new to international tribunals; they have no connection with the parties and serve the Court exclusively but without taking part in the deliberations preceding judgment.[47]

The independence of both judges and advocates-general is secured by their exclusion from participation in a case in which they have previously participated in one capacity or another (Statute, Art. 16); by excluding them from holding any political or administrative office or engaging in any paid or unpaid professional activities (Statute, Art. 4), by the grant of privileges and immunities (Art. 3), by the security of tenure of a judge unless removed from office by the unanimous vote of his fellow-judges, and by the payment of salaries and pensions from the budget of the Community. A striking corollary to the independence thereby secured is the total lack of any reference to the nationality of the judges, except in the negative sense that no party can invoke the

[45] See *ante*, p. 199, for a description of these organisations.
[46] v *European Yearbook* 587.
[47] See, more fully, Donner, "The Court of Justice of the European Communities" (1961) I.C.L.Q. Supp. No. 1, 66.

nationality of a judge, or the absence of a judge of his own nationality, as a reason for changing the composition of the Court; the "national" and "ad hoc" judge is unknown in this Court.

2. Procedure

The procedure is markedly like that of the European Court of Human Rights. It comprises two stages, written and then oral,[48] which are in principle before the full Court with a minimum quorum of nine judges. However, there is provision for the establishment of two Chambers of three judges to deal with the "instruction" stage and certain other matters, but a full Court is obligatory whenever proceedings are begun by a Member State or an organ of one of the Communities, or when the issue is a preliminary one affecting the interpretation of the Treaties, the validity of acts of the organs of the Communities or interpretation of their statutes. There are also certain special procedures to allow the President to order interim measures of protection, to allow intervention by interested parties, and withdrawal of the suit from the Court when both parties agree. A quite remarkable feature for an international tribunal is the provision of legal aid for indigent parties (Rules of Court, Art. 76). Hearings are in public, but the deliberations of the Court are in private and judges are sworn to secrecy. All parties, whether States, organs, or private entities, can be legally represented.

3. Jurisdiction

The jurisdiction of the Court is complex not only because it can sit in three capacities, *i.e.* as the Court of each of the Communities, but also because it comprises several different kinds of proceedings. These are virtually different ways in which the Court discharges it primary function of ensuring the rule of law in the interpretation and application of the treaties and any regulations made for their execution.[49] It may be noted that, whilst nothing prevents the application of international law, the primary sources of law applied by the Court are the Treaty provisions of the

---

[48] Statute Art. 18. There can be an "instruction" stage in between, conducted by a Chamber or by a Judge, to hear witnesses, examine documents, examine the *locus in quo*, etc.
[49] ECSC, Art. 31; EEC, Art. 164; Euratom, Art. 134.

Communities and "Community Law" which derives not only from these treaties but from acts of Community institutions, the jurisprudence of the Court itself and the general principles of law reflected in the municipal law of the Member States.

(a) *Appeals for annulment (recours en annulation)*

This type of proceeding is a kind of judicial review of administrative action modelled on that of the French Conseil d'Etat, used mainly to challenge the legality of decisions by the executive organs of the Communities. The jurisdiction of the Court is however limited *ratione materiae, ratione personae,* and *ratione temporis.*

Turning to the first limitation, it may be observed that in the ECSC what can be challenged are the *deliberations* of the Council and the Assembly (although only by the Commission and Member States) and the *decisions*[50] or *recommendations* of the Commission.[51] In the EEC and Euratom all *acts* of the Commission or the Council which have binding force are challengeable[52]; this will therefore include *regulations, directives* and *decisions* but not recommendations and opinions. Failure to act can be challenged, as well as positive action,[53] although this is restricted in the EEC and Euratom where the challenge is by private persons (natural or legal) in that they must show that the executive organ has failed to address a decision to them. They cannot challenge inaction so freely as do States in EEC and Euratom, or even enterprises and associations in the ECSC.

So far as the *grounds* of challenge[54] are concerned, as against the deliberations of the Assembly or Council of ECSC these are

---

[50] See *Dutch Govt.* v. *High Authority of ECSC,* Case 28/66.

[51] Under Art. 14 the former are "binding in every respect"; the latter are "binding with respect to the objectives they specify but shall leave to those to whom they are directed the choice of appropriate means for attaining these objectives." It is the "opinions" which are not binding.

[52] EEC, Art. 173; Euratom, Art. 146. See, for example, *Italian Govt.* v. *Council and Commissions of EEC,* Case 32/65. The hierarchy of decisions is different to that in the ECSC; see EEC, Art. 189 and Euratom, Art. 161. Note that, under Art. 180 of EEC, it is the "conclusions" of the Board of Governors or the Board of Directors of the European Investment Bank which can be similarly challenged, either by Member States, the Commission, or the Board of Directors.

[53] ECSC, Art. 35; EEC, Art. 175; Euratom, Art. 148. On the application of Article 175 see *Holtz* v. *Council* [1974] E.C.R. 1.

[54] ECSC, Art. 33; EEC, Art. 173; Euratom, Art. 146.

but two: incompetence or violation of substantial procedural requirements. But as against the High Authority (now the Commission) there are four. First, violation of the Treaty and of any legal provisions relating to its application; secondly, errors of substantial form (such as failure to give reasons for a decision, or neglect to consult other organs when the Treaty requires this); thirdly, incompetence, or lack of jurisdiction; and fourthly, abuse of power (*détournement de pouvoir*) as where a power is exercised for an end other than the one for which it was conferred, or is motivated by ulterior motives or in a discriminatory way. This last notion is never an easy one to apply, and, in so far as it is used to challenge the exercise of a discretionary power of the High Authority in the ECSC, it is limited by the specific provision that "the examination by the Court may not include an assessment of the situation arising from facts or economic circumstances in view of which the said decisions or recommendations were taken . . . " (Art. 33).

The second limitation concerns the entities which are capable of making this challenge before the Court. In principle the right to challenge is always available to the Member States and the executive organs of each Community. That in itself goes far beyond traditional practice, for, as we have seen, the I.C.J. has no power of judicial review over actions by organs of the UN, nor can the organs of the UN challenge each other's acts or the acts of Member States before that Court. However, the more remarkable feature is the grant of a right to challenge to private persons and entities. This is, in a sense, a logical step once the executive bodies are given supra-national powers so that they can by-pass the Member States and address their regulations and decisions directly to their subjects; nevertheless, it is a step which demonstrates the degree to which integration in these Communities has progressed. In the EEC and Euratom the general phrase "any natural or legal person" is used[55]; in the ECSC an attempt is made to define more narrowly these potential appellants. The "enterprises or associations" must be "engaged in production in the field of coal and steel within the territories" (of Member States) or "engaged in

---

[55] EEC, Art. 173; Euratom, Art. 146. The difficulties over Article 173 have arisen not so much over decisions addressed to a person, but more over decisions addressed to a person other than the plaintiff but of "direct and individual concern" to the plaintiff: see *Société C.A.M.* v. *Commission* [1973] E.C.R. 1393.

distribution other than sale to domestic consumers or to craft industries" (Art. 80) or be "buyers" (Art. 63 (2)). In every case where a private entity is the appellant, it must show that it was directly or indirectly affected by the decision or other act in question.

The third limitation refers to the imposition of time-limits within which the acts or decisions must be contested. In general the ECSC Treaty stipulates a one-month period, whilst the EEC and Euratom Treaties stipulate a two-month period.[56] The periods are short, but necessarily so once one grasps the fact that the economic régime with which the Treaties deal is a dynamic thing which cannot be altered long after the event by appeals against decisions taken.

(b) *General jurisdiction*

(i) *Appeals against sanctions and penalties ordered by the executive organs.* All three treaties give to the executive organs of the Communities powers to impose penalties against Member States and private entities within those States; these powers are subject to judicial review by the Court.

In the ECSC, under Article 36, any "interested party" may appeal to the general jurisdiction of the Court against "the pecuniary sanctions of this Treaty"; and, in support of this appeal, the petitioners may also "contest the legality of the decisions and recommendations which they are charged with violating." Also, under Article 88, a State may appeal against a decision of the Commission suspending the payment of sums due to the State as a penalty for non-fulfilment of an obligation of the State under the Treaty. The Court has, in all cases, power to annul or amend the sanction ordered by the executive organ.

In the EEC Article 172 speaks in more general terms of regulations being made pursuant to the Treaty so as to confer upon the Court "full jurisdiction in respect of penalties provided for in such regulations." Article 83 of Euratom gives the Commission broad powers to impose penalties on "persons or enterprises," and Article 144 gives to the Court full jurisdiction over appeals against them.

(ii)*Proceedings to enforce the non-contractual liability of the*

---

[56] See the table of time limits given in *Juris Classeur,* Fasc. 161–F, V, s. 7.

Community. Under ECSC, Article 34 provides for "appeals for damages" by an enterprise or group of enterprises which have not been given equitable redress for injuries caused to them by a decision or recommendation of the Commission when such decision or recommendation has been previously annulled by the Court. Article 40 gives jurisdiction to the Court to assess damages against the Community when injury has resulted "from a wrongful act performed on behalf of the Community in the carrying out of the present Treaty," and also to assess damages against the Community, "in cases where injury results from a wrongful act of a servant in the performance of his duties." This is clearly a jurisdiction over acts when a kind of vicarious liability[57] exists in the Community.

In EEC Article 215 provides that "as regards non-contractual liability, the Community shall, in accordance with the general principles common to the laws of Member States, make reparation for any damage caused by its institutions or by its employees in the performance of their duties"; Article 178 gives the Court jurisdiction to hear cases relating to compensation for damages as provided for in Article 215.[58] In Euratom Articles 188 and 174 provide for a similar jurisdiction.

(iii) *Proceedings to enforce the contractual liability of the Community.* Although, normally, contractual liability will be enforced by the municipal courts of the Members, Articles 42 of ECSC, 181 of EEC, and 153 of Euratom provide that the Court will have jurisdiction where an arbitration clause specifically vests jurisdiction in the Court, and whether the contract be concluded under public or private law.

(c) *Jurisdiction as an administrative tribunal*

Whereas in other international organisations special tribunals have had to be created to deal with appeals by staff members against decisions of the administration (since such individuals had no *locus standi* before the I.C.J.), these three Communities have had no hesitation in giving individuals access to the Court and it is

---

[57] It is more accurately the distinction in French administrative law between a *faute de service* and a *faute personnelle*.

[58] See on the application of Article 215 *Holtz* v. *Council and Commission* [1974] E.C.R. 675 where the Court held that, in adopting an economic policy, the Community is liable for damage to individuals only where there is a flagrant violation of a superior rule of law for the protection of the individual.

therefore used as an administrative tribunal. This jurisdiction rests, in the ECSC, on the rather general provisions concerning contractual and non-contractual liability of the Community in Articles 42 and 40 and, more specifically, on the Staff Regulations. In EEC and Euratom, Articles 179 and 152 provide quite specifically for this jurisdiction. The nature of this administrative jurisdiction is more fully described in the next chapter dealing with Administrative Tribunals.

(d) *Proceedings against members of the executive and judicial organs*

Articles 157 of EEC and 126 of Euratom provide that, on the application of the Council or Commission, the Court may entertain proceedings arising from allegations against members of the Commission for breach of their obligations and may order the member's removal from office or forfeiture of pension rights. There is no similar provision in ECSC. There is, however, a similar provision in Articles 4 and 6 of the Statute of the Court, enabling the Court to act against its own judges.

(e) *Jurisdiction over preliminary questions raised before municipal tribunals (recours à titre préjudiciel)*

In so far as the Treaties form an integral part of the municipal law of the Member States,[59] and decisions of the executive organs have executory force within those States, the situation may well arise in which a municipal court is seised with a case which concerns the interpretation of the Treaty, or the validity of acts by the organs of the Community; indeed, a defendant may well attempt to justify his conduct on the ground that he was implementing a decision addressed to him. Hence, some system had to be devised to enable the Court exclusively to decide certain questions arising before municipal tribunals.

In the ECSC, Article 41 provides that "when the validity of resolutions of the High Authority or the Council is contested in litigation before a national court, such issue shall be certified to the

[59] The supremacy of Community law over the national laws of the Members is beyond question, and this applies equally to subsequent national legislation: *Costa* v. *ENEL* [1964] C.M.L.R. 429. In 1974 the Federal Constitutional Court of Germany inclined to the view that a member State's constitution would prevail over Community law, but the European Commission communicated to the German Government its disagreement and "grave concern" over that view.

Court, which shall have exclusive competence to rule thereon."
Articles 177[60] of EEC and 150 of Euratom are more detailed but
provide for a similar kind of exclusive jurisdiction over such
preliminary questions, compelling any municipal court whose
decisions is final to first refer the matter to the Court, almost by
way of case stated.

(f) *Appeals against Member States*
   (i)*By organs of the Community*. Under Article 88 of the ECSC,
the Commission is given power to decide on the compatibility of
the States' actions with its obligations under the Treaty[61] and to
order sanctions, and it is left to the State to appeal against the
decision of the Commission. In the EEC and Euratom, as a
corollary to the comparatively diminished power of the executive
bodies as compared with that in ECSC, a different procedure is
followed whereby the prior approval of the Court is required for
any sanctions ordered by the Commission against States, and it is
for the Commission to cite the State before the Court for breach of
its obligations (Art. 169, EEC; Euratom, Art. 141).[62] Thus the
onus of appealing to the Court is placed on the Commission and

---

[60] "The Court of Justice shall have jurisdiction to give preliminary rulings
concerning:
   (a) the interpretation of this Treaty;
   (b) the validity and interpretation of acts of the institutions of the Community;
   (c) the interpretation of the statutes of bodies established by an act of the
        Council, where those statutes so provide.
Where such a question is raised before any court or tribunal of a Member State,
that court or tribunal may, if it considers that a decision on the question is
necessary to enable it to give judgment request the Court of Justice to give a
ruling thereon.
Where any such question is raised in a case pending before a court or tribunal of
a Member State, against whose decisions there is no judicial remedy under
national law, that court or tribunal shall bring the matter before the Court of
Justice." For applications of this see *Société Albatross* v. *SOPECO,* Case 20/64;
Schwarze v. *EVSt.,* Case 16/65. For a decision by the English Court of Appeal on
the effect of Article 177 see *Bulmer and Showerings* v. *Bollinger and Champagne*
[1974] 3 W.L.R. 202; [1974] 2 C.M.L.R. 91.

[61] And see *Humblet* v. *Belgium,* Case 6/60, December 16, 1960, where the Court
also accepted jurisdiction in a case brought against a Member State by an official
of the ECSC, claiming that he had been denied the tax exemptions to which he
was entitled under the Protocol on Privileges and Immunities.

[62] Under Art. 180 of EEC the Board of Directors of the European Investment
Bank has the same powers to cite Member States. And note that in *Commission*
v. *France* [1974] E.C.R. 359 the Court held that the Commission did not have to
show a specific interest to bring suit, since it represented the general interest of
the Community.

not on the States as in the ECSC. The EEC and Euratom, in having this procedure, which is the reverse of the ECSC procedure, thus give a kind of "federal" jurisdiction to the Court.

(ii)*By other Member States.* In what is a truly "international" jurisdiction, the Court can decide disputes between Member States. Article 89 of the ECSC gives to the Court compulsory jurisdiction over Inter-States disputes "concerning the application of this Treaty," and a permissive jurisdiction (based on consent of all parties) over disputes "related to the purpose of this Treaty." Article 87 excludes the jurisdiction of the I.C.J.

Articles 170 of EEC and 141 of Euratom similarly give compulsory jurisdiction over inter-States disputes as to the fulfilment of obligations under the Treaty, subject to prior reference to the Commission; Articles 182 and 154 of the two Treaties give a similar permissive jurisdiction over disputes "in connection with the object of this Treaty." The jurisdiction of the I.C.J. is excluded by Article 219 of EEC and Article 193 of Euratom.

(g) *Advisory jurisdiction*

Since the organs of the Communities, and to some extent individuals also, have direct access to the Court as parties it is not to be expected that the advisory jurisdiction of the Court will be comparable in importance to that of the I.C.J. However, the Court has a very limited[63] advisory jurisdiction. In the ECSC Article 95 (4) envisaged that amendments to the Treaty proposed jointly by the High Authority and the Council should be submitted to the Court for an opinion; the Court will be concerned to examine whether they "modify the provisions of Articles 2, 3 and 4, or the relationship between the powers of the High Authority and those of the other institutions of the Community." Curiously enough, the Court is not brought into the Treaty-amending process of the EEC and Euratom, but in Article 228 of the EEC its opinion can be sought on agreements contemplated between the Community and States or international organisations; the criterion for the Court is compatibility with the Treaty, and when a negative opinion is given the Community can only proceed under Article

---

[63] It is very doubtful whether the general terms of ECSC, Art. 31, or EEC, Art. 164, or Euratom, Art. 136 can be construed as giving a wide general advisory jurisdiction.

236 by amending the Treaty. The provision in Euratom is different again, for Article 103 envisages that draft agreements between Member States and non-Member States, international organisations or nationals of non-Member States shall, when they concern the "field of application of this Treaty," be first submitted to the Commission and then to the Court for an opinion by the Member-States after receiving the comments of the Commission; again the criterion is compatibility with the Treaty.

It may be said, in conclusion of this brief survey of the Court's jurisdiction, that no international tribunal has ever been equipped with so varied a jurisdictional competence as has the Court of the European Communities.

4. The judgments of the Court[64]

Against non-State entities and individuals the judgments of the Court have executive force in each Member State; the municipal authorities, upon the request of the successful party, simply verify the judgment and then enforce it through the ordinary municipal procedures for enforcement as if it were a judgment of their own courts. This is an advantage which no other international tribunal has in the actual enforcement of its judgments.

The judgment of the Court is a single judgment and, contrary to usual practice in international tribunals, no separate or dissenting judgments are allowed. It is a final judgment, creating a *res judicata* (but not a binding precedent) which is not appealable. There is, however, procedure for the interpretation of a judgment (Art. 40, Statute) and for the revision of a judgment upon the discovery of new facts "capable of exercising a decisive influence" provided a request for review is made within ten years from judgment (Art. 41, Statute).

III. THE COMMISSION OF MEDIATION, CONCILIATION AND ARBITRATION OF THE OAU[65]

Article III (4) of the Charter of the Organization of African Unity prescribes as one of the principles of the Organization, "peaceful

---

[64] Since this chapter has to combine brevity with concentration on the institutional aspects of the Court, no references can be made to the body of substantive case-law being evolved by the Court. This can, however, be consulted in the official *Recueil de la Jurisprudence de la Cour de la Communauté Européenne*.

[65] Elias, "The Commission of Mediation, Conciliation and Arbitration of the OAU" (1964) 40 B.Y.B.I.L. 336 (this includes a text of the Protocol).

settlement of disputes by negotiation, mediation, conciliation or arbitration." This principle is reaffirmed in Article XIX of the Charter which states that, "Member States pledge to settle all disputes among themselves by peaceful means and to this end decide to establish a Commission of Mediation, Conciliation and Arbitration, the composition of which and conditions of service shall be defined by a separate Protocol to be approved by the Assembly of Heads of State and Government. The said Protocol shall be regarded as forming an integral part of the present Charter." Under Article VII, the Commission is established as one of the principal institutions of the Organization. The Protocol was eventually signed at Cairo in July 1964.

1. Composition

The Commission is to consist of 21 members elected by the Assembly of Heads of State and Government. The Members are to be persons with recognised professional qualifications and are elected for a term of five years and are eligible for re-election. A President and two Vice-Presidents are to be elected by the Assembly from among the Members of the Commission as full time members and constitute the Bureau of the Commission and have the responsibility of consulting with the parties concerning the appropriate mode of settling the dispute in accordance with the Protocol. The members are obviously to be regarded as independent experts and not as government representatives.

2. Jurisdiction

The jurisdiction of the Commission is limited to disputes between States which are referred to it by the Assembly of Heads of State and Government, the Council of Ministers, or one or both parties to the dispute. There is some ambiguity on whether the Commission's jurisdiction is based on consent. But having regard to the fact that if one or more of the parties refuse to submit to the jurisdiction of the Commission the Bureau is to refer the matter to the Council of Ministers for consideration, it seems clear that jurisdiction is dependent on the consent of the party or parties concerned and that the Protocol does not establish a system of compulsory jurisdiction.

Under Article XVIII, the parties involved in a dispute and all other Member States undertake to extend to those conducting an investigation or inquiry, for the purpose of elucidating facts or circumstances relating to a matter in dispute, the fullest co-operation in the conduct of such investigation or inquiry. However, it is doubtful whether this confers a right of entry into a party's territory without specific consent. For the settlement of a dispute, the parties may agree to resort to any one of the modes of settlement: mediation, conciliation and arbitration.

(a) Mediation. The President of the Commission, with the consent of the parties, appoints one or more members of the Commission to mediate the dispute. The role of the mediator is confined to reconciling the views and claims of the parties and he is to make written proposals to the parties as soon as possible.

(b) Conciliation. If the request in the form of a petition is made by one party, then that party is to indicate that prior written notice has been given to the other party, and the President must satisfy himself that both parties are agreed on conciliation. The President, in agreement with the parties, is to establish a Board of Conciliators, of whom three are to be appointed by the President from among the Members of the Commission, and one each by the Parties.

The function of the Board of Conciliators is to clarify the issues in dispute and to endeavour to bring about an agreement between the parties upon mutually acceptable terms. The Board has power to undertake any inquiry or hear any person capable of giving relevant information concerning the dispute.

At the end of the proceedings the Board makes a report stating either that the parties have come to an agreement, and, if necessary, the terms of the agreement and any recommendations for settlement made by the Board, or that it has been impossible to effect a settlement. The Report is then communicated to the parties and the President of the Commission, although it may only be published with the consent of the parties.

(c) Arbitration. Here again the agreement and consent of the parties is emphasised. Under Article XXIX the parties in each case are to conclude a *compromis* specifying the undertaking of the parties to go to arbitration and accept as legally binding the decision of the Tribunal; it is also to state the subject matter of the controversy and the seat of the Tribunal. The *compromis* may also specify the law to be applied by the Tribunal and the power, if the parties so agree, to adjudicate *ex aequo et bono*. If the parties do

315

not make any provision concerning the applicable law, the Tribunal is to decide the dispute according to treaties concluded between the parties, International Law, the Charter of the Organization of African Unity, the Charter of the United Nations, and, if the parties agree, *ex aequo et bono*. Hearings are to be *in camera*, unless decided otherwise, and the award, in writing, is to state the reasons concerning every point decided.

The Arbitral Tribunal is composed as follows. Each party designates one arbitrator from among the Members of the Commission having legal qualifications; these two arbitrators then, by common agreement, choose from among the Members of the Commission a third person who shall act as Chairman of the Tribunal. Where the two arbitrators fail to agree, within one month of their appointment, in the choice of the person to be Chairman of the Tribunal, the Bureau shall designate the Chairman. The President may then, with the agreement of the parties, appoint two additional Members to the Arbitral Tribunal who need not be Members of the Commission but who are to have the same powers as the other Members of the Tribunal. The arbitrators are not to be nationals of the parties and are all to be of different nationalities.

It is clear that, as is commonly the case, there are no specific provisions on the enforcement of any award. However, it cannot be doubted that it would be for the Assembly or Committee of Ministers of the OAU to consider what political action would be expedient in relation to a party failing to accept the recommendations of the Commission (in relation to mediation or conciliation) or an arbitral award by the Commission. The other comment which must be made is that, in the first 15 years of its history, the Commission appears to have been little used, and arbitration not at all. Disputes there have certainly been, but following a pattern already clear in the UN, the OAS and the Arab League, the Member States have shown a marked preference for political settlement as opposed to the more formal, expert (and quasi-judicial) techniques available in the Commission. Thus, the Somali/Kenyan and Somali/Ethiopia disputes, the Algerian/Moroccan dispute (territorial disputes) the Ivory Coast/Guinea disputes (detention of diplomats) and Western Sahara dispute have been dealt with outside the Commission.

CHAPTER 10

ADMINISTRATIVE TRIBUNALS

THE creation of international civil services, or secretariats, whose members are bound to the organisation by a contractual relationship, made desirable the establishment of special tribunals competent to determine disputes arising from that relationship, once the view was accepted that the members acquired legal rights which ought to be protected by a system of administrative justice, on the continental pattern, and not left to the unfettered discretion of the executive as is largely the practice in the Anglo-American systems. Direct submission of such disputes to the P.C.I.J., or now the I.C.J., was impossible in view of the fact that the parties were individuals on the one hand and international organisations on the other, neither having any *locus standi* before these courts in contentious cases. Submission to municipal courts was inappropriate, for it conflicted with the general immunity from local jurisdiction claimed by the organisations and, moreover, the dispute generally involved a question of the internal, administrative law of the organisation and not local law; municipal courts were themselves generally reluctant to assume any jurisdiction over such disputes even when no agreement on immunities existed.[1] Hence, if the acquired rights of the staff members were to be protected by an impartial judicial body, special tribunals had to be created.

In the League a system of appeal to the Council was, in 1927 replaced by a permanent administrative tribunal, used also by the ILO, and this tribunal continues today as the ILO Administrative Tribunal. The International Institute of Agriculture in Rome established a tribunal in 1932, after the Italian courts had declined jurisdiction over disputes between staff and the Institute.[2] The United Nations did not continue with the League's tribunal but, after considerable opposition to the idea of a tribunal, established its own tribunal in 1949. The Statute of the ILO Tribunal was

---

[1] See Bastid, "Tribunaux administratifs internationaux et leur jurisprudence" (1957) 11 R.C. 354–370.
[2] *Institut d'agriculture c. Profili*, Cour de Cassation, (1929–30) A.D., Case No. 254.

317

amended in 1949 to enable other international inter-governmental organisations to use the Tribunal as their administrative tribunal, and WHO, UNESCO, ITU, WMO, FAO, CERN (European Organisation for Nuclear Research) IAEA, UPU and GATT have taken advantage of this.[3] Similarly Article 14 of the UN Tribunal's Statute enables the competence of that Tribunal to be extended to any specialised agency, although most of these agencies, being European-based, have preferred to utilise the ILO Tribunal; however, because of the common pensions scheme, some have accepted the jurisdiction of the UN Tribunal for pensions disputes. The IBRD established its own tribunal in 1980, and this will also serve the IDA and IFC. The Court of the European Communities acts as an administrative tribunal[4] and the I.C.J. is empowered to establish a procedure for dealing with disputes between the Registrar and the staff of the Registry.[5] OEEC (now OECD) established an Appeals Board for the same purpose in 1950 as a body of final resort and capable of giving judgments binding on staff member and organisation alike. WEU, the Council of Europe and NATO have also established administrative tribunals. Apart from these, and the organisations which make use of either the UN Administrative Tribunal or the ILO Administrative Tribunal, the other international organisations have no independent, permanent judicial machinery for settling such disputes and rely on internal administrative procedures or ad hoc arbitration. The differences between the existing administrative tribunals are so slight in comparison to the broad similarity of purpose and jurisdiction that it is proposed to deal with them on a comparative basis.

I. COMPOSITION

The fact that these Tribunals are international tribunals[6] has influenced their composition in the sense that the judges (called

---

[3] The ILO Tribunal (and its predecessor under the League) has also been used as a "panel" of arbitrators to form an arbitral body for staff disputes by the Institute for the Unification of Private Law, the International Institute for Intellectual Co-operation, the Nansen Office and the International Institute for Educational Cinema.

[4] *Ante*, p. 309.

[5] See Art. 17 of the Staff Regulations, (1946–47) *Yearbook of the Court 66;* disputes over pensions, however, are referred to the UN Administrative Tribunal. This is an exceptional situation of the Court being open to individuals, although there does not yet appear to have been an instance of its use.

[6] See (1956) *I.C.J. Reports* 97.

"members" in the UN Administrative Tribunal) must be of different nationalities. Their number varies; the UN has 7, the ILO and OECD have 3 and 3 deputies. They are elected for 3, 3, and 2 years respectively by the political organs of the organisations concerned, by the General Assembly of the UN, the Conference of the ILO and the Council of OECD. The judges do not have to have legal qualifications; Lord Crook, for example, a former member of the UN Tribunal, had instead experience in industrial arbitration, and this kind of administrative experience forms a useful addition to the purely legal experience of most members. The judges are all independent of the organisations concerned[7] and, in the UN, dismissal by the Assembly is conditional on the agreement of all the other members of the Tribunal (Art. 3 (5), Statute). They benefit from the privileges and immunities accorded to experts on missions and are paid a *per diem* rather than a salary in view of the irregularity of their sittings.

Each Tribunal is assisted by its own secretariat or registry, normally supplied by the organisation but controlled by the Tribunal itself, and this functions continually in between the sittings of the Tribunal which are called by the President of the Tribunal as business requires.

The Court of the European Communities, though it functions as an administrative tribunal, is a rather special case by reason of its other functions and its permanence. As we have seen, the ten judges do have to be lawyers and are elected for six years by unanimous agreement of the Member governments.

II. PROCEDURE

The Tribunals sit with a quorum of three (nine in the European Court), holding their proceedings in public as a general rule but with discretion to hold private sessions.[8] The procedure is

---

[7] Prior to 1956 the OEEC Appeals Board was composed of a President nominated by the Council from outside the organisation, one member nominated by the Sec.-Gen. (in practice the nominee was the legal adviser of the Secretariat) and one member nominated by the staff. Since 1956 all three have been completely independent persons nominated by the Council, so that the Commission changed from a body analogous in composition to the UN Joint Appeals Board to one analogous to the UN Administrative Tribunal. For the texts of the Staff Regulations, Rules of Procedure of the Appeals Board and the Resolution of the Council on the Operation of the Appeals Board of January 30, 1962 see (1966) XIV *European Yearbook* 147.

[8] But the OECD Appeals Board sits in private: Art. 7 of 1962 Resolution.

predominantly modelled on the French system and is based very much on the written briefs lodged by the parties; this first stage is followed by a second, oral hearing, at which counsel for both parties can be heard and even witnesses produced, but this is largely by way of supplementing the original written brief or in order to answer supplementary questions posed by the Tribunal itself. There is a right of intervention for all persons having access to the Tribunal and whose rights are likely to be affected by the judgment; the UN Tribunal's rules of procedure even allow for hearing representatives of the Staff Association (Rule 19 (2)) though the ILO had rejected this except when they wished to appear in their individual capacity.

The applicant must in all cases show that he is appealing against a *final* decision of the administration which has caused him some injury; this is confirmed as a rule of general application by the jurisprudence of the tribunals.[9] This requirement is consistent with the notion that the Tribunals are normally the body of last resort and this is further emphasised by the requirement that the applicant must first have exhausted all remedies within the organisation itself. In the UN Tribunal, for example, prior recourse to the Joint Appeals Board is a necessary pre-condition to the jurisdiction of the Tribunal except when both applicant and the Secretary-General have agreed to dispense with it (Art. 7 (1)). The ILO has similar internal procedures which must be exhausted, OECD envisages appeal to the Secretary-General and CERN, which uses the ILO Tribunal, even provides for arbitration by a body constituted from within the organisation.

Secondly, the applicant must submit his request to the Tribunal within a prescribed time, running from the date on which he was notified of the final decision against which he is appealing; this is ninety days in the ILO and the UN (although the UN Tribunal has power to extend the period, Art. 7 (5)), and two months in the OECD and the European Court. This limitation on jurisdiction, *ratione temporis,* and the first limitation involved in the rule of

---

[9] See, for example, ILO Tribunal, Judgment No. 15 (*Leff*); UN Tribunal, Judgment No. 56 (*Aglion*). Note that Art. 7 (2) of the UN Tribunal's Statute treats failure to act by the Secretary-General in accordance with the opinion of the Joint Appeals Board favourable to the applicant as equivalent to a "decision" by the Sec.-Gen. so as to allow the Tribunal to receive the application.

exhaustion of internal remedies, may be viewed either as requirements of procedure or as pre-conditions to the jurisdiction of the Tribunal.

III. JURISDICTION

The jurisdiction of the Tribunals is largely confined, *ratione personae,* to disputes between *officials* of the organisation and the organisations themselves. The rank of the official,[10] or the duration of his contract, is irrelevant, but he must normally be or have been an official in the technical sense; hence temporary experts or consultants, or locally recruited personnel such as gardeners, cleaners, etc., are usually excluded,[11] for they do not enter into a contract which incorporates the Staff Rules and Regulations and will rely for a remedy upon arbitration or recourse to local courts before whom the organisation will waive immunity.[12] The UN officials will include for this purpose officials of agencies like the Office of the High Commissioner of Refugees, UNICEF, or UNRWA; whether the defendant is the Secretary-General of the UN or the agency will depend on the degree of autonomy of the agency, and in the case of UNRWA applications are against UNRWA itself and not the Sec.-Gen.[13] The jurisdiction of the Tribunals is extended to successors in title to a deceased official.

The more difficult limitation on jurisdiction is the limitation *ratione materiae.* Article 2 (1) of the UN Tribunal's Statute provides:

> "The Tribunal shall be competent to hear and pass judgment upon applications alleging non-observance of con-

---

[10] Hence a former Secretary-General of the League became an applicant in *Joseph Avenol* c. *Caisse des Pensions S.D.N.,* ILO Tribunal, Judgment No. 2 (1947). An existing Secretary-General would be an unlikely applicant, since he is normally the nominal defendant, but presumably he could contest a decision of the Organisation affecting him.

[11] But note that the jurisdiction of the OECD Appeals Board has been specifically extended to Council Experts and Consultants and to Auxiliary Staff. The distinction between an official and an expert is elaborated in the decision of the Court of Justice of the European Communities in the *Roemer case* (Aff. 26–68 Vol. XV, p. 145)and of the OECD Tribunal in the *Rufo* case (dec. No. 41). But OPEX personnel are treated as officials.

[12] Bastid, *loc. cit.,* pp. 444–450.

[13] *Hilpern* c. *UNRWA,* UN Tribunal, Judgment No. 57.

tracts of employment of staff members of the Secretariat of the United Nations or of the terms of appointment of such staff members. The words "contracts" and "terms of appointment" include all pertinent regulations and rules in force at the time of the alleged non-observance, including the staff regulations."

The ILO Tribunal's Statute, Article 2, is more complex but not essentially different and in OECD and the European Court the formulation is briefer and more general.[14] Basically, however, the task of the Tribunals is to adjudicate disputes arising from the terms of the contracts of employment.[15]

The problems arising from the execution of this task are really twofold. The first, a problem common to administrative tribunals generally, even in municipal systems, is how far the tribunal is competent to question the exercise of administrative discretion. The second, a problem peculiar to international administrative tribunals, is what law is to be applied to these contracts.

The first problem is the crucial one, for these Tribunals do not have the same general power of review over administrative decisions for *détournement de pouvoir* as do some municipal tribunals; they (and also the I.C.J.) have recognised that they are Tribunals of "limited" jurisdiction.[16] In general, therefore, they are not entitled to challenge the disciplinary action of the administrative heads of the organisations against staff members, or to substitute their views of what is administratively convenient or desirable.[17] Hence much of the criticism of the UN Tribunal's judgments Nos. 29–37, the "5th Amendment Cases," rested on the view that the Tribunal had challenged the Sec.-Gen's disciplinary discretion; in form, however, the Tribunal had merely held that, as a matter of interpretation of the Staff Regulations, the staff members had not committed the "serious misconduct"

---

[14] OECD, Staff Reg. 22 also refers specifically to the Board's power to "annul" and to order the Organisation "to redress the damage."

[15] ILO Tribunal Judgment No. 66 (*Press*) indicates that it will nevertheless assume jurisdiction over the statutory rights of the official vis-à-vis the organisation, even if no specific provision of the staff regulation, rules or contract can be invoked.

[16] (1956) *I.C.J. Reports* 97.

[17] See UN Tribunal, Judgments No. 21 (*Rubin*), No. 43 (*Levinson*), No. 48 (*Wang*). ILO Tribunal Judgments No. 65 (*Morse*), No. 32 (*Garcin*), No. 69 (*Kissaun*); Court of the European Committees, aff. 35/62, 26/63.

which alone gave the Sec.-Gen. power to terminate their contracts summarily.[18] Again, in the ILO Administrative Tribunal (UNESCO) Judgments Nos. 17, 18, 19 and 21 the Tribunal's view that the staff members were entitled to renewal of their fixed term contracts (which had not been renewed as a result of their refusal to testify before the U.S. Loyalty Board) was challenged by the Director-General as an interference with his own discretion as to what was "for the good of the service and in the interests of the Organisation." It must be recalled that the I.C.J. refused to give an opinion on this particular point since it lay outside the scope of matters on which, under Article 12 of the Tribunal's Statute, opinions could be requested.[19] The line between matters properly within the jurisdiction and those matters in which interference with the discretion of the administration is improper is always difficult to draw. What has emerged is that the Tribunals will assume jurisdiction to challenge a discretionary power when there has been a failure by the administration to observe the procedures specified, such as the requirement of prior consultation of the Joint Disciplinary Committee, or such other procedures as are inherent in the notion of "due process,"[20] which Jenks has said "may well prove to be the basic concept of international administrative law."[21] The Tribunals will either nullify the decision taken or remit the case with an order that the prescribed procedure be followed. The Tribunals will also challenge an *excès de pouvoir*, when the administration goes beyond its powers,[22] or an *abus de pouvoir*, where the power is exercised for improper motives[23] or to achieve a purpose for which the power was not intended.

It may also be noted that this problem equally affects the relationship between the administrative tribunals and the political

---

[18] See *ante*, pp. 97, 103.

[19] See *post*, p. 327.

[20] Originally the UN Tribunal held that the Sec.-Gen. was required as a matter of principle to give reasons for termination (Judgment No. 5 (*Howrani*)); the Assembly amended the Staff Regulations (Regulations 9.1 (*c*)) in 1952 to allow a termination of appointments other than fixed-term "if, in his opinion, such action would be in the interest of the United Nations." The Tribunal has held itself estopped by this amendment (Judgments Nos. 19–27).

[21] *The Proper Law of International Organisations*, p. 129.

[22] See OECD Appeals Board, decisions Nos. 7–11, March 10, 1951.

[23] UN Tribunal Judgment No. 18 (*Crawford*); ILO Tribunal Judgment No. 13 (*McIntire* v. *FAO*).

organ of the Organisation responsible for establishing the staff regulations. In 1946 the Assembly of the League had refused to give effect to the League Tribunal's judgment in *Mayras v. S.G. of the League* which purported to interpret the Assembly resolutions (erroneously in the view of the Assembly). In 1953 certain Member States of the UN were prepared to oppose the supplementary appropriations in the budget necessary to implement the awards of compensation by the UN Administrative Tribunal in the "5th Amendment Cases." Fortunately the issue was referred by the Assembly to the I.C.J. for an advisory opinion which, being given on July 13, 1954,[24] stated that although the Tribunal was a subsidiary organ created by the Assembly (and capable of suppression by the Assembly) this did not imply subordination of the judgments of the Tribunal to subsequent decisions of the Assembly; on the contrary, the Assembly had established a judicial body capable of rendering judgments in the nature of a *res judicata,* which the Assembly was under a legal duty to accept and give effect to. It was a result of the dissatisfaction of certain Member States with this position that provision for a kind of appeals procedure to the I.C.J. was made under the new Article XI of the UN Tribunal's Statute.

One further aspect of this problem of the relationship between the Tribunal and the Assembly is the question of how far the Assembly can, by amendment of the Staff Regulations, affect the rights of existing staff members. The League Assembly had taken the extreme view that, by invoking its legislative authority, it could derogate from contractual rights.[25] The compromise view taken by the UN Tribunal has been to distinguish between the "contractual" and the "statutory" elements in the legal relationship of staff members; the latter are alone capable of amendment by the Assembly.[26] This distinction, however difficult to draw in practice, is clearly designed to afford protection on to the "acquired rights"

---

[24] *A.O. on Effect of Awards of Compensation made by the UN Administrative Tribunal,* (1954) *I.C.J. Reports* 47.

[25] *Official Journal, Special Supplement* No. 194, p. 262.

[26] UN Tribunal Judgment No. 19 (*Kaplan*); see *ante,* pp. 100, 103. It was the League Tribunal's interpretation of the League Assembly's resolution of December 14, 1939, to the effect that no interference with acquired rights was intended, which caused the Assembly to decline to give effect to the decision in *Mayras v. Sec.-Gen.* (see *A.D.* 1946, Case No. 91). See generally on this problem Jenks, *op. cit.* pp. 63–60; Akehurst, The Law governing employment in international organisations (1967).

of staff members.[27] The Appeals Board of OECD and the ILO Tribunal have attempted to give the same protection via the doctrine of *bouleversement imprévisible,* derived from French law, which envisages compensation for a variation of the economic benefits derived from the contract of employment to the disadvantage of the employee.[28]

The second problem is that of the law to be applied by the Tribunals. Admitting the inappropriateness of either municipal or international law as such, there has developed of necessity a body of "internal administrative law" of the Organisation concerned which comprises the terms of the particular contract in question and the relevant Staff Regulations, Staff Rules and Administrative Instructions. These last three sources are in a hierarchy to which the *ultra vires* doctrine applies, so that the Regulations established by the Assembly govern the legality of the Rules promulgated by the Secretary-General and both, in turn, govern the Administrative Instructions. In the event of any lacuna, or as an aid to the construction of the relevant contractual provisions, the Tribunals make reference to such other sources as the UN Charter, the principles applied in municipal law or "general principles of law."[29] None of these Tribunals adopt the principle of *stare decisis,* so that no judgment ever becomes a binding precedent; however, as the body of case-law develops, the Tribunals do develop a "jurisprudence constante" to which repeated reference is made in subsequent cases.

IV. THE JUDGMENTS

The judgments of the Tribunals must be reasoned and, except for the UN Tribunal which allows dissenting judgments, they are single majority judgments. In form they follow the continental style of a recital of the facts and a series of conclusions. When the judgment is against the Organisation the normal order (and the primary remedy of the applicant) is one of annulment of the contested decision or a decree for specific performance of the

---

[27] Baade, "The acquired rights of international public servants" (1966–67) 15 A.J. Comp. Law 251.

[28] OECD Appeals Board Decision No. 24, February 21, 1957; *Lindsey* v. *I.T.U.,* ILO Tribunal Judgment No. 61, *Archer et al.,* OECD Appeals Board Decision No. 37, January 9, 1964.

[29] See Bastid, *loc. cit.* Chap. V; Jenks, *op. cit.* pp. 25–62.

obligation of the Organisation towards the staff member.[30] An award of compensation does not follow as a matter of right,[31] but may follow, in the case of the ILO Tribunal, when annulment or specific performance "is not possible or advisable" (Art. 9). In the case of the UN Tribunal and the OECD Appeals Board it is clearly for the Sec.-Gen. to decide whether or not to take the action required by the annulment or decree of specific performance; only if he decides *not* to take such action does the amount of compensation fixed by the Tribunal become due to the applicant as a kind of secondary remedy. The UN Statute also fixes the normal limit of compensation as the equivalent of two years' net base salary, but gives the Tribunal power to fix a higher sum upon reasons being stated (Art. 9 (1)). The only Tribunals with a specific power to award costs are the Court of the European Communities and the OECD Appeals Board, but in fact both the ILO and the UN Tribunal have assumed such power to award costs against the Organisation.[32]

Application can be made to the Tribunals subsequently for the *interpretation* of a judgment; the power is specific in the Court of the European Communities but assumed as inherent in their jurisdiction in the other cases. Application can also be made for the revision of a judgment upon the discovery of some new fact of such a nature as to be a decisive factor.[33]

V. REVIEW OF JUDGMENTS

To establish a procedure for the review of judgments is, of course, totally different from establishing a procedure whereby the tribunal concerned can interpret or revise its own judgments; a review procedure presupposes review by some organ other than the tribunal giving the judgment, and to that extent means that the

---

[30] See Art. 9 (1) of the UN Tribunal's Statute: "If the Tribunal finds that the application is well founded, it shall order the rescinding of the decision contested or the specific performance of the obligation invoked."

[31] Except, possibly, in the Court of the European Communities.

[32] No costs are awarded against staff members; a requirement that the staff member deposits a sum as security for costs was deleted from the old League Statute in 1946; it remains, however, a requirement in Art. 2 (d) of the OECD Appeals Board, and the deposit is forfeited where the appeal is an "abuse of process."

[33] UN Tribunal, Art. 12; Court of the European Communities, Art. 38; assumed as inherent power by the ILO Tribunal. Rule 5 (c) of the OECD Appeals Board's Rules of procedure is limited to revision for "clerical or accidental error."

judgment of the tribunal is not a final judgment from which no appeal can be made.

Under the League, as now in OECD and in the Court of the European Communities, the judgments of the administrative tribunals were final. In 1946, however, the Statute of the ILO Tribunal was re-drafted to include a new Article 12[34] allowing for what is virtually a limited right of appeal by the Governing Body or Administrative Board of the Pensions Fund of the ILO by means of a request for an advisory opinion from the I.C.J., that advisory opinion being treated as binding. In 1955, following the dissatisfaction of certain States with the UN Tribunal's judgments in 1953 in the "5th Amendment" cases, a dissatisfaction rendered the keener by the I.C.J.'s opinion in 1954 that the judgments were binding on the Organisation, the General Assembly amended the Statute of the Tribunal so as to make the judgments no longer "final and without appeal," but rather subject to a review procedure similar to that in the ILO. The new Article 11 gives the right to any Member State, the Secretary-General or the individual claimant objecting to a judgment to request that an advisory opinion be sought from the I.C.J.; this is, therefore, much wider than the ILO, which limits the right to the Governing Body or the Administrative Board of the Pension Fund. There is established a special Committee on Applications for Review of Administrative Tribunal Judgments, composed of 21 States, which receives the request and decides whether or not the opinion should be sought. The grounds upon which an opinion may be sought are wider than those in the ILO Statute and are that the Tribunal has "exceeded its jurisdiction or competence or . . . has failed to exercise jurisdiction vested in it, or has erred on a question of law relating to the provisions of the Charter of the United Nations, or has committed a fundamental error in procedure which has occasioned a failure of justice . . . ." Once an advisory opinion is given "the Secretary-General shall either give effect to the opinion of the Court, or request the Tribunal to convene specially in order that it

[34] "In any case in which the Governing Body of the International Labour Office or the Administrative Board of the Pensions Fund challenges a decision of the Tribunal confirming its jurisdiction, or considers that a decision of the Tribunal is vitiated by a fundamental fault in the procedure followed, the question of the validity of the decision given by the Tribunal shall be submitted by the Governing Body, for an advisory opinion, to the International Court of Justice. The opinion given by the Court shall be binding."

shall confirm its original judgment; or give a new judgment, in conformity with the opinion of the Court"; the opinion is, therefore, to be treated as binding.

It is, of course, entirely a question of policy at which stage in a judicial hierarchy decisions are to be regarded as final, and there is perhaps little objection in principle to the Court assuming, in this roundabout way, an appellate jurisdiction from administrative tribunals. A more controversial point is the interposition in this hierarchy of a political body which takes the decision[35] on whether an appeal shall be allowed, a decision clearly involving an appreciation of purely legal questions. In *Application for review of Judgment No. 158 of the UNAT,* the I.C.J. dismissed this objection.[36] There is little doubt, in the case of the UN, that the sponsors of the amendment wished to place some form of political supervision over the Administrative Tribunal.

It may be noted, in conclusion, that the principle that individuals have no *locus standi* before the I.C.J. is undergoing modification, however indirectly. Not only is the Court able to decide disputes (other than pension disputes) between the Registrar and the staff of the Registry of the Court, in its capacity as an administrative tribunal, but it is also, by way of advisory opinions, becoming a kind of appellate court from the administrative tribunals of the ILO and the UN under the post-war review procedure. This development is not without its procedural complications, as we have seen[37]; it is nevertheless a development well worth attention. It may also be noted that in the Court's opinion of July 12, 1973, Judge Lachs suggested the desirability of unifying the U.L.O. and UN systems of administrative tribunals.

---

[35] This is so with the UN Committee on Review; in the case of the ILO the Governing Body does not appear to act as a "screening body," but simply as the body formally competent to request the opinion. In its opinion in 1954 the I.C.J. had said "the Court is of opinion that the General Assembly itself, in view of its composition and functions, could hardly act as a judicial organ . . . all the more so as one party to the disputes is the United Nations Organisation itself" ((1954) *I.C.J. Reports* 56). However, in *Jurado* v. *ILO,* ILO Tribunal Judgment No. 83, it appears that the ILO Secretariat declined to accede to the complainant's request to the Governing Body that an advisory opinion be requested from the I.C.J. The complainant appealed the refusal and the Tribunal held it had no power to review the decisions of the Governing Body.

[36] (1973) *I.C.J. Reports,* para. 25. This was the first of some 16 applications to be referred to the Court.

[37] *Ante,* p. 282.

Bibliography

Arbitration
BASTID: *"L'arbitrage international"* Juris Classeur, Fasc. 246–249.
CARLSTON: The Process of International Arbitration (1946).
DAVID DAVIES MEMORIAL INSTITUTE: Report of a Study Group on the Peaceful Settlement of Disputes (1966).
FRANCOIS: *"La Cour pérmanente d'arbitrage"* (1955) 90 R.C. 541.
HUDSON: International Tribunals, Past and Future (1944).
JOHNSTON: *"The Constitution of an Arbitral Tribunal"* (1953) 30 B.Y-.B.I.L. 152.
RALSTON: International Arbitration from Athens to Locarno (1929).
SIMPSON and FOX: International Arbitration (1959).
Convention for the Pacific Settlement of International Disputes 1899–1907: Scott, The Hague Conventions and Declarations of 1899 and 1907 (1915), p. 41; (1898–99) 91 B.F.S.P. 970 and (1906–07) 100 B.F.S.P. 298.
General Act for the Pacific Settlement of International Disputes 1928: 93 L.N.T.S. 343 *or* Hudson, International Legislation, Vol. IV, p. 2529.
Revised General Act of 1949: 71 U.N.T.S. 102.
European Convention for the Peaceful Settlement of Disputes, 1957: 5 European Yearbook 347.
International Law Commission, Model Rules on Arbitral Procedure: Report of the I.L.C. covering the work of its tenth session (A/3859).
VAN MANGOLDT: "Arbitration and Conciliation" in Judicial Settlement of International Disputes (1974), Symposium of the Max Planck Institute, 419.

The International Court of Justice
ANAND: Compulsory Jurisdiction of the International Court of Justice (1961).
CRAWFORD: "The legal effect of automatic reservations to the jurisdiction of the I.C.J." (1979) 50 B.Y.B.I.L. 63.
I.C.J.: Yearbook (consult the current Yearbook of the Court for the Statute, Rules, state of the list of pending cases, financial regulations, and the texts of instruments conferring jurisdiction on the Court).
JENKS: The Prospects of International Adjudication (1964).
KEITH: The extent of the Advisory Jurisdiction of the I.C.J. (1971).
MERRILLS: "The Optional Clause To-day" (1979) 50 B.Y.B.I.L. 87.
REISMAN: "The enforcement of international judgments" (1969) 63 A.J.I.L. 1–27.
ROSENNE: The International Court of Justice (1957).
STONE: *"The International Court and World Crisis"* (1962) International Conciliation
WALDOCK: *"The Decline of the Optional Clause"* (1955–56) 32 B.Y.B.I.L. 244.

European Commission and Court of Human Rights
Council of Europe: The European Convention on Human Rights (1968).
Council of Europe: Yearbook of the European Convention on Human Rights, 1958 (Part I contains texts of the European Convention for the Protection of Human Rights and Fundamental Freedoms, Protocol to the Convention, Reservation, Declarations by States, rules of procedure of the Commission; Part II contains the decisions of the Commision and Court).
ROBERTSON: *"The European Court of Human Rights"* (1960) 9 A.J. Comp. Law 1.
ROBERTSON: The Law of International Institutions in Europe (1961), Chap V.
Union Internationale des Avocats: Les Jurisdictions Internationales (1958) p. 72.
VASAK: *"The Court and Commission of Human Rights"* Juris Classeur, Fasc. 155 F.
WALDOCK: *"The European Convention for the Protection of Human Rights and Fundamental Freedoms"* (1958) 34 B.Y.B.I.L. 356.

Court of Justice of the European Communities
BROWN and JACOBS: The Court of Justice of the European Communities (1977).
EUROPEAN ECONOMIC COMMUNITY: Receuil de la Jurisprudence de la Cour.
LECOURT: L'Europe des Juges (1976).
MANN: The function of Judicial Decision in European Economic Integration (1972).
PLENDER and USHER: Cases and Materials on the Law of the European Communities (1979).
SCHERMERS: Judicial Protection in the European Communities (1979).
Union Internationale des Avocats: Les Jurisdictions Internationales (1958) pp. 114, 222 (in French and English).
VALENTINE: The Court of Justice of the European Communities (1965), 2 vols.
VALENTINE: *"The Jurisdiction of the Court of Justice of the European Communities to annul executive action"* (1960) 36 B.Y.B.I.L. 174.
WALL: The Court of Justice of the European Communities (1966).

Administrative Tribunals
AKEHURST: The Law governing employment in International Organisation (1967).
BASTID: Le Tribunal administratif des Nations Unies (1970).
BEDJAOUI: *"Les Tribuneaux Administratifs internationaux,"* Juris Classeur, Fasc. 230–231.
DEHAUSSY: *"Procédure de réformation des jugements du tribunal administratif des Nations Unies"* (1956) Annuaire Francais 468.
ECSC: *Cour de Justice de la C.E.C.A.,* Règlement de la procédure de la Cour pour les litiges prévus à l'article 58 due Statut du personnel de la

Communauté, arrêté fevrier 21, 1957; J.O. C.E.C.A. March 11, 1957, pp. 110–157. Recueil de la jurisprudence de la Cour.

ILO: Statute and Rules of the Administrative Tribunal (1954).

ILO: Judgments of the Administrative Tribunal.

JENKS: The Proper Law of International Organisations (1962), Part II.

OEEC: Statute of the Appeals Board, Clunet 1953, pp. 450–458.

OEEC: Internationale des Avocats: Jurisdictions Internationales (1958), pp. 240, 306.

UNITED NATIONS: Statute of the Administrative Tribunal.

UNITED NATIONS: Judgments of the UN Administrative Tribunal, Nos. 1–70 (1950–57), New York (1958) (and in mimeograph as AT/DEC/ 1—).

WOLF: Le Tribunal administratif de l'OIT (1970).

International Centre for the Settlement of Investment Disputes

BROCHES: "The Convention on the Settlement of Investment Disputes between States and Nationals of other States" (1972) R.C. II 337–409.

AMERASINGHE: "The jurisdiction of ICSID" (1979) 19 *Indian Journal I.L.* 166–227.

O'KEEFE: "The ICSID" (1980) *Yearbook of World Affairs*.

SUTHERLAND: "The World Bank Convention on the Settlement of Investment Disputes" (1979) 28 *I.C.L.Q.* 367–400.

PART FOUR

Common Institutional Problems

CHAPTER 11

INTERNATIONAL PERSONALITY

I. Nature and Consequences of the Concept

BY 1945 considerable controversy existed over whether public international organisations could be regarded as possessing legal personality.[1] Such personality had been claimed by writers for organisations like the International Commission for the Cape Spartel Lighthouse, the Bank for International Settlements,[2] the Reparation Commission and the European Commission of the Danube: in the case of the League of Nations, the *modus vivendi* of 1926 with Switzerland proclaimed in Article I that the League "which possesses international personality and legal capacity, cannot, in principle, according to the rules of international law, be sued before the Swiss courts without its express consent."[3] In drafting the UN Charter, and apparently due to a wish to avoid any implication that the UN was a "super-state,"[4] the somewhat timid compromise was adopted of recognising in Article 104 that

> "the Organisation shall enjoy in the territory of each of its Members such legal capacity as may be necessary for the exercise of its functions and fulfilment of its purposes."

The provision on privileges and immunities in Article 105 was similarly restricted in the form of a grant "in the territory of each of its Members." Similarly, Article 1, section 1 of the General Convention on Privileges and Immunities of 1946 seems to be concerned primarily with the position of the Organisation under municipal rather than international law. The question therefore arose as to whether the Organisation only had personality under municipal law, or also, to some degree, under international law; of the former interpretation Jenks stated that "it is as inherently

---

[1] See the formidable bibliography on this question cited by Jenks, "The Legal Personality of International Organisations" (1945) 22 B.Y.B.I.L. 267.
[2] Granted full personality by a constituent charter granted by the Swiss Government.
[3] (1926) 7 O.J.L.N., Ann. 911a, 1422.
[4] *Report to the President on the results of the San Francisco Conference,* Dept. State Publication 2349, (1945) Conference Series 71, 157.

fantastic as it is destructive of any international legal order to regard the existence and extent of legal personality provided for in the constituent instrument of an international organisation as being derived from, dependent upon, and limited by the constitution and laws of its individual member States."[5]

The answer to that question, so far as the UN is concerned, was authoritatively given by the I.C.J. in the Advisory Opinion on *Reparations for Injuries suffered in the Service of the United Nations.*[6] The Court found it necessary to affirm the *international* personality of the UN, before going on to consider whether the Organisation had the capacity to bring an international claim. It stated that such personality was "indispensable" to achieve the purposes and principles of the Charter, and that the functions and rights of the Organisation "can only be explained on the basis of the possession of a large measure of international personality."[7] The Court continued:

> "That is not the same thing as saying that it is a State, which it certainly is not, or that its legal personality and rights and duties are the same as those of a State. Still less is it the same thing as saying that it is a "super-State," whatever that expression may mean . . . . What it does mean is that it is a subject of international law and capable of possessing international rights and duties, and that it has capacity to maintain its rights by bringing international claims."[8]

Moreover, the Court held that "fifty States, representing the vast majority of the members of the international community, had the power, in conformity with international law, to bring into being an entity possessing *objective* international personality, and not merely personality recognised by them alone . . . ."[9]

The *indicia* of personality which the Court noted were the obligations of members towards the Organisation, the legal capacity and privileges provided for in Articles 104 and 105, and its treaty-making capacity. At this stage, however, a certain logical

[5] *Loc. cit.* pp. 270–271. See (1971) U.N.J.Y. 215 for a legal opinion on the question whether an agreement between central banks and monetary authorities could make an international person, a Clearing Union, under international law.
[6] (1949) *I.C.J. Reports* 174.
[7] *Ibid.* 179.
[8] *Ibid.*
[9] *Ibid.* 185, emphasis added.

difficulty must be noted, for whereas it is possible to refer to *specific* powers as indications of personality, the Court also went on to stress that other powers (such as the power to bring an international claim) not specifically granted in the constituent treaty could be *implied* from the very fact of personality. It stated that

> "the rights and duties of an entity such as the Organisation must depend upon its purposes and functions as specified *or implied* in its constituent documents and developed in practice."[10]

The danger is, therefore, that one might be tempted to deduce, say, a general treaty-making power, from the very fact of personality, even though personality is itself deduced from a specific treaty-making power[11]: in other words, one becomes involved in a circular argument *unless* great care is taken to restrict implied powers to those which may reasonably be deduced from the purposes and functions of the organisation in question. Therefore the test is a functional one; reference to the functions and powers of the organisation exercised on the international plane, and not to the abstract and variable notion of personality, will alone give guidance on what powers may properly be implied.[12] Nevertheless, these functions and powers are often described in very general terms, so that they leave considerable scope for extension in practice. In the Advisory Opinion on *Namibia* in 1971 the I.C.J. was concerned with Security Council resolutions which were not expressly covered by the wording of the provisions in Chapters VI and VII (such as the reference to the termination of the mandate or the continued presence of South Africa being illegal). The Court took the view that the Council had, in addition to its specific powers, certain general powers under Article 24 (1): obviously "primary responsibility for the maintenance of international peace and security" can cover a very wide range of actions. There yet remains the question whether one can imply only such powers as arise by necessary intendment from

---

[10] *Ibid.* 180, emphasis added.
[11] See Parry, "The Treaty-making power of the UN" (1949) 26 B.Y.B.I.L. 108.
[12] Weissberg, *The International Status of the UN* (1961), p. 24, classifies functions as "original" or "derivative"—or "primary" and "secondary": this is certainly more realistic than Kelsen, *Law of the UN* (1950), p. 330.

the constitutional provisions[13] or whether a more liberal approach is permissible so that powers *relating to* the purposes and functions specified in the constitution can be implied. There would seem little doubt that, in practice, organisations take the latter view and instances abound of organisations acting in a manner which is neither specifically envisaged in their constitutions nor *necessary* to give effect to them. Perhaps the prime example is the development of peace-keeping by the General Assembly: significantly, in the *Expenses Case,*[14] the I.C.J. showed no inclination to ask whether the establishment of UNEF was *necessary*.

The attribution of implied powers as a result of a liberal interpretation of the purposes and functions of an organisation has certain consequences which should be recognised. It means that the organisation is conceived as a dynamic institution, evolving to meet changing needs and circumstances and, as time goes by, becoming further and further removed from its treaty base. Moreover, if, as in the UN, there is no judicial organ with power of review (otherwise than by advisory opinions), the practice of the various organs is presumed to be *intra vires* and is, in effect, an expression of the will of the majority: the dissenting minority may appeal to the original meaning of their treaty commitments in vain. And if there is radical disagreement over the purposes of the organisation (as there is in the UN), the pursuit of a liberal approach to those purposes by the majority will ultimately lead to a confrontation between majority and minority which, ultimately, might leave the minority with no alternative but to withdraw from the organisation.

---

[13] See Seidl-Hohenveldern in (1961) *Österreichische Zeitschrift für öffentliches Recht,* 497. For an influential view see Seyersted, *United Nations Forces* (1966) pp. 143–161, who argues that intergovernmental organisations, like states and other self-governing communities, in principle are general and objective subjects of international law. They have an inherent capacity (not implied in any particular articles of their constitution) to perform any sovereign or international act which they are in a practical position to perform and which is not precluded by any provision of their constitution. Their position thus differs from that of states in fact rather than in law. In the *Expenses Case* I.C.J. Reports 1962, p. 168 the Court seems to have shared Seyersted's view, and certainly accepted his view that action taken by the wrong organ would not necessarily be invalid in relation to third parties. See also Rama-Montaldo, "International legal personality and implied powers of international organisations" (1970) 44 B.Y.B.I.L. 111–155, Schermers, International Institutional Law (1980), I, 154–7.

[14] (1962) *I.C.J. Reports.*

However, to return to the more general question of personality, it seems that whilst specific acknowledgment of the possession of *international* personality is extremely rare,[15] it is permissible to assume that most organisations created by a multilateral inter-governmental agreement will, so far as they are endowed with functions on the international plane, possess some measure of international personality in addition to the personality within the systems of municipal law of the members which all the agreements on privileges and immunities (and often the basic constitutions) provide for. Possession of such international personality will normally involve, as a consequence, the attribution of power to make treaties, of privileges and immunities, of power to contract and to undertake legal proceedings: it will also pose a general problem of dissolution, for in the nature of things the personality of all such organisations can be brought to an end. It is with the usual attributes of international personality that the remaining sections of this first part are concerned: before proceeding to these however, mention must be made of certain special attributes of personality, or manifestations of personality, attaching to the United Nations.[16] These, as will be seen, are consequent upon the very wide functions and powers of the United Nations, and it is by no means certain that these same attributes could attach to other organisations of less comprehensive aims.

The first, and most obvious, example is the power to maintain an international force.[17] The differing character of the UN Command in Korea, UNEF, UNOGIL, ONUC, UNYOM and UNFICYP will have been apparent from the first part of this book.[18] Yet, of whatever character, the capacity to maintain an

---

[15] But see, for example, Art. 2 of the WMO/Switzerland Agreement of March 10, 1955: 211 U.N.T.S. 278.

[16] Note that certain of the operating agencies of the UN make treaties on their own account: *UNRWA/Jordan Agreement on Privileges and Immunities of* 1951, 120 U.N.T.S. 282; UNICEF agreements, *e.g.* 243 U.N.T.S. 319; 227, 348; Special Fund/Guatemala, 383 U.N.T.S. 68. To this extent it it tempting to regard them as having some measure of independent intenational personality. This is reinforced by the fact that some of these treaties contemplate arbitration by the agency.

[17] See Seyersted, "Some Legal Problems of the UN Force" (1961)37 B.Y.B.I.L. 435 *et seq.* Bowett, *U.N. Forces* (1964), Chap. 8.

[18] *Ante*, pp. 41, 42, 53. The League had established an "international" detachment in connection with the Leticia dispute: (1933) 14 O.J.L.N. 977–979; and in 1934 the Council sponsored an international force to police the Saar plebiscite (1934) 15 O.J.L.N. 1729–1730.

armed force under a United Nations command utilising a United Nations flag,[19] to which (in so far as the force engages in belligerency) the rules of war apply, is a striking attribute of international personality. As a second example one might take the capacity to exercise jurisdiction over territory; this is clearly anticipated in Article 81 of the Charter[20] and was contemplated as a solution to the Trieste[21] and Jerusalem[22] problems; it became an accomplished fact when the UN took over the interim administration of Weŝtern New Guinea pending the formal transfer to Indonesia on May 1, 1963.[23] It is also implicit in the General Assembly's establishment of the U.N. Council for Namibia (S.W. Africa) in resol. 2248 (S-V) of May 1967 that the Assembly has power to administer territory.

A further example is the capacity for functional protection of its agents. This, it will be recalled, was directly raised in the *Reparations Case* in that the question (to which the Court gave an affirmative answer) was whether an international claim could be brought not only in respect of the damage caused to the UN, but also in respect of damage caused to the victim or to persons entitled through him. The Court held that functional (as opposed to diplomatic) protection was a power implicit in the purposes and functions of the Organisation and that, even though the agent might possess the nationality of the defendant State, the rule of nationality of claims could present no obstacle to this protection. It may well be that this particular attribute of international personality is not confined to the UN and the specialised agencies[24]: yet even this can only be definitely answered by means of the functional test, by reference to the purposes of the organisation in question. Certainly instances abound in which the UN has exercised this right of functional protection. The question of the

---

[19] Resol. of Security Council of July 7, 1950 (UN Doc. S/1587): note also the recognition of the right of international organisations to fly their flag on vessels at sea in Art. 7 of the High Seas Convention, (1958) 257 U.N.T.S. 75.

[20] *Ante*, p. 73.

[21] *Off. Rec. S.C. Second Year,* 89th Mtg., Jan. 7, 1947, pp. 4–19, and 91st Mtg., Jan. 10, pp. 44–61.

[22] G.A. Res. 181 (II).

[23] Agreement between Netherlands and Indonesia of August 15, 1962 (A/5170 and Corr. I and Add. I).

[24] For example, Art. 5 (b) of the OECD Staff Regulations provides that the staff shall be entitled to the protection of the Organisation when carrying out their functions.

forum appropriate to entertain claims by an organisation is, of course, a distinct question and is dealt with later under section IV.

In conclusion, therefore, the concept of international personality appears as a firmly established, albeit infinitely variable, concept: yet from it flow certain consequences, certain attributes, which are fairly common to all international, inter-governmental organisations: it is to these that we now turn.

II. TREATY-MAKING POWERS

Treaties to which international organisations are a party, whether they be agreements between different organisations, between States and international organisations, bilateral or multilateral, are now commonplace and, whilst these may be found prior to the establishment of the United Nations, it is undoubtedly within the United Nations and the specialised agencies that the treaty has become a common form of establishing a relationship, or creating rights and duties, under international law. This is recognised in the work of the International Law Commission on Treaties concluded between States and International Organisations or between International Organisations.[25]

It may be recalled that in the *Reparations Case*[26] the Court affirmed the international personality of the United Nations and found evidence of that personality in, *inter alia*, the treaty-making powers conferred upon the Organisation under the Charter; having cited specifically the Convention on Privileges and Immunities of 1946, the Court concluded that "it is difficult to see how such a convention could operate except upon the international plane and as between parties possessing international personality."[27] However, whilst treaty-making power is clearly evidence of international personality, the reverse may not be true, for, as has been indicated above, "personality" is an infinitely variable concept and it does not in the least follow that every international person has capacity to make treaties. As the International Law Commission has pithily put it: " . . . all entities having treaty-making capacity necessarily (have) international

[25] See Draft Articles adopted by the I.L.C. at its 26th, 27th, 29th and 30th sessions 1979, Art. 6. For a comprehensive survey of practice see Detter, *Law Making by International Organisations* (1965).

[26] (1949) *I.C.J. Reports* 175.

[27] *Ibid.* 179.

personality. On the other hand it (does) not follow that all international persons (have) treaty-making capacity."[28]

Whether or not any given international organisation has treaty-making power can only be determined by reference to the constitution or other rules of the organisation. This is not to adopt the somewhat narrow view of Kelsen to the effect that such treaty-making power must be expressly given[29]; but rather to state that such power must be conferred expressly or by reasonable implication as a competence required to enable the organisation to discharge its functions effectively.[30] This is clearly so in practice; if one looks at the Charter there are specific categories of treaties envisaged; for example the relationship agreements between the UN and the specialised agencies under Articles 57 and 63,[31] the trusteeship agreements under Chapter XII,[32] agreements under Article 43, and the conventions concerning privileges and immunities referred to in Article 105 (3).[33] Yet there are many agreements concluded by the UN which rest on no such specific grant of power. The succession treaties of 1946 by which the United Nations assumed assets and functions of the League,[34] the agreements on technical assistance and the Children's Fund (UNICEF) which implement Chapter IX of the Charter, and the agreements made between the Secretary-General and States contributing armed forces to UNEF are clear illustrations. Reference has been made earlier to the international agreements with States concluded by UNRWA, UNICEF and the Special Fund; here the power must necessarily be implied since these agencies were never expressly contemplated in the Charter.

The contrast between express and implied powers is not one found only in the Charter. In the Council of Europe, for example, whereas Article 40 of the Statute envisages agreements for the

---

[28] A/4169, p. 10, para. 8 (a). See also Parry, "The Treaty-making power of the UN", (1949) 26 B.Y.B.I.L. 147; Kasmé, *Le Capacité de l'ONU de conclure des traités* (1960).

[29] *Law of the United Nations* (1950), p. 330; also Lukashuk, "An international organisation as a party to international treaties" (1960) Soviet Y.B.I.L. 144.

[30] See Weissberg, *The international status of the UN,* p. 37; Lauterpacht, "The development of the law of International Organisations by decisions of International Tribunals" (1976) R.C. IV, 388–478.

[31] *Ante,* p. 65.

[32] *Ante,* p. 76.

[33] *Post,* p. 347.

[34] *Post,* p. 379.

conferment of privileges and immunities, and a special agreement with France as host country, nothing is said of agreements with other inter-governmental organisations, akin to the "relationship agreements" concluded by the UN. In fact, however, many such agreements have been made under the authorisation of a resolution of the Committee of Ministers adopted in May 1951.[35]

The exercise of an *implied* treaty-making power may well give rise to doubts over its legality. These doubts could relate to whether the treaty was *ultra vires* the organisation or *intra vires* the particular organ concluding the treaty. Theoretically it would be open to any organisation having the right to request an advisory opinion from the Court to get such an opinion on a draft treaty before the organisation formally bound itself to the treaty. In the Treaty constituting the European Community (although here the treaty-making power is *express*),[36] Article 228 specifically envisages a reference of a "contemplated agreement" to the Court of the Community for an opinion on its compatibility with the constituent treaty; a negative opinion involves an appropriate revision of the constituent treaty under Article 236 before the Community may proceed with the contemplated agreement. This kind of "legal" approval is quite distinct from the "political" approval which the Assembly of the Community gives to an agreement negotiated by the Commission and finally concluded by the Council on behalf of the Community (Article 228); the latter is akin to the parliamentary approval often required in municipal constitutions as a pre-condition to ratification of a treaty by the executive. In the United Nations practice a similar kind of political approval is often evident; the trusteeship agreements are approved either by the General Assembly or the Security Council, and the relationship agreements, which are in practice negotiated by the Secretariat, are approved by both ECOSOC and the General Assembly.

It may finally be observed that the notion of a treaty-making power implies participation in the treaty *as a party*; as such it should be sharply distinguished from the function of a quasi-legislative character possessed by many organisations by which the organisation becomes the sponsor or the deliberative or negotiat-

[35] *Ante*, p. 179.
[36] Treaties made by EEC are directly binding on organs of the Community and on Member States, without any requirement of ratification (Art. 228 (2)).

ing forum of a treaty between States. The distinction cannot always be drawn with ease. Whilst the I.C.J. clearly took the view that the UN is a party to the Convention on Privileges and Immunities of 1946, as did the Secretariat in registering the instrument *ex officio*, the matter is not free from doubt since there are no signatories (the Convention was approved by the Assembly and acceded to by Member States) and Article 105 (3) suggests that it was for the Assembly to "propose conventions to the Members," a phrase which on one construction could exclude actual participation as a party.[37] Similarly, the participation by the United Nations in the trusteeship agreements as a party is not entirely clear.[38] This other "quasi-legislative" function has already been discussed in relation to the specialised agencies.[39] It may be noted that the UN has no comparable function, and, indeed, a proposal to empower the General Assembly to "adopt" conventions in the same way as the ILO Conference was rejected at San Francisco.[40] There are, however, the general powers under Article 13, conferred on the Assembly, and the specific power conferred on ECOSOC under Article 62 (3).[41] The Assembly for some time abandoned the practice of drafting law-making treaties itself (a practice used with the Genocide Convention of 1948)[42] and confined itself to adopting or approving conventions drafted in some other body[43] or to deciding to convene a special ad hoc conference to undertake the task of preparing a convention. Thus, with the drafts emerging from the International Law Commission[44] on the Law of the Sea, Statelessness, and Diplomatic and Consular Relations, and Treaties, successive codification conferences were convened in 1958, 1959, 1960, 1961, 1964, 1968

---

[37] See Parry, *loc. cit.,* pp. 142–145; Weissberg, *loc. cit.,* pp. 62–63.

[38] See Kelsen, *op. cit.,* pp. 586, 608–609; Parry, "The Legal Nature of the Trusteeship Agreements" (1950) 27 B.Y.B.I.L. 185; Schachter, (1948) 25 B.Y.B.I.L. 130–131; Toussaint, *The Trusteeship System of the UN* (1956), p. 78.

[39] *Ante,* p. 140. See also *ante,* p. 177 for a description of the Council of Europe's activities.

[40] UNCIO, Vol. 9, pp. 77–81.

[41] See *ante,* p. 65.

[42] Resol. 362 (IV) formally disapproved of it as too time-consuming.

[43] See generally Rosenne, *The International Court of Justice* (1957), pp. 316–326.

[44] For an excellent survey of the work of the Commission see Rosenne, "The International Law Commission, 1949–50" (1960) 36 B.Y.B.I.L. 104; and Briggs, *The International Law Commission* (1964).

and 1969.[45] However, in recent years the Assembly has assumed a far more active role in adopting either declarations of legal principle or actual conventions.[46] The Charter does not, of course, contain the kind of legal obligations for Members, consequent upon such adoption, as are seen in the ILO, UNESCO and WHO, but the difference is one of degree only.

III. PRIVILEGES AND IMMUNITIES

The advent of the international organisation as an international person and the attribution to it of functions often analogous to those of sovereign States which, for their effective exercise, require the concession of privileges and immunities from States, has led to the creation of a considerable body of law concerned with the privileges and immunities of international organsiations, their premises, their staff, and Members' representatives to these organisations. The analogy of diplomatic privileges and immunities immediately suggests itself as a basis for this development, and to some extent this analogy has been accepted. However, certain major differences exist between diplomatic and international immunities: first, international immunities may well be most important in the case of relations between an official and his own national State, whereas a national of the receiving State is, for the purposes of diplomatic immunity, accepted as a member of a foreign mission only by express consent and with a minimum of privileges and immunity in respect of official acts only[47]; secondly, whereas the diplomat who is immune from the jurisdiction of the receiving State is under the jurisdiction of his own sending State, no comparable jurisdiction exists where an official of an international organisation is concerned; and, last, whereas observance of diplomatic privileges and immunities is ensured through the operation of the principle of reciprocity, an international organisation has no such effective sanction. These differences, coupled with a trend towards the diminution of privileges and immunities

---

[45] The extent to which such conferences are autonomous in matters of procedure, representation of States, subject-matter, etc., is arguable: see statement by Feller in G.A.O.R. (IV) 6th Committee, 348.
[46] *Ante*, p. 46.
[47] See the Vienna Convention on Diplomatic Relations of 1961 (A/Conf. 20/13), Arts. 8 (2), 38 (1).

generally, have been reflected in the greater emphasis placed upon the functional basis for international privileges and immunities.

Hence, Article 105 (1) of the Charter provides that "The Organisation shall enjoy in the territory of each of its Members such privileges and immunities as are necessary for the fulfilment of its purposes"; so, too, in Article 105 (2), the representatives of Member States and officials of the Organisation are to enjoy only "such privileges and immunities as are necessary for the independent exercise of their functions in connection with the Organisation." Such provisions, with their emphasis on the functional basis of privileges and immunities, are now almost common form in the constitutions of international organisations. The more detailed provisions of the agreements and national legislation supplementing these basic constitutional texts bring out even more forcibly the functional basis of immunities, as will be seen in due course in examining particular problems.

It is not to be expected that a basic constitutional text would deal in detail with privileges and immunities, although the degree of detail does vary and one finds in the constitutions of the Fund, Bank and Finance Corporation far more detailed provisions than in the Charter or the constitutions of the other specialised agencies. Hence the general tendency is to supplement the basic texts by a detailed agreement. For the United Nations that detailed agreement is normally the General Convention on the Privileges and Immunities of the United Nations,[48] approved by the General Assembly on February 13, 1946, and now acceded to by more than 60 States. A separate Convention on the Privileges and Immunities of the Specialised Agencies[49] was similarly approved on November 21, 1947, subject to variations for each specialised agency which are determined by the agency concerned and set out in a special annex. These two conventions formed a model for later agreements made by other organisations such as the League of Arab States, the Organisation of American States,[50] the Council of Europe,[51] Western European Union,[52] and, to a far

---

[48] I U.N.T.S. 15–32.
[49] 33 U.N.T.S. 261–302.
[50] (1949) I *Annals of the OAS*, No. 3, 271–274.
[51] I *European Yearbook*, 297–307; 250 U.N.T.S. 12–31.
[52] *Ibid.* Vol 3, 173.

lesser extent, the three European Communities (ECSC, EEC and Euratom).[53]

Whilst these agreements are of a multilateral character, it has normally been found necessary to conclude a special, bilateral agreement with the host State in whose territory the headquarters or other offices of the organisations are maintained. The Headquarters Agreement between the UN and the U.S.A.,[54] the UN and Switzerland,[55] the Council of Europe and France,[56] the ILO and Mexico (in respect of its Field Office)[57] are but a few examples of this kind of agreement. A similar special agreement will also be necessary in cases such as UNEF, where an agreement between the UN and Egypt of February 8, 1957[58] provided for the status of the Emergency Force, its property and personnel; similar agreements were negotiated with the Republic of the Congo[59] and with Cyprus governing ONUC and UNFICYP respectively.[60]

Clearly these agreements, whether multilateral or bilateral, impose legal obligations on States under international law[61]; it has normally been necessary for States to implement these obligations by passing municipal legislation. The International Organisations Immunities Act of December 29, 1945, in the United States,[62] or the International Organisation (Privileges and Immunities) Act of July 12, 1950, in the United Kingdom are two typical examples of such municipal legislation.[63] Whatever view the municipal courts

---

[53] *Ibid.* Vol. 1, 429–435; Secretariat of the Interim Committee for the Common Market and Euratom, *Treaty and related Documents,* Protocol on Privileges and Immunities of EEC, 321–331.

[54] II U.N.T.S. 11–41.

[55] I U.N.T.S. 163–186.

[56] 249 U.N.T.S. 207–213.

[57] 208 U.N.T.S. 225–237.

[58] 260 U.N.T.S. 61–89.

[59] *Annual Report of the Sec.-Gen.,* 1961 (A 4800), p. 170: UN Doc. S. 5004.

[60] S/5634.

[61] See the A.O. on the Interpretation of the WHO/Egypt Agreement *I.C.J. Reports* (1980), 1, in which the Court held that such an agreement could not be terminated at will but imposed mutual obligations of consultation on the parties.

[62] Public Law 291, 79th Congress, 59 Stat. 669.

[63] For the most comprehensive collection of national legislation and international agreements concerned with the privileges and immunities of international organisations see *Handbook on the Legal Status, Privileges and Immunities of the United Nations* (1952) (ST/LEG/2), *and Legislative Texts and Treaty Provisions concerning the Legl Status, Privileges and Immunities of International Organisations,* UN. ST/LEG/SER. B/10 & 11; these two volumes of the UN legislative Series give nearly all the texts of the agreements referred to in this chapter.

take, such legislation is not the source of the State's international obligations; that source remains the constituent texts and such supplementary agreements as may exist.

One further general question remains, namely, whether in the absence of a treaty obligation a State is under any duty to concede privileges and immunities to an international organisation. The situation has, indeed, arisen in the Congo in which the UN placed a force in the territory of the Republic before it became a Member of the UN. Whilst it may be difficult to argue that privileges and immunities vest by virtue of a rule of customary international law,[64] as is the case with diplomatic privileges and immunities, it may well be that once a State has consented to the presence of the United Nations on its territory for a particular purpose it is bound, by the principle of good faith, to extend all such privileges and immunities as are necessary for the proper functioning of the UN and the achievement of that purpose.[65] The same argument would be valid for any international organisation.

Turning from these general questions to specific aspects of immunities, it will be convenient to deal separately with immunities attaching to the organisation as such, and immunities attaching to personnel.

1. Immunities attaching to the Organisation

(a) *Immunity from jurisdiction*

The General Convention of 1946 provides in section 2 that "the United Nations, its property and assets, wherever located and by whomsoever held, shall enjoy immunity from every form of legal process, except in so far as in any particular case it has expressly waived its immunity." A substantially similar provision is found in the specialised agencies convention and in the various headquarters agreements with countries like Canada, France, Switzerland and Italy.[66] In the European Communities, the position is radically

---

[64] See Liang, (1957) I *Yearbook of the I.L.C.*, 5; but *contra* Lalive, (1953) 84 R.C. 304–305.

[65] See the Basic Agreements of July 27, 1960, with the Congo (A/4800, p. 170); the Congo was not formally admitted to the UN until September 20, 1960.

[66] The UN/U.S.A. Headquarters Agreement contains no such provision.

different because of the special competence of the Court of Justice; in principle "cases to which the Community is a party shall not for that reason alone be excluded from the competence of domestic courts or tribunals."[67] The Court of the Communities, however, has exclusive jurisdiction over any questions of the interpretation of the treaties or the validity of acts of the Communities, so that a national court is required to obtain a ruling from the Court of the Communities before making any final decision.[68] Further, "the property and assets of the Community may not be the subject of any administrative or legal measures of constraint without the authorisation of the Court of Justice."[69]

The jurisdictional immunity enjoyed under the General Convention and similar agreements is quite comprehensive[70] and extends to "every form of legal process"; the authority to waive it would presumably rest with the administrative head of the organisation, and a separate waiver would be required to permit measures of execution against the organisation's property. The justification for this comprehensive immunity is primarily the undesirability of having courts of many different countries determine, possibly in different senses, the legality of acts of the organisation; there may well be, in some countries, the further need to protect the organisation against prejudice in national courts, or baseless actions by individuals. The IBRD is, however, exceptional in that Article VII (3) of its Articles of Agreement allows it to be sued (although its property and assets are immune from execution). The reason for this is that the Bank's lending

---

[67] Art. 183, EEC; Art. 155, Euratom; Art. 40, ECSC.
[68] *Ante*, p. 310.
[69] Art. 1, Protocol on the Privileges and Immunities of the European Economic Community.
[70] But see *Branno* v. *Ministry of War* (1955) I.L.R. 756–757 where the Italian Court of Cassation suggests that immunity attaches to acts of the organisation *jure imperii* but not *jure gestionis*. In *Broadbent* v. *O.A.S.* (1980) the U.S. Court of Appeals avoided the somewhat similar question of whether the restriction of immunity to non-commercial activities under the U.S. Foreign Sovereign Immunities Act of 1976 also applied to international organisations. It held that the relations between the organisation and its staff were in any event non-commercial: see (1980) 19 I.L.M. 208.

operations made it desirable to allow suit by creditors and bondholders.[71]

(b) *Inviolability of premises and archives*

The inviolability of premises and archives is a principle found in all the agreements; it figures even in the Protocol on Privileges and Immunities of the European Economic Community, so that the principle has no necessary connection with jurisdictional immunity. Authorities of the host State may not enter the premises, even for the purpose of effecting an arrest or serving a writ, without the consent of the administrative head. Moreover, since inviolability is to be secured against all persons, and not merely the authorities of the host State, it is usual to find in any headquarters agreement an undertaking by the host State to exercise due diligence in the protection of the premises. Examples of breaches of the inviolability of UN premises are happily rare: but UNRWA has a history of incidents of this kind and, during the 1967 conflict in the Middle East, both UNRWA, UNEF and UNTSO premises suffered attacks and other violations.

The principle of inviolability necessarily raises problems once it is accepted that the organisation is not sovereign over the territory occupied by its premises, but merely has control and authority, and moreover, that the organisation possesses no body of law to replace that of the host State in respect of civil or criminal offences committed within the premises. Admittedly the organisation may have power to lay down regulations "operative within the headquarters district for the purpose of establishing therein conditions in all respects necessary for the full execution of its functions,"[72] and such regulations will override any inconsistent local law, but the only effective sanction for their breach is expulsion from the premises, carried out either by a Headquarters Guard Force, such as the UN possesses, or by the local authorities who may be requested to enter for that purpose. It is important, therefore, that the territory should remain under the law and the

[71] Note that in *Lutcher* v. *Inter-American Development Bank,* U.S. Court of Appeals, D.C. Circuit, 1967, under a similar provision it was held that the waiver of immunity was general and not limited to suits by bondholders.

[72] UN/U.S.A. Headquarters Agreement, s. 8. This "legislative" power may be exercised for purposes other than security; the UN has promulgated regulations for a social security (insurance) system, for permitting the practice of certain professions within the district, and for the provision of amenities and services.

jurisdiction of the host State, and the agreements so provide.[73] A crime committed on the premises will therefore normally be appropriately dealt with by the local courts; in 1928 the assailant of the representative of Hungary within the Palais des Nations was arrested and tried by the Swiss courts. Indeed, some of the agreements specifically provide that the organisation is under a duty to prevent the headquarters district from becoming a refuge for persons avoiding arrest or the service of legal process.[74] Whether there is a right for the organisations to grant asylum in cases falling outside this particular duty must be regarded as an open question, for none of the agreements specifically recognise such a right. There is certainly a strong argument for the right of the organisation to afford asylum to its own officials against measures by the local authorities which are themselves a violation of the immunities of the organisation and of the official.[75]

The inviolability of archives has never raised any special problems; without such inviolability the confidential character of communications between States and the organisation, or between officials within the organisation, would be endangered.

(c) *Currency and fiscal privileges*

Many organisations now dispose of considerable funds, and, in view of the geographical deployment of their activities, the mobility of such funds is often essential to the proper functioning of the organisation. Hence the General Convention recognises that the UN may "hold funds, gold or currency of any kind and operate accounts in any currency" and shall be free to "transfer its funds, gold or currency from one country to another . . . without being restricted by financial controls, regulations or moratoria of any kind."[76] The purchase of differenct currencies will not normally subject the organisation to the possibility of a prejudicial differential exchange rate, since these differential rates are inconsistent with the obligations of Members of the International Monetary Fund, but the agreement between the UN and Egypt

---

[73] *Ibid.* s. 7.
[74] *Ibid.* s. 9 *(b)*
[75] Jenks, *International Immunities,* pp. 51–52.
[76] s. 5. There is no comparable provision in the Headquarters Agreement with the U.S.A., but other agreements have such a provision.

over the status of UNEF did provide that the most favourable exchange rate should be available to the UN.[77]

Exemption from direct taxation of the organisation, its assets, income or property, is now normal[78]; it is equally normal for this *not* to extend to taxes which are in fact charges for public utility services enjoyed by the organisation. The principle is exactly the same with a diplomatic mission. An equally common privilege is the exemption from customs duties and import and export restrictions on articles required for official use and the publications of the organisation. In contrast there is no right to exemption from excise duties or sales taxes which are included in the price of property purchased; the General Convention, for example, provides only that "Members will, whenever possible, make appropriate administrative arrangements for the remission or return of the amount of duty or tax."[79]

(d) *Freedom of communications*

The freedom of communications rests on three principles, all of which are embodied in the General Convention,[80] in the Special-ised Agencies Convention and several headquarters agreements: these are (1) the absence of censorship over official communica-tions, (2) the right to use codes, couriers and bags (equivalent to the "diplomatic bag" or "pouch"), and (3) treatment for their communications by national administrations as favourable as that accorded to any government. It is, curiously enough, on this last principle that difficulty has been encountered by the specialised agencies due to the opposition of the I.T.U. to this equality of treatment for specialised agencies—even though it has been conceded to the UN and its organs.[81]

The UN/U.S.A. Headquarters Agreement provides that the UN may establish and operate radio facilities,[82] and similar provisions were inserted in agreements with States where a UN Force was

---

[77] Para. 35.
[78] General Convention, s. 7. By "direct" taxes is meant those taxes which ultimately fall upon the Organisation for payment. The characterisation of the tax as "direct" or "indirect" in the particular State's municipal law is irrelevant: see U.N.J.Y. 1964, 220–221.
[79] s. 8.
[80] ss. 9 and 10.
[81] See Jenks, *op. cit.* pp. 69–71.
[82] s. 4.

operating, such as Korea and Egypt. The UN also has its own postal service (operated in the Headquarters District by the U.S. Post Office Department). The UN has also used its own aircraft and even vessels, flying the United Nations flag.

2. Immunities attaching to personnel

The distinction between the immunities of the organisation as such and those of the personnel attached to it is, in one sense, an unreal one, for the principle which emerges from the many agreements is that the personnel enjoy privileges and immunities, not for their personal benefit, but for the purpose of exercising their functions in relation to the organisation. This is expressly stated, for example, in the General Convention, both in relation to officials of the organisation[83] and even the representatives of Members[84]; thus waiver becomes a *duty* for the Secretary-General or the Member State, as the case may be, whenever the immunity would impede the cause of justice and can be waived without impeding the functions of, or the relations of, the United Nations. The categories of personnel connected with international organisations are so varied as to prevent uniform treatment: they therefore have to be discussed separately.

(a) *Representatives of Member States*

The immunities and privileges accorded to this category are, not unnaturally, very much akin to those accorded to the traditional diplomatic agent but with rather greater emphasis on the functional necessity for the privileges. Article 4 of the General Convention and section 15 of the UN/U.S.A. Headquarters Agreement are somewhat at variance, for whereas the latter accords diplomatic privileges and immunities, the General Convention specifies immunity from legal process only "in respect of words spoken or written and all acts done by them *in their capacity as representatives,*" which is narrower than the general diplomatic immunity. There is also immunity from arrest, seizure of personal baggage, immigration restrictions or national service obligations, inviolability of papers and documents, the right of communication, and exemptions from customs duties (but only in respect of

[83] s. 20.
[84] s. 14.

personal baggage as opposed to all imports for personal use).[85] The Vienna Conference of 1975 produced a comprehensive Convention on the representation of States in their relations with international organisations of a universal character.[86] Its utility and likely effect are difficult to estimate. The majority succeeded, by voting power, in securing privileges and immunities for missions of members to the headquarters of international organisations far more extensive than the "host" States were prepared to concede. If, as seems likely, the major host States do not ratify, the convention will represent somewhat wasted effort.

It must be remembered that the representatives are not accredited to the host State, but rather to the organisation; nevertheless, in the UN/U.S.A. Headquarters Agreement, apart from the principal permanent representatives or permanent repesentatives with the rank of ambassador or minister plenipotentiary, the staff of any given mission have to be agreed upon between the host State, the Secretary-General and the sending State.[87] This is very similar to the "agrément" in diplomatic practice and, once given, the names are placed in the "Bluebook" issued by the United States Mission to the UN. A further consequence of non-accreditation to the host States is the inapplicability of the remedy of declaring a representative *persona non grata*.[88] The Specialised Agencies Convention, unlike the General Convention, does deal with this to the extent of allowing expulsion for activities outside the representatives' official functions. Yet another consequence is the fact that representatives may be received from governments not recognised by the host State. In the Headquarters Agreement with the U.S. privileges and immunities are granted to such persons only within the Headquarters district, or in transit between the district and residences or offices, or whilst at such residence or office[89]; other

---

[85] For a review of some of the U.S. decisions on immunities of representatives see Jenks, *loc. cit.* pp. 86–88.

[86] [1975] U.N.J.Y. 87.

[87] s. 15.

[88] On similar reasoning a host State cannot apply reciprocity to the treatment of such representatives, as it may to persons accredited to it: see the U.N. Secretariat opinion in (1967) 2 *Y.B.I.L.C.,* 154, 177–8.

[89] On the right of access to headquarters of international organisations see Goy, "Le droit d'accès au siège des organisations internationales" (1962) 33 R.G.D.I.P. 357–370.

agreements tend to specify that immunities and privileges shall be granted irrespective of the relationship between sending State and host State.

The host State's obligation to afford personal protection to the representatives of members (and also to officials of the Organisation) has been reinforced by the 1973 UN Convention for the Prevention and Punishment of Crimes against Internationally Protected Persons,[90] which includes those within that category. Several States have introduced legislation making assault, coercion or harrassment of such persons a crime under municipal law.[91]

Special problems arise in organisations in which a delegation from a State is not confined to governmental representatives. In the ILO the Employers' and Workers' delegates receive the same immunities and privileges as governmental representatives, save the right to use codes, couriers or sealed bags; waiver of immunities is by the Governing Body. In the inter-parliamentary assemblies of the Council of Europe and the European Community the immunities are carefully defined and their functional basis is emphasised by their being modelled, not on diplomatic immunities, but more on parliamentary immunities in municipal law.[92]

(b) *Officials of the organisation*

Jurisdictional immunity varies according to the rank of the official. It is now usual to find the chief administrative officer and his deputies or assistants accorded full diplomatic immunity, whereas all other officials enjoy immunity only in respect of their official acts.[93] This raises the problem, to which there is no clear solution, of who decides the official or private character of a particular act; a municipal court could well accept as conclusive a statement by the organisation, or by the executive of the State in

---

[90] (1974) 13 I.L.M. 41.
[91] See the 1976 U.S. Act: 18 *U.S.C.A.* s. 112.
[92] See Council of Europe Agreement, Arts. 13–15; European Economic Community Protocol, Arts. 7–9.
[93] General Convention, ss. 18 and 19; Specialised Agencies Convention, s. 21; OEEC, Arts. 14 and 15; Council of Europe, Arts. 16 and 18. The same principle is followed in most headquarters agreements except for the UN/U.S.A., which contains no mention of the immunities of officials, so that, in the absence of U.S. accession to the General Convention, their immunities rest on the U.S. International Organisations Immunities Act, 1945.

which the matter has arisen, or proceedings might be stayed whilst the matter went to arbitration. Certainly a conflict of view between the organisation and domestic courts is possible; in *Westchester County* v. *Ranollo*[94] the City Court of New Rochelle convicted the Secretary-General's chauffeur of speeding despite a plea of immunity based on the fact that the accused was in the course of his duty, driving the Secretary-General; the Court suggested that it would require certification from the State Department that immunity was in the public interest. It may be noted that the case of the European Communities is quite exceptional in that officials, of whatever rank, have no complete immunity from the jurisdiction of national courts, but only immunity from legal process for acts performed by them in their official capacity. There is, of course, a jurisdiction in the Court of the Communities to entertain proceedings against a Community or an official for official or personal fault.[95]

Exemption from taxation on salaries paid to officials is a further privilege to be found in the General Convention,[96] the Specialised Agencies Convention[97] and virtually all other agreements, including the Protocols on the privileges and immunites of the European Communities. The notable exceptions are the UN/U.S.A. Headquarters Agreement, which is completely silent on the point, and the agreements between ICAO and Canada, IMCO and the United Kingdom, and the NATO Agreement in which the exemption is qualified. In these exceptional cases the exemption from taxation is denied to nationals of the host State, and, as we have seen,[98] in the case of the UN led to the adoption of the Staff Assessment Plan as a clumsy expedient for securing equality of

---

[94] A.D. 1946, Case No. 77. Contrast *Curran* v. *City of New York, Trygvie Lie et Al.,* 119 N.Y.L.Q. Jan. 2, 1948, where the Court accepted the plea of immunity raised by the Organisation as defendant on a suit by a taxpayer to set aside grants of land and easements by the City to the Organisation; the Dept. of State did, however, "suggest" to the Court that immunity be granted. In *U.S.* v. *Coplon and Grubitchev,* A.D. 1949, Case No. 102, no immunity was requested for a citizen of the U.S.S.R. who was an official of the UN indicted for espionage; clearly, "official acts" could never include espionage.

[95] *Ante,* p. 309.

[96] s. 18 *(a).* The salary cannot be sequestered, nor even taken into account in calculating taxation on income from other sources: see (1969) U.N.J.Y. 239, 243.

[97] Art. 19 (b).

[98] *Ante,* p. 102.

treatment for officials, an expedient necessary only because of the refusal of the U.S.A. to accept the simple principle of exemption irrespective of nationality. It must be remembered that exemption from taxation is not designed to create a privileged class, but simply to secure equality of salary treatment to officials, regardless of nationality, and to avoid the payment to individual Member States of large sums by way of taxation on their nationals' salaries from funds contributed by the totality of the Members for the general purposes of the organisation. Other "economic" privileges are those relating to the free importation of personal and household effects at the time of taking up an appointment, and privileges in respect of exchange facilities comparable to those enjoyed by diplomatic personnel of equivalent rank.

A similar discrimination against their own nationals is to be found practised by some States in respect of the immunity from national service obligations, provided for in section 18 (c) of the General Convention. The justification for this immunity is less obvious, and, certainly in time of peace, it will cause relatively little diminution of essential personnel since the service is commonly undertaken at an early age, before recruitment into an international secretariat is likely to occur. The Specialised Agencies Convention is therefore far less categorical, and this particular immunity is confined to officials whose names have been agreed with their national State.[99] A similar approach is seen in the Agreement on the Privileges and Immunities of the Arab League[1] and in the headquarters agreements between various organisations and Switzerland, France, Italy and Austria. The agreements on the privileges and immunities of OECD, Council of Europe, the European Communities and NATO contain no exemption from national service obligations.

The refusal to grant to nationals of the host State the privileges and immunities normally accorded to officials is not confined merely to the immunities from taxation on salaries and national service obligations. Canada, France and the United Kingdom, in relation to ICAO, UNESCO and IMCO respectively deny jurisdictional immunity to the senior officials who are their nationals. Other States have maintained that "locally-recruited staff" are not covered by the protection of the 1946 Convention, a

[99] s. 20.
[1] Art. 21.

357

contention quite contrary to the G.A. resol. 76 (I)—which excluded solely those employees paid at hourly-rates.[2] Indeed, the discrimination against their own residents or nationals by States is perhaps the largest problem in relation to the immunities and privileges of officials; it implies a failure either to understand or accept the principle so clearly formulated by Jenks:

> "The purpose of international immunities is to protect (their) international responsibilities and they require protection against the State of which the official is a national as fully as, and perhaps more fully than, against any other State."[3]

One last privilege, of dubious value, is the privilege of transit which the "Laissez-passer" is designed to secure. The General Convention provides that it shall be recognised and accepted as a valid travel document by the authorities of Members.[4] Although in a number of headquarters agreements (not the UN/U.S.A.) the States agree to treat the laissez-passer as equivalent to a passport, in the practice of some UN Member States the document does not permit travel independently of national passports and visas. The laissez-passer may well be useful in securing the speedy issue of visas, or other special travel facilities.

There are, as we have seen earlier,[5] certain categories of persons employed by international organisations who are not "officials" in the accepted sense. Experts are one such category, and the General Convention[6] and most recent instruments do provide for privileges and immunities for them; these represent an amalgam of diplomatic and officials' privileges and immunities. One difficulty in providing for standard privileges and immunities is that the functions of experts vary enormously; those with quasi-judicial functions may well need different immunities from those with quasi-political functions. A newer category is that of contractors, such as those engaged by the UN for the clearance of the Suez Canal; the agreement with Egypt of January 8, 1957, extended the General Convention to cover them. The standard

---

[2] See U.N.J.Y., 1965, pp. 264–265.
[3] *Op. cit.* p. 112.
[4] s. 24.
[5] *Ante*, p. 321. But note that the experts engaged on technical assistance by the UN and the specialised agencies are regarded as officials.
[6] ss. 19 and 20.

basic agreement with governments receiving assistance from the UN Special Funds also provides for privileges and immunities.

It follows from the fact that international officials are not accredited to States (as diplomats are), that the principle of *persona non grata* is not applicable to them. The proper procedure is for the host State to make its representations to the S.G. who alone can decide whether they shall be withdrawn from the territory.[7]

(c) *Holders of judicial offices*

Initially, once the need for immunities for persons holding international judicial office had been realised, the solution adopted was to confer diplomatic immunities and privileges. This was the solution in the Hague Conventions on the Pacific Settlement of Disputes of 1899 and 1907 for the Permanent Court of Arbitration, and was the solution of 1928 for the P.C.I.J. It is basically still the solution adopted for the I.C.J., both in its Statute[8] and in the 1946 agreement between the Court and the Netherlands as host State, although these diplomatic privileges are enjoyed only whilst engaged on the business of the Court. In 1946, by resolution 90 (I), the General Assembly made certain recommendations to secure to the judges an extension of these diplomatic privileges to any country where they resided for the purpose of holding themselves permanently at the disposal of the Court, to secure transit facilities for the judges and also to secure for agents, counsel and advocates before the Court transit facilities and the immunities provided in the General Convention for representatives of Members. Waiver of the immunities of a judge is a matter for the Court; in the case of agents, counsel or advocates it is a matter for the State they represent.

Taxation of salaries and allowances of judges is forbidden by Article 32 (8) of the Statute of the I.C.J., although it is by no means clear that all the parties to the Statute so provide in their municipal legislation.[9] The judges themselves, in 1949, firmly rejected any suggestion that the Staff Assessment Plan of the UN should apply to them.

---

[7] U.N.J.Y. 1964, pp. 262–263.
[8] Art. 19.
[9] The U.K. legislation does so provide: S.R. & O. 1947 (No. 1772). Whether the immunity extends to pensions or not is an open question; in principle it clearly should.

In contrast to the I.C.J., where diplomatic immunities are broadly conferred, other tribunals such as that established by the OECD Convention on the establishment of a security control in the fields of nuclear energy, or that established by Western European Union for the control of armaments, and the Court of Justice of the European Communities have been accorded privileges and immunities based on a far more functional test, with the analogy that of the privileges and immunities conferred on courts in municipal law. Hence immunity from legal process exists, and continues after the term of office expires in respect of words spoken or acts done in the course of their judicial duties.[10] Waiver is by the Court, and only the national courts with competence to judge members of the highest national judiciary may assume criminal jurisdiction over judges of the Court of the European Communities, whose immunity has thus been waived. Salaries are tax free. Privileges and immunities are accorded to counsel and advocates comparable to those enjoyed before municipal tribunals, and may be waived by the Court. Somewhat oddly, the European Court on Human Rights was in the unsatisfactory position of having its privileges and immunities governed only by the general provisions of Article 40 of the Statute of the Council of Europe which, since that article was designed for representatives and officials, was scarcely adequate. However, an agreement on privileges and immunities has now been concluded, as was done in the case of the European Commission on Human Rights in December 1960.[11]

(d) *International armed forces*

Whilst customary international law recognised a certain immunity from the supervisory jurisdiction of the host State for friendly forces stationed on its territory, the complexities of the relationships involved demanded more specific regulation, and the Second World War and the post-War era have witnessed a considerable number of treaties to govern this problem, of which the NATO Status of Forces Agreement of 1952[12] is a prime

---

[10] See *Zoernsch* v. *Waldock* [1964] 1 W.L.R. 675 (the defendant being the President of the European Commission on Human Rights).

[11] *European Commission of Human Rights,* (1955–57) Documents and Decisions, 86: Fourth Protocol to the General Agreement of 1949, signed December 16, 1961 (U.K. Misc. No. 6 (1962), Cmnd. 1696).

[12] 199 U.N.T.S. 67.

example. In principle, when an international organisation places an armed force in the territory of a State, with its consent, the need for immunities and privileges is even greater than that of the friendly State which does so; moreover, there is no customary international law applicable to this relationship of organisation and host State, since the phenomenon of the truly international armed force is a novel one. In Korea no single agreement was concluded, but rather a complex of bilateral agreements and arrangements, and even with Japan the agreement regarding the status of UN Forces[13] was concluded by the governments of States contributing contingents, and not by the UN as such. The first real status of forces agreement concluded by the UN was the agreement with Egypt of February 8, 1957.[14]

The terms of this agreement reveal the extent to which the experience with agreements such as the NATO Status of Forces Agreement had been relied on in assessing the needs of an international armed force. The obligation to respect the local law is stressed, but total immunity from the local criminal jurisdiction is conceded (such jurisdiction rests exclusively with the States contributing the forces); immunity from civil jurisdiction lies only in respect of acts relating to official duties, and the certificate of the Commander is conclusive on the official or non-official character of an act. Other provisions cover an enormous range of matters such as taxation, customs, communications of all kinds, public utility services, freedom of movement, uniform and arms, identification, use of flag and official markings, protection and immunity of property and assets, and settlement of disputes and claims. Doubtless this agreement will form a model for future agreements, and the agreement with the Republic of the Congo of November 27, 1961, has, with certain marked differences, followed the UNEF model.[15]

[13] 214 U.N.T.S. 51. There was an agreement with Korea, constituted by an exchange of letters of September 21, 1951, but this related to UN Civilian personnel, experts and representatives of Members (ST./LEG/SER/B/10, p. 256); a similar agreement existed with Japan (*ibid.* p. 266).

[14] 260 U.N.T.S. 61.

[15] UN Doc. S/5004. The main differences are the absence of the technique of incorporating the General Convention of 1946 by reference (perhaps because the Congo was not a party thereto), the absence of any jurisdiction in the local courts (presumably because they were not functioning), a wider freedom of movement clause and a more detailed liaison clause. See generally Bowett, *U.N. Forces* (1964), Chap 13.

In concluding this brief survey of the immunities and privileges accorded to international organisations it is proper to emphasise again the extent to which the functional test has become adopted; yet there still remains on the part of the States a certain distrust of these immunities. This is very largely due to their failure to grasp the principle so well expounded by Jenks that:

"The proper measure of international immunities is what is necessary for the impartial, efficient and economical discharge of the functions of the organisation concerned, and in particular what contributes to the effective independence of the organisation from the individual control of its separate members exercised by means of their national law and executive authority as distinguished from their collective control exercised in a regular manner through the appropriate international organs."[16]

It may well be that, in addition to their functional basis, a further development may occur in introducing into international immunities the distinction between acts *jure imperii* and *jure gestionis* which is increasingly appearing in the immunities of States[17]; the wider range of activities of international organisations becomes, the greater justification for this distinction there will be. However, one of the more immediate problems, which will be dealt with in the following part, is the provision of procedures whereby disputes about the extent of immunities and claims which are barred by the pleas of immunity may be adjudicated. This appears, at first sight, to be simply a jurisdictional issue. It will be seen, on closer examination, to involve a more general discussion of the law governing the responsibility arising from the activities of international organisations, for it is part of that larger problem. It is to the two issues of responsibility and operative law that we now turn.

IV. RESPONSIBILITY OF INTERNATIONAL ORGANISATIONS

Legal personality implies not only the capacity to bring claims, as in the *Reparations Case*, but also the responsibility of the

[16] *Op. cit.* p. 167.
[17] See Jenks, *op. cit.* p. 151 and *ante*, p. 349, footnote 70.

organisation for its own illegal acts.[18] The existence of immunities
from the jurisdiction of municipal courts should never be allowed
to obscure the fact that the organisation remains responsible for
the consequences of its actions. Thus, there have evolved various
devices for ensuring an impartial adjudication of questions of fault
and for according a remedy to parties aggrieved by the acts or
omissions of international organisations.

Administrative tribunals,[19] Claims Commissions,[20] Arbitration
clauses in contracts,[21] and even bilateral negotiations between
States or individuals on the one hand and the Organisation[22] on
the other all afford means whereby the responsibility of the
organisation can be determined. In general, wherever a means has
been established for giving a definitive, binding decision on
responsibility for illegal acts and appropriate redress, no real
problem arises.

There are, however, considerable areas of potential dispute
about the constitutional legality of the acts of international
organisations in so far as these acts affect Member States where no
judicial machinery exists capable of rendering a definitive judgment. The European Communities are exceptional in this respect,
for there the Court of the European Communities has precisely
this function.[23] By and large, however, international organisations
have no "supreme court," capable of adjudicating constitutional
disputes. The I.C.J. has a function confined to giving advisory
opinions, not definitive judgments.[24] The utility, and the deficien-
cies, of this system can be seen by comparing the I.C.J.'s
contribution to the settling of the disputes in the *IMCO Case*[25] and
the *Expenses Case*.[26] In the former the IMCO Assembly accepted

---

[18] Garcia Amador, "State Responsibility: some new problems" (1958) 94 R.C.
410; Eagleton "International Organisation and the law of responsibility" (1950)
76 R.C., Chap. IV.
[19] *Ante,* Chap. 10.
[20] *Post*, p. 376.
[21] *Post*, p. 376.
[22] See Exchange of letters constituting an Agreement between the UN and
Belgium relating to the settlement of claims filed against the UN in the Congo by
Belgium Nationals, U.N.J.Y. 1965, 39.
[23] *Ante*, p. 305.
[24] Unless, as in the 1946 Convention on Privileges and Immunities, the parties
agree to treat the opinion as binding.
[25] *Ante*, p. 133.
[26] *Ante*, p. 51.

the opinion and re-constituted the new Maritime Safety Commit-tee in accordance with the Court's opinion without treating as a nullity the previous Committee and its acts. In the *Expenses Case,* although the General Assembly accepted the Court's opinion, the refusal of the Soviet bloc and of France to accept it as determining their own financial obligations produced a crisis[27] which the Assembly avoided by declining, in practice, to implement the opinion. Moreover, in so far as the Court's opinion was not, *per se,* binding on individual Members, it could not be said that members refusing to accept it acted illegally. Thus, given real opposition[28] to any interpretation of its legal powers by any organ of the UN—or for that matter of the specialised agencies or the regional arrangements—there is no final "supreme court" for resolving the issue.

Of course, the Member State might withdraw in protest or might be expelled for persistent failure to fulfil its obligations (or suffer some other sanction) but these consequences ought in principle to be avoided and, deriving from a political decision, afford no substitute for a judicial determination of a constitutional issue.

On the other hand, as already indicated,[29] there is much to be said for avoiding reference to a judicial body of issues which are essentially political conflicts, even though these may turn upon the construction of the constituent treaty provisions.

Moreover, if the I.C.J. is right in placing crucial emphasis on the *practice* of the political organ itself as a determining factor in questions of constitutionality—and this arises from the presump-tion of legality which the Court in the *Expenses Case* applied to the Assembly's conduct[30]—the difference between a political and a legal decision on the legality of an organ's conduct may not be as great as might be imagined.

Quite distinct from the question of by what means an organisa-tion tests the legality of its acts is the question of what

[27] See *post,* p. 418.
[28] Acquiescence in or failure to protest against a particular interpretation might prejudice a Member's position in this regard: see Lauterpacht, "The Legal Effects of Illegal Acts of International Organisations" in *Cambridge Legal Essays* (1965) 117–119.
[29] *Ante,* p. 278.
[30] (1962) *I.C.J. Report,* 168. Note, however, that this presumption applies only where the action taken is "appropriate for the fulfilment of one of the stated purposes of the United Nations."

consequences flow from an illegal act. The *Expenses Case* suggests[31] that an act illegal in terms of the internal operation of an organisation (*i.e.* an exercise by one organ of powers properly belonging to another) will not necessarily be illegal *vis-à-vis* third parties. Certainly it would be extraordinary if, in the event that the General Assembly's establishment of UNEF had been held *ultra vires*, contracts with third parties for supplies and services to UNEF were to be held illegal and unenforceable as against the UN. Indeed, the analogy between an international organisation and a public company whose powers are presumed to be known to the general public by virtue of the registration of its Memorandum of Association (and who cannot therefore rely on an *ultra vires* act) is probably unsound. The correct rule is probably that third parties are never to be penalised as a result of an *ultra vires* act of an organisation unless they knew of the illegality.

Finally, as to whether the *ultra vires* act is to be regarded as void *ab initio*, or merely voidable, it is clear that the notion of a "voidable" act presupposes some machinery capable of adjudicating on an allegation of illegality. Yet it is unlikely that Organisations will regard illegal acts as void *ab initio, i.e.* complete nullities, in all circumstances if only because in so many cases it will be impossible to set the clock back and undo what has passed. Certainly in the *IMCO Case* the Assembly looked to the future, not the past, and made no attempt to introduce further complications by nullifying the entirety of the work of the previous Maritime Safety Committee.

V. The Law Governing the Activities of International Organisations

The attribution to an interntional organisation of legal personality, both under international and municipal law, should not be allowed to obscure the fact that there is no single, comprehensive body of law to govern its transactions and activities; unlike the corporation in private law which has a personal law (whether based on the test of place of incorporation, place of control or siège social), the international corporation has in general no personal law or "law of incorporation." It is, of course, open to an organisation to adopt a specific system of municipal law for this purpose; this was done in

[31] *Ibid.*

the case of the Bank for International Settlements, incorporated under Swiss law.[32] The solution is not, however, likely to be satisfactory as a general rule for, not only might this endanger the international character of the organisation, but it will often fail to answer the needs of an organisation whose activities are global in operation and infinitely varied in kind. To the extent that the activities are internal activities, relating to the functions of the organs of the organisations, these will generally be adequately covered by the constitutional texts of the organisation. It is when the activities become external in the sense of affecting third parties, be they States, other international organisations or even private entities, that the constitutional texts may afford no guidance to the problems raised. The problems are either choice of law problems or jurisdictional problems.

1. Choice of law

Accepting that an international organisation may own or lease property, contract for supplies and services, use agents, armies, ships and aircraft, it needs little imagination to envisage the host of legal problems arising from these activities. In seeking the law appropriate to govern its relations with outside entities, an organisation may, according to the circumstances, turn to international law, including possibly conventions to which it is not a party,[33] or general principles of law (including general principles of the conflict of laws), to the "domestic law" of the organisation itself or even to systems of private law.[34]

---

[32] See, for earlier precedents, Jenks in (1945) 22 B.Y.B.I.L. 268, note 2; and see generally Parry, "The International Public Corporation" in *The Public Corporation* (1954), ed. Freidmann, at pp. 512–515. Some of the newer ventures, like *Eurofima* or *Eurochemic* are exceptional; to take the latter, this was organised by an agreement of December 20, 1957, between States and has juridical personality; the company "shall be governed by the present Convention, by the Statute, and, residuarily, by the law of the State in which its Headquarters are situated, in so far as the present Convention or the Statute do not derogate therefrom" (Art. 2 (a)—see V *European Yearbook*, 305). Thus the Company has a *residuary* personal law, that of Belgium.

[33] As in the "adoption" of the Geneva Convention of 1949 to govern its armed action in Korea; and see s. 44 of the UNEF Regulations (ST/SGB/UNEF/1) providing that "The Force shall observe the principles and spirit of the general international Conventions applicable to the conduct of military personnel."

[34] For an excellent, detailed treatment of this problem see Seyersted, "Applicable law in relations between IGOs and Private Parties" (1967) R.C. 434–624.

In relation to the immovable property owned or leased by an organisation, such as its headquarters site, good sense and the analogy of the rules of the conflict of laws suggest the general application of the *lex situs*. Hence the titles of the UN to its property in New York and Geneva derive from New York and Swiss law respectively, and are so registered in the appropriate Land Registries. Whereas the agreement between organisation and host State may well govern their relations, and is subject to international law, the rights of the organisation as owner or occupier *vis-à-vis* other persons may need reference to another law which, in principle, is best the *lex situs*[35]; the application of this law will nevertheless be subject to the jurisdictional immunity of the organisation when it is not prepared to waive it.[36] Specific reference to the local law is in fact rare; but there are exceptions such as the series of agreements of 1960, including a protocol to which the Swiss Confederation, the Republic and Canton of Geneva and WHO are parties, whereby WHO acquired a real right of user of land for an indefinite period; a deed provided for arbitration and specified that "it shall be interpreted in accordance with the Swiss law applicable to the case and thereafter to the extent necessary according to the general principles of law."[37]

Contracts concluded by international organisations are of an infinite variety, ranging from contracts for the purchase and hire of goods, contracts for services, charter-parties, contracts of insurance, loan agreements and bond transactions. Basically, the rule is that the parties may express their own choice of law to govern the contract; which law will be chosen will depend on the circumstances. Of course, the contract of employment concluded with an official employed with the organisation will be governed, as we have seen,[38] by the body of administrative law applicable to that particular category; in this respect a coherent body of law is fast developing. Other contracts will be governed by a system of law often varying according to the nature of the other party. When the

---

[35] The UN has voluntarily used the New York Workmen's Compensation law procedures and is also insured against injuries suffered by visitors to its premises.

[36] *Post*, p. 336.

[37] Similarly the WMO lease from the Canton of Geneva; both examples cited by Jenks, *The Proper Law of International Organisations* (1962), p. 136.

[38] *Ante*, p. 325. And not by local law: see (1970) U.N.J.Y. 189.

contract is between an organisation and a State or even another international organisation, the contract may well be a treaty, governed by international law; the various headquarters agreements or the "relationship agreements" between the UN and the specialised agencies, clearly agreements of a "public law" character, may be so regarded. The loan agreements between the International Bank and States are governed by international law[39]; they embody the provision of the Loan Regulations that the rights and obligations of borrower and lender "shall be valid and enforceable in accordance with their terms notwithstanding the law of any State, or political subdivision thereof, to the contrary."[40] However, agreements between international organisations and States can equally well be made subject to some system of municipal law. The Loan Agreement between the Swiss Confederation and the ILO of March-April 1957 provides that in all matters not specified therein the Swiss Code of Obligations shall apply.[41] The local municipal law may well apply to certain transactions on the basis of the normal principle *locus regit actum.* Hence the agreement between Egypt and FAO of August 17, 1952, provided that "Except as otherwise provided in this Agreement, the national, State and local courts . . . shall have jurisdiction, as provided in applicable laws, over acts done and transactions taking place in the Regional Office Seat."[42]

Where the contracts are between an international organisation and an entity lacking international personality, say a private corporation, there cannot be a treaty. It is, however, open to the parties to "internationalise" their agreement by making it subject

[39] See Broches, "International Legal Aspects of the Operations of the World Bank" (1959) 98 R.C. 339–355; Sereni, "International Economic Institutions and the Municipal Law of States," *ibid.* (1959) Vol. 96 *passim;* and see generally Salmon, *Le rôle des organisations internationales en matière de prêts et d'emprunts* (1958), especially Part II; Valticos, 57th Ann. de l'Institut de D.I. (1977) I, 1–191.

[40] s. 7.01 of Loan Regulations No. 3, June 15, 1956. The agreements are registered under Art. 102 of the UN Charter. The earlier practice with the loan agreements was to provide that they were to be interpreted according to the law of New York; there was uncertainty as to whether this meant that New York law was the proper law of the agreement or merely that its rules of interpretation applied; the practice is now discontinued.

[41] ILO (1957) 40 *Off. Bulletin* No. 8, 352–353, Art. 3; Jenks, *op. cit.* p. 183, regards this as an unfortunate precedent.

[42] ST/LEG/SER. B/11, p. 213.

to international law or, more often, "general principles of law."[43] The drawback to this is perhaps the inherent vagueness of the reference, since "general principles of law" are not a *system* of law and one would not expect international law, or even "general principles of law," to yield the kind of specific definition of rights and duties of the parties desirable, say, in a contract of insurance or a charter-party. The more usual course, since the agreements are of a "private law" character, will be to choose a system of municipal law: it will be recalled that in the European Communities their contractual liability "shall be governed by the law applying to the contract concerned,"[44] and this undoubtedly means one of the municipal law systems of the parties. The International Finance Corporation's contracts stipulate New York law and the European Investment Bank the local law of the borrower.[45] The International Bank loans are of interest in that, whereas the guarantee by the State is registered as an international agreement and presumably governed by international law, the instruments regulating the relationship between the Bank and the private enterprise, the actual borrower, are not so registered and are presumably not governed by international law.

It need hardly be added, for anyone familiar with the conflict of laws, that the real difficulty will arise when the contracts contain no express choice of law clause. All that can be said (accepting the "subjectivist" approach) is that it will then be for a court to determine what law the parties *intended* to apply and, lacking other indication, the submission to a particular jurisdiction will tend to be taken as evidence of submission to the law of that jurisdiction. To this extent the jurisdictional and choice of law problems merge, and the selection of the former may well give the solution to the latter.

Tortious liability can exist equally well as contractual liability, and yet the constitutions of the European Communities are unique in international law in their express provision for this; the law to be

---

[43] See Mann, "The Proper Law of contracts concluded by International Persons" (1959) 35 B.Y.B.I.L. 34–57; and see Jessup, *Transnational Law* (1956), Chap. 3. For a contrary view, Sereni, *loc. cit.* p. 207; Delaume, "The proper law of loans concluded by international persons: a restatement and a forecast" (1962) 56 A.J.I.L. 63.

[44] EEC, Art. 215; Euratom, Art. 188.

[45] Nurick "Choice of Law clauses and International Contracts" (1960) *Proceedings of A.S.* 61.

applied is not, however, the *lex loci delicti commissi,* but rather the "general principles common to the laws of Member States."[46] It is tempting to suggest that, subject to immunities, the local law will apply to torts committed within a headquarters district.[47] However, much may depend on who the tortfeasor is, and whereas this rule would be reasonable in the case of a casual visitor to the building, it would be unreasonable in the case of an official or representative of a member.[48] It is at this kind of point that, again, choice of law and jurisdictional questions merge into a single question of convenience. Pragmatic solutions may well have to be adopted, as when the United Nations deals with torts against the civilian population committed by members of UNWRA or UNEF, apparently without overmuch concern with what law governs the issue other than a reference to the local law in order to arrive at a just assessment of the quantum of damages. Torts on UN aircraft or vessels will pose similar problems, to which no answer seems to have been made as yet, unless the aircraft or vessel retains a registration in a place within the jurisdiction of a State and therefore has the law of that State to fall back upon.

Criminal liability is a similar problem; no organisations have their own systems of criminal law, hence the need for the provisions in the agreement between the UN and Egypt that members of UNEF shall be under the exclusive criminal jurisdiction of the States contributing the member. There is, however, every reason to suppose the application of the local criminal law to crimes committed within headquarters districts by persons having no connection with the organisation.[49] Crimes on UN aircraft or vessels will presumably fall under the jurisdiction of the State of the nationality of the offender, unless a place of registration in a particular State is maintained.

These, then, are the choice of law problems raised by an extension of the activities of international organisations which has outstripped the development of legal principles; it is for this reason

---

[46] EEC, Art. 15; Euratom, Art. 188.
[47] Brandon, "The Legal Status of the Premises of the UN" (1951) 28 B.Y.B.I.L. 100; this is largely on the basis of provisions in the Headquarters Agreements making local law applicable within the district except where otherwise provided. See *ante,* p. 350.
[48] Jenks, *op. cit.* p. 215.
[49] *Ante,* p. 351.

that Jenks has recently pleaded for a completely new thinking on the nature and scope of the conflict of laws.[50]

2. Choice of Jurisdiction

To assert that an organisation has sufficient legal personality to enable it to both bring and defend legal claims is not to draw any conclusion about the *forum conveniens* in which such claims may be heard. The choice of a particular forum will depend upon a whole range of interrelated factors: who are the parties, what is the law to be applied, what is the substance of the dispute, and so on. We have already seen how arbitration or reference to the I.C.J. by way of a request for an advisory opinion is a means commonly employed for resolving disputes over the interpretation of constitutional texts.[51] What remains to be seen is the variety of jurisdictions used by international organisations for settling disputes of a far wider variety, disputes, for example, over the privileges and immunities of the organisations or over contracts made by the organisation. It has already been emphasised[52] that the immunity of organisations from the jurisdiction of the local, municipal courts has a purpose which does *not* demand the exclusion of disputes relating to privileges and immunities from any kind of judicial settlement: on the contrary, States may be readier to concede immunity from the jurisdiction of their own courts provided they are satisfied as to the existence of some other forum in which disputes can be settled. The preceeding discussion of the choice of law problem will have sufficed to show a broad distinction between disputes of a *public* law character and disputes of a *private* law character. Admittedly, the first category must be taken as embracing not only those disputes which are governed by international law *stricto sensu,* but also those between an organisation and its officials which are governed by a kind of public administrative law. Moreover, the tendency to "internationalise" agreements which, prima facie, because of the lack of international personality of one party, cannot be governed by international law in the accepted sense makes the distinction increasingly artificial. Yet it is believed the distinction retains

---

[50] *Op. cit. passim.*
[51] *Ante*, pp. 147–150.
[52] *Ante*, p. 363.

sufficient validity to enable its use for the purpose of illustrating the different jurisdictions available according to the nature of the dispute.

(a) *Disputes of a "public law" character*

The International Court of Justice, as a *forum conveniens,* is, as we have seen,[53] limited in its applicability to international organisations by the terms of Article 34 of the Statute. Hence its use is at present confined to questions put by way of a request for an advisory opinion on a matter relating to international law; it is not a procedure appropriate for disputes of a private law character. The disadvantage that the advisory opinion is not binding can, moreover, be overcome by the device of providing in advance for the acceptance of the opinion by the parties as binding upon them. Section 30 of the General Convention on Privileges and Immunities accordingly provides that " . . . If a difference arises between the United Nations on the one hand and a Member on the other hand, a request shall be made for an advisory opinion on any legal question involved in accordance with Article 96 of the Charter and Article 65 of the Statute of the Court. The opinion given by the Court shall be accepted as decisive by the parties." Section 32 of the Specialised Agencies Convention is almost identical, as is Article 9 of the IAEA Agreement on Privileges and Immunities. The last does, however, contain a clause providing for prior consultation between the State and the organisation whenever the former alleges an abuse of privileges, and this very sensible clause figures in at least one of the Headquarters Agreements which provide for eventual recourse to the I.C.J.[54] There is, however, a marked difference in the general pattern of the Headquarters Agreements as contrasted with the main agreements on privileges and immunities, for the former tend to adopt arbitration as the principal means of settlement, using reference to the I.C.J. as a means of securing an advisory opinion

---

[53] *Ante,* p. 268. Note that the Model Text of the Basic Agreement concerning Technical Assistance between the UN or the specialised agencies and a particular government, s. 13, provides for reference of disputes to the I.C.J. without mentioning that this will be by way of an advisory opinion (ST/LEG/SER/B/10, p. 374); yet it cannot be otherwise. See generally Seyersted, "Settlement of Internal Disputes of Inter-governmental Oganisations by Internal and External Courts" (1964) 24 Z.f.a.ö.r.u.V., 1–121.

[54] ICAO/Canada, s. 28.

on a legal question arising during the course of the arbitration proceedings; the arbitration tribunal gives only an interim decision pending receipt of this opinion.[55]

Apart from the I.C.J., which can only be used in this indirect way, there are very few international courts before which any organisation has a direct *locus standi* in a contentious case: to date the Court of Justice of the European Communities is the prime example of such a court. The nature of its jurisdiction to deal with disputes between States and the three Communities has already been examined in some detail.[56] The European Nuclear Energy Agency Tribunal is another example of a court competent to adjudicate disputes of a public law character between States and the organisation.[57] The various administrative tribunals are also tribunals (or courts) before which the organisation has a direct *locus standi,* but they deal primarily with disputes between the organisation and its officials and apply what is really their own body of administrative law as opposed to international law *stricto sensu.*[58] No clearer example than the administrative tribunals can be given of the need to suit the jurisdiction to the nature of the parties and of the subject-matter (and therefore the "proper law" of the relationship).

Turning then to arbitration as the obvious solution to the problem of lack of procedural capacity before the I.C.J., it may be pointed out again that international arbitration is to be contrasted with judicial settlement only as a different *process* of settlement; there is no inherent difference in the law applicable.[59] Hence it is a process perfectly suited to the adjudication of disputes of a public law nature, according to international law, and between international persons. The various Headquarters Agreements almost invariably provide for arbitration between the organisation and host State; usually there are to be three arbitrators, although the

[55] UN/U.S.A., s. 21; UN/Ethiopia, s. 21; ICAO/Canada, s. 31; UNESCO/France, Art. 29. This device may perhaps be compared with the "recours à titre préjudicial" used in the Court of the European Communities, *ante,* p. 310.

[56] *Ante,* p. 311. It is possible that the projected Arab Court of Justice might be given competence to entertain proceedings to which the Arab League is a party; see Art. 33 of the Convention on the Privileges and Immunities of the League of Arab States of May 10, 1953.

[57] Convention of December 20, 1957, Art. 13 and Protocol of the same date, Art. 10: V *European Yearbook* 291, 301.

[58] *Ante,* p. 325.

[59] *Ante,* p. 257.

ICAO/France Agreement[60] envisages but one, and it is customary to find the device of reference to the President of the I.C.J. when agreement on the third arbitrator, or single arbitrator, cannot be reached. As we have seen, some agreements combine a request for an advisory opinion from the I.C.J. with the arbitration process. The traditional disadvantages of arbitration, namely, the need to establish the tribunal *de novo,* with each dispute, is sought to be counteracted in the different headquarters agreements concluded by Switzerland, which provide for the constitution of the tribunal on the coming into force of the agreements, and therefore prior to any dispute. However, it is not believed that tribunals have been so constituted,[61] and the paucity of actual arbitration over privileges and immunities is excellent witness to the restraint of both parties and the efficacy of their processes for amicable settlement without resort to arbitration. Apart from disputes relating to privileges and immunities, or to the general régime of the headquarters agreements, there is another class of disputes of a public law character which are normally referred to arbitration: this is the class of disputes arising from the loan agreements between the financial organisations and States.[62]

There has been far less inclination to adopt arbitration as the appropriate means for settlement of disputes outside the UN framework: the headquarters agreements between France and the Council of Europe, or OECD, and between the U.S.A. and the Organisation of American States, for example, contain no provisions for arbitration. The other class of agreements which might be expected to use arbitration, in that they are international agreements between international persons is the "relationship agreements" between the UN and the specialised agencies; they do not provide for arbitration and, presumably, the A.C.C.[63] will be the body in which the solution of differences will be negotiated in the last resort.

(b) *Disputes of a "private law" character*

The reference of disputes of a "private law" character, to which an international organisation is a party, to a regularly established

---

[60] Art. 20.
[61] Jenks, *International Immunities* (1961), p. 23.
[62] *Ante*, p. 368.
[63] *Ante*, p. 90.

international court is quite exceptional.[64] The I.C.J. clearly cannot be so used, and it is only in the newer European experiments that one finds this made feasible. The Court of the European Communities has such a competence,[65] and so does the Tribunal established by the convention of December 14, 1957,[66] for the protection of private interests against the control measures to be taken by the Agency for the Control of Armaments established within Western European Union. Both courts will entertain actions brought by private entities against the organisation concerned, or against the officials of the organisation. There is also the competence of the ILO Administrative Tribunal, highly unusual for an administrative tribunal and so far unused, to determine "disputes arising out of contracts to which the International Labour Organisation is a party . . . ."[67]

In the absence of a court of this kind other procedures must be devised. It may be noted that under section 29 of the General Convention of 1946,

> "The United Nations shall make provisions for the appropriate modes of settlement of:
>
> (a) Disputes arising out of contracts or other disputes of a private law character to which the United Nations is a party;
>
> (b) Disputes involving any official of the United Nations who by reason of his official position enjoys immunity, if immunity has not been waived by the Secretary-General."

The Specialised Agencies Convention has an identical provision and so do most of the agreements between organisations and host States. These provisions simply emphasise the point that, whilst the immunity from national jurisdictions of both organisation and officials precludes that particular jurisdiction, the principle of liability remains and an alternative jurisdiction or procedure must be established so as to enable claims against the organisation to be dealt with justly.

---

[64] We treat the disputes between organisations and their officials as being of a "public law" character.

[65] Ante, p. 305.

[66] V *European Yearbook* 245.

[67] Art. II (4) of the Statute.

Arbitration is a useful alternative in the absence of an established court, and is equally applicable to disputes of a private law character as to disputes of a public law character, except that in the former case, with which we are now concerned, it will be arbitration according to some system of municipal law. It is, for example, common form to insert in contracts of a private law nature made by the UN (*e.g.* for film distribution or supply of services) a clause providing for arbitration according to the rules of the American Arbitration Association.[68] Arbitration is similarly used in the agreements of the International Bank with private borrowers.[69]

A not dissimilar procedure is to establish the kind of Claims Commission envisaged in the agreement between the UN and Egypt over UNEF.[70] The disputes provision is worth particular attention since it illustrates the different procedures envisaged for different categories of disputes. Whereas, under section 39, disputes between the UN and Egypt over the question of privileges and immunities are dealt with under the procedure of section 30 of the General Convention, that is to say by reference to the I.C.J., and under section 40 all other disputes by arbitration—these both being of a "public law" character—the disputes of a private law character are dealt with under section 38 by reference to a Claims Commission[71] or, when they concern employment of locally recruited personnel, by an administrative procedure settled by the Commander, or by some other appropriate mode of settlement provided by the UN. In practice settlements are reached informally, between the parties directly, or between the Egyptian liaison office and UNEF subject to the approval of the individual claimant.

The above procedures for settlement of disputes all presuppose that the jurisdiction of the local national courts is not applicable.

---

[68] Eagleton, "International Organisation and the Law of Responsibility" (1950) 76 R.C. 392. Also U.N.J.Y. 1964, p. 223 which indicates that for persons not resident in the U.S.A., the rules of the International Chamber of Commerce are used.

[69] Broches, *loc. cit.* p. 371; and Akehurst, "Settlement of claims by individuals and companies against international organisations" in (1969) *Ann. de l'Assoc. des Auditeurs de l'Academie de la Haye*, 69–98.

[70] ST/LEG/SER. B/10, p. 295.

[71] This deals, not with all private law disputes, but only those defined in s. 38 *(b)*. See Bowett, *U.N. Forces* (1964), 149–151 (UNEF) and 242–248 (ONUC).

However, there may be circumstances in which the local national courts are appropriate in disputes of a private law character. First, the organisation is entitled to immunity as a general rule but not *bound* to claim it; to this extent a waiver will open up this particular means of settlement, and it will be recalled that waiver is often a duty imposed upon the organisation whenever to claim immunity would impede the course of justice and a waiver will not impede the functioning of the organisation.[72] Secondly, the organisation is always free to commence an action, as plaintiff, before the local courts: this is one of the consequences of the possession of juridical personality under municipal law. Hence in *I.R.O.* v. *Republic S.S. Corp. et Al.*[73] a United States Court of Appeals concluded that the attribution of capacity to institute legal proceedings in the United States International Organisations Immunities Act "means by necessary implication, that Congress has opened the doors of the federal courts to suits by such international organisations." Thirdly, immunity from the local jurisdiction may not be contemplated at all. We have seen that the European Communities have no general immunity from local jurisdiction.[74] Moreover, the financial organisations have no general immunity: the Bank, for example, may be sued in the municipal courts of any Member country where the Bank has either an office, or has appointed an agent to accept service of process or has issued or guaranteed securities; provided, however, the plaintiff is not a Member State or someone claiming through a Member State.[75]

VI. DISSOLUTION OF INTERNATIONAL ORGANISATIONS AND PROBLEMS OF SUCCESSION

Whether or not a particular organisation will wish to provide in its constitution for the contingency of dissolution will depend upon

---

[72] *Ante*, p. 353.
[73] (1951) I.L.R., Case No. 140.
[74] *Ante*, p. 349.
[75] Art. VII (3). See Broches, *loc. cit.* pp. 309–310. Also Seyersted, *loc. cit.* pp. 78–84 who accepts the jurisdiction of municipal courts in cases where the Organisation claims an "extended" jurisdiction but who denies it in "internal, organic disputes" of the Organisation.

political factors: it is somewhat unlikely in the case of an organisation like the UN where permanence is the aim. It was similarly not provided for in the League, and we shall discuss shortly the means whereby it was in fact accomplished in 1946.

Dissolution is, however, very sensibly anticipated in the constitutions of the financial agencies, for such agencies will inevitably face the problem of distributing the financial assets. Hence, in Article 6 (5) of the Bank Agreement there are detailed provisions providing for dissolution by a vote of the majority of the Governors, exercising a majority of the total voting power. The analogy of the winding-up of a company in municipal law is striking[76]: payment of creditors and claims takes priority over distribution of assets, and this distribution is in proportion to the shareholding of a Member. The Fund contains a special Schedule E dealing with dissolution, or "liquidation" as it is called, and Article 7 (5) of the International Development Association equally contains detailed provisions, modelled on the Bank's. It was in the absence of any constitutional provision for dissolution that the League Assembly, without any formal convening of the Council, dissolved the League by its own resolution of April 18, 1946; all that survived was a Board of Liquidation, established for the sole purpose of liquidating the affairs of the League.[77] A similar, and perhaps even more questionable, method was adopted in relation to the P.C.I.J., dissolved by resolution of the same date; one might have expected this to have been done by the States parties to the Statute, acting as such.

Succession is, of course, not necessarily connected with dissolution; it presupposes that a political decision has been taken to transfer the functions, assets and liabilities of the one organisation to another (whether already in existence or new) either in whole or in part. The complicated nature of the problems involved can perhaps be illustrated by recounting briefly the methods used in

---

[76] See the provision that liability for uncalled subscriptions shall remain until all claims by creditors, and all contingent claims, have been discharged (Art. 6 (5) (c)).

[77] Prior to the dissolution on April 18, the Assembly by resolution of April 12 decided to "assume the functions falling within the competence of the Council," with the concurrence of all the Members represented at the session.

the succession of the UN to the League[78] and, in part by way of contrast, of OECD to OEEC.

With the League it was known, in 1946, that, politically speaking, the UN was the successor to the League even though neither the Atlantic Charter nor the Dunbarton Oaks proposals referred to the League. So far as a transfer of functions was concerned, the Preparatory Commission of the UN, which had before it a report of the League's own Executive Committee, declined to accept the idea of a transfer of functions *en bloc*[79] and, instead, a review of the many functions was undertaken to ascertain those which it was desirable the UN or the specialised agencies should undertake. The review of "political" functions was undertaken by the General Assembly and the review of "technical and non-political" functions by ECOSOC; the acceptance of the transfer of any particular function was done by resolution of the Assembly. In fact no political functions were assumed in the sense of a jurisdiction over political problems which had been before the League. With the Mandates system, as we have seen,[80] the transfer to the new Trusteeship system was a matter for the administering authority to decide; similarly with the bureaux in relationship with the League under Article 22 of the Covenant, a new agreement had to be negotiated with the UN. Where, under treaties,[81] the League or related organisations had exercised administrative functions, the transfer of these required consent of the parties to the treaties so that, in the case of the agreements on narcotic drugs, for example, these had to be amended by a Protocol between the parties, substituting references to the UN and WHO for those to the League and the

---

[78] See Mackinnon Wood, "The Dissolution of the League of Nations" (1946) B.Y.B.I.L. 317; Myers, "Liquidation of the League of Nations' Functions" (1948) 42 A.J.I.L. 320; Parry, (1949) B.Y.B.I.L. 133–135; Rosenne, (1954) 2 R.C. 394; Chiu, "Succession in International Organisations" (1965) 14 I.C.L.Q. 83.

[79] The U.S.S.R., having been expelled from the League, disliked this notion of almost automatic succession.

[80] *Ante*, p. 73.

[81] The League had published three publications on its functions under treaties: *Powers and Duties attributed to the League of Nations by International Treaties* (C.3, M.3, 1944, VI); *List of Conventions with Indications of the Relevant Articles conferring Powers on the Organs of the League* (C.100, M.100, 1945, VI); and *The Committee of the League of Nations: Classified List and Essential Facts* (C.99, M.99, 1945, V2).

International Office of Public Hygiene.[82] The assumption of depositary functions in relation to treaties was more simply accomplished by a resolution of the General Assembly expressly stating the UN's willingness to assume these functions.

In dissolving the P.C.I.J. care was taken to provide for the continuance of acceptances of the Court's jurisdiction by including in the new Statute of the Court Articles 36 (5), 37; and the judges' pension scheme was entrusted to the ILO. The ILO itself was, of course, carefully preserved; finance was transferred to it in the form of the Working Capital Fund and measures were taken by the League to vest in the ILO full ownership of its land and buildings and to preserve certain facilities for the use by it of the League's own buildings which were due for transfer to the UN.

The transfer of the physical assets, including buildings, equipment, archives, libraries, etc., was provided for in the "Common Plan," and payment for them was made by the UN. The adoption of the Common Plan was by resolution of the UN Assembly on February 12, 1946. All staff were discharged, although some were taken on under new contracts by the UN.[83]

The "reconstitution" of OEEC into OECD[84] terminated the 1948 Convention by which OEEC had been established contemporaneously with the coming into force of the new 1960 Convention. Yet, as distinct from the dissolution of the League, the personality of the old organisation was continued in the new. Article 15 of the 1960 Convention[85] provided:

"When this Convention comes into force the reconstitution of the Organisation for European Economic Co-operation

---

[82] 12 U.N.T.S. 179.

[83] This seems a fairly normal procedure, although in the transfer of UNRRA's functions and assets to the UN consequent upon its dissolution in 1948, the staff was taken over by the UN. The Agreement between UNRRA and the UN of September 27, 1948 (27 U.N.T.S. 350) is another useful case-study on succession: the treaty deals with settlement of claims, assignment of contracts, a very complicated accounting, and the usual problems of transfer of functions and physical assets.

[84] See *ante*, p. 189. This course was necessitated, it is believed, by the constitutional position in the U.S.A. It should be distinguished from the simpler course, adopted when the Brussels Treaty Organisation became Western European Union, of amending the earlier treaty and inviting new Members to accede: see 2 *European Yearbook*, docs. relating to the revision and extension of the Brussels Treaty, pp. 313–340.

[85] *U.K. Treaty Series* No. 21 (1962), Cmnd. 1646.

shall take effect, and its aims, organs, powers and name shall thereupon be as provided herein. The legal personality possessed by the Organisation for European Economic Co-operation shall continue in the Organisation, but decisions, recommendations and resolutions of the Organisation for European Economic Co-operation shall require approval of the Council to be effective after the coming into force of this Convention."

The method by which the reconstitution was to be effected was to establish a Preparatory Committee by a Ministerial Meeting of July 22–23, 1960, with power to review the acts of OEEC to decide which should be recommended for approval. Moreover, the members of the Council *agreed in advance* to accept these recommendations.[86] So far as the structure of OEEC was concerned, the changes were not startling and have been reviewed in the earlier part of this book.[87] The review of functions and previous acts was done in the form of dividing them into four categories: the first included acts to be retained without any modification of substance, the second of acts to be retained but with substantial modifications, the third of acts not be retained but which embodied certain activities, principles or rules worthy of retention, and the fourth of acts that should lapse completely.[88]

Treaties and private-law contracts were continued[89] although the contracts of employment with officials were terminated under the conditions governing notice, and the officials were recruited again as necessary with the specific proviso that the terms of service with OEEC were to count towards service with OECD.

Whether one organisation has been dissolved and replaced by a new legal entity depends upon the intention of the Member States as reflected in the instruments effecting the constitutional change. For example, the changes to the constitution of the UPU as

---

[86] Memorandum of Understanding on the Application of Art. 15 (reproduced in the "Bluebook," the publication of OEEC in 1960 entitled *The Organisation for Economic Co-operation and Development*). The U.S.A. and Canada entered into a much less binding commitment.

[87] *Ante*, p. 189.

[88] Part II of the *Report of the Preparatory Commission,* contained in the "Bluebook."

[89] Hahn, "Die Organisation für wirtschaftliche Zusammenarbeit und Entwicklung" (1962) 22 Z.a.o.r.v. 56.

between 1874, 1878, and 1957 were simply amendments: in contrast, the ITU Convention of 1932, replacing the 1865 Convention, created a new legal entity which fused the personality of the old ITU with the former International Radiotelegraphic Union. Similarly, the 1962 Wheat Agreement, replacing the 1959 Agreement, was not regarded as having been intended by the parties to create a new régime and thus end all obligations under the 1959 Agreement.[90] In contrast, the two organisations ESRO and ELDO were replaced in 1975 by one, new organisation ESA (European Space Agency) which was stated expressly to "take over all rights and obligations."[91]

It may be doubted whether practice to date provides any firm rules on succession of international organisations. However, certain principles would seem to emerge from practice and the law of treaties.

(i) The capacity of a successor organisation to accept a transfer of functions may arise either from express or implied powers. Some constitutions contain express provisions [*e.g.* WMO Art. 26 (c), WHO Art. 72, UNESCO Art. 11 (2)] but the UN acceptance of transfers of functions and assets from the League rested on implied powers. So did the General Assembly's succession to the supervisory functions under the Mandate for S.W. Africa.[92]

(ii) The obligation of States to recognise the effectiveness of such a transfer depends upon their consent, express or implied.

(iii) There is, as yet, no rule of "automatic" succession.[93]

(iv) The form of transfer therefore should be such as to indicate consent and can therefore be expressed in either parallel resolutions of the two organisations *or* in amendment to or specific enactment in the constitutions of both organisations.

---

[90] International Wheat Council, 1962: Minutes of the 36 Session. This affected *inter alia,* the question whether arrears of assessments were to be nullified or continued over under the new Agreement.

[91] Art. XIX. Treaty of May 30, 1975: U.K. Misc. Ser. 24 (1975) Cmnd. 6272.

[92] See the S.W. Africa Cases, (1950) *I.C.J. Reports* 128; (1952) 319.

[93] Fitzmaurice (1952) 29 B.Y.B.I.L., 8–10 argues that the S.W. Africa Case, supports the view that there can be *automatic* devolution: this view is refuted by Chiu, *loc. cit.* 103–106.

CHAPTER 12

THE IMPACT OF INTERNATIONAL ORGANISATIONS ON THE DOCTRINE OF SOVEREIGN EQUALITY OF STATES

THE sovereign State not only tended, in the nineteenth century, to be thought of as the only real subject of international law, but, in the context of the nineteenth-century conferences, which represented the beginnings of international organisation, equality meant "the right of every interested State to participate on an equal footing, (and) conceding to the delegations of every State an equality of voting strength whenever votes are taken and requiring unanimity for all important decisons and . . . limiting the assembly to decisions *ad referendum*. . . . "[1] The assumptions that only States ought properly to be represented in the international sphere, that States should enjoy complete equality of vote, and that decisions required unanimity could, if carried to their logical conclusions, well-nigh stultify the promotion of common interests through the medium of international organisations. Our present purpose, therefore, is to show how far, by a constant process of development and experiment, these supposed consequences of the doctrine of sovereign equality have been evaded by different techniques of membership, representation, voting and the like.

I. MEMBERSHIP OF INTERNATIONAL ORGANISATIONS

A good deal has already been said of admission to membership in the first, descriptive part of this book in so far as the membership provisions of the various organisations have been mentioned in dealing with specific organisations.[2] It will have become apparent that universality of membership does not exist in the sense of a

---

[1] Dickinson, *The Equality of States in International Law* (1920), p. 280; see also Bengt Broms, *The Doctrine of Equality of States as applied in International Organisations* (1959); Boutros-Ghali, "Le principe d'Egalité des Etats et les Organisations internationales" (1960) 100 R.C. 1; Drago, "La pondération dans les organisations internationales" (1956) 2 *Ann.fr.de.dr.int.*; Padirac, *L'égalité des Etats et l'organisation internationale* (1953); Kooijmans, *The Doctrine of the Legal Equality of States* (1964).

[2] *Ante*, pp. 42, 118, 171, 218, 229.

sovereign State having a right to membership of an organisation[3]; even in the United Nations, where much has been said of the avowed aim of universality, admission is not an automatic consequence of statehood, but conditional on the fulfilment of the conditions of Article 4 of the Charter and subject to the approval of both Security Council and General Assembly.

The exception to this, found in those organisations which link membership, is apparent rather than real. In the cases where membership of the UN gives a right to membership of certain of the specialised agencies, or membership of, say, the Bank gives a right to membership of the other financial organisations such as the Fund, the IFC and the new International Development Association, there is still the initial hurdle of membership of one organisation to be surmounted, whether in the form of receipt of an invitation to become an original signatory or of subsequent admission.

Membership of certain organisations is necessarily limited by their very character. No one would expect to find regional organisations open to States outside the region, and thus organisations like the Council of Europe (Art. 4), or the European Economic Community (Art. 237), or the Council for Mutual Economic Aid (Art. 2 (2)) limit admitted Members to European States. Even in the military pacts such as NATO and the Warsaw Treaty Organisation, although there is no geographical limitation built into the admission clause, admission of new Members is subject to the unanimous approval of existing Members who may be expected to apply some kind of geographical and political criteria of suitability.

Unless the constitution allows States, in applying for membership, to make reservations to their acceptance of the constitution, the presumption must be that such reservations are not permitted. It was on this ground that, in 1953, the Director-

---

[3] No more than it existed in the sense of a right to participate in a Conference in the nineteenth century: see Dickinson, *Equality of States in International Law* (1920), pp. 281–282. The usual practice in convening UN Conferences is to limit participation to Members of the UN or of any of the specialised agencies or to signatories of the Statute of the I.C.J. ICAO is an exceptional case in that it is open to "members of the United Nations and States associated with them, and States which remained neutral in the present world conflict" (Art. 92 (a)). The exception is explicable by the fact that ICAO preceded the establishment of the UN.

General of the ILO refused to accept the Soviet Union's application for membership, this application having stated that the Soviet Union could not accept Article 37 (1) and (2) of the Constitution. Subsequently, the Soviet Union withdrew the reservation and was admitted.[4] The rule in Article 20 (3) of the Vienna Convention on the Law of Treaties required that a reservation be accepted by "the competent organ," and this corresponds with the practice of the WHO in 1948 in formally recognising the reservation made by the U.S.A. in its acceptance of the WHO constitution. However, the "competent organ" may not be obvious, and there remains the question of by what vote the reservation must be accepted: by unanimity or majority? For a reservation of some consequence, there is much to be said for unanimity.

Membership is not necessarily confined to States[5] and even in those organisations where it is so confined a very variable concept of statehood is applied in practice: it would seem that a less rigorous interpretation of the term "State" is used when admission to certain specialised agencies is accorded than when admission to the United Nations is sought.[6] Hence the Republic of Vietnam is a Member of the ILO, UNESCO, WHO and UPU; Monaco is a Member of UNESCO, WHO and UPU.

In some organisations the admission of non-autonomous territories is expressly provided for: this is the case with the UPU, the ITU, WMO and GATT. These are all cases where the territories operate as independent units in the fields in question—postal, telecommunications, meteorological services and trade—so that good sense dictates their being accorded full membership.

The device of "associate" membership is quite commonly used, connoting limited rights of participation. In WHO this associate membership is open to non-autonomous territories, in ITU to such territories and even independent States, and so too in the Council of Europe and OECD.

---

[4] Whiteman, *Digest,* 13, 213 and, generally, Mendelson (1971) 45 B.Y.B.I.L. 137. The application of the rule on reservations in Article 20 (4) of the Vienna Convention on Treaties would produce chaos. A State cannot be a member *vis-à-vis* some members but not *vis-à-vis* others, so a collegiate system is essential.

[5] *Ante,* p. 119, and *post,* p. 397.

[6] Cohen, "The Concept of Statehood in United Nations Practice" (1961) 109 *Univ. of Pennsylvania L.R.,* 1156–1161.

II. Suspension from the Privileges of Membership

Not all international organisations utilise suspension as a means of securing compliance by a Member with its obligations; ITU has no provision for suspension, nor has UNESCO any independent power of suspension, since suspension occurs only as the automatic result of suspension from the UN. Moreover, in the European Communities, where a Court has been established with compulsory jurisdiction over Members in questions involving non-fulfilment of the treaty obligations, suspension has not been thought necessary.

However, in the many organisations which do have powers of suspension, the circumstances in which such powers may be exercised vary considerably; and so may the degree of suspension vary from loss of voting rights to loss of the right to attend meetings of one or more organs. Suspension is generally used as a sanction for non-fulfilment of financial obligations. Article 19 of the Charter provides for suspension in the sense of deprivation of a vote in the Assembly when a Member is in arrears with its budgetary contributions to an amount equal to the contributions due for the preceding two full years.[7] The ILO similarly adopts two years, whereas IMCO (Art. 42) allows only one year's grace and ICAO refers only to "a reasonable period" (Art. 62). Other organisations extend the category of defaults for which suspension is a sanction, so that in WHO it applies "in other exceptional circumstances," and WMO refers to a Member who "otherwise fails in its obligations under the present Convention" (Art. 31); moreover, under Article 5 of the Charter suspension will be a possible sanction against a Member "against which preventive or enforcement action has been taken." The three financial organisations, the Fund, Bank and IFC, also have power of suspension for breach of obligations towards the organisation generally. The

---

[7] This sanction has been applied to Haiti in 1963 and to the Dominican Republic in 1968 (see A/7146 and the 1671 and 1672 Plen. Mtgs. of G.A., June 12, 1968). The fact that it was not applied in 1965 over the arrears of peace-keeping contributions was due to the particular constitutional conflict over this vexed issue. To avoid a "confrontation" over this, the General Assembly operated during the 19th Session by "consensus," avoiding any vote. Indeed, the U.S.A. and U.S.S.R., the main protagonists over the constitutional issue, joined in opposing Albania's attempt to force a vote. See Padelford, Financing Peace-Keeping: Politics and Crisis (1965) 19 *Int. Orgs.* 444.

Council of Europe can suspend a Member for having "seriously violated Article 3," this being the article enjoining acceptance of the rule of law and observance of human rights. A significant new development has been the amendment by the ILO and WHO of their constitutions in order to suspend or expel States subject to suspension or expulsion from the UN and to enable suspension of a State found to be flagrantly and persistently pursuing a policy of racial discrimination or apartheid from any further participation in the Conference. These new powers of sanction are based upon the organisation's desire to assume greater powers against South Africa and followed heated debates over the question whether, without amendment of the constitution, such sanctions were possible.

Not only is there this broad distinction between organisations having power to suspend for non-fulfilment of financial obligations, and those having wider powers, but it will also be seen that the *effect* of suspension varies considerably. In the UN, suspension under Article 19 involves merely loss of vote in the General Assembly, although suspension under Article 5 involves loss of the "rights" and "privileges of membership" generally, presumably, therefore, depriving a Member of representation as well as vote in all organs. The ILO confines the effect of suspension to loss of vote, but extends it to the Conference, the Governing Body, any committee or in the elections of members of the Governing Body (Art. 13 (4)).[8] WMO refers to the suspension of rights and privileges "as a member" (Art. 31),[9] and the Council of Europe provision clearly covers loss of representation as well as loss of vote.

Those organisations which provide services or more tangible advantages have the more effective sanction in using suspension in that it may bring about suspension of these services and advantages. The WMO speaks of loss of voting privileges "and other services," and all the financial organisations have similarly comprehensive sanctions. The Fund is in a very strong position in

---

[8] This suspension of privileges should be sharply distinguished from the refusal to approve the credentials of the delegates from a Member State, such as occurred in 1958 and 1959 when the General Conference of the ILO rejected the credentials of government, employers' and workers' delegates from Hungary; see further, *post*, p. 395.

[9] So, too, UNESCO (Art. 2 (3)).

being able to sanction any use of the resources contrary to the purposes of the Fund by either limiting the Member's use of the Fund or even declaring it ineligible to use those resources.[10] Similarly the IFC in Article V (2) has a quite general power of suspension from membership, the totality of rights and privileges, for a failure to fulfil "any of its obligations to the Corporation," and this suspension becomes a cessation of membership one year from the date of suspension unless the Member is restored to its "good standing" by a decision of the Governors. The Bank's Article 6 (2) is similar, and obviously formed the model for it. The extremely effective sanction in the hands of the financial agencies is all the more effective when it is recalled that the three organisations link suspension and cessation of membership, so that to lose the privileges of membership of the IFC and cessation of membership of the Fund, generally involves cessation of membership of the Bank.

It is clearly desirable that suspension should follow, not as a matter of course upon the occurrence of some event, but rather as a result of the exercise of a discretion by a competent organ; that it should be *permissive* rather than *mandatory*, in other words. This is generally so; the apparent exceptions in Article 19 of the Charter, or 13 (4) of the ILO, are not true exceptions, for in both cases there is a proviso for waiver of the sanction when failure to pay is "due to conditions beyond the control of the Member."[11] A truer exception is seen in those cases where suspension from one organisation brings about automatic suspension from another.

The actual procedure for effecting suspension also varies. It is generally entrusted to the main plenary organ, although in Article 5 of the Charter the recommendation of the Security Council is a prior condition; moreover, since suspension of a Member is eminently a matter for the Member States to decide, in organisations like the Council of Europe, where the Assembly is not

---

[10] As is also the International Atomic Energy Agency which can enforce the observance of its provisions on safeguards by either suspending all privileges and rights of membership or by curtailing or suspending assistance provided by the Agency or even recalling materials and equipment provided: Statute, Arts. 19 (B) and 12 (A) (7) (Peaslee, p. 926).

[11] However, the S.G. has taken the view (opposed by the U.S.S.R.) that the suspension is automatic unless (a) a challenge is made to the accuracy of the computation of the assessment or (b) the Member State petitions the Assembly to use its discretion to waive the sanction (A/7111, A/7146).

composed of State representatives, the decision is entrusted to the Committee of Ministers. The vote required varies, and, although normally a two-thirds majority is required, a simple majority suffices in ICAO and WHO, for example. Recent years have seen acute controversies in organisations in which an attempt was made to exclude South Africa from participation in meetings although the constitutions of those organisations confined the power of exclusion, or suspension from participation, to very limited circumstances such as non-payment of contributions. The ILO, WHO, UNESCO and even technical organisations like ITU and UPU faced concerted moves of this kind.[12] As indicated above, certain of these organisations have made constitutional amendments to give them wider powers of suspension. An attempt to exclude South Africa from UNCTAD in 1968 was rejected by the General Assembly, and ICAO rejected a proposal to exclude South Africa in 1965. However, in 1975 WMO did suspend South Africa's membership on the highly dubious reasoning that the practice of apartheid was not conducive to the fulfilment of the objectives of WMO. The link between meteorology and racial discrimination defies definition. There has thus been no consistent practice on this matter.

Surprisingly enough, the requirement of prior notice to the offending Member, and the affording to it of a chance to state its own case, are rarely found as essential parts of the procedure except in the financial organisations. In the absence of a specific power of suspension it may be doubted whether an organisation can exercise such a power against a Member, hence the various "constitutional crises" referred to above.

It may finally be noted that suspension does not free a Member from its obligations, but merely suspends the exercise of rights or privileges of one kind or another.

---

[12] In 1965 ITU resolved to exclude South Africa from Regional Conferences in Africa and all Plenipotentiary Conferences even though, in 1964, this had led to a major constitutional crisis in which the European Members withdrew and the Conference adjourned *sine die*. The year 1966 saw a similar clash in UPU. In 1966 WHO suspended Portugal from participation in the Regional Committee for Africa and suspended technical assistance to Portugal in accordance with G.A. resol. 2107 (XX), para. 9. For the refusal of the Bank to do so see, *ante*, p. 67.

III. TERMINATION OF MEMBERSHIP[13]

Apart from the case of dissolution of the organisation, termination of membership is likely to arise in three different ways: by withdrawal, as the voluntary act of the Member; by expulsion, as a measure taken by the organisation against a Member; and by the loss of membership consequent upon a Member's refusal to accept an amendment to the constitution of the organisation.

1. Withdrawal.

A specific right of withdrawal is found in the constitutions of most of the specialised agencies, although not in WHO, UNESCO (prior to 1954) or the UN itself. There is, however, considerable variation in the conditions attached to the right of withdrawal. Whereas the financial organisations allow withdrawal simply upon submission of written notice, and allow this withdrawal to take effect immediately, other organisations impose clear limitations on withdrawal. In some cases it is not permited during an initial period, so as to allow the organisation time to become establishɔd; this period may range from four years in the case of FAO (Art. 19) to 50 in ECSC (Art. 97). Sometimes a period is prescribed between the giving of notice to withdraw and the coming into effect of withdrawal, a kind of "cooling-off" period to allow for reconsideration (and possibly a change of government) or even necessary budgetary readjustments[14]; this is one year in WMO and two years in ILO.[15]

A fourth condition sometimes attached to withdrawal is that outstanding obligations must be fulfilled before withdrawal is effective. In general the obligations specified are simply the financial obligations incurred as part of the budgetary commit- ment; thus Article 9 of FAO, Article 5 of ILO, or Article 1 (3) of the League Covenant suspend effectiveness of withdrawal until financial obligations are fulfilled. When an organisation has an operational budget, as is the case with the financial organisations, the settlement of accounts with a withdrawing Member is even

---

[13] See generally Nagendra Singh, *Termination of Membership of International Organisations* (1958).

[14] As in the Council of Europe, Art. 7, where withdrawal takes effect only "at the end of the financial year."

[15] South Africa withdrew in 1964 following the sanctions of suspension threatened against it.

more complicated. To take the Bank by way of example, under Article 6 (4) the Member remains liable for direct obligations to the Bank and for contingent liabilities to the Bank so long as its loans or guarantees remain outstanding; the Member's shares are re-purchased by the Bank at their book value subject to the Bank's right of set-off for amounts due under loans or guarantees. In some cases the fulfilment of obligations other than financial ones is specified; this was true of Article 1 (3) of the Covenant, somewhat ineffectively, since withdrawing Members of the League usually settled their debts but rarely made amends for breaches of other obligations. The ILO is a very special case in providing (perhaps *ex abundante cautela*) that withdrawal shall not affect the continued validity of obligations arising under any international labour convention to which the Member withdrawing is a party (Art. 5). Evidently the need to impose this fourth condition is not widely felt, since several of the specialised agencies do not contain it (ICAO, WMO, UPU). It is, of course, clear that withdrawal could not in any event affect the obligations already incurred; these would still subsist, at least in the case of the financial obligations. It is simply that a State might be more ready to pay if its effective withdrawal depended on settlement.

Considerable problems arise in the absence of any withdrawal clause. Prima facie a State must be deemed to be free to withdraw unless it has surrendered that right expressly or impliedly.[16] Therefore, in the absence of a withdrawal clause one is left with the problem of ascertaining what obligations the parties intended to assume in this respect. In the case of the UN, which contains no withdrawal clause due to the desire of the parties to emphasise their aspirations to stability and permanence, it is nevertheless clear from the *travaux préparatoires* that the right to withdraw "in exceptional circumstances" (to use the phrase of the report of Committee I/2) was conceded.[17] The decision of Indonesia to "withdraw" from the UN (and also the specialised agencies) in January 1965 was eventually followed by a decision in September 1966 to "resume full co-operation" and the General Assembly concurred in the S.G.'s view that Indonesia's absence was to be

---

[16] For the contrary argument see Feinburg, "Unilateral Withdrawal from an International Organisation" (1963) 39 B.Y.B.I.L. 215.
[17] UNCIO, Doc. 1178, I/2/76(2), p. 5; see generally Kelsen, *Law of the UN*. Chap. 7.

regarded as a cessation of co-operation, not withdrawal.[18] Again, in the absence of any provision, Members have withdrawn from WHO and UNESCO, although their subsequent re-entry makes it possible to regard this as a temporary rather than permanent decision.[19] A clear provision that a treaty such as a military alliance, creating an organisation, was to be of a fixed duration might also imply a surrender of the right to withdraw.[20] What is certainly clear is that mere silence on the question of withdrawal is not adequate to deprive a Member of the right to withdraw.

2. Expulsion

The compulsory cessation of membership as a result of the decision of the organisation is by no means generally envisaged in constitutions of international organisations. Article 6 of the Charter contemplates expulsion for persistent violation of the principles of the Charter, the Council of Europe for a "serious violation" of the fundamental principles of the organisation as set out in Articles 1 and 3, and, of the specialised agencies, UNESCO (Art. 2 (4)) and IMCO (Art. 11) link expulsion from those organisations with expulsion from the UN. The ILO and WHO have recently amended their constitutions to provide a similar link, as well as establishing a separate ground for expulsion, namely the flagrant and persistent pursuit of a policy of racial discrimination or apartheid. The three financial organisations also contemplate expulsion in the sense that, in the Bank and the IFC, a suspension automatically ripens into expulsion after one year

---

[18] The S.G. negotiated a financial settlement whereby Indonesia paid 10 per cent. of its usual assessemnt for 1965 and 25 per cent. for 1966. See Livingstone, "Withdrawal from the UN" (1965) 14 I.C.L.Q., 637 and Blum, *ibid.* (1967) 16 I.C.L.Q. 522. Contrast the position in IMF and IBRD, both having an express withdrawal clause: Indonisia withdrew in 1965 and was formally re-admitted in 1967.

[19] The Soviet bloc "withdrew" from WHO between 1949 and 1955; Poland, Hungary and Czechoslovakia "withdrew" from UNESCO between 1952–4. In both cases the Organisations regarded these States simply as having temporarily ceased to participate and in fact a nominal budgetary contribution was exacted when they resumed participation to cover their years of absence.

[20] The proposed EDC Treaty was silent on withdrawal and was expresssed to be for 50 years; this probably prevented withdrawal. A provision similar to Art. 13 of NATO allowing denunciation after twenty years must be regarded as an express provision preventing withdrawal during that period. But see *ante,* p. 181 on the French decision to withdraw from participation in certain activities of NATO without formally withdrawing from the Organisation.

unless the Governors decide to restore the Member to good standing (Art. VI (2)), and in the Fund a Member which persists in its failure to observe its obligations can be "compelled to withdraw" (Art. XV (2)). Expulsion is always discretionary and never automatic.

In the absence of an expulsion clause it may be doubted whether, in general, an organisation has the power to expel a Member.[21] There is, however, the decision of the Meeting of Consultation of Ministers of Foreign Affairs of January 31, 1962,[22] to exclude Cuba from participation in OAS, a decision taken without specific constitutional power to expel; a number of the abstaining Members, and Cuba itself, expressed misgivings over the legality of this step. Similar misgivings have been expressed over decisions within various of the specialised agencies, such as ITU and UPU,[23] to exclude South Africa from participation in certain agencies. Of a similar kind was the decision by UNESCO to exclude Israel from the European Group in 1974. Because of doubts over the legality of this decision, France and the U.S.A. reduced their contributions to UNESCO, and in 1977 Israel was re-admitted to the European Group. In 1979 the UPU took the final step of expelling South Africa. The member States of the European Community issued a joint declaration, claiming that this step was illegal, since the UPU constitution has no provision for expulsion: they therefore consider South Africa to be still a member and will treat her as such.

This action supports the view that, in the absence of an express constitutional power to expel, the general rule is that a member cannot be expelled. The possible exception to the general rule might be the case where a Member, having accepted by the constitution a procedure for amending the constitution without the consent of all the Members, declines to recognise an amendment constitutionally effected.

It may well be that expulsion and even suspension, at least for a political organisation, are of doubtful value. The danger is, of

---

[21] But see the somewhat roundabout way of expulsion envisaged by the resolution of the ILO Conference on June 29, 1961, condemning the apartheid policies of the Republic of South Africa and requesting the Governing Body to advise the Republic to withdraw from membership: *Parl. Papers,* Cmnd. 1514, p. 26.

[22] *Dept. State Bull.,* Vol. 46, No. 1182, 281.

[23] The 1969 UPU Congress actually expelled South Africa: see (1969) U.N.J.Y. 118. An attempt to expel her from the UN was vetoed in October 1974.

course, that except when a Member has very decided advantages to lose by suspension or expulsion, as may be the case with the financial organisations, the suspension or expulsion simply removes the recalcitrant Member from the very pressures of general opinion which, constantly in play within the organisation, are perhaps the best means of securing a return to fulfilment of obligations. In 1942, C. W. Jenks, although writing with expulsion for non-payment of financial obligations in mind, made this observation, an observation which can well be applied to suspension or expulsion in general:

> "International institutions are not clubs from which unpleasant and disagreeable members can be blackballed to the general advantage; they are an attempt to create machinery of government for a world where the unpleasant and the disagreeable cannot be assumed not to exist. Denationalisation is not normally regarded as an appropriate remedy when an individual fails to pay his income tax, and expulsion from an international institution is no more appropriate as a remedy when a Government defaults upon a payment due to the international fisc."[24]

3. Non-ratification of an amendment to a constitution

It is very rare to find specific provisions governing this matter. Article 26 of the Covenant of the League did provide that amendments were to take effect when ratified by all members of the Council and a majority of the members of the Assembly, but that they should not bind dissenting Members who "shall cease to be a Member of the League." Article 94 of ICAO provides that, in recommending the adoption of an amendment, the Assembly may provide that a Member which has not ratified the amendments within a specified period shall cease to be a Member.

There are, as we shall see in discussing amendments later,[25] broadly two types of amendment procedures: those which adopt the "legislative" principle of allowing amendments by a majority, with binding effect on *all* Members, and those which make the amendment binding on individual Members only with their consent. In the first category there is much to be said for providing

[24] Jenks, "Financing of International Institutions" (1943) 38 T.G.S. 111.
[25] *Post*, p. 408.

expressly for compulsory withdrawal of the Member, since it is declining to accept the will of the majority which it agreed in advance to accept; it may well be that, even without express provision, an organisation would be justified in expelling in such circumstances.[26] In the second category the dilemma is posed that the Member has not agreed to be bound except with its consent, and yet in practice it is unwise to admit that any one Member can either veto an amendment or remain a Member under the terms of the old constitution whilst the majority continue under the amended constitution. In such a case withdrawal should be permitted, and probably compelled.[27]

This is essentially a problem facing the large, multipartite constitutions; in smaller organisations, such as the European Communities, acceptance of amendments by all Members is so essential to the wellbeing of the organisation that ratification by *all* Members is made a pre-condition to the entry force of the amendment.

IV. REPRESENTATION OF MEMBERS

The representation of a Member should be sharply distinguished from the question of admission to membership; the former presupposes admission and is concerned with the question of which representatives shall be recognised as entitled to represent a Member within the organs of the organisation. This question can best be illustrated by the problems arising from the competing claims of the Nationalist Government and the Government of the Chinese People's Republic to represent China within the United Nations.

In practice the question is dealt with under the rules of procedure of each organ; it is not directly dealt with in the Charter. Hence, within the Security Council, representation was treated as a matter of credentials and under Rule 17 a representative to whom objection has been made continues to sit until the

---

[26] Contrariwise, when power to withdraw exists, a member would *not* be justified in withdrawing because of such an amendment. But note that Committee I/2 at San Francisco instanced inability to accept an amendment as a possible "exceptional circumstance" justifying withdrawal.

[27] IMCO, in adopting the constitutional amendments of 1964, resolved that members failing to accept them must withdraw: A/ES. 11/Res. 69 and A IV/Res. 70.

Council, by a simple majority vote, decides to expel him. Hence the Nationalist representative continued to sit until nine Members were prepared to oppose him. Within the Assembly the vote on Chinese representation was initially regarded as procedural, but in 1962 was resolved to be an "important question" requiring a two-thirds majority for any change.[28]

Various attempts were made to discuss the substantive issues which lie behind this question which is treated as procedural. A memorandum of the Secretary-General in 1950[29] attempted to distinguish representation from the question of recognition by other Member States and suggested that competing claims by two rival governments should be resolved according to the test of effectiveness. Opposition to CPR representation was led by the U.S.A. but support for this position dwindled until, finally, on October 25, 1971 the General Assembly recognised the representatives of the People's Republic as "the only legitimate representative of China" and that the People's Republic is "one of the five permanent members of the Security Council."[30] The Assembly thus rejected any idea of Taiwan being given separate representation. As a result, the Assembly's own decision was quickly accepted and followed in the Security Council and the various specialised agencies.[31]

Whilst the Chinese problem has been the crucial one, it is not unique. Similar difficulties arose, for example, over Hungary and, since the representatives of the new régime were the only feasible representatives, they were allowed to sit but formal approval of their credentials has been withheld in the UN by the Credentials Committee of the Assembly taking no decision regarding the credentials (but not opposing them). Clearly the problem is not confined to the UN. Reference has already been made to the independent action of the General Conference of the ILO in

---

[28] (1962) *UN Review*, Jan., 38.

[29] S/1466. In connection with the Chinese representation problem see Quincy Wright, "The Chinese Recognition Problem" (1955) 49 A.J.I.L. 320; O'Connell, "The status of Formosa and the Chinese Recognition Problem" *Ibid.* (1956) Vol. 50, 405; Steiner "Communist China in the world community" (1961) 533 *Int. Concil.*; Stone, *Legal Controls of International Conflict* (1959), pp. 238–242; Fitzmaurice, "Chinese representation in the UN" (1952) Y.B.W.A. 36.

[30] Resol. 2758 (XXVI).

[31] (1971) *UN Yearbook* 126–137. Although the P.R.'s acceptance into the other agencies was not immediate in all cases, depending on China's own wishes. For the arrangements with the IBRD in 1980 see (1981) 20 I.L.M. 777.

rejecting the credentials of Government, Employers' and Workers' delegates from Hungary in 1958 and 1959.[32]

Prior to 1974, the view had been taken, both in the UN and in the specialised agencies, that failure to approve the credentials of South Africa (because of its refusal to comply with resolutions on Namibia) did not affect the rights and privileges of membership: that is to say, the non-approval of credentials, a procedural matter, could not be made an indirect way of achieving the same results as sanctions under Article 5, or 6, or 19 of the Charter. In 1974, having failed to get adopted a resolution to expel South Africa, the Afro-Asian bloc succeeded in having the General Assembly interpret the non-approval of credentials as, in effect, suspending South Africa from any participation in the session. That action was unconstitutional and reflects no credit on the organisation.

V. THE REPRESENTATION OF NON-STATE INTERESTS

One of the most striking developments in international organisation has been the gradual breakdown of the monopoly once enjoyed by States in representation in international organisations. This has been achieved in various ways.

First there has been the use of the device of "associate membership" to secure representation of non-State entities; the prime examples are the Council of Europe, OECD, UPU, WMO and ITU.[33] Whilst this is not confined to non-political organisations, so that one finds associate members contemplated in Article 5 of the Statute of the Council of Europe,[34] this category is not likely to appeal to sovereign States in a political organisation, the more so since it usually carries diminished rights.

The granting of observer status is yet another way of allowing the representation of non-State interests, for this status commonly allows a non-State entity to submit documents or speak in debate, though without the right to vote.

However, in an organisation with membership confined to

---

[32] *Ante*, p. 387, f.n. On the procedure of the ILO (somewhat complicated because of the tripartite structure) see Jenks, *The International Protection of Trade Union Freedom* (1957), Chap. 4. And in March 1971 the OAU failed to agree when faced with rival delegations from Uganda.

[33] *Ante*, p. 120.

[34] *Ante*, p. 171; W. Germany and the Saar were at one time associate Members.

sovereign States, the matter can be controversial. Thus, the General Assembly's invitation to the Palestinian Liberation Organisation in 1974 to participate as an observer in the Assembly and in its international conferences was disputed, as was the Security Council's invitation to the PLO to participate in its debate on the Lebanese complaint of an Israeli air attack on Palestinian refugee camps in 1975.[35]

The PLO has also been admitted as an observer to the ILO Conference and, indeed, the Conference in 1975 amended its Standing Orders to allow repesentation of liberation movements recognised by either the OAU or the Arab League.

Secondly there has been the tendency to establish organs in which non-State representatives appear, either to the exclusion of State representatives or together with them.[36] The reasons for this may well vary. If one takes the Secretariats, the reason is to ensure the "international character" of the organ and immunise it from the political control of individual States. With organs like the I.C.J. or the I.L.C. the reason is to secure an independent body of experts, capable of looking at international law objectively and representing the principal legal systems of the world rather than specific States; whether this ideal is in fact achieved by the systems of elections in the political organs of the United Nations is another matter. In some organs the reason is to secure technical direction rather than political discretion; hence in the Commission of the European Communities[37] or the quasi-executive Boards under OECD,[38] the members, whilst appointed by governments, sit in their individual capacities as experts. Within the specialised agencies, as we have seen in examining the organs of limited composition,[39] a compromise between the traditional diplomatic representation and expert repesentation is attempted by requiring the governments to appoint technically qualified representatives

[35] Much of the argument in the Security Council turned on the fact that Rules 37 and 39 of the Rules of Procedure did not cover or allow for such participation. Yet, if an organ is master of its own procedure that argument is trivial: the more fundamental point was whether the decision was contrary to the Charter's limitation of membership to States.

[36] See Myers, "Representation in Public International Organs" (1914) 8 A.J.I.L. 81; Sereni, *Organizzazione internazionale* (1959), p. 282.

[37] *Ante*, p. 210.

[38] *Ante*, p. 193.

[39] *Ante*, p. 129.

and requiring the organ to exercise its functions on behalf of the plenary organ rather than on behalf of the individual States which the members represent; this is the case with UNESCO, WHO, ITU, and to a lesser extent UPU and the financial agencies. In general, however, the use of experts is confined to subsidiary bodies acting in an advisory capacity in relation to the main political organs. Thus the largely technical bodies comprising the economic and financial organisation of the League, or administrative bodies like the Permanent Mandates Commission or the Permanent Central Opium Board or the International Commission of the Saar,[40] were the bodies in which the experts came into their own, often, significantly, voting by majority rather than the traditional unanimity of the political organs.[41] Within the UN the use of non-State representation, normally by experts, is fairly restricted; the I.L.C. is an example already mentioned, and others have been the UN Commission on the Racial Situation in the Union of South Africa, the Italian-Libyan Mixed Arbitration Commission, and the UN Administrative Tribunal.[42]

A quite distinct reason from the desirability of expert direction or advice is the recognition that individuals may represent a set of interests, distinct from State interests, which ought to be represented in the organisation if the organisation is to achieve its purpose. Hence the tripartite system of representation in the Conference and Governing Body of the ILO[43] is a recognition of the necessity to represent the interests of workers and employers separately from the representation of the State to which they may belong and which is represented by the governmental delegates. Yet another example of this kind of *raison d'être* is the parliamentary representation found in the Consultative Assembly

---

[40] Established by the Treaty of Versailles to govern the territory on behalf of the League, it consisted of one citizen of France, one Saar inhabitant (not French), and three persons of neither French nor German nationality, all five being appointed by the Council of the League.

[41] It may be recalled that many people regarded as retrogressive the decision at San Francisco to have the functional commissions of ECOSOC manned by government representatives rather than independent experts; see *ante*, p. 70.

[42] A list of all bodies established under Art. 22 of the Charter, giving their composition, can be found in the *Repertory*, Vol. 1, Annex to comment on Art. 22.

[43] *Ante*, p. 121. Another example can be seen in the representation of private operating agencies by their own experts in the Consultative Committees of the ITU; *ante*, p. 128.

of the Council of Europe[44] and, even more so, in the European Parliamentary Assembly[45]; in both cases the aim is to represent opinion in the national legislatures (or ultimately the opinion of the people, if direct suffrage is achieved), as opposed to the opinion of the government of the State.

VI. REPRESENTATION OF THE REAL INTERESTS OF STATES

1. The composition of organs as a reflection of real interest

Within the UN itself, the Security Council with its permanent membership by the "Big Five" and its non-permanent membership by States elected having regard to contribution to the maintenance of international peace and security, to the other purposes of the Organisation, and to equitable geographical distribution represents a striking example of a departure from literal adherence to "sovereign equality"; it also represents an attempt, however inadequate, to represent the States with real responsibility for the maintenance of international peace and security. In fact the difficulty is not so much one of principle as of finding the criteria appropriate to select the States which merit representation. The farther removed from the political arena, the easier such criteria are to establish. Hence the Trusteeship Council's composition of half administering authorities and half non-administering authorities, combined with the guarantee of membership for the Big Five, strikes one immediately as less open to criticism in principle. Within the specialised agencies, as we have seen,[46] the formulae vary from the 10 States "of chief industrial importance" guaranteed repesentation by governmental representatives on the Governing Body of the ILO to the complicated Article 17 of IMCO breaking up the representation of States into three categories to give a total of eighteen in the Council, and the special guarantee of membership to "eight from among the ten largest ship-owning states" in the Maritime Safety Committee. The Council of ICAO is composed of three distinct categories: States of "chief importance in air transport," other States which make the "largest contribution of the provision of

---

[44] *Ante*, p. 174.
[45] *Ante*, p. 206.
[46] *Ante*, p. 129.

facilities for international civil air navigation," and other States designated to ensure representation of the major geographical areas, totalling twenty-seven States but without assigning numbers to any given category. The UNCTAD Trade and Development Board of fifty-five Members, all elected by the Conference, has a detailed provision which ensures election in four groups—those being entitled to twenty-two, eighteen, nine and six seats respectively. The groups of States are listed in four Annexes and broadly correspond to Developing Countries, Developed Countries, Latin-American Countries and Socialist Countries. So also in the Governing Council of UNDP the allocation of the thirty-seven seats is governed by a separate Annex to General Assembly resolution 2029 (XX) of November 22, 1965. It is very largely the question of function of the organisation which determines if this kind of formula can be adopted: UNESCO, for example, is an organisation which in terms of functions defies any attempt to compose the Council by formulae other than those relating to geographical distribution.

2. Voting techniques

(a) *The decline of the rule of unanimity*
    The abandonment of the rule of unanimity, and the movement towards the rule of majority, was a necessary pre-condition to the development of voting techniques designed to represent States according to their real interests. The majority rule is first seen to be accepted in arbitral bodies,[47] though perhaps more as a submission to the idea of "neutral"determination than to that of majority rule. Within the ad hoc political conferences it remained, virtually throughout the nineteenth century, acceptable for adoption of agendas or procedural questions generally, but not for substantive questions.[48] It was within the more technical public unions that the majority rule came into general use and, significantly, especially in those which favoured technical or expert representation rather than diplomatic representation. The UPU (1874) and the International Commission for Aerial Navigation

---

[47] *Ante*, p. 259.
[48] Dickinson, *op. cit.* Chap. 8; Riches, *Majority rule in international organisation* (1940), *passim;* Wellington Koo, *Voting procedure in international political organisations* (1947), *passim.*

(1919)[49] even exercised a certain legislative power by majority; the ITU, the Metric Union, the International Office of Public Health (1907) and the ILO also adopted majority voting, although they only had powers to act *ad referendum,* so that no Member became bound by the majority decision. Bodies with administrative functions such as the Commission for Cape Spartel Lighthouse (1865), the Central Commission for the Navigation of the Rhine (1815), the Governing Commission under the Saar Statute (1919), the Permanent Sugar Commission (1902) and the Permanent Central Opium Board (1925) similarly adopted a majority vote. In the few cases where unanimity was preserved (together with diplomatic representation), notably the Union for the Protection of Industrial Property (1883), the Union for the Protection of Literary and Artistic Works (1886) and the International Institute of Agriculture (1905), the rigours of the unanimity rule were mitigated by the practice of abstention from voting, by the authorisation of "partial" agreements[50] and allowing States to enter reservations in respect of agreements or conventions concluded.[51]

In the political conferences progress was necessarily slower. The rules of procedure of the great conferences at The Hague in 1899 and 1907 required unanimity on all really important questions, although this met with criticism at the time,[52] and at the Paris Peace Conference of 1919 unanimity was preserved in respect of the States entitled to take decisions.[53] In the course of drafting the Covenant of the League Lord Robert Cecil declared that "all international decisions must by the nature of things be

---

[49] Established by the Paris Convention, this body used a majority vote varying from three-quarters to simple majority according to the nature of the question, *i.e.* two-thirds for the budget adoption, three-quarters for amendment of the Annexes, simple majority for recommendations to Members.

[50] See Art. 15 of the Industrial Property Convention; note that the same technique is used even to-day to avoid the restrictions of the unanimity rule in the Committee of Ministers of the Council of Europe, *ante*, p. 173.

[51] See Art. 17 of the Convention of the Union for the Protection of Literary and Artistic Works; the unsatisfactory result of breaking up the unity of the agreements concluded led to a severe reduction of the capacity to enter reservations in 1928: see Riches, *op. cit.* p. 46.

[52] Riches, *op. cit.* p. 287; committees could, however, make recommendations to the plenary by majority.

[53] Participating States were divided into three groups, of which only the first (U.S.A., Britain, France, Italy and Spain) were entitled to attend all sessions: for the rules of procedure see (1919) 13 A.J.I.L. Suppl. 109.

unanimous,"[54] so that it is not surprising to find the unanimity rule generally preserved in the Covenant in Article 5. However, within the Assembly, on certain matters a majority sufficed[55] and the express provisions of the Covenant (*e.g.* admission of new Members, Article 1 (2); amendments, Article 26 (1); procedural questions, Article 5 (2); election of non-permanent members of the Council) were supplemented by practice; hence abstention developed as a matter of practice, as did the distinction between decisions and a "voeux" (the latter requiring only a majority), and committees normally took decisions by a majority. The Council adhered even more strictly to the unanimity rule, but exceptions did exist, as in the making of reports on disputes likely to lead to a rupture (Art. 15 (4)), and in the exclusion from the vote of any party to a dispute (Art. 15 (6)). The treaties of peace also imposed on the Council a number of functions to be exercised by majority vote. Yet these were the exceptions; the normal rule was most certainly one of unanimity.

It is in the light of this that the UN Charter appears as a fairly radical break with tradition, for there the majority vote becomes the rule and only in respect of permanent Members, voting on a non-procedural question within the Security Council, does unanimity remain as the kind of defensive mechanism which is seen operating in the veto. Unanimity has, as we have seen,[56] virtually disappeared from the specialised agencies. It remains in a few organisations of limited membership, as for example in the Committee of Ministers of the Council of Europe, the Council of

---

[54] Miller, *The Drafting of the Covenant,* Vol. 1, p. 161.

[55] For a full list of such matters see Riches, *op. cit.* pp. 20–29; and see Stone, (1933) 14 B.Y.B.I.L. 18.

[56] *Ante,* pp. 129–139. In conferences convened under the auspices of an international organisation the general tendency is to adopt rules of procedure modelled on those of the organisation, but the nature of the conference may well be the determining factor; see statement by Yuen-li Liang on the UN practice, sometimes adopting simple majority, sometimes two-thirds, in' (1959) 1 *Yearbook of the I.L.C.* 50. This was made in connection with the statement that the simple majority was the *normal* rule at international conferences drafting treaties in the Fitzmaurice *Report on the Law of Treaties* (A/CN.4/101), new Art. 6; for the discussion thereon see *ibid.* pp.40–54. The abandonment of unanimity in codification conferences goes back to The Hague in 1930; it may well not be an unmitigated blessing since it may produce a text which a large minority may be unable to ratify, or can only ratify with reservations. See Rosenne, *loc. cit.* pp. 314–315; Johnson, "The Conclusions of International Conferences" (1959) 35 B.Y.B.I.L. 1.

OECD, the Councils of the European Communities (but only in respect of the most important decisions), the Council of the Arab League, COMECON and the Political Consultative Committee of the Warsaw Treaty Organisation. Obviously, the smaller the membership the more justification, in principle, for the retention of the unanimity rule.

The adoption of equality of voting and the majority rule is not without its problems. In the General Assembly it has led to some unrealism in the resolutions adopted. The first UNCTAD Conference in Geneva produced an imposing set of "principles,"[57] adopted by the overwhelming vote of the developing countries, which for their execution required the active assistance of the developed countries but which were, by and large, unacceptable to them. In this connection it is of extreme interest to note that General Assembly resolution 1995 (XIX), in providing a constitution for UNCTAD, maintained equality of voting and a two-thirds majority rule on matters of substance but, at the same time, established an elaborate system of conciliation procedures which can be requested by groups of members *before* any vote on a substantive matter occurs. The conciliation committee's essential task is to produce proposals which have a realistic chance of true acceptance by the Conference (or Board)—"true" being used in the sense of support from members having the capacity to give effect to the proposals—and to avoid proposals which, whilst capable of securing the two-thirds majority, could never find such true acceptance. This is symptomatic of the present trend towards a search for "consensus" as opposed to a simple reliance on the results of formal voting.[58]

A few organisations allow for postal voting; for example, the IMF (Art. XII, 2 (f)), Bank (Art. V, 2 (e)), WMO (Art. 5 (b)). Somewhat surprisingly, IMCO, which in Article 43 uses the phrase "present and voting" and thus would seem to exclude such a technique, has since 1970 used postal voting in the Council on a trial basis.

---

[57] (1964) *UN Year Book* 198–201.
[58] See Jenks, "Unanimity, the veto, weighted voting, special and simple majorities consensus as modes of decision in international organisation" in *Cambridge Legal Essays* (1965), 48. The conciliation technique, aiming at consensus, was adopted in the Rules of Procedure of the UN Law of the Sea Conference: A/CONF. 62/30/Rev. 2, Rule 37.

(b) *Variations in the rule of equality of voting power*

Departures from the somewhat unrealistic rule of "one State—one vote" were made in two ways, and again it fell to the technical international public unions to pave the way along which political organisations followed very much more slowly.

The first way was by allowing separate representation to some of the colonies or separate territorial units of a State; this device we have already noted as a means of breaking through the monopoly of State representation. The other effect of the device, with which we are now concerned, was that it introduced a system of plural voting. Organisations like the UPU, ITU, Metric Union, International Institute of Agriculture, International Wine Office and International Office of Chemistry, amongst others, adopted this device. Occasionally, as in the International Wireless Telegraph Union of 1906, a limit (in that case six) would be placed on the number of votes so acquired. In one sense the separate repesentation of the members of the British Commonwealth in the League of Nations, or the separate representation of Byelorussia S.R. and Ukraine S.R. in the UN may be regarded as a perpetuation of this technique, yet it clearly becomes a matter of separate representation *simpliciter,* and not plural voting, when the separate entities act independently and not as additional votes automatically cast with the former parent State.

The second way was by weighting the votes of Members to represent their real interest. Weighting has been defined as "a system which assigns to members of international organisations votes proportioned on the basis of predetermined relevant criteria."[59] The crucial problem is, of course, to find acceptable criteria by which the weighting can be done. A simple solution, adopted at an early stage in the International Office of Public Health and in the International Institute of Agriculture and now continued in the financial agencies of the UN, is to weight the voting powers of a Member according to its financial contribution. The I.I.A. had five classes for the purpose of budgetary contributions and, whilst a Member was free to select its own class,

[59] McIntyre, "Weighted voted in International Organisations" (1954) 8 *International Organisation,* 484; see also Sohn, "Weighting of votes in International Assemblies" (1944) *Am. Pol. Sci. Review,* 1192, and "Multiple representation in International Assemblies" (1946) 40 A.J.I.L. 71; Weinschel, "The Doctrine of Equality and its recent modifications" *ibid.* (1951) Vol. 45, 417.

the votes ranged from five to one according to the class selected. The system had the merit of linking power with financial responsibility. Within the present financial agencies of the UN the votes are weighted according to the share of a Member in the operating capital (not the budget); for example, in the Bank each member of the Board of Governors has 250 votes plus one additional vote for each share of stock held (par value $100,000).[60]

In the International Telecommunications Satellite Organisation (INTELSAT)[61] the voting power of each Governor is determined by the investment share of the Signatory (or group of Signatories) he represents: and these investment shares in turn are based upon the degree of usage by the Signatory of the space segment for communication purposes, subject to the maximum limit of 40 per cent. of the votes for any one Governor (thereby preventing U.S. dominance). The International Maritime Satellite Organisation (INMARSAT)[62] gives to each representative on the Council a voting participation equal to the investment share or shares he represents, but subject to a maximum of 25 per cent. If his share exceeds 25 per cent. the signatory he represents must either offer the excess share for sale to other signatories, or distribute the excess votes equally to all other signatories.

The new International Fund for Agricultural Development (IFAD)[63] has a novel distribution of votes in the Executive Board. A bloc of votes is allocated to each region (OECD, OPEC, Developing Countries 600 votes each bloc) and then, within the region, the bloc vote is divided amongst the members of the bloc by a dual formula: a certain percentage of votes being divided equally, the remainder according to financial contribution. The system is very far removed from the traditional one State—one vote rule.

Another, basically similar but simpler technique is seen in the

---

[60] Art. 5 (3); compare Art. 6 (3) of the International Development Association (500 votes plus one additional vote for each £5,000 of subscription), and Art. 12 (5) of the Fund (same as Bank), and Art. 4 (3) of the I.F.C. (250 votes plus one for each share of $1,000). Note that the European Investment Bank does not adopt this technique but weights by the number of Directors allowed to each Member.

[61] 23 U.S.T. 3813, Agreement of August 20, 1971, Art. 9.

[62] (1976) 15 I.L.M. 1052, Agreement of September 3, 1976, Art. 14.

[63] A new specialised agency established by Agreement of December 20, 1976: (1976) 15 I.L.M. 922.

commodity councils such as the Wheat and Sugar Councils. For example, in the International Wheat Agreement of 1959[64] the Exporting countries are assigned 1,000 votes in the Council, and the Importing countries 1,000. The allocation of specific numbers of votes to particular countries is by reference to the guaranteed sales or purchases for the current year.

In some cases a specific number of votes is assigned to each participating Member in the basic agreement. This technique goes back to the Central Commission for the Navigation of the Rhine (1815) which allocated unequal votes for the purpose of electing the Chief Inspector. Today this is done in the European Communities and in the Consultative Assembly of the Council of Europe. To take the European Economic Community by way of example, in the Parliament, the Members are accorded a number of representatives, each with one vote, varying from 81 in the case of France, Germany and Italy to 6 in the case of Luxembourg. In the Council of Ministers the votes are weighted amongst the Ministers, ranging from ten votes to two.[65] Decisions require 45 votes out of the total of 65 although, in the case of a decision where no proposal has been made by the Commission, at least 6 Members must vote in favour.[66] A similar technique is seen in the 1964 Agreement establishing interim arrangements for a global commercial communications system.[67] Within the Interim Committee established by this treaty the votes are allocated according to budgetary quotas, and whilst the Committee is directed to "endeavour to act unanimously" (Art. V), in cases where this is not possible there is a detailed category of decisions which can be taken only if the decision has "the concurrence of representatives whose total votes exceed the vote of the representative with the largest vote by not less than 12.5."

It is notable that, outside the financial organisations and IFAD, no specialised agency has adopted a weighted voting system of the kind illustrated above. Weighting is achieved indirectly in allocating only to certain Members a right to representation in various

[64] Peaslee, Vol. 11, p. 1528. See footnotes 61–63.
[65] Arts. 138, 148.
[66] Compare Art. 28 of ECSC which, for decisions other than those requiring unanimity or a qualified vote, requires the vote of one repesentative of one of the States producing 20 per cent. of the total value of coal and steel produced in the Community (*i.e.* France or Germany).
[67] Convenient text in Jenks, *Space Law* (1965), Appendix V.

organs,[68] just as it is achieved indirectly in the Security Council by giving to the vote of the permanent Members more *effect* (*i.e.* the veto) than the vote of other Members. Otherwise the tendency has been to rely more on the requirement of specific majorities for certain decisions, in part because in many organisations the success of a resolution may depend more on the number of States supporting it than on the weight of votes that can be collected for it.[69] It is probably for this reason that, in some cases where weighted voting does exist, as in the Board of Governors of the Bank, a formal vote is rarely taken, and the preferred method is for the Chairman to take the sense of the meeting. However, the larger part of the explanation must remain the impossibility of getting criteria for weighting accepted in a political organisation.[70]

VII. AMENDMENT PROCEDURES

The essentially dynamic character of a constitutional text, as opposed to the normal multilateral treaty, has led to a general recognition of the need for a specific clause envisaging revision or amendment of the text.[71] The procedures for revision are by no means uniform but may be appropriately discussed at this juncture since they illustrate yet another sphere in which inroads have been made on the principle of State equality. Before proceeding to a discussion of the three main types of amendment clause, two general observations may be made. First, whilst amendments are usually carried out by the established organs of the organisation, it is sometimes envisaged that a special "review conference" may be convened to deal with any comprehensive proposals for amendment: this is precisely what is envisaged in Article 109 of the Charter, in Article 18 (B) of the IAEA Statute, and in Article 236 of EEC. The extreme contrast is afforded by the technique in the UPU whereby, in the intervals between the meetings of Congress,

---

[68] *Ante*, p. 407.

[69] See the statement by the spokesman for the Dept. of State in the Hearings of the Senate Financial Committee on the proposed ITO Charter: *U.S. Congress (80th, 1st Sess.) Senate, Committee on Finance, Hearings* (1947), pp. 532–533.

[70] For the democratic, but politically unacceptable, formula which would base votes in the General Assembly on population figures, see Clark and Sohn, *World Peace through World Law* (1960), 2nd ed. revised, pp. 20–23, 25–31.

[71] Phillips, "Constitutional Revision in the specialised agencies" (1968) 62 A.J.I.L. 654; Zacklin, *The amendment of the constitutive instruments of the UN and Specialised Agencies* (1968).

amendments may be proposed by Members and agreement is obtained by circulation of the proposals by the Bureau.[72]

The second general observation is that normally the amendment procedure involves two stages: the first is the vote of adoption within the organ or conference, the second is the depositing of ratifications by Members. In some cases it will be observed that though unanimity is not required for the first, it is for the second in that ratification by all Members is required for the entry into force of the amendment; hence one is dealing with a "consent" principle and not a "legislative" principle. At the other extreme only the first stage is required in that the amendment enters into force upon adoption by the organ, and there is no second stage[73]: the first stage may be either by majority vote or by unanimity, *i.e.* either the "legislative" or the "consent" principle.

1. The "consent" principle

As might be expected, the principle that amendments to the constitution require the consent of all the Members is the older principle. It was to be found in the League (Art. 26)[74] and is still found in Article 94 (a) of ICAO which specifies that an amendment adopted by a two-thirds vote of the Assembly (first stage) comes into force only when ratified by not less than two-thirds of the Members (second stage) and then only "in respect of States which have ratified such amendment." The Council of Europe which, in Article 41, envisages amendments coming into force upon ratification by two-thirds of the Members, does so on the condition that the first stage of adoption by the Committee of Ministers has been by *unanimous* vote; even under the alternative procedure for amendments to Articles 23–25, 38 and 39 (where only the first stage is required in that the amendments come into force, once adopted by the Committee and

---

[72] Arts. 29 and 30. Amendments to the proposals circulated are, naturally enough, not admitted. For general discussion of amendment procedures see Schwelb, "The Amending procedure of constitutions of international organisations" (1954) 31 B.Y.B.I.L. 49.

[73] As in Art. 95 of ECSC; Art. 235 of EEC; Art. 41 of the Council of Europe; Art. 20 of FAO.

[74] A revision of Art. 26, allowing the Assembly to adopt amendments by a three-quarters majority vote, including the votes of all members of the Council, such amendments to come into force when ratified by a majority of the Assembly, including all the Council, never came into effect: it failed to do so because of the stringency of the old amendment clause.

the Assemby, by certification by the Secretary-General) the unanimous vote of the Committee again ensures that all Members agree to the amendment. Similarly in EEC, whether the amendments are enacted by the Council on a unanimous vote (Art. 235), or adopted in a special conference and then ratified by all Members (Art. 236), the requirement of consent is there.

2. The "legislative" principle

The contrasting principle is that which allows a majority of Members to adopt an amendment which becomes binding on the dissenting minority. This is the principle adopted in the UN in that, under Article 108, after adoption by two-thirds of the Assembly and ratification by two-thirds of the Members including all the permanent Members of the Security Council, amendments enter into force for *all* Members. WHO (Art. 7), UNESCO (Art. 13)[75] and the IAEA (Art. 18) all envisage entry into force of amendments for *all* Members even when adoption, or ratification where necessary, has been by only two-thirds of the Members.

3. A combination of the two principles

A very rational development has been that of differentiating between amendments so as to govern the minor amendments by the legislative principle but the major amendments by the consent principle. To take the example of FAO, Article 20 distinguishes between amendments not involving new obligations for Members which enter into force for all Members upon adoption by two-thirds of the Conference, and other amendments which require the same adoption but followed by ratification by two-thirds and subject to the condition that amendments enter into force for each Member ratifying and thereafter for each Member on accepting the amendment. WMO (Art. 28) is similar; and the Convention, the General Regulations and the Agreements of UPU differentiate by stating the articles requiring unanimity and providing for a two-thirds or even a simple majority in other defined cases. The Fund (Art. 17) and the Bank (Art. 18) also distinguish between amendments requiring majority approval and

[75] Here the second stage of "acceptance" is only necessary for amendments involving "fundamental alterations" to the Constitution or new obligations for Members: other amendments enter into force upon adoption by two-thirds of the Conference.

those requiring unanimous approval. In ECSC the consent principle, involving ratification by all Members, is applied to normal amendments (Art. 96), but a special procedure is envisaged under Article 95 for modifications arising out of "unforeseen difficulties" revealed in the experience with the treaty or due to profound changes in economic or technical conditions. This special procedure envisages proposal of the amendments by five-sixths of the Council and Commission jointly and approval by three-quarters of the Assembly, including two-thirds of the total membership.[76] The amendments then enter into force for all.

4. The problem of the Members declining to accept an amendment

The refusal of a Member to accept an amendment can occur either in the case where the consent principle is applied but, a number having voted for an amendment, ratification is refused (as might happen under the League formula)[77] or, more commonly, where the legislative principle is applied and a Member refuses to accept the will of the majority. The inconvenience of allowing a minority of Members to continue their membership under conditions no longer obtaining for the majority needs no stress, and its solution lies, as we have seen, either in having a withdrawal clause which allows the Member to withdraw or, to deal with the recalcitrant Member, an expulsion clause. As we have seen,[78] considering the generality of the problem, these clauses are found relatively infrequently and this suggests that a good deal of faith is placed in the powers of political persuasion as opposed to clear-cut legal powers of terminating membership.

5. Variation as distinguished from amendment

Very exceptionally, authority is given to some organ to apply a principle or rule different from the one established in the constitutional text. There is no change of the text, so that the process is not strictly one of amendment; yet a variation from the

---

[76] A reference to the Court intervenes between the proposal and the adoption to ensure that, in fact and in law, the amendment is to deal with the "unforeseen difficulties" referred to in the article.

[77] Or under the Antarctica Treaty Organisation, Art. 12 (1), which provides for amendment by unanimous vote but compulsory withdrawal of a non-ratifying Member: Peaslee, Vol. 1, p. 29.

[78] *Ante*, pp. 390, 392.

constitutional text is permitted. Examples can be seen in Arts. V, ss. 7 and 9, and XXVI, s. 3 of the IMF, where such power of variation is conferred on the Board of Governors or Executive Directors acting by special majorities.[79]

VIII. BUDGETS[80]

There is a certain attraction in the idea of a common budget for the UN and the entire family of specialised agencies. Certainly some degree of liaison between them and the UN on budgetary matters seems desirable. Hence, whilst in the constitutions of the Fund and the Bank nothing is said on this score, the constitutions of other agencies reflect to a greater or lesser extent this idea of budgetary co-operation. The ILO envisages "such financial and budgetary arrangements with the UN as may appear appropriate" (Art. 13 (1)); UNESCO anticipates that any agreement with the UN may "provide for the approval and financing of the budget of the Organisation by the General Assembly of the United Nations" (Art. IX). As has been seen, the agreements with the UN concluded by the various specialised agencies envisage varying degrees of budgetary co-operation, ranging from full budgetary integration to the mere submission of the budget to the General Assembly, the latter having the right to make recommendations to the specialised agency concerned, although even this is lacking in the agreements with the Fund and Bank which stress the "autonomy" of the agencies and contemplate the submission of copies of the budget for information purposes only.[81] At the present, therefore, there is no common budget and the agencies are virtually autonomous. There are, of course, practical difficulties in the way of a common budget; for example, membership is not uniform. The overriding obstacle is more likely to be the desire for independence of the agencies.

In dealing with budgetary problems our main emphasis will

---

[79] See Gold, "The amendment and variation of their Charters by International Organisations" (1973) 1 *Revue Belge de D.I. 50.*

[80] See generally Singer, *Financing International Organisation: The UN Budget Process* (1961); Mangone and Srivastava, "Budgeting for the UN" (1958) 12 *International Organisation,* 473; Stoessinger, "Financing the UN" (1961) 535 *International Conciliation;* Jenks, "Financing of International Institutions" (1943) 38 T.G.S. 93.

[81] *Ante,* p. 68.

necessarily, if only for reasons of space, be placed on the UN: reference to other organisations will, however, be made by way of contrast where important differences exist.

1. The budget programme

The budget of an international organisation will normally include the administrative costs of running the organisation (salaries of staff, printing, costs of conference services, etc.) and costs which result from a decision of policy that a particular activity be undertaken. Within the United Nations the relation between policy and cost is emphasised by the provisions in the Financial Regulations which provide that no organ "shall take a decision involving expenditure unless it has before it a report from the Secretary-General on the administrative and financial implications of the proposal,"[82] and that, where the proposed expenditure cannot be made from existing funds, it shall not be incurred until the General Assembly has made the necessary appropriation.[83]

The preparation of the budget estimates is the task of the Secretary-General; such estimates will include the original estimates representing the cost of implementing decisions taken during the financial year to which the budget relates, revised budget estimates to cover new decisions, and supplementary estimates to cover "unforeseen or extraordinary expenses" arising after the budget has been voted.[84] In fact the Secretary General is authorised in advance to spend up to $2 million on such expenses, drawing on the Working Capital Fund.

The estimates are reviewed successively by the Advisory Committee on Administrative and Budgetary Questions, composed of nine representatives of States, the Fifth Committee of the Assembly, and finally by the Assembly. In one sense the Advisory

---

[82] Financial Reg. 13.1.
[83] Financial Reg. 13.2. There is an express exception for the case when the Sec.-Gen. certifies that provision can be made under the head "unforeseen and extraordinary expenses". The Assembly's concern over the Organisation incurring large, unforeseen expenses as a result of decisions taken by the Security Council in order to maintain international peace and security can be seen in its resolutions in the 15th and 16th Sessions requiring a special session of the Assembly to be convened where more than $10 m. is involved.
[84] The financial year begins on January 1 but most organisations now operate on a biennial budget cycle, although supplementary estimates are voted for one year at a time.

Committee and the Fifth Committee duplicate each other's functions—the former has been called "little more than a Fifth Committee in microcosm"[85]—yet the limited size of the former does enable it to spend more time on the budgetary problems than a plenary committee could manage. A critical question has always been how far the Advisory Committee and the Fifth Committee can, by reducing or eliminating an appropriation, interfere with or reverse a policy decision of another Main Committee or even the Assembly itself; in principle they should have no such power, and in the last resort the Assembly would be free to overrule and re-instate any items so affected. Clearly the final approval of the budget is, under Article 17 (1) of the Charter, a matter for the General Assembly, acting by a two-thirds majority vote.

Within the specialised agencies the preparation of the estimate is, similarly, a task of necessity entrusted to the administrative head of the organisation. This is expressly recognised in the constitutions of the ILO, FAO, WHO and IMCO. Even in organisations like ICAO, where it is said that the Council submits the budget, in practice the preparation of the initial proposals must lie with the Secretary-General. The actual approval or acceptance of the budget is a different matter, and this, without exception, is a matter for the plenary organ. Where variation does occur is in the extent to which some organ of limited composition intervenes in the process. For example, whereas in the ILO and the FAO the Director-General submits directly to the plenary organ, in WHO and IMCO the executive head submits through the Board and Council respectively. In IMCO, where, as we have seen, the Council is given a strong position generally in relation to the Assembly, the former is expressly empowered to submit its comments and recommendations to the Assembly (Art. 40).

2. Apportionment of expenses

It will rarely be necessary to apportion the total cost of the activities of an organisation amongst the Members, for most will have, on the credit side, a limited income from sales of publications or even of stamps. The European Communities afford the prime example of organisations with sources of income independent of the contributions of members. This income is

[85] Singer, *op. cit.* p. 176.

derived from agricultural levies, the external tariffs, and part of the value-added tax. The collection of these taxes is done by Member States, who deduct ten per cent. to cover their Administrative costs.[86] Certain activities may be self-supporting, as for example when the UN raised funds for the clearance of the Suez Canal in 1956 by levying a tax on shipping through the Canal. Exceptionally an organisation may be entirely self-supporting, and even have to deal with the problem of allocation of net income. The Fund, Bank and IFC are all operating agencies which derive an income from charges on transactions, income from certain short-term investments and, in the case of the IFC, more general investments.[87] They therefore have no need to resort to budgetary contributions from Members, and the *contributions* of Members to these organisations, in the form of quotas or shares, should be distinguished sharply from the budgetary contributions made by Members in other organisations, for they are not used for the upkeep of the organisation itself, but rather form the backing for the financial operations of the organisation. The European Coal and Steel Community is also self-financing by means of the levy on coal and steel production paid by enterprises to the Commission.

By and large, however, international organisations necessarily depend on contributions from Members for the financing of their activities. Whilst the size of their budgets makes a favourable comparison with the expenditure of States on armaments, the total figures are not inconsiderable. For the biennium 1980/81 the General Assembly appropriated over $1 billion.[88]

The problem therefore arises of how the net cost shall be divided between Members, and it is at this stage that one appreciates how very far the principle of equality of States is from affording a workable solution to this problem.

The ITU and UPU follow a system whereby a number of

---

[86] *Ante*, p. 212. One must distinguish loans from income: the loans will have to be serviced from income and serve only as a temporary means of acquiring capital; for example, see the Bond issues by the UN to the value of $200 m. (authorised by the G.A. in 1961 by Resol. 1739 (XVI) to relieve the pressure caused by defaults on contributions towards UNEF and ONUC) carrying 2 per cent. interest and repayable over 25 years. For a survey of such borrowing techniques see Salmon, *Le rôle des organisations internationales en matière de prêts et d'emprunts* (1958).

[87] For a list of organisations which have in the past derived an income from their activities see Jenks, *loc. cit.* p. 93.

[88] Resol. 34/303 of December 20, 1979.

"classes" are established, fourteen in the case of ITU and seven in UPU. Each Member or associate Member is, according to the class in which it finds itself, obliged to pay so many "units" of the total budget. In the ITU the Members, on joining, simply inform the Secretary-General of the class in which they wish to be included. In the UPU the class is agreed upon between the applicant for membership and the Swiss Government.

The more usual solution is to fix a percentage quota for each Member: this may be done in the constituent instrument, as in Article 200 of the European Economic Community, or more usually it may be done by the plenary organ[89] and made subject to review in the light of fluctuations in the number of Members or the relative prosperity of the Members, as is the case under Article 17 (2) of the Charter.

In general nothing is said of the criteria by which the plenary organ shall determine the respective quotas of the Members. Within the UN the criterion adopted has been "capacity to pay,"[90] this being deduced from total national income, *per capita* income, and from evidence of economic dislocation due to war and ability to acquire foreign currency. The United States, which has in practice borne the major burden of financing the UN, argued that the principle of sovereign equality called for maximum and minimum limits to a Member's contribution. By 1973 the Assembly had accepted the principle that one-quarter of the budget should be the maximum that any one Member should be required to pay, and from 1955 the Assembly accepted the further principle that the *per capita* contribution of any Member should not exceed the *per capita* contribution of the Member bearing the

---

[89] It may be noted that, in the ILO, it is by a two-thirds vote of the *government* delegates that all budgetary questions are settled, hence the "tripartite" vote is ousted in view of the fact that it is the governments alone which assume the financial responsibilities. Organisations such as ICAO, IMCO or WMO, for example, in which the plenary organ does not meet annually either have to vote a budget on a biennial basis or delegate to an executive organ the power to approve expenditures within limits imposed by the plenary organ.

[90] This is not the only feasible basis, of course. Contributions to the Pan-American Railway Congress were based on miles of railroad in operation in each country; population has provided the basis for the Inter-American Statistical Institute; equal apportionment was used in the Central Rhine Commission and the Caribbean Commission.

highest assessment (*i.e.* the U.S.A.).[91] So far as a *minimum* contribution is concerned, the Assembly has determined this at 0.01 per cent. Revision of scales is, in practice, an annual task of the Committee on Contributions, even though the Assembly's rules of procedure (Rule 161) contemplate revision only every three years.

It need not be assumed that *all* expenses of an organisation have to be brought within one overall budget to be apportioned according to one set of scales. The ITU had to deal with the problem of financing the different levels of conferences (plenipotentiary, administrative and regional), the Board and the Consultative Committee; this became a problem because the participation of Members was not uniform, nor was it even confined to Members or Associate Members, for private operating agencies and international organisations took part in the Consultative Committees.[92] Hence the solution was adopted of distinguishing "ordinary expenses" from "extraordinary expenses." The first category included expenses arising from meetings of the Administrative Council, the salaries of the staff and other expenses of the General Secretariat, the International Frequency Registration Board, the International Consultative Committee, and laboratories and technical installations created by the Union. Such "ordinary" expenses were borne by all Members and Associate Members. The "extraordinary" expenses pertained to plenipotentiary conferences, administrative conferences, meetings of the International Consultative Committees or special tasks entrusted to the Bureau and were borne by Members according to the contribution class into which they have been placed by Congress; private operating agencies and international organisations also contributed on the basis of participation and according to the class they had chosen.[93]

Within the United Nations certain programmes were set aside as "extra-budgetary" programmes to which Members would contribute voluntarily and not as part of their normal budgetary commitment: UNICEF, UNRWA, UNITAR are cases in point.

---

[91] The largest contributors are U.S.A. (25 per cent.), U.S.S.R. (11.1 per cent.), Japan (9.58 per cent.), F.R. Germany (8.31 per cent.). Over 70 Members pay the minimum contribution.

[92] *Ante*, p. 128.

[93] See Art. 21 of the UPU Regulations of 1964.

417

Some programmes were in part financed in this way: the Expanded Programme of Technical Assistance, the ofice of the UN High Commissioner for Refugess are examples. The crucial financial issue which arose for the UN became, however, the financing of UNEF and ONUC. For UNEF a "special account" was opened, and for ONUC an "ad hoc" account. In relation to UNEF the Assembly decided to apportion expenses "in accordance with the scale of assessments adopted by the General Assembly for contributions to the annual budget . . . ."[94] Whilst this did not attempt to account for the entire cost (for considerable voluntary subscriptions were also made) the pattern was clear, and it was this same pattern which was eventually adopted for ONUC.[95] It was implicit in this pattern (and had been contended by the Secretary-General all along) that the expenses of both operations were "expenses of the Organisation" within the meaning of Article 17 (2) of the Charter and for which, therefore, a legal obligation to pay existed. By the end of 1961 the UN faced a deficit of $150 m. due to defaulting Members. The reasons for refusal to pay varied[96]; some States opposed the legality of the operations, some the principle that the cost of the operations was a collective responsibility to be assumed on the normal basis for assessment. Finally the matter was referred to the I.C.J. by the General Assembly in the form of a request for an advisory opinion on whether the expenditures authorised by the successive resolutions of the General Assembly "constitute 'expenses of the Organisation' within the meaning of Art. 17 (2) of the Charter of the United Nations."

The opinion of the Court[97] of July 20, 1962, on *Certain Expenses of the United Nations* distinguished three possible questions: first, the identification of what are "expenses of the Organisation";

[94] Resol. 1089 (XI), December 21, 1956.
[95] Resol. 1619 (XVI), April 21, 1961; however, by para. 7 Belgium was called on to make a "substantial" contribution, and by para. 8 the assessments of Members whose normal assessments ranged from 0.04 to 0.25, or who received technical assistance under the Expanded programme in 1960 were reduced by 80 per cent.; Members receiving technical assistance and assessed normally above 1.26 were reduced by 50 per cent.
[96] See the full analysis in the *Report of the Working Group of Fifteen on the Examination of the Administration and Budgetary Procedure of the UN* (A/4971), November 15, 1961.
[97] (1962) *I.C.J. Reports* 155. On the question of the division of powers between the S.G. and the G.A., with which the opinions dealt at length, see *ante*, p. 51.

secondly, the question of apportionment; and, thirdly, the interpretation of the phrase "shall be borne by the Members." The Court stressed that it was concerned with only the first of these questions. The Court rejected the distinction alleged by some States between "administrative" and "operational" budgets, just as it rejected the Soviet contention that financing of measures designed to maintain international peace and security was a matter for the Security Council and not the General Assembly. It then proceeded to examine whether the particular expenses incurred fell within the purposes of the United Nations, for it conceded that they would have to do so to qualify as "expenses of the Organisation." Applying a presumption that the actions taken were *intra vires* (since it fell to each organ to determine, in the first place, its own jurisdiction), the Court found that the expenses of both UNEF and ONUC were "expenses of the Organisation" within the meaning of Article 17 (2) which, therefore, the Assembly had the right to apportion. The Court did *not* advise that the method of apportionment must be the same as that for the regular budget.

3. The effect of apportionment

At least until the dispute over UNEF and ONUC, the principle had generally been accepted that, once apportioned, the budgetary contribution became payable as a matter of legal obligation.[98] In the *Expenses* case the Court did not, strictly, deal with this question, although it instanced decisions under Article 17 as examples of decisions of the Assembly which have "dispositive force and effect,"[99] and referred to its previous opinion[1] that once

---

[98] For this reason the kind of provision which is found in Art. 16 (9) of the ITU General Regulations, imposing an interest rate of 3 per cent. p.a. for the first six months and 6 per cent. p.a. from the beginning of the seventh month on amounts due from Members is, whilst exceptional, perfectly logical. Once paid, the sums become the property of the organisation in question and do not remain the property of the contributor entrusted to the organisation for the achievement of its aims and purposes.Hence it should follow that any surplus is not, as a matter of right, returnable to contributing Members; however, the League's financial regulations provided for such a return, and have been criticised on that account. Similarly, when withdrawal is permitted, it is frequently provided that this is subject to the fulfilment of any outstanding financial obligations of the Member towards the organisation; there is no question of a right to a refund.

[99] p. 163.

[1] *Effect of Awards of the UN Administrative Tribunal* (1954) *I.C.J. Reports* 59.

obligations towards third parties are incurred by the Secretary-General, on the authority of the S.C. or G.A., the Assembly "has no alternative but to honour these engagements."[2] In his separate opinion Sir Gerald Fitzmaurice regarded the legal obligation as arising from the decision to take a given course of action, and not from the decision on apportionment: hence, in his view, the obligation arose from Article 25 when such decisions were taken by the S.C. Even when action was undertaken on a mere recommendation of the G.A., then, for Sir Gerald, the obligation was equally imposed on all Members, whether dissenting or not, for such was the essence of a majority vote.[3]

Despite this, certain Member States, which are not strictly bound by an advisory opinion,[4] did not regard this opinion as imposing a legal obligation to pay the contributions, and even though the Assembly "accepted" the opinion by resolution of December 19, 1962, by 76 votes to 17, with eight abstentions. The crucial test came in 1965 when the S.G. reported that 16 States, including France and the U.S.S.R., were in arrears in an amount exceeding their assessed contributions for the preceding two years. However, as we have seen[5] the General Assembly declined to apply the sanction of deprivation of vote in the Assembly under Article 19 of the Charter. It may be added that the Committee of 33 has so far failed to produce an acceptable formula for the financing of peace-keeping operations.[6] Some subsequent peace-keeping operations, like UNYOM and UNFICYP, have had to be financed on a purely voluntary basis, although the later operations like UNEF II, UNDOF and UNIFIL have involved compulsory assessments.

It may nevertheless be asserted that the numerous provisions on suspension or even expulsion from membership as a sanction for non-payment of budgetary contributions[7] reinforce the view that the obligation to pay is a legal obligation. The refusal to pay

[2] p. 170.
[3] p. 208 *et seq*. Note his qualifications where the resolution consists solely of the provision of finance, or when the functions are merely permissive and not mandatory.
[4] *Ante*, p. 277.
[5] *Ante*, p. 386 f.n.
[6] For an excellent summary of the essence of the problem see Falk and Mendlovitz, *The Strategy of World Order* (1966), Vol. 3, Chap. X.
[7] *Ante*, pp. 386, 393.

peace-keeping expenses has arisen because of the constitutional controversy over the powers of the Assembly and Security Council and is thus a "special case." As we have seen, in other cases of default, the sanction of Article 19 has been applied. A particularly glaring case of budgetary default arose in 1970 when the U.S.A. stopped contributions to the ILO in an attempt to coerce the Director-General over his appointment of a Soviet Assistant D.G.[8]

[8] See Schwebel, "The United States assaults the ILO" (1971) 65 A.J.I.L. 136.

INDEX

423

431